D1349112

Common Market Digest

An information guide to the
European Communities

David Overton

LA
THE LIBRARY
ASSOCIATION
LONDON

© Cyril David Overton 1983

Published by Library Association Publishing Limited, 7 Ridgmount Street, London WC1E 7AE.
Typeset by TJB Photosetting Limited, South Witham, Lincolnshire and printed and bound in
the United Kingdom by the Pitman Press, Bath.

First published 1983

British Library Cataloguing in Publication Data

Overton, David
  Common Market digest: an information guide to the European Communities
  1. European Economic Community—Information services   2. European Economic
Community—Bibliography
  I. Title
  382'. 9142'07   HC241.2

ISBN 0 85365 553 7

Contents

Introduction

The Common Market has brought together ten advanced nations each with a long history of independence. This could be called the most challenging economic and political task attempted in modern times. But it is happening successfully in Europe today.

As the European Communities (EC) develop, they affect increasingly the lives of 270 million people. For over 30 years now, the EC legislation programme has been trying to bring an even greater degree of unity to the laws of those separate nations. This change is working gradually and is being given authority by its incorporation into the body of laws of each national administration.

For most people the growth of the EC legislation is hardly noticed and its incorporation into the law of the land goes unremarked by the majority of the peoples affected by it. In spite of this its effect on the peoples living within the Communities increases from day to day.

Purpose of the Digest

The Common Market Digest is a guide and aide mémoire to these fundamental changes. The complex structure of the EC has resulted in a mass of published material both officially and commercially produced. As the EC is in process of development in response to new circumstances and the demands put upon it, this book charts changes in the major institutions and administrative arrangements. Most of the existing aspects of life in the Communities have been touched upon and, where possible, future developments are identified.

This process of bringing together existing legislation, known as 'harmonization', is a long term project. In addition, the legislation on many of these subjects requires enhancement to bring it into line with the changing and developing needs of the peoples served.

As will be clearly seen, this is a reference book whose aim is to provide each enquirer on a Community topic with a starting point. It attempts to give a modicum of information which will be all that is needed in some cases. It also makes provision for those who wish to undertake deeper research by giving precise references to both primary and secondary source material.

It will be seen therefore that a guide such as this Digest also needs to keep in touch with the changes and developments in the European Communities and bring itself up to date at regular intervals.

The users of the Digest

The business man – whose work is affected by Community legislation, who wishes to export to other EC countries, who wishes to take part in the trade benefits negotiated by the Community or who wishes to know about aid to industry or agriculture in development regions of the country.

The local authority or civil servant – who wishes to know where to seek information on Community assistance for developments being proposed or regions with which they are concerned.

The student – who finds that his project or his studies involve information on an aspect of Community work, or on a subject with which the Community is also concerned.

The lecturer or teacher – who cannot afford not to be up-to-date with EC developments now that he is living in one of the major areas of the Common Market.

Those whose time is limited – who are appalled at the welter of primary and secondary publications on the Community and want a short cut to the information they seek.

The general enquirer – who has come across a reference to an aspect of the Communities and without too much time or trouble, wishes to find out more.

Arrangement of the information

The easiest way to arrange material is in one alphabetical sequence, which everyone can use. There are some enquiries which could benefit by having related material close together instead of separated by an alphabetic sequence.

This Digest tries for the best of both worlds by grouping articles on a subject basis. The broad subjects have been listed by chapter on the Contents page at the front of the book. At the beginning of each chapter there is a more detailed breakdown to assist the enquirer. Each subject entry is self-contained.

It will be found that a certain number of points are referred to in more than one chapter, and to provide for this an alphabetical index has been compiled. As this is considered of prime importance to the user it has been printed on yellow paper and placed in a key position at the front of this book. At the beginning of the index there is a brief note on the various types of references to be found.

Help to the user

The development of the Communities must inevitably result in a growing bureaucracy which has been described in the Digest. At the same time, an attempt to overburden the user with too much detail has been avoided. Instead guides are given to where this additional information may be found, if required.

Where appropriate a degree of uniformity has been given to each subject covered by this book. Firstly, there is basic information which usually concerns the EC authority resting on the text of the treaties setting up these Communities. The subject is then dealt with by key development in an evolutionary order. Where appropriate, examples are given, usually from the United Kingdom or the Republic of Ireland as this book has been produced for an English speaking market.

One or two sections of general application have been grouped together in Chapter 8 – such as a list of holidays in the Community, a chronology, a list of initials and abbreviations used in the Community and mentioned in the Digest. Another tabulation is a general reading list on the Communities which was thought most appropriate in Chapter 1, a short biography section of key European civil servants at the end of Chapter 2, and at the beginning of Chapter 4 a list of industry and trade organizations in Europe.

How to use the Digest

Users are encouraged to go directly to the index on the yellow pages after reading the section above, 'Arrangement of the information.' Please note the few words at the beginning of the index listing the types of references included. Turn directly to the page you think most appropriate to your enquiry, and work outwards within the chapter or to other references mentioned in the index.

The written text merely gives the background to what is usually a developing problem. It is expected that the references in the text or under further reading will be used frequently. None of these is difficult to acquire and 99% will be found in any European Documentation Centre (EDC) (see list in Chapter 4 for your nearest EDC) or in the larger public reference libraries or university libraries. This is a growing subject and it will be to the enquirer's advantage to contact the local expert. She or he will be the Librarian-in-charge of the EDC or the special collection housing this type of material. In addition the librarian will have the latest information and books on the subject which concerns you, either immediately to hand or, rather more likely, will know where and how to find the additional information you require.

As far as possible the information in this publication includes changes which have been issued up to the end of June 1982. Users will realize however that there are delays in manuscripts submitted, publishing and despatch so that some of the changes made within the last few weeks or months can only be included in the next issue. The author would be very pleased to have suggestions for improving the next edition for with this type of publication improvements are always possible.

Acknowledgements

It is always a pleasing task to thank those who have helped with the production of a book.

In this case much of the work was undertaken in the European Documentation Centre of Sheffield City Polytechnic. I am most grateful to the staff in the Pond Street Library who allowed me to take up a reading space in their busy section and use their stock as much as I wished.

The Sheffield City Libraries, in particular the Commerce and Technology library, have drawn my attention to many recent publications and developments in the Communities and were most helpful with all my queries.

The European Communities Office in Nairobi where I started this compilation, was concerned with one aspect of the EC's work and it was useful to be able to browse amongst their collection of publications.

Inevitably the Communities Office in London has an outstanding collection of publications, and here again the Librarian was helpful in allowing me to use the collection and answering my queries.

I am sure if I had had the time to visit them I would have been helped by all the other EDCs and other libraries with collections of Common Market material, throughout the country. However, I would like to thank Salford University's EDC librarian with her well organized material and runs of pre-1973 documents. I should not fail to mention the EDC newsletter compiled by Mrs Anne Ramsay and issued by Newcastle upon Tyne Polytechnic, which kept me well informed and up-to-date whilst I was overseas.

Whenever I have wished to discuss this volume with the publisher Charles Ellis, he has always kindly arranged to be available and frequently included others who are interested. From these meetings I have received help from Joe Wormald, the Librarian of HM Treasury and Cabinet Office for which I am grateful.

The very considerable assistance which my wife has given me over this publication, should also be recorded. Her advice and diligence in bringing new EC publications to my attention, have been a continuing aid.

Index

Notes

The arrangement of this index is by the most usual system known as 'word by word'.
Under this method the arrangement would be:

Europe + 30 project
European Economic Community
Eurostatics

Entries have been made for the following:

- subjects, eg Steel, Aerospace, etc
- titles of articles and books mentioned in the text are in inverted commas, eg 'Action programme for the European aeronautical sector' (titles found under 'Further information' have been recorded in the reading list in Chapter 1)
- countries and places eg Algeria
- persons (surnames first) eg Cheysson, Claude
- titles of committees, associations, etc eg Apprenticeship working party
- titles of section entries have been set in italic eg *Advisory committee on transport*, or are prefaced by a –
- *major references have had the pagination set in italic eg Agriculture 128, 129, 130, 131,* 132
- abbreviations have been listed separately in Chapter 8. The full title will be found in this index.

1 The European Communities

'Common Market', is the popular term for:-
   The European Coal and Steel Community
   The European Economic Community
   The European Atomic Energy Community

Of these three the best known is the European Economic Community (EEC) with which the term 'Common Market' is most frequently associated. This first chapter includes general descriptions of each of these three Communities plus related sections.

The first of the European Communities to be established was the :

- **European Coal and Steel Community** (ECSC) (pages 2–4) which entered into force in 1952. The participating countries were, France, the Federal Republic of Germany, Italy, Holland, Belgium and Luxembourg. On 21 December 1974 Britain signed a treaty of association with the ECSC.

Two other sections which can best be included in this chapter are:

- **Consultative committee of the ECSC** (pages 4–5)
- **ECSC – financial assistance** (pages 5–8)

The second and third Community treaties concern the :

- **European Economic Community** (EEC) (pages 8–11)
- **European Atomic Energy Community** (EURATOM) or (EAEC) (pages 11–12)
  European atomic energy Community – financial assistance (pages 12–14)
  Euratom supply agency (pages 14–16)

both of these treaties came into force in 1958.

All three Communities are working towards an improved and prosperous Europe which collectively could play a more helpful and positive role in world affairs. It seemed logical, therefore, that the administration of these three should be unified. This was accomplished in 1965 by the :

- **Merger treaty** (pages 16–17) which brought together the institutes and organizations details of which will be found in Chapter 2 .

FOR A DETAILED INDEX SEE THE YELLOW PAGES.

The Communities are controlled by the European Council which, since 1974 meets regularly, three times each year, to assess progress and agree objectives. It is concerned with Community and foreign policy matters. Details of its meetings will be found in Bulletin of the European Communities, section 1.3.1 – and in the, General reports on the activities of the European Communities, in Chapter 1 section 2 – Council. These include a brief summary of the work of both the European Council and the Council of Ministers (qv). The European Council consists of the Prime Ministers or Heads of states together with the President of the Commission. In 1976 the European Council decided that an annual survey of progress produced by the Commission, would be helpful in charting progress towards the ultimate goal of European union. Details of this may be found under the heading:

● **European union** (page 17–18)

Brief details of participating states:

● **Member states** (page 18–19)

Finally there is a selected list of books taken from the many hundreds which have been written on the Common Market. Whilst this book is being printed, others will have been published. Why not consult your nearest European Documentation Centre Librarian (for details see yellow index pages) or your local University or Public Librarian, who are willing to help you with details of the latest publications. (Pages 19–26)

European Coal and Steel Community (ECSC)

Basic information

Jean Monnet (qv), known as the 'Father of Europe', wrote when he drafted the Schuman (qv) Declaration which led to the foundation of the ECSC, 'By the pooling of basic production and the establishment of a new High Authority, whose decisions will be binding on France, Germany and the countries that join them, this proposal will lay the first concrete foundations of the European Federation which is indispensable to the maintenance of peace'. This Community, set up by the Treaty of Paris signed on 18 April 1951, was the first of the three European Communities and its immediate effect was to secure future supplies of coal and steel, vital to economic recovery after the second world war.

Purpose of the ECSC

The preamble to the treaty reflected the current fear that peace could be only safeguarded by efforts to overcome the divisions in Europe and the dangers from outside. The treaty itself (see, Further information) emphasized:

- by the introduction of a common market there should be an economic expansion, growth of employment and a rising standard of living for the Community as a whole
- the conditions aimed at should ensure the most rational production and productivity whilst safeguarding employment and the smooth development of the economies of member states
- consumers in the ECSC should have equal access to the sources of production, fair prices, a considered use of natural resources, improved standard of living for workers, promotion of international trade and the modernization of production, all part of the development of these two industries

Members of the Community

The first members were the original six of the Community who ratified the Paris treaty by the Spring of 1952.

- Belgium
- France
- Germany
- Italy
- Luxembourg
- Netherlands

The treaty entered into force on 27 July 1952.
As the Communities expanded in size so member states participated in the work of the ECSC.

Steel industry

For over twenty years the steel industry boomed after the foundation of the ECSC. During the 1970s and early 1980s there was a downturn in the demand for steel products. Price restraint has been abandoned and because voluntary restraint of production failed, mandatory quotas were introduced in 1980 (qv Steel industry).

The Commission, which took over from the High Authority of the ECSC under the, Merger treaty (qv), has declared the steel industry to be in a state of manifest crisis and is attempting to deal firmly with an extremely difficult situation. Its main aid in the restructuring of the industry is finance, or withholding the very large sums of money required for changes in this industry when these are not in conformity with its plans (qv Steel industry).

Coal industry

After a period of restriction of coal output to keep in line with national needs and exports, the two major oil crises of the 1970s led to an emphasis on the need for coal production (qv Energy objectives, Energy policy). By the year 2000 the ECSC wants to double the Community's coal consumption in power stations and reconvert some of the existing stations from oil to coal burning. A second programme of research on safety in mines was submitted to the ECSC Consultative committee on 11.3.82. The approval of the Council has to be obtained.

Further information

Diebold, William
Schuman plan, a study in economic co-operation 1950–9
    New York: Praeger for the Council on Foreign Relations, 1959. 750p
European Coal and Steel Community, financial report
    Luxembourg: Office for official publications of the European Communities, annual
General report on the activities of the European Communities
    Luxembourg: Office for official publications of the European Communities, annual
Treaties establishing the European Communities
    Luxembourg: Office for official publications of the European Communities, 1973. 1502p
Hallstein, Walter
Europe in the making
    London: Allen and Unwin, 1973. 343p
Hopkins, Michael
Policy formation in the European Communities
    London: Mansell, 1981. 339p. ISBN 0–7201–1597–3
Investment in the Community coalmining and iron and steel industries, report on the 1981
    survey Luxembourg: Office for official publications of the European Communities, 1982.
    107p. ISBN 92–825–2751–4 Catalogue number CB–33–81–085–EN–C

Consultative Committee of the European Coal and Steel Community (ECSC)

Basic information

Established in 1957 under article 19 of the Treaty of Paris setting up the European Coal and Steel Community (ECSC). Amended after the first expansion of the Community by Council decision (OJ L73 27.3.72) and again in 1981 (OJ L58/30 5.3.81) (Decision 81/84/ECSC).

Consultative Committee – representation

The Committee is attached to the High Authority of the ECSC. Its membership consists of not less than sixty or more than eighty-four. With the three members appointed in 1981 to represent Greece the total membership is now eighty-four covering producers, workers, consumers and dealers.

Work of the Consultative Committee

It has set up a series of sub-committees:

- general objectives
- markets and prices
- research projects
- labour problems

The aims of the Committee are laid down under article 19 of the Treaty of Paris.

Further information

Treaties establishing the European Communities
  Luxembourg: Office for official publications of the European Communities, 1973. 1502p
Community advisory committees for the representation of socio-economic interests
  Farnborough: Saxon House for EC Economic and Social Committee, 1980. 215p.
  ISBN 0-566-00328-7

European Coal and Steel Community (ECSC) – Financial Assistance

Basic information

The second paragraph of article 2 of the ECSC treaty lays down the principles under which the industries should be organized. Article 56 mentions new activities capable of absorbing redundant workers.

Projects benefiting under the Community

Loans are for investment projects only and cover the following:

- investments which keep in line with Community policy for the industries, covering capital goods, buildings, supply installations, environmental protection, etc

- works and installations to increase production, reduce costs or facilitate marketing

Whilst recipients need not necessarily be coal and steel undertakings they should be connected to or working for these industries or providing further employment for former workers in these industries.

Projects benefiting under the ECSC financial assistance

- housing construction or modernization schemes for coal and steel industry workers. Funds allocated on a member state basis and with the agreement of the employers and workers involved plus the government department responsible for housing
- technical research in the industries
- development of other industries in coal and steel areas with high unemployment
- workers redeployment and retraining
- modernization of plant
- construction of new collieries and new pits in existing collieries

Rates of grants and loans

The Commission determines the proportion of investments eligible for ECSC assistance on a case-by-case study

- 40% or less of the cost of fixed investments is granted as a loan on conversion programmes
- global loans are granted in regions where coal and steel are the predominant industries

For 50% loans on fixed investments, interest rates are based on those current in the member state concerned. These may be lowered by 3% for all or part of the loan in the case of industrial programmes with recognized priority status.

- 20% or less of the cost of new low-cost housing for coal or steel employees
- 35% or less of the cost of conversion or modernization of housing for coal or steel employees

For these loans the interest rate is usually 1% and repayment over 20 years.

During 1980 1.73 million EUA were loaned to British coal and steel workers for assistance in low-cost housing.

- 60% grants are allowed for expenditure directly incurred for research purposes. This includes staff, equipment and operating expenses. A programme of research in the steel industry for 1980–5 is available (OJ C232/1–141 4.10.76)

Non-repayable grants to workers affected by redeployment. The ECSC may provide grants at the request of the government of the member states towards:

- tide over allowances to employees
- resettlement allowances
- financing of vocational training for those who have to change employment

The United Kingdom received benefits under these proposals. For example, in May 1982 the Commission decided to contribute 27,579,000 ECU towards the cost to workers affected by closures and cutbacks (*Bulletin of the European Communities* **15** (5) 1982 point 2.1.33).

On 29.4.82 the Commission approved a 5 year programme designed to develop new economic activities in certain areas of the UK affected by the reorganization of the steel industry. 33 million ECU are being given by the Community and £19.8 million by the UK Government. The Community participation is from the non quota section of the ERDF (*Bulletin of the European Communities* **15** (4) 1982 point 2.1.38).

Submission of applications

- details of requests for **industrial loans** to be sent in triplicate to Commission of the European Communities, Directorate-General for Credit and Investments, Jean Monnet Building, Luxembourg.
- applications for **conversion loans**, including global loans, should be sent to the national ministry responsible (in Britain it is the Department of Industry – London or regional offices or the Scottish Economic planning department or the Welsh Office or the Department of Commerce for Northern Ireland).
- loans for house-building to be submitted by the person concerned to their employer. They are then sent to regional committees to determine priorities and make financing proposals, and from there to the Commission for a final decision. Requests for non-repayable grants for the redeployment of workers are channelled through the Department of Employment, London, to the ECSC
- applications for financial aid covering technical research on coal and steel is available to undertakings, institutes, research centres, or individuals. The applicant need not necessarily be directly concerned with the coal and steel industries. Applications should be sent to the Commission (OJ C139/1–8 12.11.74)

Further information

Grants and loans from the European Community
   Luxembourg: Office for official publications of the European Communities, 1981. 83p.
   (European Documentation series 7-8/1981) ISBN 92-825-2633-X. Catalogue number
   CB-NC-81-008-EN-C
Ninth programme of ECSC low cost housing 1979-83
   Luxembourg: Office for official publications of the European Communities, 1979.
Scott, Gay
Guide to European Community grants and loans – 2nd ed
   Biggleswade: Euroinformation Limited, 1981. 111p. ISBN 0-907304-01-X
Official sources of finance and aid for industry in the UK
   London: National Westminster Bank Limited, Commercial information market intelligence
   department, 1981. 67p

European Economic Community (EEC)

Community treaties with member states

1957 25 March	European Economic Community (EEC) treaty signed in Rome: France, Germany, Italy, Holland, Belgium and Luxembourg
1957 25 March	European Atomic Energy Community (Euratom) treaty signed in Rome: France, Germany, Italy, Holland, Belgium and Luxembourg
1958 1 January	Rome treaties, ratified by parliaments of the Six, come into force
1959 4 February	Britain and Euratom sign a co-operation agreement
1961 9 July	Greece signs an association agreement
1965 8 April	Merger Treaty between Communities signed
1972 22 January	Treaty of accession between the Six and Britain, Denmark, Norway and the Republic of Ireland signed
1972 1 July	Portugal as part of EFTA signed a trade agreement with the EEC
1973 1 January	Community of Nine. Norway opted out
1975 12 June	Greece submitted an application to accede to the European Communities
1977 28 March	Portugal submitted an application to accede to the European Communities
1977 28 July	Spain submitted an application to accede to the European Communities

1979 28 May	Greece signs treaty of accession in Athens
1980 3 December	Portugal signed an agreement to provide pre-accession aid from the EEC
1981 1 January	Greece becomes the 10th member state
1981 1 January	Portugal pre-accession aid agreement enters into force
1984	Portugal expected to become the 11th member of the Communities

Aims of the Community were:

To lay down the foundations of a European Union which would rule out conflict between its members and provide the countries concerned with a voice in the world at least equal to the major continental powers.

To provide for economic development through the creation of a common market starting with the coal and steel sector.

From the common market it was expected that there would be economic expansion and higher standards of living and during the 1960s and early 1970s this happened. The economic crisis of the middle and late 1970s caused a slackening of this expansion and this was continued into the early 1980s.

Political union of the Community was obtained through Parliament.

Throughout the last three decades the work of the Common Market has helped to develop interdependence between Community countries by:

- The free movement of people and services has been facilitated by equal treatment over wages, social security and trade union rights. Developments are taking place to harmonize national professional criteria and qualifications.
- European competition rules have been implemented
- Common prices have been introduced in Agriculture
- A common customs tariff has been introduced

Trade development between member states of the community has increased very considerably:

- By 1980 43% of British exports went to European Community member states. This was worth £20.4 billion. Exports to Commonwealth countries form 13% of UK trade in 1980
- Trade between the six rose from 7 billion European Units of account (EUA) in 1958 to 54 billion EUA in 1973. By 1977 this had risen to 168 billion amongst the nine countries of the Community. By 1981 and 1982 the Commission was drawing attention to the obstacles to internal trade still existing 25 years after the Economic Community had been

established. The European Council called for a special effort to strengthen the internal market (*Bulletin of the European Communities* **14** (6) 1981 point 2.1.11). By June 1982 as mentioned in the previous point, 2.1.10, the Commission had approved:

- a draft Council resolution to relax frontier checks within the Community
- a proposal for the simplification of formalities over trade within the Community
- a proposed 14th Council directive on the harmonization of turnover tax
- emphasis on an earlier proposal to simplify frontier crossings for the carriage of goods (OJ C127/6–8 18.5.82)

On an international trade basis the Community has:

- Attempted to improve the liberalization of international trade. Free trade zones have been set up with other Western European countries. A regular dialogue has been started with the other major powers. By 1979 100 states have concluded trade arrangements with the EC or are in the process of so doing. In 1979 the Community had 20% of all world trade compared with the United States' 14% and the Soviet Union's 5%.
- An attempt to encourage the development of the Third World has been made by the two Lomé (qv) Conventions. Community aid to the countries now participating in Lomé amounted to 3.4 billion EUA between 1976 and 1980

The economic problems of the 1970s have given new objectives to the Community including:

- A European monetary system (currently excluding the pound sterling and the Greek drachma)
- A more effective co-ordination of national economic policies
- Joint action to resolve structural inbalances
- A more effective use of the European Investment Bank whose loans (8 billion EUA between 1958 and 1977) have helped support investment in the poorest regions

Within the Community interdependence has been strengthened by the gradual growth of the following:

- The development of harmonization and standardization throughout member states in the mass production goods market
- Environment and consumer protection. For example the development of harmonization between European car manufacturers of anti-pollution and safety equipment
- Regional policy to assist in the development of economically disadvantaged areas. During 1981 the UK received 23.80% of the European Regional Development Fund
- Social policy to co-ordinate Community social measures throughout the industrial field and prevent any one country being at a disadvantage
- Science policy development by co-ordinating research efforts in laboratories and research stations throughout the community
- Industrial policy by encouraging the importation of raw materials,

energy supplies, etc. By developing a co-ordinated approach to production and development, for example in aerospace, data processing, etc

Further information

A European Community – Why?
    Brussels: EC Directorate-General for further information, 1979. 8p.(European File 1/79) Catalogue number CC–AD–79–001–EN–C
The European Community in the 1980s
    Brussels: EC Directorate-General for information, 1980. 7p.(European File 1/80) Catalogue number CC–AD–80–001–EN–C
British business in Europe; businessmen's guide to the European Communities
    London: HMSO for the Departments of Industry and Trade, 1981. 80p. (Published with the 26 June–2 July issue of *British business*)

European Atomic Energy Community (EAEC) (Euratom)

Basic information

Because of the great potential of nuclear energy with its present high costs and the limited amounts of other existing fuels, it was thought necessary to establish a separate Community. This was the European Atomic Energy Community which was established at the same time as the European Economic Community – 1957. It is known as EURATOM. A reference where the terms of the Euratom treaty can be read will be found under, Further information, below.

Purpose

Under the EAEC treaty the duties allocated included:

- promotion and co-ordination of nuclear research and development within the Community
- the development of a training programme
- establishment of safety standards within nuclear energy. These were improved by a new directive in 1980 (OJ L246/1–72 17.9.80) (Directive 80/836/EURATOM)
- distribution of information on European atomic energy
- assisting with the development of nuclear research for peaceful purposes in the Community – finance, information, technical support
- development of commercial outlets for research and sources for material used
- establishment of international links

Work undertaken

- A supply agency has been established (qv Euratom supply agency)
- Aid for the development of all aspects of the peaceful uses of atomic energy has been given to member states (qv European atomic energy community – financial assistance)
- In 1977 a joint undertaking was commenced to initiate the Joint European torus (JET), an experiment in controlled fusion at Culham in Oxfordshire (qv Joint Research Centre). The 1982–6 R & D programme in the field of controlled thermonuclear fusion should also cover the completion of the construction phase of JET (*Bulletin of the European Communities* **15** (5) 1982 point 2.1.148). (Willson, Denis. *A European experiment, the launching of the JET project.* Bristol: Adam Hilger, 1981. 181p. ISBN 0–85274–543–5)
- New safety standards to safeguard the public and workers in the nuclear field were approved by Council in 1980 (see above) and came into force on 3.12.82, as far as most EC members are concerned

Information on all nuclear safeguard matters can be obtained in the UK from the Co-ordinating Unit of the Safeguards Office, Atomic Energy Division, Department of Energy, Thames House South, Millbank, London SW1P 4QJ.

Further information

General report on the activities of the European Community [European Atomic Energy Community]
   Luxembourg: Office for official publications of the European Communities, annual 1958 – until the General report covered all three Communities

European Atomic Energy Community (Euratom) – Financial Assistance

Basic information

The purposes of Euratom research loans are:

- to promote the use of nuclear energy in order to reduce dependence on external energy supplies
- to ensure the optimum safety precautions are known and brought into use

In many cases the research work involved is undertaken by contracts. In the case of the decommissioning of nuclear power plants programme the decision specifically refers to this work being undertaken at the Joint Research Centre (qv)

Projects benefiting under EURATOM

- those relating to the production of electricity from nuclear sources
- industrial nuclear fuel cycle installations
- radiation protection programme
- management and storage of radioactive waste
- decommissioning of nuclear power plants
- safety of thermal water reactors

Resources allocated

- under a 1977 decision the Council allocated a maximum of 500 million EUA to the Commission for Euratom financing (OJ L88/9–10 6.4.77) (Decision 77/270/Euratom)
- in 1979 the ceiling for loans was increased to 1,000 million EUA (OJ L12/28 17.1.80) (Decision 80/29/Euratom)
- under the radiation protection programme, 59 million EUA were allocated for this work over a five year period commencing 1.1.80 (OJ L78/19–21 25.3.80) (Decision 80/342/Euratom)
- under the management and storage of radioactive waste programme, 43 million EUA were allocated for this work over a 5 year period commencing 1.1.80 (OJ L78/22–3 25.3.80) (Decision 80/343/Euratom)
- under the decommissioning of nuclear power plants programme, 4.7 million EUA were allocated to run from 1979–83 (OJ L83/19–20 3.4.79) (Decision 79/344 Euratom)
- under the safety of thermal water reactors programme 6.3 million EUA were allocated for this work over a 5 year period commencing 1.1.79 (OJ L83/21–2 3.4.79) (Decision 79/345/Euratom)

Rates of loans

- loans normally do not cover more than 20% of the project cost
- in the case of the radiation protection programme, the contribution usually lies between 25% and 40% of the costs
- interest rates reflect those in the country receiving the loan

Submission of applications

Firms or authorities should apply to:

- Commission of the European Communities
  Directorate-General for credit and investments
  Jean Monnet Building
  Luxembourg – Kirchberg
  Luxembourg

In the use of grants and loans for technological developments in the hydrocarbon sector or uranium prospecting projects, grants may be obtained from:

- The Commission of the European Communities
  Directorate-General for energy
  rue de la Loi 200
  1049 Brussels
  Belgium

Further information

General report on the activities of the European Communities
  Luxembourg: Office for official publications of the European Communities, annual
Grants and loans from the European Community
  Luxembourg: Office for official publications of the European Communities, 1981. 83p. (European documentation series 7–8/1981) ISBN 92–825–2633–X. Catalogue number CB–NC–81–008–EN–C
Scott, Gay
Guide to European community grants and loans – 2nd ed
  Biggleswade: Euroinformation Limited, 1981. 111p. ISBN 0–907304–01–X

Euratom Supply Agency

Basic information

The Agency was formed under articles 52, 53, 60 and 222 of the Treaty of Rome (EURATOM) (1957).

The statutes of the Euratom supply agency were published by the Council in 1958 for the EAEC (OJ L27/534–539 6.12.58) and brought into force by a decision on 1.6.60 (OJ L32/776 11.5.60).

Euratom Supply Agency – representation

The Director-General and Deputy Director-General are appointed by the Commission. The former is responsible for managing the Agency.

An Advisory Committee was set up comprising 24 members for the Six, the larger member states having six members and Belgium and Holland three each. This was later expanded as the Community grew. With the Community of 9 a total of 33 members were appointed (OJ L83/20 30.3.73) (Decision 73/45/EURATOM).

Purpose of the Advisory Committee

Its duties are to:

- assist the Agency in carrying out its tasks acting as a link between the users or sections and the Agency
- assist the Director-General whenever it is approached on matters within its remit of duties
- give advice over a range of subjects on which it has to be consulted by the Director-General
- issue opinions provided it has the support of 10 of its members

Purpose of the Supply Agency

This is outlined in Article 53 of the EAEC Treaty. It is necessary to read the statutes of the Agency in conjunction with EURATOM treaty chapters concerned.

The Agency is under the supervision of the Commission which has the powers to adjudicate in disputes between the Agency and a third party.

The Agency has the right to use and consume materials owned by the Community under the provision laid down in Chapter VII of the Euratom treaty.

Producers of materials have the right to sell outside the agency if:

- their ores are not required by the Agency
- if their ores do not fall under the definition of special fissile materials

Potential users shall periodically inform the Agency of the supplies they require.

The Agency has the exclusive right in the Community to enter into contracts with third states or international organizations to purchase ores, source materials or special fissile materials.

Articles 67–9 of the Euratom treaty (1957) deals with prices.

The Agency has the right to store material preparatory to its use.

The manner in which the supply of ore's is balanced against the demand was detailed in 1960 (OJ L32/777–8 11.5.60).

The address of the Agency is:
  rue de la Loi 200
  1049 Brussels
  Belgium

Further information

General report on the activities of the European Communities, section 12 Energy–Supply
Agency
    Luxembourg: Office for official publications of the European Communities, annual

Merger Treaty 1967

Basic information

Three Communities were established each with its own administrative organization. The
first treaty was the European Coal and Steel Community (ECSC) and it was signed in Paris
in 1951. It included amongst its institutions:

- a High Authority
- an Assembly
- a Council
- a Court

The second was the European Economic Community (EEC) and it was signed in Rome in
1957. It included amongst its institutions:

- an Assembly
- a Council
- a Commission
- a Court of Justice
- an Economic and Social Committee, etc

The third treaty was the European Atomic Energy Community (EAEC) also signed in Rome
in 1957. It included amongst its institutions:

- an Assembly
- a Council
- a Commission
- a Court of Justice
- an Economic and Social Committee, etc

Unification of institutions

Under the Convention on certain institutions common to the European
Communities, signed at Rome in 1957, the heads of the six member
states decided to create certain single institutions including:

- a single Assembly for both the EEC, the EAEC and the ECSC
- a single Court of justice for the Communities
- a single Economic and Social Committee for the EEC and the EAEC

A part of this Convention was superseded by the Merger treaty. Finally a
Treaty establishing a single Council and a single Commission of the
European Communities, known as the Merger treaty (OJ L152/2 13.7.67)
(Treaty 67/443/EEC) was signed at Brussels on 8 April 1965 and brought
into force on 1 July 1967.

Under this treaty the new Council takes the place of the ECSC Council and serves all three Communities. Those sections of the ECSC treaty referring to a Council were repealed.

Also under this Merger treaty a new Commission takes the place of the High Authority of the ECSC and the Commission of the EEC and EAEC and serves all three Communities.

Similar action was taken linking the Court and the Courts of Justice, the Economic and social committees, etc.

Further information

Treaties establishing the European Communities
    Luxembourg: Office for official publications of the European Communities, 1973. 1502p.
    [texts of treaties, conventions, etc]
Guide to EEC legislation
    Amsterdam: North-Holland publishing company, 1979. 2 v. ISBN 0–44–85320–0

European Union

Basic information

On 29 December 1975 Leo Tindemans produced a report *(Bulletin of the European Communities* supplement 1/76) which defined an overall approach to the subject, providing a framework for future relevant action by member states. At the same time it gave a number of practical measures which would have to be adopted if Union were to be accomplished. This report also included a proposal that there should be periodic reports on the progress of the Communities towards European Union (page 23).

In the following year the European Council whilst at the Hague, requested the Commission to report to it annually on progress during the past year and in the future, towards the ultimate goal of European union.

The annual reports

Starting in 1977 these included sections by the Minister of Foreign Affairs and by the Commission.

Further information

European Union, annual reports for 1977
Bulletin of the European Communities supplement 8/77

European Union, annual reports for 1978
Bulletin of the European Communities supplement 1/79
European Union, annual reports for 1979
Bulletin of the European Communities supplement 9/79
European Union, annual reports for 1980
Bulletin of the European Communities supplement 4/80
European Union, annual reports for 1981
Bulletin of the European Communities supplement 3/81

Member States
Basic information

Very brief information follows on member states as the whole book charts the journey they are taking towards a single entity.

European Coal and Steel Community (qv)

In May 1950 Belgium, France, the Federal Republic of Germany, Italy, Luxembourg and The Netherlands started negotiations leading to the first Community covering coal and steel. The Treaty of Paris was signed on 18 April 1951 and came into force on 27 July 1952.

These same six countries negotiated, signed and brought into force two further Communities in 1958 under the Treaty of Rome:

- European Economic Community (qv)
- European Atomic Energy Community (qv)

Enlargement of the Communities

After several false starts negotiations began on 30 June 1970 for the first enlargement of the Community. A treaty was signed on 22 January 1972 and on 1 January 1973 the United Kingdom, Denmark and the Republic of Ireland became the next three members of the Communities. Norway (qv) which participated in the negotiations withdrew before ratification.

Second enlargement of the Communities

On the 28th May 1979 an accession treaty with Greece (qv) was signed. It entered into force, after ratification by member states and Greece, on 1 January 1981.

Further Community members

Two further members of the Community are likely to be Portugal (qv) and Spain (qv).

Withdrawal from the Community

On 23 February 1982 a referendum was organized by the Greenland executive which produced a majority in favour of seeking withdrawal from the Communities and negotiating a new type of relationship. This was noted by the Commission.

In April 1982 Denmark informed the member states that Greenland wanted OCT (qv) status. The Council noted this and requested opinions from Parliament and the Commission on 8 June 1982 (*Bulletin of the European Communities* **15** (2) 1982 point 2.4.1, **15** (4) 1982 point 2.4.1, **15** (5) 1982 point 2.4.1 and **15** (6) 1982 point 2.4.3).

European Communities References

Basic information

A number of general guides has been produced on the Community and doubtless will be issued whilst this booklet is in course of publication. To find the latest book, your nearest Librarian – public, academic or special – should be able to advise you.

The following is a grouping of general and reference books which the author has found useful. It is by no means an exhaustive list.

Bibliographic and source guides

Alerting services covering European Communities documentation
   London: British Library, Official publications library, 1982 (?). 5p
European Communities Yearbook, and the other European organisations 1982.
   Epping, Essex: Bowker, 1982. 600p. ISBN 2–829–0031–5
Jeffries, John
Guide to the official publications of the European Communities, 2nd ed.
   London: Mansell, 1981. 178p. ISBN 0–7201–1590–6
Palmer, Doris M (ed)
Sources of information on the European Communities
   London: Mansell, 1979. 230p. ISBN 0–7201–0724–5
Publications and documents of the EC received by the Library

Luxembourg: Office for official publications of the European Communities for the EC library, 1981. not paged (supplement 1981/1). ISBN 92–825–2840–5.Catalogue number CB–35–82–053–7C–C

Publications of the European Communities, catalogue . . .
Luxembourg: Office for official publications of the European Communities, annual

Scott, Gay

The European Economic Community: a guide to sources of information
London: Capital planning information, 1979. 72p. ISBN 0–906011–04–3. (also available on microfiche)

Treaties establishing the European Communities
Luxembourg: Office for official publications of the European Communities, 1973, 1502p

European Community, member states, regions and administrative units (map, coloured)
Luxembourg: Office for official publications of the European Communities, 1979. scale 1:2,000,000 (Wall map) [later editions to include Greece, Portugal and Spain]

Booklets on a variety of subjects are available from the European Community Office, 20 Kensington Palace Gardens, London W8 4QQ (nearly all of these are free).

General guides

A number of leaflets have been published by the EDC Librarians in their 'How to' series, eg 'How to find out about the Court of Justice of the European Communities'. All are dated 1982 and vary between four and five pages. Available from any EDC Librarian.

Effects on the United Kingdom of membership of the European Communities
Luxembourg: European Parliament, Directorate-General for Research and Documentation, 1975. various pagings:

The Community today
Luxembourg: Office for official publications of the European Communities, 1980. 226p. ISBN 92–825–0785–8

Europe today, state of European integration 1980–1
Luxembourg: Office for official publications of the European Communities, 1981. 617p. ISBN 92–823–0037–4.Catalogue number AX–30–80–972–EN–C

General report on the activities of the European Communities
Luxembourg: Office for official publications of the European Communities, annual

Hallstein, Walter

Europe in the making
London: Allen and Unwin, 1973. 343p

Hopkins, Michael
Policy formation in the European Communities
    London: Mansell, 1981. 339p. ISBN 0–7201–1597–3
Morris, Brian and others
European Community, the practical guide for business and government
    London: Macmillan, 1981. 303p. ISBN 0–333–26205–0
Myles, Gregg
EEC Brief
    Belfast: Locksley Press, 1979. 2v. (loose leaf)
Noël, Emile
The European Community: how it works
    Luxembourg: Office for official publications of the European Communities, 1979. 97p. (European perspectives series) ISBN 92–825–1015–8. Catalogue number CB–28–79–390–EN–C
Ramsay, Anne
'European Communities information – how to track it down and keep pace with it'
Refer 1 (3) Spring 1981 p.4–7 (Part 1)
       1 (4) Autumn 1981 p.3–5 (Part 2)
Shlaim, Avi and G N Yannopoulos
The EEC and Eastern Europe
    Cambridge: CUP, 1978. 251p. ISBN 0–521–22072–6
Sjostedt, Gunnar
External role of the European Community
    Farnborough: Saxon House for the Swedish Institute of International Affairs, 1977. 274p. ISBN 0–566–00172–1
Spain, Portugal and the European Community
    London: University Association for Contemporary European Studies, 1978. 62p. ISBN 0–906384–01–X
Taylor, Phillip
When Europe speaks with one voice, the external relations of the European Community
    London: Aldwych Press, 1979. 237p. ISBN 0–86172–001–6
Tsoukalis, Loukas
The European Community and its Mediterranean enlargement
    London: Allen and Unwin, 1981. 273p. ISBN 0–04–382030–1
Twitchett, Carol and Kenneth J
Building Europe: Britain's partners in the EEC
    London: Europa Publications Limited. 1981. 262p. ISBN 0–905118–61–8
Twitchett, Kenneth J (ed.)
Europe and the world, the external relations of the Common Market
    London: Europa Publications, 1976. 197p. ISBN 0–900–36278–2

Organization of the Community

Parliament

Englefield, Dermot
Parliament and information
   London: Library Association, 1981. 132p. ISBN 85365–570–7 [section
   on EC Parliament]
Europe's Parliament
   London: European Parliament information office, 1981. 32 slides, lecture
   notes and tape commentary:
Official handbook of the European Parliament
   Luxembourg: Office for official publications of the European Commu-
   nities, 1981.(looseleaf)
The Times guide to the European Parliament . . .
   London: Times Books Limited, 1979. 267p. ISBN 0–7230–0231–2

Law

*Competition law in the European Economic and the European Coal and
Steel Communities*
   Luxembourg: Office for official publications of the European Commu-
   nities, 1981. 134p. ISBN 92–825–2389–6·Catalogue number CB–30–
   80–576–EN–C
Encyclopedia of European Community law
   London: Sweet and Maxwell, 3v.(looseleaf service)
*EEC checklist of Community legislation and legislative proposals of
concern to financial institutions and markets*
   London: British Bankers association, 1981.(looseleaf)
Guide to EEC legislation
   Amsterdam: North Holland publishing company, 1979. 2 v. ISBN
   0–444–85320–0
Louis, Jean-Victor
Community legal order
   Luxembourg: Office for official publications of the European Commu-
   nities, 1980. 145p. ISBN 92–825–1053–0·Catalogue number CB–28–
   79–407–EN–C
Mathijsen, P S R F
Guide to European Community law, 3rd ed.
   London: Sweet and Maxwell, 1980. 256p. ISBN 0–421–25900–0
Parry, Anthony
EEC law
   London: Sweet and Maxwell, 1973. 511p. ISBN 421–17390–4

Biography

*European Communities and other European organizations who's who
1980–1*
   Brussels: Editions Delta, 1981. 237p. ISBN 2–8029–0017–X

Economic and agricultural development

Economics

Directory of the professional organizations set up at Community level
    Brussels: Editions Delta, 1981. 818p. ISBN 2–8029–0025–0

Drew, John
Doing business in the European Community
    London: Butterworth, 1979. 280p. ISBN 0–408–10631–X

European Investment Bank, *Annual Report*
    Luxembourg: The Bank, annual

Exporting to the European Community, information for foreign exporters
    Luxembourg: Office for official publications of the European Communities, 1977. 71p. Catalogue number CB–23–77–526–EN–C

Lewis, D E S
Britain and the European Economic Community
    London: Heinemann, 1978. 125p. ISBN 0–435–84560–8

Monetary policies in the countries of the European Economic Community, institutions and instruments
    Luxembourg: Office for official publications of the European Communities for the Monetary committee, 1972. 436p. supplement 1974 not paged

Noelke, Michael and Robert Taylor
Spanish industry and the impact of membership of the European Community
    Brussels: European Research Associates, 1980. 559p

Report on competition policy
    Luxembourg: Office for official publications of the European Communities, annual 1970–

United Kingdom medium term economic trends and problems
    Brussels: Commission of the European Community, 1982. 128p. (Economic Papers series no. 7) (Internal paper, EEC Library, London)

Vaulont, Nikolaus
Customs union of the European Economic Community
    Luxembourg: Office for official publications of the European Communities, 1981. 89p. (European Perspectives series). ISBN 92–825–1911–2. Catalogue number CB–30–80–205–EN–C

Grants and loans

Donovan, Michael H
Official grants and financial aids to business in Western Europe
    London: Graham and Trotman Ltd, 1977 + supplements 1978 and 1979. ISBN 0–86010–057–X

The European social fund, what it does, who can apply, how to apply
    London: Department of Employment, 1981. 28p

Grants and loans from the European Community
    Luxembourg: Office for official publications of the European Communities, 1981. 83p. (European documentation series 7–8, 1981) ISBN 92–825–2633–X. Catalogue number CB–NC–81–008–EN–C

Official sources of finance and aid for industry in the UK
London: National Westminster Bank Limited, Commercial information market intelligence department, 1981. 67p
Scott, Gay
Guide to European Community grants and loans, 2nd ed
Biggleswade: Euroinformation Limited, 1981. 111p. ISBN 0–907304–01–X
Vade-Mecum of contract research (indirect action)
Luxembourg: Commission of the EEC. 1981. 46p

Agriculture

AGREP, permanent inventory of agricultural research projects in the European Communities
Luxembourg: Office for official publications of the European Communities, 1977. 2v. (updated by the monthly periodical Euroabstracts)

The agricultural situation in the Community ... report
Luxembourg: Office for official publications of the European Communities, annual

Energy policies

Solar energy for development, proceedings of the international conference held at Varese, Italy, March 26–9 1979 by the Commission of the European Communities
The Hague: Martinus Nijhoff for the Commission of the European Communities, 1979. 240p. ISBN 90–247–2239–X

Social and environmental development

Social

Community advisory committees for the representation of socio-economic interests
Farnborough: Saxon House for the European Communities Economic and Social Committee, 1980. 215p. ISBN 0–566–00328–7
Consumer protection and information policy
Luxembourg: Office for official publications of the European Communities, annual. 1977–
Economic and social committee of the European Communities, annual report
Luxembourg: Office for official publications of the European Communities, annual, 1974–
The European social budget 1980–75–70
Luxembourg: Office for official publications of the European Communities, 1978. 183p. ISBN 92–825–0913–3. Catalogue number CB–25–78–704–EN–C

Higher education in the European Community, a handbook for students
  Brussels: Directorate-General for research, science and education, 1977. 177p. Catalogue number CT–22–77–451–EN–C
Hospitals in the EEC, organization and terminology
  Copenhagen: Gyldendalske Broghandel Nordisk Forlay AS. 1978. 464p. ISBN 87–01–59851–1
Practical handbook of social security for employed persons and their families moving within the Community
  Luxembourg: Office for official publications of the European Communities, 1973– (looseleaf). Catalogue number CE–28–79–035– EN–C
Report on social development
  Luxembourg: Office for official publications of the European Communities, annual
Social indicators for the European Community, 1960–75
  Luxembourg: Office for official publications of the European Communities, 1977. 488p
Systems of education and vocational training in the member countries of the European Communities
  Luxembourg: Office for official publications of the European Communities, for the Economic and social committee, 1976. 114p
Williams, Michael (ed)
Directory of trade unions in the European Economic Community
  London: Graham, Trotman, Dudley publishers limited, 1978. 124p. ISBN 0–86010–118–5

Environment

Bridgewater, A V and K Lidgren
Household waste management in Europe, economics and techniques
  London: Van Nostrand, 1981. 249p. ISBN 0–442–30464–1
Cramp, Stanley
Bird conservation in Europe, a report prepared for the Environment and Consumer Protection Service of the Commission of the European Communities
  London: HMSO, 1977. 58p. ISBN 0–11–700258–5
Environmental impact of energy strategies within the EEC
  Oxford: Pergamon Press for the Commission of the European Communities, 1980. 155p. ISBN 0–08–025681–3
Johnson, Stanley P
Pollution control policy of the European Communities
  London: Graham and Trotman, 1979. 157p. ISBN 0–86010–136–3
State of the environment
  Luxembourg: Office for official publications of the European Communities, annual. 1977–

Technology and research

Aims and priorities of a common research and development policy
 Brussels: General Secretariat of the Economic and Social Committee,
 1982. 59p
Danzin, A
Science and the second renaissance of Europe
 Oxford: Pergamon Press for the Commission of the European Commu-
 nities, 1979. 125p. ISBN 0–08–022442–3
Europe plus thirty report.
 Luxembourg: Commission of the European Communities, 1975. various
 pagings
First European congress on information systems and networks ...
 Munich: Verlag Dokumentation for the Commission of the European
 Communities, 1974. [plus subsequent congresses]
Operation of nuclear power stations
 Luxembourg: Office for official publications of the European Commu-
 nities, annual
*Patent information and documentation, an inventory of services available
to the public in the European Community*
 Munich: Verlag Dokumentation for the Commission of the European
 Community, 1976. 173p. ISBN 3–7940–5167–X
Transfer and exploitation of scientific and technical information,
proceedings of the symposium ...
 Luxembourg: Office for official publications of the European Commu-
 nities, 1982. 363p. ISBN 92–825–2837–5
Vade-mecum of contract research (indirect action)
 Luxembourg: Commission of the EEC, 1981. 46p

External affairs

ACP states yearbook.
 Brussels: Editions Delta, 1981. 600p. ISBN 2–8029–0014–5

2 The Organization of the Communities

With the signing of the Merger treaty in 1965 (qv) a rational and more cost-effective method of administering the three Communities was evolved.

The inter-relationship of the main institutions is shown in diagrammatic form after this introduction to Chapter 2:

- **European Communities institutions – inter-relationship** (pages 30–1)

For those who wish to know the sequence of Presidents of the Commission a list in date order has been provided. Biographical details of each will be found in the short biographical section at the end of this chapter:

- **Presidents of the European Commission** (page 28)

After these two preliminaries, sections on each of the major administrative organizations will be found starting with the Council of Ministers which has the major area of responsibility within the Communities:

FOR A DETAILED INDEX SEE THE YELLOW PAGES.

Reform of the Community institutions in order to ensure an effective and efficient government has been undertaken:

- **Commission reform** (pages 61–2)
- **Committee of three wise men** (pages 62–3)

The administrative action of the EC institutions directly affects the 300 million people of the Communities through the legislation which is issued. Currently this is brought into force by the legislative process of each member state:

- **Legislation of the European Communities** (pages 63–6)
  Legislative process (pages 66–8)
  Official journal of the European Communities (pages 68–71)

The budget of the EC has evolved with the development of the organization and grown with the current expansion of member states from six to ten and with the possibility of a further growth to twelve in the near future:

- **Budget of the European Communities** (pages 71–5)
  Budgetary policy committee (page 75)

Senior Community officials have been listed at the end of this chapter. They are in alphabetical order of surname. The list includes only Presidents of the Communities and members of the current Commission. This brief listing attempts to include names which are most frequently in the Press (pages 76–92)

Presidents of the European Commission

1958–60	Robert Schuman
1960–2	Hans Furler
1962–4	Gaetano Martino
1964–5	Jean Duvieusart
1965–6	Victor Leemans
1966–9	Alain Poher
1969–71	Mario Scelba
1971–3	Walter Behrendt
1973–5	Cornelis Berkhouwer
1975–80	Roy Jenkins
1981–	Gaston Thorn

Council

Basic information

Articles 145–54 of the Treaty of Rome establishing the EEC, are concerned with the Council. A number of these articles have been amended by the Merger treaty (qv) 1972.

At the Paris Summit Conference 9–10 December 1974, it was decided that regular meetings should be held of Heads of Governments. These were subsequently called the European Council.

Membership

The European Council will normally consist of Heads of Governments. The Council consists of representatives of the governments of the member states of the EC. Each government normally sends one of its ministers, though on occasions there may be more than one member present. Its membership thus varies according to the matter under consideration.

The Foreign Minister is normally regarded as his country's main representative on the Council.

Meetings of the Council

The function of the Council in its various forms is to direct the overall policy of the Community. One of the ways in which this is accomplished is to make decisions on Commission proposals.

At the 1974 Summit meeting, the Heads of Government agreed to meet at least three times a year in a Community Council. These meetings are currently described as sessions of the European Council. They are usually held in Brussels where the permanent secretariat is located.

Members of the Council will also take part regularly in European parliamentary debates, question time, etc., and will meet with appropriate Committees. The chairmanship of the Council rotates between the member governments at six-monthly intervals in the following order – Belgium, Denmark, Germany, Greece, France, Ireland, Italy, Luxembourg, Netherlands, United Kingdom.

Voting of the Council

When decisions are taken by majority vote the four larger countries –

(*continued p. 32*)

European Communities Institutions – Inter-Relationship

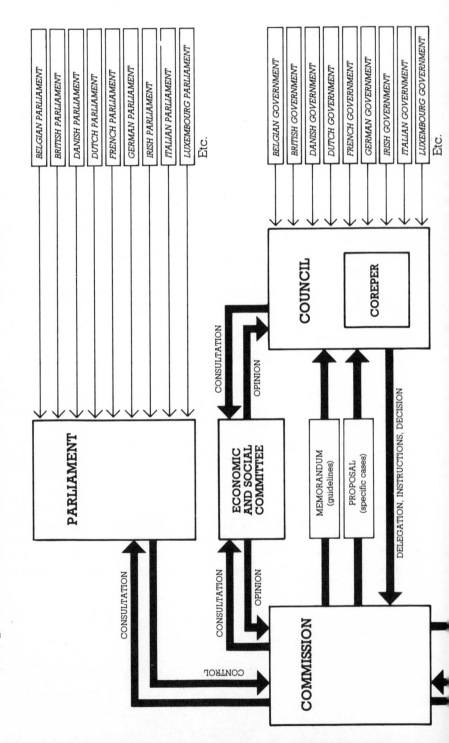

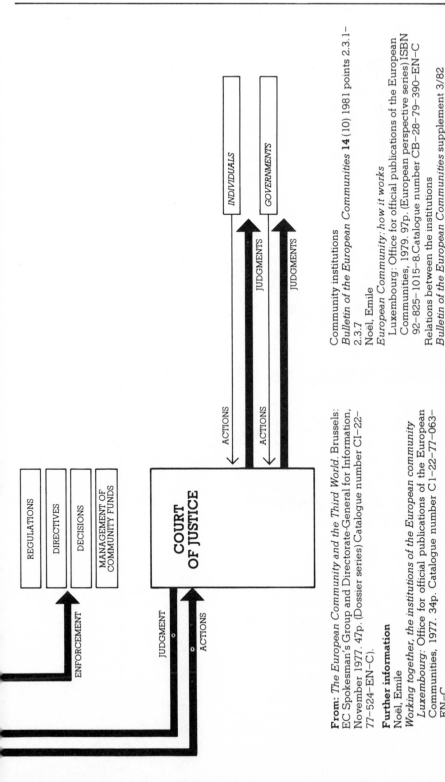

REGULATIONS

DIRECTIVES

DECISIONS

MANAGEMENT OF COMMUNITY FUNDS

ENFORCEMENT

COURT OF JUSTICE

JUDGMENT

ACTIONS

ACTIONS

ACTIONS

JUDGMENTS

JUDGMENTS

INDIVIDUALS

GOVERNMENTS

From: *The European Community and the Third World.* Brussels: EC Spokesman's Group and Directorate-General for Information, November 1977. 47p. (Dossier series) Catalogue number CI–22–77–524–EN–C).

Further information
Noël, Emile
Working together, the institutions of the European community
Luxembourg: Office for official publications of the European Communities, 1977. 34p. Catalogue number C1–22–77–063–EN–C

Community institutions
Bulletin of the European Communities **14** (10) 1981 points 2.3.1–2.3.7
Noël, Emile
European Community: how it works
Luxembourg: Office for official publications of the European Communities, 1979. 97p. (European perspective series) ISBN 92–825–1015–8. Catalogue number CB–28–79–390–EN–C
Relations between the institutions
Bulletin of the European Communities supplement 3/82

Germany, France, Italy and the United Kingdom – have ten votes each, Belgium, Greece and the Netherlands have five votes each, Ireland and Denmark three each and Luxembourg two. A total of 63 votes. For a proposal to be passed by a qualified majority vote, 45 votes in favour are needed in those cases where the Treaties require acts of the Council to be adopted on a proposal from the Commission. In other circumstances 41 votes in favour cast by at least six member states are required.

The special majority required under the last paragraph of article 95 of the ECSC treaty for certain amendments to the treaty is now nine-tenths as against the previous majority under the Community of 9 of eight-ninths.

Passports

The Council adopted a resolution on 23 June 1981 concerning a European passport of uniform pattern (OJ C241/1–7 19.9.81). A further resolution (OJ C179/1–2 16.7.82) specified its format and endorses the findings of a working party regarding colour of the covers and pages, security protection and material to be used.

Further information

Noël, Emile
The European Community: how it works
  Luxembourg: Office for official publications of the European Communities, 1979. 97p. (European perspective series) ISBN 92–825–1015–8. Catalogue number CB–28–79–390–EN–C

Permanent Representatives Committee (COREPER)

Basic information

Instituted by article 3 of the Merger treaty (qv). COREPER (Acronym from the French version of the title of this committee) is the second most important of the many committees advising the Council.

It consists of the Brussels Ambassadors of member states, who call upon appropriate national civil servants to assist them when specialized subjects are being dealt with.

Purpose of COREPER

To carry out tasks assigned to it by the Council. To prepare advice on reports presented to the Council and to feed them with advice on appropriate subjects of current interest.

Method of work

To undertake its duties the Committee meets in two parts:

- COREPER One consisting of Deputy Permanent Representatives is is concerned with technical questions, in the main
- COREPER Two consisting of Ambassadors is concerned with political matters

The president of the Committee is the Ambassador of the member state holding the office of President of the Council at the time.

Further information

General report on the activities of the European Communities
  Luxembourg: Office for official publications of the European Communities, annual
Noël, Emile
The European Community: how it works
  Luxembourg: Office for official publications of the European Communities, 1979. 97p. (European perspective series) ISBN 92-825-1015-8. Catalogue number CB-28-79-390-EN-C

Commission of the European Communities

Basic information

Under the Treaty of Rome (1957) a Commission was authorized. Article 155 lays down its authority and activities. Articles 156-63 concerning the Commission were repealed by article 19 of the Merger treaty (1972) and replaced by articles 10-18 of that treaty. Articles 189-192 give legal force to the measures inaugurated by the Commission.

The Commission is the guardian of the treaties setting up the European Community and is responsible for seeing that the treaties are implemented.

The Commission therefore proposes Community policy and is responsible for the administration of the Community.

Structure of the Commission

The Commission has 14 members chosen by agreement of the Community governments. Two each from Britain, France, Germany and Italy and one from other members. Commissioners are obliged to act in the Community's interests and not in the interests of the country from which they come. Commissioners are appointed for four years and can only be removed during their term of office by a vote of censure from the European Parliament. A quorum is eight members. The Chairman and five vice chairmen chosen from the Commissioners for two year renewable periods.

Work of the Commission

Each Commissioner with his chief of staff heads a department. For details of these departments see under Commissioners of the European Communities. He has special responsibilities for one or more areas of Community policy, such as economic affairs, agriculture, the environment, etc. Regular discussions are held between a Commissioner's department and interested parties in member states and within the Community's administrative services (plus Parliament). As a result of these discussions the Commissioner formulates draft proposals which he believes will help to improve the quality of life of Community citizens. For details as to how these proposals receive the force of law, see under Legislative process.

The Commission produces a directory of its staff and an annual report on the work of the Communities, see under Further information below.

Further information

General report on the activities of the European Communities
    Luxembourg: Office for official publications of the European Communities, annual
Directory of the Commission of the European Communities
    Luxembourg: Office for official publications of the European Communities, usually biennial
Programme of the Commission
    Luxembourg: Office for official publications of the European Communities, annual
Scott, Gay
European Economic Community
    London: Capital Planning Information, 1979. 72p. ISBN 0-906011-04-3
Noël, Emile
The European Community: how it works
    Luxembourg: Office for official publications of the European Communities, 1979. 97p. (European perspective series) ISBN 92-825-1015-8. Catalogue number CB-28-79-390-EN-C

Commissioners

Basic information

There are 14 Commissioners chosen with the agreement of the Community governments. They act in the Community's interest only. They are appointed for a period of four years and can only be removed during their term of office by a vote of censure from the European Parliament. The President was appointed for the period 6 January 1981 to 5 January 1983. The quorum at Commission meetings is eight.

14 Commissioners

(as at January 1981 plus one amendment May 1981 and one on 1 April 1982)

President:

Gaston Egmont Thorn	General Secretariat
	Legal Service
	Spokesman's group
	Cultural Matters
	Security Office

Members:

François-Xavier Ortoli Vice-President	Economic and Financial Affairs Credits and Investments
Wilhelm Haferkamp Vice-President	External Relations Nuclear Matters
Poul Dalsager	Agriculture
Lorenzo Natali Vice-President	Special responsibilities for institutional questions pertaining to enlargement Overall Mediterranean policy Information
Ivor Richard	Employment and Social Affairs Tripartite Conference Education and Vocational Training
Edgard Pisani	Development
Richard Burke	Delegate of the President Statistical Office Official Publications Office Personnel and Administration

Antonio Giolitti	Co-ordination of Community Funds Regional Policy
Franciscus H J J Andriessen	Competition Relations with the European Parliament
Georgios Contogeorgis	Co-ordination of Matters relating to Tourism Transport Fisheries
Karl-Heinz Narjes	Internal Market and Industrial Innovation Customs Union Service Environment and Consumer Protection Nuclear Safety
Etienne Davignon Vice-President	Research and Science Euratom Supply Agency Energy Joint Research Centre Industrial Affairs
Christopher Samuel Tugendhat Vice-President	Budget and Financial Control Financial Institutions Taxation

Further information

Directory of the Commission of the European Communities
Luxembourg: Office for official publications of the European Communities, usually biennial

Directorates-General of the Commission

Basic information

The Commission is divided into 25 Directorates-General and other services each of which is sub-divided into a number of Directorates with responsibility for an area of Commission policy.

Directorates-General
DG1 External Relations
  Director-General: Sir Roy Denman
DG11 Economic and Financial Affairs
  Director-General: T Padoa-Schioppa
DG111 Internal Market and Industrial Affairs
  Director-General: Fernand Braun
DG1V Competition
  Director-General: Manfred Caspari (15.4.81)
DG V Employment and Social Affairs
  Director-General: Jean Degimbe
DG V1 Agriculture
  Director-General: Claude Villain
DG V11 Transport
  Director-General: John R Steele (1.7.81)
DG V111 Development
  Director-General: Klaus Meyer
DG 1X Personnel and Administration
  Director-General: Jean-Claude Morel (1.4.81)
DG X Spokesman's Group and Directorate-General for Information
  Director-General: Franz Froschmaier (15.4.81)
DG X11 Research, Science and Education
  Director-General: Günter Schuster
DG X111 Information Market and Innovation
  Director-General: Raymond Appleyard
DG X1V Fisheries
  Director-General: Eamonn Gallagher
DG XV Financial Institutions and Taxation
  Director-General: O Bus Henriksen
DG XV1 Regional Policy
  Director-General: Pierre Mathijsen
DG XV11 Energy
  Director-General: John Christopher Audland (2.4.81)
DG XV111 Credit and Investments
  Director-General: Antonino Nicoletti
DG X1X Budgets
  Director-General: Daniel Strasser
DG XX Financial Control
  Director-General: Carlo Facini
Legal Service
  Director-General: Claus D Ehlermann
Statistical Office
  Director-General: Aage Dornonville de la Cour
Administration of the Customs Union Service
  Director: Friedrich Klein
Environment and Consumer Protection and Nuclear Safety
  Director-General: Athanassios Andreopoulos (27.5.81)
The Secretariat-General of the Commission
  Secretary-General: Emile Noël

Further information

Directory of the Commission of the European Communities
   Luxembourg: Office for official publications of the European Communities, usually biennial. Latest changes appear in the *Bulletin of the European Communities*.

Parliament

Basic information

The Treaty of Paris 18 April 1951 founding the ECSC, made provision for a Common Assembly which held its first sitting in Strasbourg on 10 September 1952, There were 78 representatives of the peoples of the member states. This first meeting formed an 'ad hoc' assembly located in Paris. A new and enlarged assembly to represent the ECSC, the EEC and EURATOM was set up at Europe House in Strasbourg 19 March 1958 and took the name of the 'European Parliament'.

The enlarged Community

With the enlargement of the European Community on 1 January 1973, the European Parliament was enlarged also to 198 members, which the nine national parliaments designated from their own members in the following proportions – France, Germany, Italy and the United Kingdom 36 members each, Belgium and the Netherlands 14 members each, Denmark and the Republic of Ireland 10 members each and Luxembourg six members. The Heads of the State or Government of the nine member states of the EC agreed on 12 July 1976 that there should be 410 representatives in Parliament.

The directly elected Parliament

On 7, 9 and 10 June 1979 elections took place for directly elected members of the European Parliament – the world's first international elections. In the new Parliament France, Germany, Italy and the United Kingdom have 81 representatives each, the Netherlands 25 representatives, Belgium and later Greece 24 representatives, Denmark 16 representatives, the Republic of Ireland 15 representatives and Luxembourg six representatives. They are elected for a period of five years. With the second enlargement of the community to include Greece on 1 January 1981, the total Parliamentary membership was 434.

The systems of voting used are – Proportional representation with national party lists in Denmark (except Greenland), France, Greece, the Netherlands and Luxembourg: proportional representation with regional party lists in Italy and Belgium: proportional representation with choice for parties of national or regional lists in Germany: single transferable vote in multi-member constituencies in the Republic of Ireland and Northern Ireland: simple majority in England, Scotland, Wales and Greenland. It is thought that later a uniform system of European elections will be worked out.

The provisional headquarters of the Parliament was in Luxembourg. Up to the end of the 1980/81 session a great deal of Parliament's work was carried out in the French city of Strasbourg where half the full sessions take place. Parliamentary committees meet in Brussels (qv Parliament location).

Work of Parliament

Parliament is the forum of the European Communities. It debates in public any issue or question of interest for the Communities. Both the Commission and Council of Ministers make major statements of policy in Parliament. It has the right to be consulted on major items of legislation, has growing powers over the Community budget and it can dismiss the Commission by a vote of censure. In January 1973 Parliament introduced Question Time which takes place on the second or third day of each sitting and lasts 1½ hours. Members may put questions directly to the Commission and a supplementary question if they wish. When five or more members do not think that a question has been answered in full they may demand an emergency debate to be held immediately afterwards. Members of Parliament may address written questions to the Commission. These together with the answers are published in the Official journal of the European Communities.

Presidents of Parliament

ECSC Common Assembly

Spaak, Paul-Henri	1952–4
de Gasperi, Alcide	1954
Fohrman, Jean	1954
Pella, Giuseppe	1954–6
Furler, Hans	1956–8

Parliament

Schumann, Robert	1958–60
Furler, Hans	1960–62

Martino, Gaetano	1962–4
Duvieusart, Jean	1964–5
Leemans, Victor	1965–6
Poher, Alain	1966–9
Scelba, Mario	1969–71
Behrendt, Walter	1971–3
Berkhouwer, Cornelis	1973–5
Spenale, Georges	1975–77
Colombo, Emilio	1977–9

The first President after the start of direct elections was Mrs Simone Veil, France–Liberal, 1979–82. She was succeeded by Mr Piet Dankert, Netherlands–Socialist, 1982–.

Further information

Official journal of the European Communities. Debates of the European Parliament
   Luxembourg: Office for official publications of the European Community. [The debates are published as an annex to the OJ. Sessions of Parliament run from March to March the following year. Sessional indexes cover names, subjects and have a list of working documents. Currently they have a publishing delay of about twelve months]
European Parliament Information, the sittings
   Luxembourg: Directorate General for Information and Public Relations, monthly (Includes a weekly and daily summary, together with an annex of resolutions adopted during the month)
Noël, Emile
Working together, the institutions of the European Community
   Luxembourg: Office for official publications of the European Communities, June 1977. 35p. Catalogue number CI–22–77–063–EN–C
Your voice in Europe, the European Parliament
   London: London Information Office of the European Parliament, March 1979. 8p.
Englefield, Dermot
Parliament and information
   London: Library Association, 1981. 132p. ISBN 85365–570–7
Europe's Parliament
   London: European Parliament information office, 1981. 32 slides, lecture notes and tape commentary:
Official handbook of the European Parliament
   Luxembourg: Office for official publications of the European Communities, 1981. looseleaf
European Parliament: towards a uniform procedure for direct elections
   Luxembourg: Office for official publications of the European Communities, 1982. 466p. ISBN 92–825–2527–9

Parliamentary Bureau

Basic information

All the activities of Parliament and its various bodies are under the direction of the President. He is assisted by twelve Vice-Presidents and five Quaestors (without the right to vote). Together they form the Bureau, an annually-elected body which is responsible for the day-to-day running of the Parliament.

The chairmen of the political groups together with members of the Bureau attend meetings of the enlarged Bureau.

Parliamentary Committees

Basic information

Until 1979 the European Parliament had twelve specialized committees each dealing with a particular area of the Community's activities. On 20 July 1979 Parliament increased these committees to 15 (EP Working document 1–235/79).

Composition of the committees

1. Political affairs (39 members)
2. Agriculture (39 members)
3. Budgets (37 members)
4. Economic and monetary affairs (35 members)
5. Energy and research (35 members)
6. External economic relations (35 members)
7. Legal affairs (27 members)
8. Social affairs and employment (27 members)
9. Regional policy and regional planning (27 members)
10. Transport (27 members)
11. The environment, public health and consumer protection (27 members)
12. Youth affairs, culture, education information and sport (27 members)
13. Development and co-operation (27 members)
14. Budgetary control
15. Rules of procedure and petitions (27 members)

These Committees usually meet in Brussels, but members may go on missions to study problems on the spot.

By the same resolution of 20 July 1979, the European Parliament decided to set up two delegations:

- 1 to the Joint Parliamentary Committee of the EEC – Greece Association
- 2 to the Joint Parliamentary Committee of the EEC – Turkey Association

Purpose of the Committees

Politically and nationally the membership of the Committees broadly reflects that of Parliament. The work of each consists of preparing the ground for debates, keeping in touch with the Commission and the Council particularly during Parliamentary recess, preparing resolutions on proposed legislation put forward by the Commission on which Parliament has been asked for an opinion.

Further information

European Parliament briefing
   Luxembourg: Directorate-General for Information and Public Relations. Weekly whilst Parliament is in session
Bulletin of the European Communities, Part 2 Section 3
   Luxembourg: Office for official publications of the European Communities. Monthly ISSN 0378–3693

Parliamentary Sessions and Procedure.

Basic information

Articles 137–44 of the Treaty of Rome establishing the EEC, are concerned with Parliament (The Assembly).

Organization of Parliamentary work

Parliament's year begins on the second Tuesday of March.

The session begins with the election of the President, Vice Presidents, which together form the Parliamentary Bureau (qv) and members of the Parliamentary Committees. It decides on its own agenda. It has published rules of procedure which were revised in 1981 (*Bulletin of the European Communities* **14** (3) 1981. point 2.3.6) On average Parliament meets for a week at a time once a month. Specialist sittings may be convened by the President at the request of the majority of its members, or at the request of the Council, or Commission.

Up to the end of the 1980/1 session about half the sittings were in Strasbourg, and the remainder in Luxembourg (qv Parliament – location).

Parliamentary sittings are open to the public but not committee meetings unless specifically so arranged.

The debates are conducted in the seven official languages of the Community:

Danish
Dutch

English
French
German
Greek
Italian

There is simultaneous translation and reports and other documents are made available in all seven languages (qv *Official Journal*).

Work of Parliament

Parliament presents reports to the Council and influences legislation proposed by the Commission.

Preparatory work for Parliamentary debates is done in the Committees (qv) who draw up reports on specific questions. The report consists of a motion, an explanatory statement and includes the result of the Committee's vote. Minority opinions are stated where appropriate. These reports are considered by Parliament which votes on the motions.

The formal powers of Parliament have been used more effectively in the late 1970s and 1980s than heretofore. This applies particularly in the budgetary field. For example owing to a disagreement between Parliament and the Commission over the 1980 budget increases, this budget was not agreed by Parliament until 9 July 1980 (*Bulletin of the European Communities* **13** (7/8) 1980 points 1.1.2 and 2.3.70). Parliament was also disturbed that it is not always consulted by the Community's institutions when necessary. It took up an example of this lack of consultation and in the Isoglucose case, after discussion, had the institutional decision reversed (*Bulletin of the European Communities* **14** (2) 1981 point 2.3.2.).

Further information

General report on the activities of the European Communities
    Luxembourg: Office for official publications of the European Communities, annual.
Scott, Gay
The European Economic Community, a guide to sources of information
    London: Capital Planning Information, 1979. 72p. ISBN 0-906011-04-3
Jeffries, John
Guide to the official publication of the European Communities
    London: Mansell, 1981. 318p. ISBN 0-7201-1590-6
Englefield, Dermot
Parliament and information
    London: Library Association, 1981. 132p. ISBN 85365-570-7

Parliamentary Political Groups

Basic information

Under the Treaty of Rome (1957), articles 137–44 are concerned with Parliament.

Up to July 1979 representation was by nomination from the Parliaments of member states.

Since July 1979 members are elected by direct universal suffrage a body of 410 members up to the end of 1980 and 434 with effect from January 1981 when the Community was enlarged to 10 members.

Organization of the political groups

During plenary sessions members sit in political not national groups. The minimum strength of a political group is 21 representatives or 15 if from at least two member states or 10 if from at least three member states.

Members are not obliged to join a group and at the 1980/81 session in October 1980 there were 10 non-attached members.

In 1981/2 session of Parliament there were the following political groups:

- Socialists (Labour Party and Social Democratic Labour Party) 113 representatives
- European People's Party (Christian Democrats) 107 representatives
- European Democrats (including Conservatives and Ulster Unionist Party) 63 representatives
- Communists and allies 44 representatives
- Liberals and Democrats 40 representatives
- European Progressive Democrats (including Scottish National Party) 18 representatives
- Group for the Technical Co-ordination and Defence of Independent Groups and Members 11 representatives

Work of the political groups

Each political group tries to present a common front on the issues arising. National preoccupations tend to take second place.

Further information

General report on the activities of the European Communities
   Luxembourg: Office for official publications of the European Communities, annual

Political groups in the European Parliament
   Luxembourg: Secretariat of the European Parliament, 1975/6.4p. [Separate pamphlet for
   each group]
Elections to the European Parliament by direct universal suffrage
   Luxembourg: Office for official publications of the European Communities, 1977. 158p.
   Catalogue number AX-22-77-241-EN-C
European Parliament rules of procedure
   Luxembourg: Secretariat of the European Parliament, 1978. 55p. [new edition in preparation.
   See OJ C77/16 6.4.81 OJ C90/48 21.4.81 (EP DOC 1-926/80)]
A parliament for Europe
   Luxembourg: Secretariat of the European parliament, 1978. 30p. [Produced in preparation
   for the first election in June 1979 with special reference to the UK constituencies]
*Guide to the European Democratic Group in the European Parliament and the role of the
Parliament in the European Community*
   London: European Democratic Group, 2 Queen Anne's Gate, London SW1H 9AA, 1980.
   47p.
Your MEP
   London: UK Information office of the European Parliament, 2 Queen Anne's Gate,
   London SW1H 9AA, 1981.
   [Includes list of UK members of the European Parliament, their constituencies, addresses
   and telephone numbers]
Official handbook of the European Parliament
   Luxembourg: Office for official publications of the European Communities, 1981. looseleaf:
   [Available in six languages. Gives biographic detail and photographs of all MPs. Also
   includes abstracts from European treaties, details of electoral laws and election results,
   political parties, parliamentary standing orders, etc]

Political Control by Parliament

Basic information

Parliament, or the Assembly as it is mentioned in the EEC Treaty of Rome (1957), does not
appear until Articles 137-44.

Its function is to exercise democratic control over the institutions and over the legislative
process (qv).

Method of Work

Before 1979 Parliament consisted of representatives nominated by the
national parliaments of member states. After the universal suffrage first
election which was held between 7th and 10th June 1979, those elected
sat in political groupings not national ones. The Communists on the left
and Liberals and Democrats on the right.

The decisions of the Community are implemented by Legislation (qv
Legislation and legislative process). Here, Parliament's role is consultative
for the most part. Before taking a final decision on a Commission proposal
Council almost inevitably consults Parliament. Under the Community
treaties the Council is not obliged to act on Parliament's reply.

It is mainly at an earlier stage of the legislation that Parliament's influence can be felt. This influence can amend or initiate legislation. It is, however, the Commission's task to formally initiate legislation. There are usually consultations at an early stage between the responsible directorate of the Commission and the appropriate Parliamentary committee (qv).

When the Commission has drafted its proposals it forwards them to the Council. The Council requests the opinion of Parliament.

The proposal goes to one of the 15 specialized Committees where a rapporteur is appointed to prepare a draft opinion and amendments. The Parliamentary political groups hold meetings to decide on the party line for each legislative proposal.

At the Committee meeting the Parliamentarians and Commission officials sit together and discuss the proposals.

The Rapporteur produces a final report which is presented to Parliament for debate. Further amendments may be made. The Commissioner responsible is present and frequently replies to the debate. Council representatives are also allowed to attend and may speak.

Parliaments's opinion is then sent to the Council. In the meantime, the Commission is likely to have incorporated some or all of the Parliament's opinions in its own proposals. The Council makes a final decision.

Another major source of political control by Parliament is through the Parliamentary Question system. Whilst this system has always been available, it was only after the first expansion of the Community member states that it began to be used as an effective means of keeping Parliamentarians up to date and bringing pressure to bear on the Commission and Council.

It should be noted that Parliament can call the Commission to account for what it has done or failed to do. In 1979 Parliament showed its disfavour with Council proposals and rejected for the very first time the Community budget. The 1980 budget was in dispute between Parliament and the Council and was not resolved until 19 July 1980 (OJ L242/1–737 15.9.80) (EP/80/782/EEC, EURATOM, ECSC). The main problem concerned Community expenditure on agriculture which Parliament wanted limited to a greater extent than the Council, reinstatement of appropriations for non-compulsory expenditure and inclusion in the budget of the European Development Fund and Community borrowing and lending operations. Whilst Parliament made progress towards its aims, they were not all reached.

Citizens and Parliament

Problems which citizens wish to have resolved or opinions which they wish to express, can be given to:

- their local Euro MP
- the European political group they support
- the rapporteur of a parliamentary committee which is preparing a report in which they are interested
- combining with others to submit a petition to the President of Parliament on an aspect of the Community's activities

Euro MPs and Parliament

A private member of Parliament can raise any point which he considers should be known. He may also do this through his political group:

- whilst Parliament is in plenary session an oral question is put down to the Council or Commission (with or without debate)
- he can also put down questions to Council or Commission for question time on the second or third sitting day. In these circumstances supplementary questions may be given if considered necessary
- he may table motions in the house for reference to the appropriate committee or for immediate consideration if thought to be urgent

Where matters raised at question time cannot be fully dealt with, five or more members of a political group may put down a motion for an emergency debate to follow at the end of question time.

Any ten members or a political group may put down a motion censuring the Commission which if carried would lead to the resignation of the whole Commission.

In addition Euro MPs may at any time:

- put down written questions to Council or Commission for a written answer to be published in the *Official Journal* (OJ)
- raise points in writing or orally in the committees on which they serve

Further information

Function of the European Parliament, procedure followed in the exercise of political control
   Luxembourg: Directorate-General for information and public relations, 1974. 21p.
Hopkins, Michael
Policy formation in the European Communities
   London: Mansell, 1981. 360p. ISBN 0-7201-1587-3

Parliament – Location

Basic information

Article 216 of the Treaty of Rome (1957), reads:
'The seat of the institutions of the Community shall be determined by common accord of the governments of the member states.'

There was no agreement when the Community was set up and Luxembourg, Brussels and Strasbourg were all used as institutional headquarters.

The European Parliament, however, moved from Luxembourg to Strasbourg and back every year.

Many European MPs wanted to locate Parliament in a single town on both convenience and cost grounds.

Action taken

In 1980 several of Europe's political groups tabled a motion article 4 of which states, 'the Secretariat of the Assembly and its departments shall remain in Luxembourg'. It requested that the governments of the member states take a decision by 15 June 1981. There were, however, insufficient members present to form a quorum. Instead the motion was debated on 12 January 1981.

On Friday 13th March 1981 Parliament decided to hold all its 1981 part sessions in Strasbourg, to organize the meetings of its committees and political groups in Brussels as a general rule and that the operation of the Secretariat and technical services of Parliament be reviewed to suit these arrangements and avoid constant travel by Parliamentary officials. There was some disagreement with these arrangements and the action taken is likely to be reviewed again at some time in the future.

Further information

Seat [of Parliament] and places of work
  Bulletin of the European Communities **14** (7/8) 1981. point 2.3.10

Court of Justice

Basic information

Article 7 of the ECSC treaty established a Court of Justice (April 1951). The Court consists of ten judges appointed jointly by all governments. Each judge serves a term of six years which is renewable. Judges are appointed by agreement between member states.

They are assisted by four advocates-general who give an independent view on cases.

The President of the Court, who is selected by the judges from amongst their number, directs the work of the court.

The court is located in Luxembourg at the Plateau du Kirchberg, PO Box 1406.

Powers of the Court

The Court of Justice is the final authority on all legal matters falling within the domain of the Treaties of Rome and Paris. It rules on cases between member states and the Commission. Its decisions are binding on member states, Community institutions and all individuals. National courts can appeal to it for rulings on how to interpret Community Law. It is a court of appeal for the staff of the Communities.

Work of the Court

The particular value of the Court of Justice, is its interpretation of Community legislation.

Whilst the Council with other Community bodies – the Commission, Parliament, the Economic and Social Council, etc., formulate the most effective legislation they can devise, it is only when it is used in practical situations that its true worth can be seen. It is then that disputes and disagreements between parties occur and it is the Court of Justice that is the final court of appeal, there being no appeal against its rulings.

The decisions of this court affect Community legislation and provide interpretations of difficult or unclear sections.

It is important, therefore, that a detailed record of cases be made available in all the official languages of the Community. Cases affecting an item of primary or secondary legislation having Community–wide implications are referred to in the legal commentaries or restatements on the laws of member states. Examples may be found in volume 42A of *Halsbury's Statutes of England* 3rd ed. 1975.

The major record of cases will be found in the series, 'Reports of cases before the Court' (European Court reports (ECR)). It is published in Luxembourg: Office for official publications of the European Communities, 1954 – ISSN 0378–7591.

There is also the *Bibliography of European judicial decisions* which was continued in 1976 by the *Bulletin bibliographique de jurisprudence communautaire.*

The monthly, *Bulletin of the European Communities* includes a listing of new cases and judgements as well as a summary of selected important cases. Some of these appear in the *Bulletin* before they are included in, 'Reports of cases before the Court.'

There are also the weekly, *Proceedings of the Court of Justice of the European Communities*, the quarterly, *Bulletin of information on the Court of Justice of the European Communities* and the annual, *Synopsis of the work of the Court of Justice of the European Communities*, all produced for the Court by the Luxembourg Office for official publications of the European Communities. (qv entry under, Law reports of the European Communities).

Further information

The Court of Justice of the European Communities, 2nd ed
   Luxembourg: Office for official publications of the European Communities, 1981. 43p.
   (European Documentation series 1/81). ISBN 92–825–2140–0. Catalogue number CB–
   NC–81–001–EN–C
Selected instruments relating to the organization, jurisdiction and procedure of the Court
   Luxembourg: Office of official publications of the European Communities, 1975. 348p.
Jeffries, John
How to find out about the Court of Justice of the European Communities
   Canterbury: University of Kent for the Association of EDC Librarians, 1982. 4p. ('How to'
   leaflets)
Register of current Community legal instruments, 2nd ed
   Luxembourg: Office for official publications of the European Communities, 1982. 2v.
   ISBN 92–825–2626–7

Law Reports of the European Communities

Basic information

Communities legislation, having the force of law in all member states, is enforced by national courts. In this process of enforcement and by the resulting appeals to higher courts, the legislation is also interpreted.

The Court of Justice of the European Community exists to interpret those points of Communities law which are referred to it by national courts. Further it has the power to determine the legal correctness of action taken by organs of the Communities and to resolve disputes between the Community and its employees.

Court decisions aim at producing uniformity in the interpretation of Communities legislation. The judgements of the Court of Justice have not quite the same standing as precedents as do similar decisions in English law.

The Law Reports series

From 1954–8 this series of reports carries the title, 'Reports of cases before the Court'. It is published for the Court of Justice of the European Coal and Steel Community (ECSC) in Luxembourg, by the Office for official publications of the European Communities. It is in two volumes both having been translated from the French.

From 1958 the series continued the title, 'Reports of cases before the Court'. It is published for the Court of Justice of the European Communities in Luxembourg by the Office for official publications of the European Communities. The ISSN is 0378–7591.

The series is published in eight, nine or ten parts with an additional part as an index, for each year.

The index consists of a number of sections:

- index of parties [alphabetical]
- alphabetical index of subject matter
- table of Community legislation [referred to in the judgements and opinions]
- table of cases reported [Chronology under date of judgement or order]
- table of cases classified in numerical order (sic)

Further information

European Community law reports are also issued as:

Common Market law reports
    London: European Law Centre Ltd. 1962 – (monthly 1962–78, thereafter weekly. Indexes in the last part of each month, cumulate throughout the year)

References to those Law Reports of the European Community which throw light on EC legislation are included in the following:

Encyclopaedia of European Community law
    London: Sweet and Maxwell, 3 vols. (a loose leaf service with regular updating) (includes references to Law reports of the European Communities)
European law digest
    London: European Law Centre Ltd. 1973 – (monthly)
Halsbury's statutes of England, 3rd ed. v 42A
    London: Butterworths, 1975 (continuation volumes) (European Communities legislation will be found in v 42A and is updated by yellow pages at the end of each set of continuation volumes. This material cumulates annually so that only the latest cumulation plus volume 42A is required. Case references from the 'Common Market Law Reports' series are included.)
Digest of case law relating to the European Communities A, B, C and D series
    Luxembourg: Office for official publications of the European Communities, 1977. ISBN 92-829-0033-9.
    [successor to *Compendium of case law relating to the European Communities*, 1973–6, compiled by H J Eversen and H Sperl
    Amsterdam: North Holland Publishing Company]

Court of Auditors

Basic information

Established under the second, Budgetary treaty (1975) and came into effect on 1.6.77.
It replaces the Audit Board of the EEC and EAEC and the Auditor of the ECSC.

Court of Auditors – representation

It has ten members appointed by the Council on a unanimous vote after consultation with Parliament.

Members appointed should have belonged to external audit bodies or be especially qualified.

They are appointed for a renewable term of six years.

They have similar conditions to those appointed to the Court of Justice.

The purpose of the Court is to keep a check on the Community's budget spending. It works closely with national audit bodies in the member states.

Purpose of the Court

It is responsible for the external audit of the Community budget and the ECSC's operational budget.

Internal audits remain the responsibility of the financial controller of each institution.

More recently, appropriate questions put by members of the European Parliament are being referred to the Court of Auditors. For example in January 1979 a question by Mr Tam Dalyell on the non-use of EC funds and another by Mr Ralph Howell on emergency aid to East and South East England were both referred.

Work of the Court

Not only is the Court responsible for an examination as to whether all revenue has been received and all expenditure made in a lawful and regular manner, but it is also designed to examine whether the financial management is sound. For example the report covering 1980 included a number of strictures (OJ C344/1–259 31.12.81).
See also last item under, Further information, below.

The audit extends to:

- the Community's institutions eg on 30.9.80 report to Council and Commission on the ECSC's financial operations in 1979
- bodies created by the Community eg Joint European Torus (JET)
- the European development fund
- the submission of observations on specific problems
- production of reports on specific subjects submitted to it eg at the request of Parliament, on Community food aid

Further information

General report on the activities of the European Communities, section 2 *Institutions and other bodies*
   Luxembourg: Office for official publications of the European Communities, annual
Myles, Gregg
EEC Brief
   Belfast: Locksley Press, 1979. 2 v: (loose leaf)
Noël, Emile
The European Community: how it works
   Luxembourg: Office for official publications of the European Communities, 1979. 97p. (European perspectives series). ISBN 92–825–1015–8. Catalogue number CB–28–79–390–EN–C
Court of Auditors, study of the financial systems of the European Communities (1981) (OJ C342/1–71 31.12.81)

Economic and Social Committee (ESC)

Basic information

The Committee was established by the Treaty of Rome (1957) articles 4 and 193–198 of the EEC treaty as amended on the accession of new countries. The EURATOM treaty 1957, articles 3 and 165–170, also applies to this committee.

This advisory body was given rules of procedure in 1959 (OJ 493 18.4.59). A set of revised rules of procedure was approved by the Council in 1968 (68/101/ EEC, EURATOM) and again in 1974 (OJ L228/1–12 19.8.74) (Act 74/428/EEC, EURATOM). An opinion of the ESC concerning its place and role in the institutional machinery was presented in 1974 (OJ C115/37–42 28.9.74).

It considered that there had been a dilution of its responsibilities.

Economic and Social Committee – representation

The Committee consists of representatives of employers, workers and interest groups in the subjects concerned. With the enlargement of the Communities to 10 the Committee has 156 members allocated as follows:

Belgium	12 members
Denmark	9 members
Germany	24 members
Greece	12 members
France	24 members
Republic of Ireland	9 members
Italy	24 members
Luxembourg	6 members
Netherlands	12 members
UK	24 members

Members of the Council and Commission may attend meetings.

Members are appointed for four years and the last change of members was 1982. A member may have an assistant who may take part in the proceedings but not vote.

A chairman, two vice chairmen and a bureau (21 members) are elected by the Committee for a two year period, the latter has the task of organizing the Committee's work. A second election takes place after two years.

The Committee is divided into sections responsible for the principal subjects covered by the Rome treaties (EEC and EURATOM). Sections may set up study groups where necessary. Experts may be appointed for specific projects.

On the initiative of the bureau, sub-committees may be set up for questions coming within the purview of two or more sections.

Groups may be set up on a voluntary basis by members. These would represent employers, workers, etc.

Purpose of the Economic and Social Committee

Under the EEC treaty the Committee has to be consulted by the Council and the Commission on questions relating to:

- agriculture
- freedom of movement for workers
- right of establishment
- transport
- approximation of laws
- social policy
- European social fund
- vocational training

Under the Euratom treaty the Committee has to be consulted on:

- certain areas of the nuclear field
- research and training programmes
- establishment of schools for training specialists

- health and safety
- investment
- access to skilled jobs
- insurance cover against nuclear risks

Further, the committee has obtained the right to advise on all questions affecting the work of the Community.

Work of the Economic and Social Committee

It has an advisory role covering a very wide range of EC activities.

Whilst many questions have to be referred to it, its opinions and recommendations do not have to be taken by the Council.

Further information

General report on the activities of the European Communities
    Luxembourg: Office for official publications of the European Communities, annual
Economic and Social Committee of the European Communities annual report
    Luxembourg: Office for official publications of the European Communities, 1974–
Economic and Social Committee
    Luxembourg: Office for official publications of the European Communities, 1976. 16p
The right of initiative of the Economic and Social Committee
    Brussels: Economic and Social Committee, 1977. 123p
Community advisory committees for the representation of socio-economic interest.
    Farnborough: Saxon House for EC Economic and Social Committee, 1980. 215p. ISBN 0–566–00328–7

European Investment Bank (EIB)

Basic information

Article 129 of the Treaty of Rome (1957) established the EIB and article 130 outlines its purpose. It was set up in 1958.

Statutes of the EIB

These will be found in the, Treaties establishing the European Communities, see, Further information.

Members of the Bank include all the Member states of the Community. The starting capital was 2,025 million units of account. Most of its later capital it raised on the money market.

Special loans may be raised by the Board of Governors for specific projects. They will not exceed a certain sum from each member on which interest will be paid. The term of the loan not to exceed 20 years.

In the event of a fall in the value of the currency of a member state, the lost value shall be replaced.

The Bank shall be directed and managed by a Board of Governors, a Board of Directors and a Management committee.

The bank to build up a reserve fund of 10% of its capital.

The statute also laid down the method by which the bank should carry out its duties.

Tasks of the EIB

Under article 130 these should be:

- to contribute to the balanced and steady development of the Common Market. Therefore it would not finance the general cash requirements of a project or an authority, but would concentrate on effective investments which are part of a well defined development.

- it shall operate on a non-profit making basis, but investments financed by the bank should contribute to the overall economic productivity of the Community.

- it shall grant loans and give guarantees which facilitate the financing of:

  - projects in less developed regions including associated third world countries
  - projects for modernizing or converting undertakings
  - projects of interest to several member states and which may be beyond the capacity of one or two of the members

Who can borrow?

- private and public enterprises including those in associated countries
- public authorities
- financing institutes such as banks, or intermediate financing institutes

How much may be borrowed?

Though the bank does not lay down a minimum amount it prefers sums of over 1,000,000 units of account. It can, of course, help finance a project which may be made up of a number of small items of less than 500,000 ECU each.

The bank rarely lends more than 50% of the cost of a project.

Currencies used

Whilst the project may be expressed in a single currency, the loan may be in one or more equivalent currencies. Currently the EIB is using the currencies of the 10 together with the Swiss Fr. and American $.

Duration of loan

The EIB makes long term loans of from 7–12 years. In the case of infrastructure loans the period before repayment may be up to 20 years.

Interest rates

Up to 1972 these were $8\frac{1}{8}$% per annum. This was continued after 1972 for loans of less than 9 years, but increased to $8\frac{1}{2}$% for funds required for longer periods.

Guarantees by the EIB

Another aid of the EIB is to support enterprises or public authorities by guaranteeing loans which they have raised on the open market or from financing institutes.

Formal approach to the EIB

The applicant should supply documentary material on the activities and financial situation of the borrower (annual report/profit and loss account). Description of the project. Prospects of profitability. The plan of financing the project. The guarantee which can be provided. This should be sent to the Head Office of the EIB:

2 place de Metz
Luxembourg

Work undertaken

In the UK, loans from EIB have assisted in the building of nuclear and other power stations, development and transmission of oil and natural gas, coal mining, power lines, transport, telecommunications, water schemes, basic industries, mechanical and electrical engineering, agriculture, and global loans (a comprehensive loan to support multiple interlinked projects whose overall purpose is approved by the EIB).

In September 1981 the bank announced loans totalling 336.4 million ECU for investments in the Community and 18.4 million ECU for investments in ACP countries. These loans included 79.1 million ECU for projects in the UK including – new British Railways rolling stock, drainage and flood prevention in Devon, a water supply system in Cornwall, road improvements and water supply in Fife, a micro-processor computer plant at Leeds, a ring road round Liverpool, a factory producing earth moving equipment, etc.

Further information

European Investment Bank, annual report
    Luxembourg: EIB, annual
Statute and other provisions governing the EIB
    Luxembourg: EIB, 1973 plus later amendment sheets
European Investment Bank Information
    Luxembourg: EIB, periodically (approximately quarterly). ISSN 0250–3891

European Investment Bank (EIB) – Financial Assistance

Basic information

The EIB was founded in 1958 under articles 129 and 130 of the Treaty of Rome (1957). The Bank grants:

- long term loans
- provides guarantees

to firms, public authorities and financial institutions to help finance investment to solve regional problems. Priority is given to those problems which concern regional development.

Projects benefiting under the EIB

The Bank is especially concerned with projects which increase productivity and provide employment such as:

- amenities
- building and plant for industry and mining
- energy infrastructure
- housing adjacent to industrial investment
- irrigation network
- sewage systems
- telecommunications
- transport
- transport equipment
- vocational training centres
- water supply and purification plant

Rates of grants

As it is a non-profit making body the Bank is able to offer reasonable terms to its clients

- the Bank normally finances up to 50% of the fixed asset project cost
- it prefers not to lend less than 1 million ECU per project
- it undertakes smaller-scale projects by means of 'global loans' to a bank or financial institution ('global', is used to refer to a number of small, linked projects) Details from the Department of Industry in the UK
- the term of the loan depends on the project but in the case of infrastructures this may be for up to 20 years. The normal period of loan is between 7 and 12 years. Loans are at a fixed interest rate and there is usually a two year deferrment of capital repayments
- loans can be made in the local currency, or the currencies of other member states or in certain third party currencies eg US $
- repayment of loans is usually in fixed half yearly instalments of the principal and interest in the currencies used for the loan
- the EIB is also able to guarantee loans for projects considered suitable which are raised by firms or institutions from commercial credit institutions

Submission of applications

Direct to the head office of the Bank:

- 2, place de Metz
  Boîte postale 2005
  Luxembourg
  Telephone: Luxembourg 43–50–11

or via the EIB's London office at:

- 23 Queen Anne's Gate
  Westminster
  London SW1H 9BU
  Telephone: 01–222 2933

Work undertaken

The United Kingdom was one of the major recipients of EIB loans in 1980 (688 million EUA). Examples include:

- British Railways, 38.6 million EUA towards 18 high speed diesel trains for NE and SW lines
- Lancashire County Council, 10.1 million EUA for the construction of a section of the M65, Calder valley motorway
- Yorkshire Water Authority, 10.4 million EUA for sewage and sewage disposal schemes in Sheffield
- Shetland Islands Council, 8.2 million EUA for roads, housing and water supply
- Rockwool Limited, 1.7 million EUA for a mineral wool factory at Bridgend, Wales

Further information

General report on the activities of the European Communities
Luxembourg: Office for official publications of the European Communities, annual
European Investment Bank, annual report
Luxembourg: The Bank, annual. [The bank also issues comparative reports covering longer periods, loans and guarantees in the member countries of the EEC: Investment in the Community and its financing (annual). Activities of the EIB in ... EIB information (quarterly)]
Grants and loans from the European Community
Luxembourg: Office for official publications of the European Communities, 1981. 83p. (European documentation series 7–8/1981) ISBN 92–825–2633–X. Catalogue number CB–NC–81–008–EN–C
Scott, Gay
Guide to European Community grants and loans, 2nd ed
Biggleswade: Euroinformation Limited, 1981. 111p. ISBN 0–907304–01–X
Official sources of finance and aid for industry in the UK
London: National Westminster Bank Limited, Commercial section market intelligence department, 1981. 67p

Commission Reform

Basic information

The Commission decided in 1977 that an informal weekend meeting away from the daily work, would allow members to sit back and take a rather more objective view of their work (*Bulletin of the European Communities* **10** (9) 1977. points 1.1.1–1.1.5). This was repeated in the following year (*Bulletin* ... **11** (9) 1978. points 1.1.1–1.1.13) and the President, Roy Jenkins, commented on the discussion.

Proposals made

Rather brief comments were made on the future of the Community budget with particular reference to the transfer of resources and the need for additional revenue.

Inevitably because of its importance, Agriculture was discussed with special reference to the surpluses which had accumulated, and it was considered a prudent policy to reduce these surpluses.

The main part of the discussion concerned the work, organization and staffing of the Commission. In their programme of work, in earlier years there had been a number of subjects considered as possibly suitable for harmonized legislation and which if undertaken might well benefit many people in the Community. However, the work involved would use an unnecessarily large part of the limited time of the officials without moving forward the major issues of European policy. It was thought that in these cases, some divergence amongst member states would not matter. It was agreed that in future years there should be a more critical appraisal of the programme of legislation work within the Community.

Another major feature of the discussion concerned the organization and staffing of the Commission. The question of the number of representatives from member states was also discussed, for in a few years there will be a Community of 12 whereas when first set up the Commission was concerned with only six countries. It was proposed that a working party to review the administrative structures and operation of the Commission, should be set up to report in six months. The review body which was established was chaired by Dirk Spierenburg.

The report of this Body was submitted to the Commission on 24 September 1979 as 'Proposals for reform of the Commission of the European Communities and its services' (*Bulletin of the European Communities* **12** (9) 1979. points 1.3.1 – 1.3.13). Its main theme was that if the Commission is to perform its vital political role to the full and engage in effective dialogue with the Council and the directly elected Parliament, it must be strengthened and its structure and workings made more efficient. The report analyses the Commission's role, certain weaknesses it has and their causes. It was particularly concerned with the size of the Commission in view of the growing number of member nations and recommended that only one Commissioner be appointed from each country. This proposal has not been accepted as yet.

Part 3 of the Spierenburg report dealt with administrative policy and the Commission appointed a working group chaired by Mr Ortoli (Commissioner for economic and financial affairs) to examine this section and report back. Based on this report in part, the Commission sent a communication to Council on convergence and budgetary questions (*Bulletin of the European Communities*, **13** (3) 1980. point 3.4.1).

Reform of the Community institutions are being dealt with in a separate report. In December 1978 the Council commissioned a committee consisting of Barend Biesheuvel, Edmund Dell and Robert Marjolin to report on this problem (*Bulletin of the European Communities* **11** (12) 1978. point 2.3.1) (qv Committee of the three wise men).

Inevitably these reports overlap to some extent.

Further information

'Proposals for the reform of the Commission'. *Bulletin of the European Communities*, **1 2** (9) 1979. points 1.3.1. – 1.3.15
Fourteenth general report on the activities of the European Communities in 1980, section 29
   Luxembourg: Office for official publications of the European Community, 1981. 360p. ISBN 92–825–2197–4.Catalogue Number CB–31–80–102–EN–C

Committee of Three Wise Men

Basic information

The three wise men were Barend Biesheuvel, Edmund Dell and Robert Marjolin.

They were asked to report on the reform of Community institutions, by the Council in December 1978. On 29 November 1979 the report was submitted to Heads of Government at their Dublin meeting, under the title, the European Institutions – present and future.

Work of the Committee

The proposals made covered the following points:

- the Commission needed to maintain an active role in the Community
- the authority of the Commission President should be reinforced

- the Commission should strengthen its collaboration with the Heads of Government
- it should play a greater part in Council meetings
- the Council had become an effective source of political guidance in the Community and should remain free to make full use of this facility
- the Council should be integrated within the normal framework of inter-institutional relations
- the Council should be free to concentrate on the genuinely political issues
- it should delegate more to the Commission
- it should give more scope for the work of the Permanent Representatives Committee and lower level bodies
- representatives of member states on the Council should accept voting as the normal practice in all cases where the Treaty does not impose unanimity
- the co-ordination of Community affairs in the capitals of member states should be improved so that representatives may be given instructions in good time
- the present special relationship between the Commission and Parliament should be replaced by a tripartite arrangement bringing in Council

See also 'Proposals for the reform of the Commission of the European Communities and its services', mentioned under the heading, Commission reform.

Further information

Thirteenth general report on the activities of the European Communities, point 8
   Luxembourg: Office for official publications of the European Communities, 1979. 346p.
   ISBN 92-825-1602-4. Catalogue number CB-29-79-522-EN-C
'Conclusions of the "Three wise men".'*Bulletin of the European Communities* 1 2 (11)
   1979. points 1.1.11 and 1.5.1-1.5.2
'Report of the "Three wise men".' *Bulletin of the European Communities* 1 2 (12)
   1979. point 2.3.1

Legislation of the European Communities

Basic information

Each European country which is a member of the Community has its own established body of legislation. To this is being added European Communities legislation as it is introduced. This new legislation is rather infrequently identical with existing legislation, occasionally it is additional to a member country's laws and more usually it amends national legislation. It takes precedence over national legislation.

Primary legislation in EC terminology refers to the treaties and protocols signed by the original member states establishing the Communities. It also includes subsequent treaties eg the 1973 Treaty of accession for the UK, Denmark and the Republic of Ireland.

Secondary legislation consists of:

- regulations, made by the Council and the Commission, which are fully binding and directly applicable to all member states
- directives, again issued on the authority of the Council and the Commission. The result of each directive is binding on each member state which is given free choice as to the method and form of implementation. (But note judgement of Court of Justice in Case 41/74 where certain provisions arising from directives have direct effects on individuals).
- decisions, taken by the Council and the Commission which are binding on those to whom they are addressed

There are other types of advice given by the Community which has not necessarily the force of law in member states. These are:

- opinions
- recommendations
- programmes

Publication of Community legislation

Primary legislation will be found in:
Treaties establishing the European Communities; treaties amending these treaties; documents concerning the accession.
    Luxembourg: Office for official publications of the European Community, 1973

This information will also be found in UK Command paper series *Cmnd. 5179*, available from Her Majesty's Stationery Office

Secondary legislation will be found in:

Official Journal of the European Communities, L series
    Luxembourg: Office for official publications of the European Communities

Notices, draft legislation, opinions, recommendations, the exchange rate for the Euro currency unit, etc will be found in:

Official journal of the European Communities, C series
    Luxembourg: Office for official publications of the European Communities

Indexes of primary and secondary legislation will be found in:

Halsbury's statutes of England, 3rd ed. v 42A and the latest continuation volumes
    London: Butterworths, 1975. (Continuation volumes)
Simmonds, K R
Encyclopaedia of European Community law
London: Sweet and Maxwell, 1973. with updating service. looseleaf 2 v. [Takes UK legislation and shows EC amendments]

Indexes to secondary legislation will be found in:

Index to the official journal of the European Communities, volume 1. alphabetical index and volume 2 methodological table
    Luxembourg: Office for official publications of the European Communities. [Indexes L and C series on a monthly basis (1975 –) cumulating annually (1952 –)]
Secondary legislation of the European Communities, subject list and table of effects
    London: HMSO for the Statutory Publications office (a general index issued monthly with annual cumulations)
European Communities secondary legislation
    London: HMSO, 1972. (lists all important Communities legislation published prior to the British entry on 1 January 1973. This is not the authentic English translation. Prior to this publication the texts were only available in German, Italian, Dutch, French)
Catalogue of Community legal acts and other texts relating to the elimination of technical barriers to trade for industrial products and nomenclature for iron and steel products (EURONORM)
    Luxembourg: Office for official publications of the European Communities, 1981. 112p. ISBN 92–825–2769–7.Catalogue number CB–33-- 81–110–EN–C
Communitatis Europaeae Lex (CELEX). A computerized documentation system of Community law currently available within the Community Institutions, made available to the public with effect from 1982.
    The host information service is EURIS.
Secondary legislation of the European Communities
    London: HMSO for the Statutory Publications office, 1974. 43 v. (The authentic English translation)

Further information

Parry, Anthony
EEC Law
    London: Sweet and Maxwell, 1973. 511p. ISBN 421–17390–4. [A legal history and description of the legal system. The range of EEC law immediately prior to the first enlargement of the Community]
Palmer, Doris M (ed)
Sources of information on the European Communities, p 10. *European Communities legislation* by L S Adler,
    London Mansell, 1979. 230p. ISBN 0–7201–0724–5
Louis, Jean-Victor
Community legal order
    Luxembourg: Office for official publications of the European Communities, 1980. 145p. ISBN 92–825–1053–0. Catalogue number CB–28–79–407–EN–C. [The development of Community law and its relations with national law]
Mathijsen, P S R F
Guide to European Community law, 3rd ed.
    London: Sweet and Maxwell, 1980. 256p. ISBN 0–421–25900–0. [A general history and description of the legal system]

European Communities legal system
    Luxembourg: Office for official publications of the European Communities, 1981. 43p.
    (European documentation series 6–1981) ISBN 92–825–2570–8
Hutchinson, E A S and Thomas, R C H
Company law in Europe; the Vth directive and the harmonization programme
    London: Institute of Directors, 1982. 69p. ISBN 0–900–939–00–21

Legislative Process

Basic information

As within any democratic process the methods of formulating policy can be complex and this is almost inevitably carried through to the legislative procedure.

This is emphasized in any organization such as the EC, which is in process of development and change. One of the fundamental changes which is gradually evolving in the Community is the power of Parliament. Another movement which is gradually taking place in the Community is the change in thought and activity from agriculture to other aspects of development. With the 1970s the comparatively small effort which was put into research and development in science and technology and the efforts made to enhance social science fields, both received a boost which has continued into the 1980s. Everyone will know of other changes which are gradually taking place each as a result of pressure groups in Parliament, or in the member states, or in committees set up by the Community executive itself to ensure that it keeps well in touch with the needs of the people.

These changes of thought from so many sides of the Community result in changes of policy which in turn lead to demands for changes in legislation. In order to ensure that the new legislation is appropriate and efficient, extensive consultation is necessary. Hence the rather complex and lengthy legislative process within the Communities.

Method of work

Under the Community treaties (Paris 1952 and the two treaties of Rome 1957) the Commission (qv) has almost complete power to initiate the Community legislative process. However, the ideas for such legislation may come from the Council, Parliament, a member state, etc.

The idea is then referred to the most appropriate Directorate-General to draw up an initial working paper. This may be a discussion document, draft proposals on which a debate may be formulated, or draft legislation in certain circumstances. At this stage there is considerable discussion with those concerned with the subject being reviewed with special reference to the positions upheld by the governments of member states. A paper is then

Initial working paper issued by the **Commission**

Meetings with national and subject experts.

produced which reflects the position of the Commission. This is published in the Commission non priced COM documents or the SEC document series of the Secretary-General. (For details of an index to COM documents see, *Bibliography of the European Communities*, entry by Pau in, Bibliographic and source guide section).

Final draft produced by the **Commission**

The paper is then sent to the Council of Ministers (qv) via the Committee of permanent representatives of member states (COREPER) (qv). If it is a technical paper it would first go to a technical committee before being forwarded to this Council. The value of COREPER is that it involves the member states at an early stage. COREPER sends copies to the European Parliament (EP) and, if appropriate, to the Economic and Social Committee (ESC) requesting opinions. Though not published at this stage copies become available in this form to the parliaments of member states, national interested bodies, European documentation centres, etc who can and do take action through their elected representatives or by direct representation.

Usually published in the **COM** or **SEC** series

COREPER Council of Permanent Representatives for the Council distributes copies
European Parliament where the papers are examined by subject committees with a Commission representative in attendance
Economic and Social Committee If the paper is concerned with these two subjects it is referred to one or more of the subject committees.

The EP (in some cases after a debate usually for matters with some political content) and the ESC prepare opinions on the draft proposal which are published in COM or SEC or OJ, C series of document. The Commission usually amends its documents in the light of these comments.

Commission considers comments made which are not, however, binding on it

The Council then considers the Commission's (revised) draft and can accept or reject it by a majority of weighted votes or amend it where there is unanimity. When accepted or amended, publication takes place in the *Official Journal*.

Council Publication of the agreed proposal in the **L** series of the **OJ**

The EC legislation now has to be incorporated in that of member states.

This can be done in the British Parlia- | **Member Parliaments**
ment by:

- administrative action where no legal sanction is necessary
- statutory instrument when the department concerned already has the authority under an enabling act
- Act of Parliament

(It should be noted that where a proposal has a substantial financial implication, Council may wish to depart from a recommendation by Parliament. In these circumstances a delegation from both sides tries to resolve the viewpoints. It should be noted that Council makes the final decision).

Further information

Scott, Gay
European Economic Community, a guide to sources of information
  London: Capital Planning Information Limited. 1979. 72p. ISBN 0-906011-043

Draft legislation in progress can be traced in:

- *British Business*, weekly
  HMSO (gives both the COM number and UK Parliamentary number)
- *London Gazette*
  HMSO
- *Weekly information bulletin*
  House of Commons ISSN 0261-9229
- London office of the European Communities Commission
  20 Kensington Palace Gardens, London W8 (tel. 01-727 8090).

Recently published legislation can be traced in:

- *Index to the official journal of the European Communities*, monthly (some delay in publication)
- *Official Journal of the European Communities* L series, daily

Hopkins, Mike
How to find out about Commission documents
  Loughborough: University of Loughborough for the Association of EDC Librarians, 1982.
  5p. ('How to' leaflets)

Official Journal of the European Communities

Basic information

The *Journal of the European Communities* can be described by section, or by its use, or by the type of information carried in each part. These will be found in the publications listed under, Further information. As an alternative and to give a different slant which may be useful in certain cases, it is described below in an historical and developmental order.

The decisions, recommendations, proposals, advice and notices of the European Communities appear in the *Official Journal* . . . (OJ)

Chronology of development and changes

The *OJ* is published every working day:

- from 30.12.52 to 19.4.58 it had the title, *Journal Officiel de la Communauté Européenne du Charbon et de l'Acier.* Publication was in the four official languages. There were annual indexes, from 1952–5 Table and from 1956–8 Table annuelle
- from 20.4.58 appeared, *Journal Officiel des Communautés Européennes.* A, Table annuelle was issued from 1958–72
- from 1962 to 1967 there was the, *Supplément agricole au Journal Officiel des Communautées Européennes.* Subsequently this information was included in the, *Journal Officiel* . . .
- from 1.1.63 the numbering of regulations started with No. 1 each year. Previously the numbering was continuous
- up to 30.6.67 the pagination of the *OJ* started afresh each year. From 1.7.67 the pagination started afresh each issue.
- from 1.1.68 the, *Journal Officiel* . . . was divided into two parts:

Legislation (L), which is in two parts.

The first consists of those Community acts which are obligatory under the EC treaties. The more important of these are listed in heavy type and prefixed by an asterisk.
The second part consists of acts whose publication is not obligatory. These are usually decisions.
Communications et informations (C) is in three parts. In the post 1973 English version:
The first carries the title, *Information* and records the current work of Community institutions. It contains the records of action by Parliament, including written questions, the Court of Justice, the Commission, the Council and the opinions of the Economic and Social Committee
The second part has the title, *Preparatory Acts* and includes Commission proposed legislation, etc
The third part has the title, *Notices* and covers tenders for contracts (until the start of the S series, see 1978 below), staff recruitment, etc

- from the European Parliament (EP) 1968/69 session, the texts of the debates have been published in an, *Annex to the Journal Officiel* . . . Prior to 1968 these texts were published by the EP. For session 1968/69 and subsequently, indexes have been issued. These are in three parts, index of names, analytical table and a list of working documents
- in 1972 Special editions of the, *Official Journal of the European Communities* appeared. These were in English and Danish and covered

major legislation issues between 1952 and 1972 and in force at the time of publication. The volumes covered chronological periods. There was a supplementary corrigenda covering the 1972 Special edition (1952–72), then a supplement 1959–72, and finally a consolidated edition of corrigenda (OJ L101/1 28.4.72) (Regulation 857/72/Euratom, ECSC, EEC) under article 155 of the Act concerning the conditions of accession and the adjustments to the Treaties, 1972

- from January 1973 the *OJ* was published in six official languages of the Community. The English version was, *Official Journal of the European Communities*, which started on 9 October 1972. Also from this date the index was divided into two sections – Alphabetical and Methodological. Monthly indexes were issued as well as annual cumulations. From January 1973–March 1975 only a methodological table was available. From April 1975 monthly alphabetical and methodological sequences were commenced.
- in 1974 a second series of the, *Special editions of the Official Journal of the European Communities*, appeared in English and Danish. These were arranged under subject headings, eg External relations and covered the same period as the first series
- from January 1978 the title, *Supplement to the Official Journal of the European Communities* was used to designate a regular publication numbered consecutively throughout the years after a prefix S and covering tenders, works contracts, supply contracts, exchange rates, European Development Fund tenders, accounts, etc. Previously the title, *Supplement* had been restricted to the indexes to the *OJ* and the occasional supplement to a particular issue
- from 1979 the, *Annual index to the Official Journal of the European Communities* appeared in two volumes, volume 1 the alphabetical index (very broad subjects only) and volume 2 the methodological table
- from January 1980 the, *Monthly index to the Official Journal of the European Communities* appeared in two volumes, volume 1 the alphabetical index (very broad subjects only) and volume 2 the methodological table
- from January 1981 written questions to the European Parliament instead of appearing in both the Alphabetical index and the Methodological table were only to be found in the latter
- from January 1981 the *OJ* was also published in Greek

Languages of the *OJ*

- from 1952 it was published in French, German, Italian and Dutch
- from 1973 English and Danish have been added
- from 1981 Greek has been added

Versions of the *OJ* and references

Microform versions of the *OJ* are available in fiche, 16 mm film and 35 mm film

References to the more important sections of the *OJ* will be found in a number of journals. One of those with a considerable coverage is, *British Business* (formerly, *Trade and Industry*).

Further information

Palmer, Doris M. (ed)
Sources of information on the European Communities
   London: Mansell, 1979. 230p. ISBN 0-7201-0724-5
Scott, Gay
European Economic Community, a guide to sources of information
   London: Capital Planning Information Ltd, 1979. 72p. (CPI Information Reviews/3) ISBN
   0-906011-04-3
Jeffries, John
Guide to the official publications of the European Communities, 2nd ed
   London: Mansell 1981. 318p. ISBN 0-7201-1590-6
How to find out – using the Official Journal of the European Communities
   Newcastle upon Tyne: Polytechnic Library, Newcastle upon Tyne, for the Association of
   EDC Librarians, 1982 (?). 5p. ('How to' leaflets)

Budget of the European Communities

Basic information

Under the Treaty of Paris (1952) the European Coal and Steel Community (ECSC) provided for its budget by imposing a levy on coal and steel production. Its purpose was to pay for the salaries and wages of administrative staff, aids for vocational training, tide-over allowances for redundant workers, and support for house building. All of which was to assist those working in the two industries. The ECSC were also empowered to raise loans.

With the treaties of Rome (1957), the Euratom treaty under article 172(4) established two budgets, an operating one and an investment budget.

Only one budget was envisaged for the EEC covering revenue, plus administrative and operational expenditures. However, the Development fund for developing nations lay outside this budget. (First development fund, 250 million ua, Second fund 730 million ua, Third fund 905 million ua, Fourth development fund 3,150 million ua.

In 1967 with the merger of the three Communities and in particular under article 20 of the Merger treaty (qv) there have developed three main financial sectors:

- the EEC budget which has both an administrative and an operational content. The latter includes the Social fund (qv), the Agricultural fund (qv Agricultural income), the Regional development fund (qv) and the EAEC research and investment budget
- the ECSC operational expenditure
- the Development fund

Financing the Communities

Originally the Community was financed by direct contributions from member states, and the Community just had to say how much it wanted. The Community is now financed from its 'own resources' consisting of customs duties and levies up to a 1% rate of VAT (not 1% of the VAT revenue). In 1980 the VAT levy was 0.73%. Estimates for future years up to 1983 show the income from a 1% rate of VAT being insufficient. It should be noted that the limit of 1% VAT was made in 1970 (OJ L94/19–22 28.4.70) (Decision 70/243/ECSC, EEC, EURATOM) and by a Council directive (OJ L145/1–40 13.6.77) (Directive 77/388/EEC) brought into force on 1 January 1978. Proposals for future financing were put forward by the Commission in a paper, 'Financing the Community budget', see Further information below.

Moves were made to alter the allocation of expenditure, cutting down the very high percentage allocated to the EAGGF (qv). This reform of the budget led to a dispute between Parliament and the Council in 1980 when the budget was rejected by Parliament and not finally approved until 9 July 1980 (*Bulletin of the European Communities* **13** (7/8) 1980 point 2.3.78).

In 1980 the budget ran to some 17,500 million EUA or about £35 per person, throughout the community. This is a very much lower figure than that for national and local government costs, covering the same year.

Budget procedure

Action taken	*Timetable for each year*
Each institution produces its estimate for the following calendar year and sends it to the Commission	1 July
The Commission produces a preliminary draft budget which it sends to the Council	1 September
Council considers modifications and consults institutions concerned. It produces a draft budget which it forwards to Parliament.	5 October
Parliament amends the draft budget acting by a simple majority and can propose modifications (based on majority of votes cast) to obligatory expenditure under the Treaty as well (article 203/4 of the Treaty of Rome). Since 1977 Parliament may reject the budget in toto and ask for a new one. Action if taken must be within 45 days.	26 November
The draft budget if agreed by Parliament shall be	

deemed to have been finally adopted. If not agreed
the draft budget, as amended or modified, goes back
to the Council.

The Council has the last word on compulsory
expenditure.

If within 15 days Council accepts the amendments   11 December
proposed by Parliament, the budget is deemed to have
been finally adopted.

If the Council modifies Parliament's amendments or
proposed modifications the draft budget is again forwarded to Parliament.

Within 15 days Parliament acts, by a majority of its   26 December
members or 3/5ths of the votes cast, on the modifications to its amendments. If there is still no agreement
the conciliation procedure between Council and
Parliament comes into play.

When this stage is completed the President of
Parliament declares the budget finally adopted.

Parliament has the last word on non-compulsory expenditure.

Purpose of the Budget

The budget is used mainly to support agricultural prices and modernize
agriculture (74%), to finance social policies (4.5%), industrial investment in
poorer regions (4%), research (2%), aid to developing nations (3%), running
costs of the EC (4%), etc (1979 figures).

This very high allocation of funds to agriculture is in the process of being
changed in the 1980s. On 30 May 1980 the Council gave a mandate to the
Commission to examine the development of Community policies ... to
prevent the recurrence of unacceptable situations. The reference was to
Britain's imbalance over payments to and financial benefits from the
Community. Commission proposals were sent to the Council on 24.6.81.
(Bulletin of the European Communities supplement 1/81). Parliament
during 1980 reduced a proposed 7.9% increase in agricultural prices to
one of 4.8% and voted for an extension of the co-responsibility levy to
more products which are being over produced. This change is an attempt
to restrict and reduce surpluses in production.

At the same time proposals for increased aid for industrial development,
regional development and social policy were envisaged (see last item
under, Further information below). The effect of this change on the UK is
likely to be considerable.

In an effort to contain agricultural spending and redistribute the money saved to other sections of the Community's budget, a special reference to the fight against unemployment was included in the 1983 draft budget. The UK pressed strongly for lower increases in farm prices during 1980 and 1981. In 1982 in view of the UK's continued insistence, the decision on the Budget's agricultural spending during 1982/83 was only agreed by a majority vote (*Bulletin of the European Communities* **15** (5) 1982 points 1.1.3 –1.1.4 and 2.1.73 and 2.1.99).

The UK's imbalance over payments to the Community was compensated by fixed amount refunds in 1980, 1981 and 1982.

Besides the relocation of the balance of expenditure which was being advocated by some member states during the latter 1970s and early 1980s, there were, from time to time, procedural disputes between some of the institutions of the Community. These have been recorded in the 13th, 14th and 15th, General reports on the activities of the European Communities. In 1982 the Presidents of Parliament, the Commission and the Council, held talks to resolve these problems. A, Joint declaration by the European Parliament, the Council and the Commission on various measures to improve the budgetary procedure, was formerly approved in July 1982 and appears in, *Bulletin of the European Communities* **15** (6) 1982 points 1.1.1 –1.1.5. (OJ C194/1–38 28.7.82).

By 1982 the Commission were of the opinion that the Mandate of 30 May 1980 had been completed, Parliament did not agree and considered that:

- there was need for further agricultural policy reform
- continued attempts to reduce budget contributions were harmful
- replacement of the 1976 financial mechanism with one having a wider validity for the whole Community on the basis of the Lange resolution (*Bulletin of the European Community* **12** (11) 1979 point 2.3.13).
- priority should be given to a social policy
- development of the Regional policy should be undertaken
- there was a need for a sound industrial strategy
- progress was needed on economic and monetary union

(*Bulletin of the European Communities* **15** (6) 1982 point 2.1.1).

Further information

General report on the activities of the European Communities
    Luxembourg: Office for official publications of the European Communities, annual
'Preliminary draft general budget of the European Communities for the financial year 1979.'
Bulletin of the European Communities supplement 6/78 [a fully laid out budget with explanations]
'Financing the Community budget: the way ahead'
Bulletin of the European Communities supplement 8/78
The European Community's budget, 2nd ed
    Luxembourg: Office for official publications of the European Communities, 1979. 37p.
    (European documentation 1/79) ISBN 92–825–0702–5

'The May mandate and the future of Europe'
Bulletin of the European Communities **1 4** (6) 1981. point 2.3.8 (comment) points 1.2.1 – 1.2.19 (summary of the Commission report)

Budgetary Policy Committee

Basic information

Under the Treaty of Rome (1957) articles 105(1) and 145 (first indent), a Council decision was enacted in 1964 setting up a Budgetary policy committee (OJ 77/1205 21.5.64).

Budgetary Policy Committee – representation

- one full member and two alternative members from each member state
- one full member and two alternative members from the Commission
- the chairman of the Monetary committee and the Conjunctural policy committee may participate at meetings either in person or through a representative
- the Committee shall elect its own officers who are in post for a two year term which is renewable

Work of the Budgetary Policy Committee

- to study and compare the broad lines of the budgetary policies of member states in order to facilitate co-ordination of economic and financial policies
- the opinion of the Committee may be obtained by the Commission or the Council
- the Committee may deliver its own opinions when it considers this necessary, without a request from the Commission or the Council

In 1974 the work of this Committee was incorporated into the Economic policy committee (qv).

Further information

General report on the activities of the European Communities
Luxembourg: Office for official publications of the European Communities, annual

Brief Biographies

This section has been limited to information on the present President of the EEC, past presidents, current members of the Commission, as well as those who were members in 1981, together with a few outstanding names connected with the Communities. The criteria for selection has been the names of those in office who appear or are likely to appear in the world press.

Readers who require more information are referred to:

Who's Who: European Communities and other European organizations, 2nd ed 1981/82
   Bruxelles: Editions Delta, 1981. 237p. ISBN 2–8029–0017–X,

as well as the major national *Who's Who,* and *Who Was Who* of the member states.

Andriessen, Franciscus H J J

The representatives of the governments of the member states, meeting on 16 December 1980, agreed on the members of the Commission of the European Communities for the period 6 January 1981 to 5 January 1985. Mr Andriessen is a member (OJ 9/41 9.1.81) (Decision 81/3/Euratom/ ECSC/EEC).

Born 2 April 1929.

Married, four children.

1951	Doctor of Law, State University of Utrecht.
1954–72	Held various posts, latterly Director, Catholic Housing Institute, Holland.
1958–67	Member of the Utrecht Provincial States.
1967–77	Member of the Lower House of the States-General (initially specializing in housing problems).
1971–7	Chairman of the KVP in the Lower House.
1977–9	Minister of Finance.
1980	Member of the Upper House of the States-General.
1981, 6 Jan	Member of the Commission of the European Communities.

Burke, Richard

The representatives of the member states agreed the proposal of the government of the Republic of Ireland that Richard Burke should replace their former representative on the Commission, Michael O'Kennedy, on 1 April 1982 (OJ L99/33 15.4.82) (Decision 82/207/EEC).

Born New York, 29 March 1932.

Married, 2 sons, 3 daughters.

Masters degree in Arts and higher diploma in Education from the University College, Dublin.

Secondary school teacher.

1969–77	Member of the Dáil Éireann for South, County Dublin.
1969–72	Fine Gael, Chief whip.
1973–7	Minister for education.
1977–81	Member of the Commission and responsible for taxation, consumer protection, transport and, until 1979, for relations with Parliament.
1981–2	Member of Dáil Éireann for West, County Dublin.
1982, 1 April	Appointed member of Commission.

Cheysson, Claude

The representatives of the governments of the member states, meeting on 16 December 1980, agreed on the members of the Commission of the European Communities for the period 6 January 1981 to 5 January 1985. Mr Cheysson was a member (OJ L9/41 9.1.81) (Decision 81/3/Euratom/ECSC/EEC).

Born 13 April 1920.

Married, six children.

1940	Ecole Polytechnique.
1943	Escaped from France via Spain. Commanded tank squadron in Free French Forces. Saw action in France and Germany. Croix de guerre, four times mentioned in dispatches, Legion of Honour.
1946	Ecole nationale d'administration.
1952	Political Adviser to the Government of Vietnam, Saigon.
1954	Member of the French Delegation to the Geneva Conference on Indochina. Chef de cabinet to Prime Minister Pierre Mendès-France.
1956	Technical adviser on the staff of Alain Savary, State Secretary for Moroccan and Tunisian Affairs; negotiations for independence of Morocco and Tunisia.
1957	Secretary-General, Commission for Technical Co-operation in Africa south of the Sahara (Cota).

1962	Director-General, Technical Organization for the Exploitation of Mineral Resources in the Sahara (an Algerian public agency established by the Evian agreements to replace the OCPS).
1966	Ambassador to Indonesia.
1970	Chairman of the Board, Entreprise minière et chimique.
1971–	Member of the Board, *Le Monde*.
1973, April	Member of the Commission of the European Communities with special responsibility for development and co-operation policy, budgets and financial control.
1977, 6 Jan to 1981, 5 Jan	Member of the Commission with special responsibility for development policy and relations with the Third World.
1981, 6 Jan to 1981, 23 May	Member of the Commission. Left to become Minister of External Relations of the French Government.

Contogeorgis, Georgios

The representatives of the governments of the member states, meeting on 16 December 1980, agreed on the members of the Commission of the European Communities for the period 6 January 1981 to 5 January 1985. Mr Contogeorgis is a member (OJ L9/41 9.1.81)
(Decision 81/3/Euratom/ECSC/EEC).

Born 21 November 1912

Married.

1935	Degree in economic and commercial sciences, University of Athens Studied in the United States (1957–8). Administrator, Ministry of Economic Affairs.
1940–1	War service.
1941–52	Principal Administrator, Ministries of Economic Affairs and Trade.
1952–64	Director, Ministry of Trade (Foreign Trade and External Relations).
1964–7	Director-General, Ministry of Trade.
1967–74	Resigned at the time of the dictatorship.
1974, Aug-Nov	Secretary-General, Greek Tourism Office.
1974–7	State Secretary for Co-ordination (Economy) and Planning.

1977   Elected member of the Greek Parliament (New Democracy
            Party).

1977–80   Minister for Relations with the European Communities.

Mr Contogeorgis led the negotiations on the accession of Greece to the
European Communities and represented the Greek Government at
several rounds of economic and bilateral trade negotiations and in
international bodies (such as OECD, GATT, FAO, UNCTAD)

1981, 6 Jan Member of the Commission of the European Communities.

Dalsager, Poul

On 20 January 1981 the representatives of the governments of the
member states appointed Mr Poul Dalsager member of the Commission
of the European Communities for the period 21 January 1981 to 5 January
1985 to replace the late Mr Finn Olav Gundelach. (OJ L21/20 29.1.81)
(Decision 81/8/Euratom/ECSC/EEC).

Born 5 March 1929 at Hirtshals, North Jutland, Denmark.

Married, two sons.

After taking an interest in political matters throughout his youth, at the
age of twenty he became chairman of the local section of the Social
Democratic Party.

1945   Joined Andelsbank, Hjorring, where he learned banking.

1956–7   Member of the Central Committee of Young Social
            Democrats.

Since 1964 Member of the Danish Parliament (Social Democratic
            Party).

1969 & 1971 Delegate to UN General Assembly.

1971–3   Chairman, Danish Parliament's Committee on the Common
            Market.

1973 & 1974 Member and Vice-President, European Parliament.

1975 Feb   Minister of Agriculture and Fisheries, Denmark.
to
1977 Feb

1977 Feb   Minister of Agriculture, Denmark.
to
1978 Aug

1978 Aug   Social Democratic Party Chairman in Danish Parliament.
to
1979 Sept

1979 Oct   Minister of Agriculture and Fisheries, Denmark.
to
1981 Jan

1981, 21 Jan European   Communities,   appointed   Member   of   the
Commission.

Davignon, Etienne

The representatives of the governments of member states, meeting on 16
December 1980, agreed on the members of the Commission of the
European Communities for the period 6 January 1981 to 5 January 1985.
Mr Davignon is a member (OJ L9/41 9.1.81) (Decision 81/3/Euratom/
ECSC/EEC).

Born 4 October 1932 in Budapest.

Married, three children.

Doctor of Law.

1959	Entered Ministry of Foreign Affairs.
1961	Attaché on the Minister's staff.
1963	Deputy Chef de cabinet to M Spaak.
1964–9	Chef de cabinet; to M Spaak until March 1966 and then to M Harme until November 1969.
1969, Nov to 1976, Dec	Director-General, Political Department.
1974, 18 Nov	Appointed Chairman of the Governing Board of the International Energy Agency.
1977, 6 Jan to 1981, 5 Jan	Member of the Commission of the European Communities with special responsibility for the internal market and industrial affairs and for the customs union.
1981, 6 Jan	Member of the Commission.

Giolitti, Antonio

The representatives of the governments of member states, meeting on 16
December 1980, agreed on the members of the Commission of the
European Communities for the period 6 January 1981 to 5 January 1985.
Mr Giolitti is a member. (OJ L9/41 9.1.81) (Decision 81/3/Euratom/
ECSC/EEC).

Born 12 February 1915.

Married, three children.

1943–4	Member of the Resistance; wounded in action and treated in French hospital.
1946	Elected member of the Constituent Assembly on the

Communist Party list and appointed State Secretary at the Ministry of Foreign Affairs in first Republican Government. Re-elected to all parliaments until 1976.

1957	Left Communist Party to become active member of Socialist Party.
1958	Member of party's Central Committee.
1964	Member of the party executive and between 1972 and 1973 Chairman of the party's Economic Committee.
1973–4	Minister for the Budget and Economic Planning in Centre-Left Governments.
1974	Represented Italy at the sixth special session of the UN General Assembly.
1974	Chairman of the OECD Council.
1977, 6 Jan to 1981, 5 Jan	Member of the Commission of the European Communities with special responsibility for regional policy and co-ordination of Community Funds.
1981, 6 Jan	Member of the Commission.

Gundelach, Finn Olav

The representatives of the governments of the member states, meeting on 16 December 1980, agreed on the members of the Commission of the European Communities for the period 6 January 1981 to 5 January 1985. Mr Gundelach was a member (OJ L9/41 9.1.81) (Decision 81/3/Euratom/ ECSC/EEC).

Born 23 April 1925 in Vejle

Married, two children.

1951, Jan	Graduated in economics from Aarhus University.
1946–7	President, Aarhus Students' Union.
1947–9	Vice-President, Danish National Union of Students.
1951–5	Ministry of Foreign Affairs (NATO and OECD matters).
1955–9	Permanent Representative of Denmark to the United Nations in Geneva.
1959–61	Director, Department of Trade Policy, GATT, Geneva.
1961	Assistant Director-General of GATT.
1962–7	Deputy Director-General of GATT (Kennedy Round).
1967–72	Ambassador, Head of Mission of Denmark to the European Communities (negotiations for the accession of Denmark, information programme prior to the Danish referendum).
1972–6	Member of the Commission of the European Communities,

special responsibility for the internal market and the customs union.

1977, 6 Jan   Vice-President of the Commission with special responsi-
to   bility for agriculture and fisheries.
1981, 5 Jan

1981, 6 Jan   Member of the Commission.

1981, 13 Jan   Died at Strasbourg. He was 55.

Haferkamp, Wilhelm

The representatives of the governments of the member states, meeting on 16 December 1980, agreed on the members of the Commission of the European Communities for the period from 6 January 1981 to 5 January 1985. Mr Haferkamp is a member (OJ L9/41 9.1.81) (Decision 81/3/Euratom/ECSC/EEC).

Born 1 July 1923 in Duisburg.

1946–9   Read economics and social sciences at Cologne University.

1950   Head, Social Policy Department, North Rhine–Westphalia Region, German Trade Union Federation (DGB).

1953–7   Member of Executive, North Rhine–Westphalia Region, DGB.

1957–63   North Rhine–Westphalia Regional Chairman, DGB.

1963–5   Member of the ECSC Consultative Committee and of the Economic and Social Committee of the EEC.

1967 July   Member of the Commission of the European Communities with special responsibility for energy, the Euratom Supply Agency and nuclear safeguards.

1970 July   Vice-President of the Commission with special responsibility for the internal market and approximation of legislation as well as the portfolios held since 1967.

1973 Jan.   Vice-President of the Commission with special responsibility for economic and financial affairs and credit and investments.

1977, 6 Jan   Vice-President of the Commission
to   with special responsibility for
1981, 5 Jan   external relations.

1981, 6 Jan   Member of the Commission.

Monnet, Jean Omar Marie Gabriel

The representatives of the governments of the member states, appointed Jean Monnet the first president of the European Coal and Steel Community in 1952.

Born 9 November 1888 in Cognac.

Married in 1934 Silvia de Bandini.

	Received a secondary education only but in later life was given honorary degrees from major British and American universities.
1906–14	In Canada in the family brandy business as a salesman.
1914	In Ministry of Commerce in Paris. Suggested an Anglo French board to allocate scarce commodities.
1916	When this was set up he was appointed to it.
1919–23	Assistant Secretary-General to the League of Nations. Went on a mission to China to plan the finance of railway development there.
1923–6	In the family business.
1926	Partner in an American investment bank.
1939	Chairman of the Franco-British economic co-ordination committee.
1940	Requested by Winston Churchill to participate in plans for an Anglo French union which was rejected by the French Government (Reynaud).
1940	Member of the British supply mission to Washington. Assisted with the planning of Roosevelt's 'Victory programme'.
1943	Mediator between de Gaulle and General Giraud after the liberation of North Africa. Worked for the establishment of the French National Liberation Committee. Was Commissioner for Supplies, armaments and reconstruction for France.
1946–50	Monumental plan for the modernization of post war France. Outlined its first five year investment programme. Appointed first Director of the, Commissariat Général au plan de modernization et d'équipement.
1950	Submitted a proposal for six major European powers to pool their coal and steel resources. This was accepted by Robert Schuman, the French Foreign Minister and led to the European Coal and Steel Community (ECSC) (1952–).
1950–52	Took an active part in the Pleven plan for a European Defence Community. Though this plan was rejected by the French it led to Western European Union.

1952	Awarded the Dutch Watteler peace prize.
1952 Aug – 1955	First President of the High Authority of the ECSC. Developed the system of 'permanent dialogue' between the international body and the national governments.
1953	Awarded the Charlemagne prize.
1955	Founded the, Action Committee for the United States of Europe which supported the foundation of the EEC and EURATOM.
1960	Played an important role in the reorganization of the Organization for European Economic Co-operation (OEEC) into the Organization for Economic Co-operation and Development (OECD) which included the United States and Canada.
	His work to the end of his life was for a United States of Europe joined in partnership to the United States of America.
1976	Published: *Les Etats Unis d'Europe ont commencé.*
1979	*Mémoirs.*
1979, 16 March	Died at the age of 90.

Narjes, Karl-Heinz

The representatives of the governments of the member states, meeting on 16 December 1980, agreed on the members of the Commission of the European Communities for the period 6 January 1981 to 5 January 1985. Mr Narjes is a member (OJ 9/41 9.1.81) (Decision 81/3/Euratom/EEC).

Born 30 January 1924.

Married, two children.

Carolinum Gymnasium in Neustrelitz

1941	Submarine officer in German Navy.
1944, Feb.	Taken prisoner by British and Canadians.
	Studied law and economics in prison camp schools in Canada and Britain.
1952	Doctor of Law (Thesis on 'Economic and customs unions as legal forms of external economic policy').
1953	Second State examination in Law.
1953–5	Administrator in Bremen Land Finance Office.
1955	Attaché in Foreign Office.
1956	Vice-Consul.

1957	Legationsrat.
1958	Seconded to EEC Commission as Deputy Chef de cabinet to President Hallstein.
1963	Chef de cabinet to President Hallstein.
1968–9	Director-General for Information at the Commission.
1969, Nov to 1973, Jan	Schleswig-Holstein Minister of Economic Affairs and Transport. and
1971, May to 1973	Member of Schleswig-Holstein Parliament.
1972–80	Member of Bundestag.
1972–6	Chairman, Bundestag Economic Affairs Committee.
1976–80	Member, Bundestag Foreign Affairs Committee; alternate member, Economic Affairs Committee.
1980	Re-elected to Bundestag.
1981, 6 Jan	Member of the Commission of the European Communities.

Natali, Lorenzo

The representatives of the governments of the member states, meeting on 16 December 1980, agreed on the members of the Commission of the European Communities for the period 6 January 1981 to 5 January 1985. Mr Natali is a member (OJ L9/41 9.1.81) (Decision 81/3/Euratom/ECSC/EEC).

Born 2 October 1922.

Married, two children.

Lawyer.

Volunteer in the Italian Liberation Corps in 1944.

Decorated for bravery in the field; wounded in action.

Member for the Abruzzi in seven consecutive parliaments.

Member of the Christian Democrat Party Executive.

State Secretary in the Prime Minister's Office, at the Ministry of Finance and at the Treasury Minister of the Merchant Marine, Minister of Tourism and Entertainment, Minister of Public Works and Minister of Agriculture.

1977, 6 Jan to 1981, 5 Jan	Vice-President of the Commission of the European Communities with special responsibility for enlargement, protection of the environment, nuclear safety and relations with the European Parliament.
1981, 6 Jan	Member of the Commission.

O'Kennedy, Michael

The representatives of the governments of the member states, meeting on 16 December 1980, agreed on the members of the Commission of the European Communities for the period 6 January 1981 to 5 January 1985. Mr O'Kennedy is a member (OJ L9/41 9.1.81) (Decision 81/3/Euratom, ECSC, EEC)

Born 21 February 1936 in Nenagh, County Tipperary, Republic of Ireland.

Married, three children.

Christian Brothers' School, Nenagh; St Flannan's College, Ennis; University College, Dublin (Ancient Classics); King's Inns, Dublin (Barrister-at-Law 1961; Senior Counsel 1973).

1965	Elected to the Senate. Spokesman on Education and Justice.
1969	Entered the Dail.
1970–2	Parliamentary Secretary to the Minister for Education.
1973, Jan–Mar	Minister for Transport and Power.
1973–7	Opposition Spokesman on Foreign Affairs.
1977–9, Dec	Minister for Foreign Affairs.
	President of the Council of the European Communities (June-December 1979).
1979–80	Minister for Finance.
1980, Jun–Dec	Chairman, Board of Governors, European Investment Bank.
1981, 6 Jan	Member of the Commission of the European Communities.
1982, 9 Mar	Resigned from the Commission on taking up his seat in the Dáil Eireann.

Ortoli, François-Xavier

The representatives of the governments of the member states, meeting on 16 December 1980, agreed on the members of the Commission of the European Communities for the period from 6 January 1981 to 5 January 1985. Mr Ortoli is a member (OJ L9/41 9.1.81) (Decision 81/3/Euratom/ECSC/EEC).

Born 16 February 1925 in Ajaccio, Corsica.

Married, four children.

Lycée Albert-Sarraut in Hanoi.

Law Faculty in Indochina: Law degree.

1947	Ecole nationale d'administration.
1948	Inspecteur des Finances.
1951	Member of the staff of the Minister of Economic Affairs, then of the Minister of Information.
1952	French Government Agent attached to the Franco-Italian Conciliation Commission.
1953	Technical adviser on the staff of the Minister of Economic Affairs.
1955	Assistant Director on the staff of the Minister of Economic Affairs.
1957–8	Head of Trade Policy Department, Office of the State Secretary for Economic Affairs.
1958–61	Director-General for the Internal Market, EEC Commission.
1961, May	Secretary-General, Interdepartmental Committee for European Economic Co-operation.
1962	Technical adviser on the staff of the Prime Minister, then Director of the staff of the Prime Minister in December 1962.
1963	State representative on the Board of Directors of the Havas Agency. State representative on the Managing Board of Urbaine.
1966–7	General Commissioner for Planning.
1967	Chairman, Advisory Committee on the Production of Electricity from Nuclear Sources.
1967–8	Minister of Public Investment and Housing.
1968 May–Jul	Minister of Education.
1968 Jun–Aug	UDR deputy for the Nord constituency.
1968 July to 1969 June	Minister of Economic Affairs and Finance.
1969 June to 1972 July	Minister of Industrial and Scientific Development.
1973–6	President of the Commission of the European Communities.
1977, 6 Jan to 1981, 5 Jan	Vice President of the Commission.
1981, 6 Jan	Member of the Commission.

President of the Administrative Council of the College of Europe, Bruges.
President of the Cancer Institute, Lille.

Honorary doctorates from the Universities of Athens (1975) and Oxford (1976).

Robert Schuman Gold Medal (1975).

Pisani, Edgard

The representatives of the governments of the member states meeting on 26 May appointed Mr Edgard Pisani Member of the Commission for the period 26 May 1981 to 5 January 1985. He succeeded Mr Claude Cheysson, who had been appointed Minister of External Relations in the French Government. Mr Pisani formally took office on 27 May and will hold his predecessor's development portfolio (OJ L168/21 25.6.81) (Decision 81/438/EURATOM/ECSC/EEC).

Born 9 October 1913.

Widower, four children.

University studies in law, political science and humanities.

1944	Entered the French civil service.
1946	Director, Office of the Minister of the Interior.
1946–54	Prefect.
1954	Senator (Democratic left).
1961–6	Minister of Agriculture.
1964–73	Departmental councillor, Maine-et-Loire.
1965–75	Mayor of Montreuil-Bellay.
1966–7	Minister of Supply.
1967–8	Member of the National Assembly.
1968 May	Resigned from the National Assembly.
1974	Senator (Socialist).
1975	Member of the Club of Rome.
1978–80	Member of the Brandt Commission.
1978–81	Member of the European Parliament.
1981 27 May	Member of the Commission of the European Communities.

Richard, Ivor Seward

The representatives of the governments of the member states, meeting on 16 December 1980, agreed on the members of the Commission of the European Communities for the period 6 January 1981 to 5 January 1985.

Mr Richard is a member (OJ L9/41 9.1.81) (Decision 81/3/Euratom/ECSC/EEC)

Born 30 May 1932.

Married, three children.

St Michael's School, Bryn, Llanelli: Cheltenham College; Pembroke College, Oxford, where he was Wightwick Scholar. Graduated in jurisprudence in 1953, was called to the Bar in 1955 and became a Queen's Counsel in 1971.

1964–74	Member of the Parliament for Baron's Court, London.
1965–8	Delegate to the Council of Europe and British representative with Western European Union.
1966–9	Parliamentary Private Secretary to the Secretary of State for Defence.
1969–70	Parliamentary Under-Secretary for Defence (Army).
1970–3	Opposition spokesman in the House of Commons on Posts and Broadcasting.
1973–4	Deputy Opposition spokesman on Foreign Affairs.
1974–9	United Kingdom Permanent Representative at the United Nations.
1979–80	In practice at the Bar.
1981, 6 Jan	Member of the Commission of the European Communities.

Schuman, Robert

Born on 29 June 1886 in Luxembourg. Studied at Bonn, Munich and Berlin Universities. He became a barrister in Metz in 1912. Was a deputy to the French Assembly for the Moselle from 1919–1963. Remained unmarried.

1919–1940	Represented Moselle as a Popular Democrat.
1940 Mar–Jul	Under Secretary of State for refugees in France. Supported Petain.
1941 Sept	Under arrest by the Germans.
1942	Escaped to unoccupied France. Stayed in monasteries until the liberation.
1945	Elected a deputy representating the Mouvement Républicain Populaire
1946 Jun – 1947 Dec	At the Finance Ministry.
1947 Dec – 1948 Jul	Head of the Government of France (Prime Minister).

1948 Jul – 1953 Jan	Foreign Minister to the Fourth Republic. During this time he accepted the Monnet plan for the European Coal and Steel Community. This was also accepted by Adenauer for West Germany.
1949	One of the signatories to the Council of Europe treaty.
1950 May	Together with Jean Monnet he proposed the formation of a Community to embrace the coal and steel resources of France and West Germany as well as any other European country which wished to join.
1950 Nov	In conjunction with René Pleven (Defence Minister) he launched a proposal for an integrated European Army but this idea was rejected by the French Government in 1955.
1955 Feb – 1956 Jun	Minister of Justice.
1958 Mar	President of the Strasbourg European Assembly. Awarded the Charlemagne prize (created in 1949. Awarded by the city of Aachen annually. Given for the outstanding contribution to European unity during the year. Value 5,000 DMk).
1960 Mar	Relinquished the post of President of the European Assembly and was made honorary President.
1962	Did not stand in the 1962 French general elections.
1963 Feb	Resigned from the European Parliament.
1963 Sept 4	Died near Metz at the age of 77.

Thorn, Gaston Egmont

The representatives of the governments of the member states, meeting on 16 December 1980, agreed on the members of the Commission of the European Communities for the period from 6 January 1981 to 5 January 1985. Mr Gaston Thorn will be President from 6 January 1981 to 5 January 1983 (OJ L9/42 9.1.81) (Decision 81/4/Euratom/ECSC/EEC).

Born 3 September 1928 in Luxembourg.

Married, one child.

1943	Arrested for political activities and sent to re-education camp at Stahleck.
1957	Obtained doctorate in law after studying at Universities of Montpellier, Lausanne and Paris. President, Luxembourg National Union of Students. President, World Conference of Students. Member of the Luxembourg Bar.

1957–69	Luxembourg City Councillor. Echevin 1961–3.
1959	Stood for Parliament and elected on Democratic (Liberal) Party list; since re-elected at every election.
1959–69	Member of European Parliament; Vice-Chairman, Liberal Group; Chairman, Developing Countries Committee; Chairman, Joint EEC–AASM Association Committee.
1959–61	General Secretary, Luxembourg Democratic Party.
1961–80	President, Luxembourg Democratic Party.
1968–74	Minister for Foreign Affairs in a Social Christian/Democrat coalition and Minister for the Civil Service, Physical Education and Sport.
Since 1970	President, Liberal International.
1974–9	Prime Minister, Minister of State and Minister for Foreign Affairs in a Liberal/Socialist coalition. From 1977 also Minister of Economic Affairs and Small firms and Traders.
1975–6	President of the thirtieth session of the UN General Assembly.
1976–80	President, Federation of Liberal and Democratic Parties of the European Community.
1979–80	Deputy Prime Minister, Minister for Foreign Affairs, External Trade and Co-operation, Minister of Economic Affairs and Small firms and Traders, Minister of Justice in a Social Christian/Democrat coalition.
1981, 6 Jan	President of the Commission of the European Communities.

Tugendhat, Christopher Samuel

The representatives of the governments of member states, meeting on 16 December 1980, agreed on the members of the Commission of the European Communities for the period 6 January 1981 to 5 January 1985. Mr Tugendhat is a member (OJ L9/41 9.1.81) (Decision 81/3/Euratom/ECSC/EEC).

Born 23 February 1937.

Married, two children.

Ampleforth College; Gonville and Caius College, Cambridge (President of Union).

1960–1970	*Financial Times* leader and feature writer.
1971	Director, Sunningdale Oils.
1972	Director, Phillips Petroleum International (UK) Ltd.
1974–1976	Member of Parliament (Conservative), Consultant to Wood

Mackenzie and Co. Stockbrokers.

1977, 6 Jan to 1981, 5 Jan	Member of the Commission of the European Communities.
1981, 6 Jan	Member of the Commission.

3 Common Economic and Agricultural Development

The purpose of the Communities is to provide a better standard of living and a fuller life for the peoples of the member states involved.

The first two chapters have outlined the Communities and their administrative organization. This chapter is the first of four which takes very broad subjects and refers to those aspects which are likely to be of interest to the general enquirer and which have been dealt with by the Community.

To co-ordinate the economic structures of ten very individual nations, with long histories of independent thought and action, is a truly formidable task. Each member nation has evolved the most appropriate economic policy to enable it to face the changing conditions of a rapidly developing world.

The nationalistic, political and economic pressures of the first half of the twentieth century have led to a co-ordination of effort in those areas of the world which already have a natural affinity of purpose.

Europe, with its long and unified cultural history, with the warnings it has had in the past from political, economic and military disputes, has a clear need to work together to preserve its heritage, maintain peace and unity within its borders and to build its own resources, as has been accomplished already by other superpowers.

The practical starting point for this development is a thriving economic community.

To reach forward towards this goal, an assessment of the present situation is necessary. The latest is:

- **Economic problems of the 1980s** (pages 95–8)

The next steps concerning a monetary policy include:

- **European monetary system** (EMS) (pages 98–9)
  Balance of payments (pages 99–101)
  New Community instrument (NCI) (pages 101–2)
  Currencies of the European Communities (pages 102–3)

FOR A DETAILED INDEX SEE THE YELLOW PAGES

To maintain a watch on the economic development and to plan for the future, a series of committees were initiated:

- **Conjunctural policy committee** (pages 103–4)
- **Short term economic policy** (pages 104–5)
- **Medium term economic policy** (pages 105–6)
- **Economic policy committee** (pages 106–7)
- **Monetary committee** (pages 108–9)

The unity of a common market is maintained by a single customs area. This has been extended from the European Communities to the European Free Trade Area (EFTA), thus making paractically the whole of Western Europe into a free trade zone:

- **Customs union** (pages 109–11)
  Advisory committee on customs matters (pages 111–12)
  Common customs tariff (pages 112–13)
  Nomenclature for the classification of goods (pages 113–14)

European trade is based on free competition. How this is being organized will be found in:

- **Competition policy** (pages 115–17)
  Stabilization of export earnings (STABEX) (pages 117–18)
  Generalized system of preferences (GSP) (pages 118–19)

An even development in all parts of the Community has to be encouraged if the human resources there are to be utilized to the full:

- **Financial aid from the European Community** (pages 120–1)
- **Regional policy** (pages 121–3)
  Regional policy committee (pages 123–4)
  European regional development fund (ERDF) (pages 124–5)
  ERDF – financial assistance (pages 125–8)

By far the biggest effort in the Community has been for farmers. Though the 1980s is seeing the beginnings of a change, with a larger proportion of resources being allocated elsewhere, yet agriculture still has a dominant place in Community activities:

- **Agriculture** (pages 128–131)
  Standing committee on agricultural research (pages 131–2)
- **Common agricultural policy** (CAP) (pages 132–4)
  Agricultural management and regulatory committees (pages 135–7)
  Farm accountancy data network (FADN) (page 138)

Financial aid to the CAP is covered by:

- **European agricultural guidance and guarantee fund** (EAGGF) (pages 138–140)
  EAGGF, – financial assistance (pages 140–2)
  'Green'exchange rates (page 142–3)

To enable farmers to counter currency fluctuation:

- **Monetary compensatory amounts (MCA)** (pages 143–4)

Subjects related to Agriculture include:

- **Forestry** (page 145)
- **Fisheries** (pages 146–7)

All pervasive subjects in the economic field which the EC have harmonized throughout the member states are:

- **Insurance** (pages 147–9)
- **Statistics** (pages 150–1)

Economic Problems in the 1980s

Basic information

Problem areas include unemployment, inflation, energy, raw materials, food supplies, industrial restructuring, international trade, social and regional inequality and many others. Whilst many of these are social, environmental or industrial yet they have their basis in the Community's economic development.

In the thirty years of its existence (ECSC treaty 1952) the simply colossal task of bringing together 270 million people, speaking many different languages, having a long history of antagonism and war, led to a vast number of problems. But these many difficulties in developing the European Economic Community are being overcome. This foundation has enabled the Community to be in an advantageous position to tackle the energy problems of 1973–4 and successive energy and unemployment problems of the late 1970s.

In its Mandate of 30 May 1980, the Council decided that structural changes to the Community budget were required. The Commission's response concerned fundamental changes in the Community and these were outlined in *Bulletin of the European Communities* supplement 1/81 and detailed in a later supplement 4/81 – *A new impetus for the common policies*. The Commission chairman stated in May 1982 that the Mandate of 30 May 1980 exercise was now completed (*Bulletin of the European Communities* **15** (5) 1982 point 2.1.1.), but the EP disagreed.

Major problems

- unemployment

    This is currently (1981) over 6 million in the EC. The European Council of Ministers in late 1979 passed two resolutions in a social remedy approach to the problem. These covered overtime, flexible retirement, part-time work, temporary work, shift work, the annual volume of work, on the job training and retraining. Further action is required to deal with the roots of the problem which are industrial and economic (qv employment, mobility of labour, etc).

- inflation

  In 1979 this led to an average rise in consumer prices of 10% though certain member countries experienced considerably higher rates than this. The Community introduced in 1979 a European Monetary System based on exchange rate stability (Currently excluding the Pound Sterling and Greek Drachma). It also included the pooling of a proportion of each country's monetary reserves. This is leading to the creation of a European currency (qv European monetary system).

- energy

  Demands in the EC were faced with a fourfold increase in the price of imported oil up to 1974, with further substantial increases subsequently in 1979. To limit the effect of this change, the EC has reached agreement with Japan and the USA over a ceiling for energy imports during the period 1980–5. Extended efforts are being made to restrict imports, to reduce consumption, to develop alternative sources of energy, to devise new sources of energy, to readjust use of energy sources from those in scarce supply to those which are more plentiful (qv Alternate energy sources, Solar energy, Research and the Community, Nuclear energy, ECSC, etc).

- raw materials

  Basic materials for industry and food for man, make the EC the foremost world importer of agricultural products. It has introduced a common agricultural policy (CAP) which contributes to food supply, security and stability. Many of the raw materials – especially minerals – come from outside suppliers. The Community under the Lomé Conventions (qv) has made agreements with 61 ACP countries which are mutually beneficial.

- industrial restructuring

  This is necessary as Europe's industrial organization has not always been sufficiently adaptable in the face of outside competition. Joint action by the EC gives greater weight to relations with the rest of the world, thus ensuring that the ten are in a strong position to take advantage of the economic upturn as soon as it comes (qv Shipbuilding, Air transport, ECSC, EIB, Medium term economic policy programmes, etc). The Commission's policy was outlined in two proposals, a policy for industrial innovation – strategic lines of a Community approach, and, a Community strategy to develop Europe's industry. Both are included in *Bulletin of the European Communities* supplement 4/81 a, *New impetus for the common policies*. In June 1982 Parliament called for specific proposals (OJ C182/57 19.7.82).

- international trade

  This represents a quarter of the gross domestic product of EC countries. The ACP states work with the Community in developing mutual trade. During the 'Tokyo Round' negotiations, concluded in 1979, the EC were able to obtain a balanced reduction of customs tariffs from various non-Community partners (qv Lomé conventions, and names of individual countries).

● harmonization

One of the largest and most difficult continuing problem of the Community is bringing together and harmonizing the legislation of individual member states. There are obvious historical and economic reasons why the legislation of one country differs from that of another. If a single entity is to be reached, a basic and universally accepted body of legislation has to be accepted by each member state and included first of all in its own legislation (qv Legislation, Diplomas and professional qualifications mutual recognition, Law reports of the EC, etc).

● research and development

If the total research effort of the 10 member states is to be co-ordinated to prevent overlapping of effort and to give a greater thrust to urgent research, eg alternative energy sources, a total linking of Community scientific and industrial research has to be organized (qv Research and the Community, European co-operation in the field of scientific and technical research (COST), Scientific and technical research committee (CREST), etc).

● single Community currency
● single Community language
● single Community foreign policy
● elimination of nationalism in member states

Further information

General report on the activities of the European Communities Chapter II Section I
Economic and monetary policy (Prior to 1977 Chapter III Section 5)
   Luxembourg: Office for official publications of the European Communities, annual
Lewis, D E S
Britain and the European Economic Community
   London: Heinemann, 1978. 125p. ISBN 0-435-84560-8
Drew, John
Doing business in the European Community
   London: Butterworth, 1979. 280p. ISBN 0-408-10631-X
The European Community in the 1980s
   Brussels: EC Directorate-General for Information, 1980, 7p. (European File 1/80). Catalogue
   number CC-AD-80-001-EN-C
Financial resources for economic development, Scotland (section C concerns the European
Community)
   Glasgow: The Planning Exchange, 1980. not paged. ISBN 0-905011-17-1
The role of the banker in industrial innovation, proceedings of a symposium . . .
   Luxembourg: Infobrief for the Commission of the European Communities, 1981. 98p.
   ISBN 3-88766-000-5
European Economic Community, Economic report 1982
   London: Lloyds Bank Group, 1982. 29p.

Dahrendorf, Ralph
Europe's economy in crisis
   London: Weidenfeld and Nicolson, 1982. 274p. ISBN 0-297-78078-6

European Monetary System (EMS)

Basic information

Early plans for monetary union in the Community included the Barre plan in February 1969, the Werner plan in 1970, the introduction of the European monetary 'snake' (a linking of currency values) in 1972 which gave experience in identifying the economic and financial conditions required before monetary mechanisms can function properly. In November 1977 a Communication on the, Prospect of economic and monetary union was published (*Bulletin of the European Community* **10** (10) 1977. point 1.2.1). In March of the following year it was translated into an action programme to be reviewed annually. On 8 April 1978 during the European Council at Copenhagen, the first decision of principle regarding a European monetary system, was taken. On 6 July the same year at Bremen the European Council meeting confirmed their decision, established the outlines of the system and the timetable. At the Council meeting in Brussels on 4-5 December 1978 a resolution on the introduction of a European monetary system and related questions was adopted with all countries except Britain, taking part. On 12 March 1979 the European Council meeting in Paris gave the go-ahead with the European Monetary System (EMS) coming into force on 13 March 1979. (OJ L379/2 30.12.78) (Regulation 3181/78/EEC).

The EMS objectives are to stabilize exchange rates between currencies, re-establish the proper functioning of the industrial and agricultural common market and establish confidence amongst investors and industrialists.

For those countries in the 'snake' at that time (13 March 1979) – Germany, Denmark, Holland, Belgium, Luxembourg – the EMS was based on the 'snake' central rates. For the Republic of Ireland, Italy and France they were derived from market rates. The UK, though it decided not to participate in the system's exchange rate mechanism, a national central rate based on the market rate was chosen for sterling for the purpose of calculating the divergence indicator. In June 1982 central rates were realigned allowing a new balance to be found within the currencies which participate. Details of the national exchange rates per ECU can be found in *Bulletin of the European Communities* **15** (6) 1982 point 2.1.3.

It is noted that in the Commission in its foreword to the draft fifth medium term economic policy programme 1981-5, stresses the importance of developing the EMS. It does this by making it the first of four main lines of action up to 1985. In forwardng this policy it aims to bring in to the EMS both the United Kingdom and Greece (*Bulletin of the European Communities* **14** (7/8) 1981. points 3.4.1–3.4.8).

Purpose of the EMS

As a result of the current economic and financial crisis, the then President of the European Commission Roy Jenkins, emphasized in the first Jean Monnet lecture in Florence on 27 October 1977 the need for the economic and monetary union of Community countries (*Bulletin of the European Communities* **10** (10) 1977 points 1.1.1–1.1.9). It is hoped that this would bring:

- monetary stability, by the progressive introduction of a European currency. This change would provide shelter for half the trade of the EC against exchange rate fluctuations, enable countries to cope more calmly with short periods of deficit, decrease speculative movement and help create a new world monetary order, based on large zones of stability
- moderating influence on inflation which could be more powerful with all the 9 Community members acting in concert than in isolation
- growth and rationalization of the economy can be undertaken on a European scale with inflation uncertainties eliminated
- employment opportunities can be improved by strengthening demand amongst the 270 million consumers of the Community
- improved regional balance should come from a monetary union

Further information

European Monetary System
Brussels: EC Directorate-General for information, 1979. 7p. (European File 7/79). Catalogue number CC–AD–79–007–EN–C
General report on the activities of the European Communities
Luxembourg: Office for official publications of the European Communities, annual
European economic and monetary union, 2nd ed
Luxembourg: Office for official publications of the European Communities, 1981. 39p. (European Documentation series 4/1981). ISBN 92–825–2589–9. Catalogue number CB–NC–81–004–EN–C

Balance of Payments

Basic information

Under article 104 of the EEC Treaty of Rome (1957) a Community loan mechanism was set up in 1975 (OJ L46/1–2 20.2.75) (Regulation 397/75/EEC). This concerns Community loans and (OJ L46/3–4 20.2.75) (Regulation 398/75/EEC) implements these facilities. This was designed to support the balance of payments of member states. Initial regulations limited borrowing operations to the equivalent of US $ 3,000 million.

During 1980 there were a number of discussions (Luxembourg in April, Venice in June) on how the balance of payments problem could be solved. In October 1980 the Council debated the question in the light of a report from the Monetary committee (qv) A draft proposal was submitted by the Commission (OJ C308/10–11 26.11.80). Parliament commented on these proposals (OJ C346/62,99,100 31.12.80).

In 1981 the Council reached agreement on the outstanding points regarding adjustment of the Community loan mechanism (OJ L73/1–2 19.3.81) (Regulation 682/81/EEC). This was the outcome of a general review of problems involved in recycling oil producers' surpluses.

Purpose of the proposals

The principles on which this new policy was based are:

- the Community is to use its credit to borrow on the world market through the, New Community instrument (NCI) (qv)
- the money received will in turn be lent to member states who are in balance of payment difficulties

The new arrangements include:

- each member state seeking a loan will first have to submit its own adjustment programme with which it must undertake to comply
- the Council will decide whether the loan is granted, the economic policy conditions (if any) which are to be attached, how the loan should be disbursed
- the ceiling for borrowings is now ECU 6,000 millions. Voting rules implementing decisions will be taken by the Council acting unanimously.

Work undertaken

A second tranche of borrowings was successfully negotiated during 1980 by the NCI. The re-loan of this money to member states for projects concerned with their economic development was a means of recycling surplus world funds to help overcome the current balance of payments problems within the Community. Much of the relending of finance is undertaken by the European Investment Bank. Examples of these are:

- loan of £5 million for improvement schemes in Northern Ireland including trunk roads, improving communications between industrial estates and Belfast, March 1981 (*Bulletin of the European Communities* **14** (3) 1981. point 2.3.44)
- loan of £1 million to finance 18,000 new subscriber telephone connections at several industrial estates at Kingston upon Hull, February 1981 (*Bulletin of the European Communities* **14** (3) 1981 point 2.3.44)
- loan of £5 million to Midland Bank Industrial Equity Holdings Ltd, for loans to small and medium sized investment, April 1981 (*Bulletin of the European Communities* **14** (4) 1981. point 2.3.56)
- a conversion loan of ECU 8.9 million was granted to Tates Circuit Foil, Silloth, through Finance for Industry, London and to the Westfalen bank in Bochum, Germany, June 1981 (*Bulletin of the European Communities* **14** (6) 1981. point 2.3.59)
- a loan of £20 million to help finance a motorway construction through Glasgow and improvements to water supply sewerage and sewarage disposal system. (This is a second loan, the first being for £32 million), May 1981 (*Bulletin of the European Communities* **14** (6) 1981. point 2.3.40).

Further information

'Community loans to provide balance of payments support', *Bulletin of the European Communities* **14** (2) 1981. 1.3.1–1.3.6

New Community Instrument (NCI) Borrowing and Lending

Basic information

Under article 235 of the Treaty of Rome (1957) establishing the European Economic Community, provision is made for the Council to act on a Commission proposal, when no specific articles cover the subject. The Community decided in 1978 that it should use available private financial resources for developing its aims (OJ L298/9–10 25.10.78) (Decision 78/870/EEC). Provision was made for loans up to 1,000 million EUA. Loans to be activated tranche by tranche. This development is also known as the 'Ortoli facility'.

Purpose

The proceeds of these loans are for:

- financing investment projects in the energy, industry or infrastructure sectors
- projects should have a regional impact and help to combat unemployment
- financing projects completely or in conjunction with other Community financing instruments
- projects approved by the Commission on guidelines laid down by the Council
- funds to be deposited with the European Investment Bank (EIB)

Action taken

The first action under the 1978 Council Decision was in the following year when a tranche of 500 million EUA was borrowed. Its purpose was also stated, covering infrastructure investment and giving guidelines for the selection of projects (OJ L125/16–17 22.5.79) (Decision 79/486/EEC).

A proposal for a second tranche of 500 million EUA was submitted by the Commission (OJ C54/4–5 4.3.80). This proposal was considered by the Council but reduced to 400 million EUA. Again the purposes of the loan were outlined in the Council decision. (OJ L205/19 7.8.80) (Decision 80/739/EEC).

The decision 80/739 above was supplemented by a second decision covering 100 million EUA (OJ L326/19 2.12.80) (Decision 80/1103/EEC). This additional sum included money for building both factories and housing. Further tranches of borrowing were made including one for 1,000 million ECU submitted by the Commission (OJ C29/5-6 6.2.82) and adopted by the Council on 26.4.82. This tranche, like earlier ones, is being used to finance investment projects on Community territory and included for the first time small and medium sized enterprises.

The Commission, finding the limit exhausted has submitted a proposal to the Council for money to be raised by the European Investment Bank without limit and loaned for projects approved by the Commission (OJ C341/18-19 31.12.80). By this means the NCI can be given greater flexibility. The Commission reports annually to the Council on its transactions (*Bulletin of the European Communities* **13** (4) 1980 point 2.1.5). This first report mentioned that by December 1979 the Commission/ EIB had signed nine loan contracts for projects in the United Kingdom, Italy and the Republic of Ireland.

Further information

General report on the activities of the European Communities
    Luxembourg: Office for official publications of the European Communities, annual
'New Community borrowing and lending instrument'. *Bulletin of the European Communities*
13 (4) 1980. point 2.1.2

Currencies of the European Communities

Explanations

The original units of account (ua) were based on gold and corresponded to FF 5.55 or FB 50.

The European unit of account (EUA), devised in 1975 and introduced on 1 January 1976, was valued each day in relation to a basket of Community currencies. It thus varies with the exchange rate and on 31.12.77 was worth £0.641652 or DM 2.58058.

With the introduction of the European Monetary System (EMS) the EUA is replaced by the ECU (European Currency Unit) with effect from 1 January 1981. The ECU was devised in 1979 for the purpose of the EMS and had been in use in a few areas before 1981, for example in the CAP in 1979.

The ECU is identical with the EUA, though its definition enables changes to be made. It is a 'basket of currencies' unit. The act of accession of

Greece specifies that the drachma be included in the ECU before 31 December 1985.

The ECU is calculated each day and exchange rates are established on each exchange market at 2.30 pm by the relevant Central Bank. On the basis of these rates the Commission establishes an ECU equivalent which is published each day in the *Official Journal of the European Communities* 'C' edition or obtained by telex on Brussels 23789 (after 3.30 pm daily, type your answer back code, followed by 'CCCC', for the automatic answering service).

Agricultural Units of Account (ua) (OJ L106/2553–4 30.10.62) were changed on 9 April 1979 to ECU. This was just after the introduction of the EMS on 13 March 1979 (qv Green currencies).

Further information

European Investment Bank, annual reports
   Luxembourg: EIB, 1958, annual
The European Community and the Third World
   Brussels: EC Spokesman's Group and Directorate-General for Information, November 1977. 47p. (Dossier series) Catalogue number CI–22–77–524–EN–C
'ECU'
Bulletin of the European Communities **13** (12) 1980. points 3.1.1. – 3.1.5

Conjunctural Policy Committee

Basic information

Article 103 of the Treaty of Rome (1957) stated that, 'Member states should regard their conjunctural policies as a matter of common concern'. The Council therefore set up a Conjunctural policy committee, attached to the Commission, to forward the implementation of this policy (OJ 31/764 9.5.60).

Conjunctural Policy Committee – representation

- three representatives from the Commission
- three representatives of each member state
- the chairman of the Monetary commission to attend ex officio
- when necessary experts may be called upon Commission agreement is necessary
- the Committee may elect its own officers and adopt its rules of procedure

Work of the Conjunctural Policy Committee

- participate in the consultations between member states and the Commission provided for in article 103 of the Treaty of Rome (1957)
- governments of member states to keep the Commission informed of the broad lines of any project which may affect the conjunctural situation of other member states
- the Commission to consider how the work of the Community and the Organization of European Co-operation (OEEC), now, Organization for Economic Co-operation and Development (OECD), can be linked

The Conjunctural policy committee became the, Short-term economic policy committee and in 1974 it was incorporated into the, Economic policy committee (qv).

Further information

General report on the activities of the European Communities
  Luxembourg: Office for official publications of the European Communities, annual

Short-Term Economic Policy Committee

Basic information

Owing to the increasing interpenetration of the economics of member states in the fulfilment of articles 103 and 105 of the Treaty of Rome (1957), a Council decision on the co-ordination of short-term economic policies was taken in 1969 (OJ L183/41 25.7.69) (Decision 69/227/EEC). This was strengthened in 1971 (OJ L73/12-13 27.3.71) (Decision 71/141/EEC). See also Conjunctural policy committee (qv).

Purpose

In 1960, in response to article 103 (1) of the founding treaty of the EEC, the Council had set up a Conjunctural policy committee. Its duty was to assist the Commission in its consultations with member states over the economic development outlined in article 103 (qv). In the main these were short-term developments.

In 1964 a Medium-term economic policy committee was formed (qv). It was inevitable therefore that an instruction on short-term economic policy, should follow.

Work on short-term economic policy

It was thought appropriate that member states should consult together in this area of economic development. The 1969 Decision laid down that prior consultations should be held on important short-term economic policy measures or decisions to be taken by a member state. Special importance was given to those short term measures likely to affect other member states and interrupt or affect medium-term economic policy that had been reached by joint consultation. These consultations are held in the, Monetary committee (qv), the Conjunctural policy committee (qv) and the Budgetary policy committee (qv). The 1971 decision laid down how the Commission should examine the progress of co-ordination throughout the years. This work was co-ordinated in 1974 by setting up the Economic policy committee (qv).

Further information

General report on the activities of the European Communities
   Luxembourg: Office for official publication of the European Communities, annual

Medium-Term Economic Policy Committee
Basic information

Economic policy programmes were envisaged under articles 105 and 145 of the Treaty of Rome (1957).

By a 1964 Council decision (OJ 64/1031 29.4.64) (Decision 64/247/EEC) a Medium-term economic policy committee was set up. Later, this was taken over by the Economic policy committee (OJ L63/21–22 5.3.74) (Decision 74/122/EEC).

Medium-Term Economic Policy Committee – representation

Membership consisted of:

- two members from each member state selected from senior officials responsible for economic policy
- two members from the Commission
- an alternative member for each full member
- their term of office is two years which is renewable

Purpose

- To effect co-ordination of the economic policy of member states
- To prepare by available information and forecasts preliminary drafts of medium-term economic policy programmes outlining in broad terms the economic policies that member states and institutions of the Community intend to follow during the period under consideration

In 1974 it was incorporated with other committees in the Economic policy committee (qv).

Further information

General report on the activities of the European Communities
   Luxembourg: Office for official publications of the European Communities, annual up to 1974

Economic Policy Committee

Basic information

The authority for this Committee under the Treaty of Rome (1957) is founded in articles 103 (conjunctural policies), 104 (a reminder to each member state that it must maintain a sound economic policy), 105 (co-ordination of the economic policies of member states), 106 (a declaration that member states will work towards a closer economic entity), 107 (exchange rates) and 108/109 (action within the Community resulting from economic difficulties in member states).

At a 1974 Council meeting a decision was agreed establishing the, Committee (OJ L63.21–2 5.3.74) (Decision 74/122/EEC). This was a result of the Commission's proposals for movement towards a second stage in an economic and monetary union (OJ L63/16–18 5.3.74) (Decision 74/120/EEC).

The Committee is a merger of:

   Short-term economic policy committee (qv)
   Budget policy committee (qv)
   Medium-term economic policy committee (qv)

The merger was undertaken to avoid overlapping of authority, duplication of effort and to prepare for the next thrust towards the goal of economic and monetary union.

Economic Policy Committee – representation

The Committee to consist of:

- four Commission representatives
- four delegates from each member state, who are concerned with short

and medium term economic policies
- a chairman to be selected from the members of the committee, to hold office for a non-renewable term of two years
- three vice chairman to be selected from the members of the committee for a non-renewable term of two years
- the Committee may meet with a reduced membership (those especially concerned) for the purpose of dealing with specific problems in the fields of short or medium term economic policies or budgetary policy.

Work of the Economic Policy Committee

The following tasks have been assigned to the Committee, to:
- assist in co-ordinating general economic policies
- examine and compare budgetary policies and their implementation in member states
- prepare the preliminary draft of medium-term economic policy programmes for the Community (1st programme 1966) as required under section 6 of Decision 74/120/EEC
- review the medium-term economic programmes of member states in the light of current Community policy (outlined in the task above)
- analyse divergencies from the programmes

The opinion of the Committee may be requested by the Commission or the Council.

The 5th medium-term economic policy programme preparation began early in 1980 and by April/May a report to the Council proposed the priorities for consideration. Consideration of these proposals was made during the following month by the Council. The second half of the year saw more detailed work by the Committee including studies on specific aspects by Commission staff. The first half of 1981 saw the preparation of the preparatory texts and by the end of May 1981 the 5th medium-term economic policy programme in a preliminary draft form was sent to the Commission. This was approved after the introduction of a foreword (*Bulletin of the European Communities* 14 (7/8) 1981 points 1.2.1–1.2.10).

Further information

General report on the activities of the European Communities
    Luxembourg: Office for official publications of the European Communities, annual
'Economic policy committee'. *Bulletin of the European communities* 6 (11) 1973. point 1109
United Kingdom medium term economic trends and problems.
    Brussels: Commission of the European Community, 1982. 128p. (Economic Papers series no. 7 (Internal paper, EEC Library, London)

Monetary Committee

Basic information

Under a Council decision of 1958 the Committee rules were established to implement articles 105 (2) and 153 of the Treaty of Rome (1957) (OJ 17/390–392 6.10.58) amended by (OJ 32/1064 30.4.62) (OJ L257/20 15.11.72) (Decision 72/377/EEC) (OJ L84/56 31.2.76) (Decision 76/332/EEC). See also last item under, Further information.

Monetary Committee – representation

- two members from each member state
  one a senior administrator and
  one from the Central Bank
- two alternate members from each member state
  one a senior administrator and
  one from the Central Bank

  { Experts in the monetary field

- term of office two years which is renewable
- the Committee shall appoint from among its members a Chairman and three vice-chairmen
- alternate members may attend meetings of the Committee when their representative is present. They shall not participate in the discussion or vote

Purpose of the Monetary Committee

- to keep under review the monetary and financial situation of member states
- it shall attempt to foresee balance of payments problems and send to Council and Commission suggestions for alleviating these problems
- it shall keep under review article 106 (1) to (3) of the Treaty of Rome (1957) regarding the general payments system of member states
- as laid down in the Treaty of Rome the Committee's opinion regarding the finances of member states must be sought by the Council and also may be obtained by both Council and Commission in other cases
- It has the authority to draw up opinions when it thinks necessary

Work undertaken

It has set up working parties, for example, the Working party on the harmonization of monetary policy instruments, which currently (1981) is considering amongst other subjects, the technical problems arising from the co-existence of monetary and exchange rate objectives within the European Monetary System. The, Working party on capital markets, is reviewing bond market trends and the capital markets of member countries. The, Working party on public finance, submits proposals for EC budget guidelines. There is also a, Working party on securities markets.

For some time there has been a movement to harmonize stock exchange rules throughout the Community. In 1979 a directive was issued on conditions governing stock exchange listing (OJ L66/21-32 16.3.79) (Directive 79/279/EEC). The following year the particulars required were amplified (OJ L100/1-26 17.4.80) (Directive 80/390/EEC) and in 1981 were given details of information which must be published on a regular basis by companies whose shares are admitted to official stock exchange listing (*Bulletin of the European Communities* **14** (12) 1981 point 2.1.51). On the 19 January 1982 the Commission sent a proposal to the Council that all three items of legislation should be given an implementation deadline of 30 June 1983. This was adopted by the Council on 26 January 1982 (*Bulletin of the European Communities* **15** (1) 1982 point 2.1.23).

The Committee produces an annual report (see Further information).

Further information

General report on the activities of the European Communities
   Luxembourg: Office for official publication of the European Communities, annual
Report on the activities of the Monetary committee
   Luxembourg: Office for official publications of the European Communities, annual
Monetary policies in the countries of the European Economic Community, institutions and instruments
   Luxembourg: Office for official publications of the European Communities for the Monetary committee, 1972. 436p. Supplement 1974 not paged
Compendium of Community monetary texts
   Luxembourg: Office for official publications of the European Communities, 1979. 177p. ISBN 92-825-1148. Catalogue number CB-28-79-504-EN-C

Customs Union

Basic information

In the original Schuman Plan for Europe, announced on 9 May 1950, one of the aims was to set up an economic community.

The Dutch government on 11 December 1952 put forward a plan for integrating the economies of the six on the basis of a customs union.

The European Economic Community treaty entered into force on 1 January 1958. Article 9 section 1 of the treaty states:

'The Community shall be based upon a customs union which shall cover all trade in goods and which shall involve the prohibition between member states of customs duties on imports and exports and of all charges having an equivalent effect, and the adoption of a common customs tariff in their relations with third countries' (Treaties establishing the European Communities . . .; or Guide to EEC legislation (v1 page 9) see, Further information).

Work undertaken

Customs duties between member states were removed and a common customs tariff introduced on 1 July 1968.

The integration of the three new member states (UK, Republic of Ireland and Denmark) into the customs union of the Community came about on 1 July 1977 with the ending of a transitional period. In December 1977 the Commission organized a conference to debate customs union. This conference published its proceedings, *The customs union today and tomorrow*. Luxembourg: Office for official publications of the European Communities, 1978. 107p. ISBN 92-825-0297-X. Catalogue number CB-24-78-047-EN-C, which showed the importance of the Commission's guidelines to complete and consolidate the Customs Union.

In 1978 a five year plan was proposed to promote economic and monetary union. The Economic and Social Committee examined the 1977 conference proceedings and EP working document 557/77 (Nyborg report), and produced an opinion on 30 March 1978 (OJ C181/31-8 31.7. 78).

This year saw a continuation of consultations begun in 1977 which aimed to reach the broadest possible consensus of ideas on future objectives. Parliament delivered its opinion in a resolution dated 12 April 1978 (OJ C108/29-31 8.5.78). The Commission in close collaboration with the national authorities set about preparing the broad lines of future policy for a customs union.

1979 led to the incorporation into Community law of the results of multilateral trade negotiations. On 31 March 1979 the Commission considered it desirable to redefine the key aspects relating to Economic Union emphasized by growing world economic problems and produced a multiannual programme for the attainment of Customs Union (OJ C84/2-10 31.3.79).

In 1980, following the multilateral trade negotiations (GATT's Tokyo Round), there was a switch to new rules for the valuation of goods for customs purposes. The Commission sent to both Council and Parliament a communication proposing a new approach to Community policy on technical barriers to trade (*Bulletin of the European Commission* 13 (1) 1980. point 1.3.1). This outlined the action taken so far and emphasized the importance of forestalling the creation of barriers to trade and the value of the co-ordination of standardization policies.

1981 saw work scheduled for 1980 still being carried out. A Parliamentary resolution passed on 16 October 1980 called for a speedier removal of the technical barriers to trade. The Commission, therefore, drew up new proposals designed to further progress towards a full customs union including proposals to strengthen the Common Customs Tariff.

The customs authorities of member states and the Commission are developing an integrated Community system of computerized data collection to provide rapid information for sound decision making. This is known as the CADDIA experiment (OJ C291/3–4 12.11.81) and (*Bulletin of the European Communities* supplement 4/81, page 54).

Further information

General report on the activities of the European Communities
  Luxembourg: Office for official publications of the European Communities, annual
Treaties establishing the European Communities
  Luxembourg: Office for official publications of the European Communities, 1973. 1502p.
Exporting to the European Community, information for foreign exporters
  Luxembourg: Office for official publications of the European Communities, 1977. 71p.
  Catalogue number CB–23–77–526–EN–C
Guide to EEC Legislation
  Amsterdam: North Holland Publishing Company, 1979. 2 v. ISBN 0–444–85320–0
Customs union of the European Economic Community by Nikolaus Vaulont
  Luxembourg: Office for official publications of the European Communities, 1981. 89p.
  (European Perspectives series). ISBN 92–825–1911–2. Catalogue number CB–30–80–205–
  EN–C
European economic and monetary union, 2nd ed
  Luxembourg: Office for official publications of the European Communities, 1981. 39p.
  (European documentation series 4 – 1981) ISBN 92–825–2589–9

Advisory Committee on Customs Matters

Basic information

Established by Commission decision in 1973 (OJ L321/37– 9 22.11.73) (Decision 73/351/EEC), amended by (OJ L362/55 31.12.76) (Decision 76/921/EEC).

Advisory Committee – representation

The Committee consists of 35 members, appointed by the Commission from professional or consumer organizations in the subject field and who are most concerned with customs matters. The subject fields covered by members include industry, craft industry, agriculture, commercial organizations, chambers of commerce and industry, rail transport, road transport, shipping, inland waterway transport, air transport, banking institutions, insurance institutions, customs agents, tourist boards. Members are appointed from representatives of workers, representatives of consumers, and others concerned with customs in these subject fields. The organizations put forward names to the Commission which makes the appointments. Appointments are for two years which may be renewed. Experts may be invited by the Committee to attend.

Work of the Advisory Committee

The Committee's duties are:

- to reply with an opinion to requests for information from the Commission, with reference to community provisions on customs matters
- to provide the section preparing customs regulations and directives (GUD8) with opinions giving a user point of view

Further information

General report on the activities of European Communities
   Luxembourg: Office for official publications of the European Communities, annual
Community advisory committees for the representation of socio-economic interests
   Farnborough: Saxon House for EC Economic and Social Committee, 1980. 115p. ISBN 0–566–00328–7

Common Customs Tariff (CCT)

Basic information

The CCT was introduced on 1 July 1968 when customs duties between member states were removed, thus implementing article 28 of the Treaty of Rome (1957).

It is the instrument through which the Community will implement the contractual undertakings it gave on tariffs in the multilateral trade negotiations.

Purpose

Possibly the most important series of changes as far as international trade is concerned, resulted from the negotiations commenced in Tokyo in September 1973 (See, Development of an overall approach to trade in view of the coming multilateral negotiations in GATT, a memorandum from the Commission to the Council submitted on 9 April 1973 and amended 24 May 1973) (*Bulletin of the European Communities* supplement 2/73). It was concluded on 17 December 1979 (OJ L71/1–2 17.3.80) (Decision 80/271/EEC). The rest of this rather large *Official Journal* includes other aspects of the GATT agreement. These were under the auspices of the General Agreement on Tariffs and Trade (GATT) and known as the Tokyo round. The results of these negotiations were implemented through the CCT by the production of a Customs valuation code and a Government procurement code. The former came into force on 1 January 1981. The uniform application of the CCT Nomenclature is of growing importance in this work. The CCT is a necessary preliminary stage leading towards full customs union. This union was started in 1979 by the institution of a multi-annual programme (OJ C84/2–10 31.3.79) (*Bulletin of the European Communities* **12** (3) 1979. points 1.4.1–1.4.5).

Further information

Thirteenth general report on the activities of the European Communities (points 142, 143, 493 and 494)
    Luxembourg: Office for official publications of the European Communities, 1979. 346p. ISBN 92–825–1602–4. Catalogue number CB–29–79–522–EN–C
Fourteenth general report on the activities of the European Communities in 1980 (points 163 – 165 and 556–564)
    Luxembourg: Office for official publications of the European Communities, 1981. 360p. ISBN 92–825–2197–4. Catalogue number CB–31–80–102–EN–C

In view of the very considerable number of regulations involved see:

Guide to EEC Legislation (Chapter 8)
    Amsterdam: North Holland Publishing Company, 1979. 2 v. ISBN 0–444–85320–0
Customs union of the European Economic Community by Nikolaus Vaulont
    Luxembourg: Office for official publications of the European Communities, 1981. 89p. (European Perspectives series). ISBN 92–825–1911–2. Catalogue number CB–30–80–205–EN–C

Nomenclature for the Classification of Goods

Basic information

Article 28 of the Treaty of Rome (1957) is concerned with the common customs tariff. The customs tariff nomenclature was authorized by a Council regulation (OJ L14/1–2 21.1.69) (Regulation 97/69/EEC).

Purpose of the nomenclatures

The customs nomenclature, frequently known as the Brussels nomenclature, is one of many in everyday use. It was devised by the, Customs co-operation council.

It is a trade classification to identify imports and exports for the purpose of payment of duty, statistics, assessment of changes in the flow of particular products over a period of time, etc. First published in 1965 it was then correctly known as the 'Brussels tariff' nomenclature (BTN) Since 1976 when the 5th edition was produced it became known as the Customs co-operation council nomenclature (CCCN).

The, Customs co-operation council (CCC) has also produced, Explanatory notes to the Brussels nomenclature, Brussels: CCC, 1966.

The EC itself through the Commission issued, Explanatory notes to the customs tariff of the European Committees
Luxembourg: Office for official publications of the EC, 1971. Catalogue number CB–24–77–205–EN–C (six monthly amendments, loose leaf).

Related nomenclatures

For trade matters the EC also has its, Nomenclature of goods for the external trade statistics of the Community and statistics of trade between member states (NIMEXE).
　　Luxembourg: European Communities statistical office, 1973 –. annual: Changes to the classification enter into force at the beginning of each year. The NIMEXE headings correspond in the main, either to the CCCN, or sub-headings in the nomenclature of the, Common customs tariff (CCT) (qv). See the useful section by Lewis Foreman in, *Sources of information on the European Communities* mentioned in, Further information.

For industrial products there is a Eurostat publication, *Common nomenclature of industrial products* (NIPRO).
　　Luxembourg: Office for official publications of the European Communities, 1975.

Further information

Palmer, Doris M. (ed)
Sources of information on the European Communities, Chapter p. 129
Sources of statistics ... by Lewis Foreman
　　London: Mansell Publishing, 1979. 230p. ISBN 0–7201–0724–5

Competition Policy

Basic information

An economic community currently of 270 million and rapidly approaching the 300 million mark, where there are no trade barriers, is an exceptional market for manufacturers and producers. Competition should provide all members of the Community with goods of improving quality and, relatively speaking, at a decreasing cost. Those responsible for the founding Treaties realized that the third largest grouping of consumers in the world would be open to adverse manipulation unless a sound competition policy was developed and enforced. Articles 65 and 66 of the ECSC treaty (1951) and 85 to 94 of the EEC treaty (1957), laid the foundation for a sound competition policy. The basic regulation implementing Articles 85 and 86 (restrictions on competition) of the EEC treaty was agreed in 1962. (OJ L13/204–210 21.2.62) (Regulation 17/62/EEC). A number of amendments have been made to this regulation. Block exemptions to these regulations can be authorized by the Council. For instance (OJ L57/849–52 25.3.67) (Regulation 67/67/EEC) exempts certain categories of exclusive dealing agreements between a supplier and a distributor. This exemption has been extended to 1982 (OJ L276/15 9.12.72) (Regulation 2591/72/EEC).

Development of the Policy

Under the Treaty articles listed above, European competition policy pursues the following objectives:

- removal of trade restrictions, cartels, market sharing agreements
- prevention of abuses by firms in dominant positions
- maintenance of fair competition and market fluidity
- prevention of aid by national authorities from distorting competition, and undermining Community policy for national gain

Work undertaken

Since 1970, the Commission has produced a separate *Report on competition policy*, published in conjunction with their, *General report on the activities of the European Community.*

This report is concerned with:

- competition policy towards enterprises (an analysis of developments in community policy, and community involvement in international trade; changes in national competition policies by member states; and finally the implications of major cases examined during the year)
- competition policy and government assistance to enterprises (an analysis of individual cases during the year reviewed)
- the development of concentration and competition in the Community (most of the reports in this section are concerned with industries rather than individual firms)

At the end of each report is a list of cases, with references. This is followed by a list of study reports published in the *Evolution of concentration and competition*, series.

Since 1962 Companies seeking to conclude agreements likely to fall within the scope of the banned agreements mentioned under the Treaty, have to notify the Commission and obtain negative clearance. During the present period of recession it is possible to obtain approval if special advantages in trade, employment, relief of unemployment in economically hard hit areas, do accrue from the proposals. Applications for exemption should be made on form A/B (obtainable from the Department of Industry or its regional offices, Scottish Office, Welsh Office, Department of Commerce for Northern Ireland or the EEC London Office). The completed forms to be sent to the EC Brussels. State ownership and private enterprise concentrations sometimes lead to abuse of their dominant positions. Here again the Community is neutral regarding ownership and both public and private organizations have to adhere to the EEC treaty rules on competition.

State aid whilst benefitting the local firm or industry may provide unfair competition to similar firms in other member states. This is checked in the interests of all. Similarly the work of the Community in Regional development has to ensure that support given does not assist in the infringement of overall Community competition policy. An example of this took place in 1978 when the Community ruled against the UK's Temporary Employment Subsidy because its use appeared to distort competition rules. On the other hand, in 1981 the Commission decided not to raise objections to the Government of Ireland's plan to reduce taxation on profits of certain service sector companies located at Shannon Airport. One of the reasons for this decision was the regions social and economic problems. However, the Commission insisted that certain provisos be included, such as each tax reduction could only apply to initial investments (new companies, etc) with less than 50 employees. (*Bulletin of the European Communities* **14** (6) 1981. point 2.1.35).

Community attitudes towards the copyright of industrial and commercial property, has been shown through a number of court cases (*Bulletin of the European Communities* **15** (6) 1982 point 2.1.43). The principles applied are generally similar to those used in Patent law, qv.

A, Business co-operation centre, whose purpose was to bring small businesses into contact with each other, has been established (*Fifteenth general report on the activities of the European Communities in 1981*, points 158 and 159).

The Community allocated a specific new budget heading in 1981 for training and informing representatives of European small business associations, on European affairs. The work undertaken was outlined in *Bulletin of the European Communities* **15** (5) 1982 point 2.1.9.

Small and medium sized enterprises, because of their importance in the

Community's industrial and commercial structure, have been the subject of special attention. Details of these have been listed in section 5 of chapter 1 of the *11th report on competition policy*, Luxembourg: Office for official publications of the European Communities, 1982. 194p. ISBN 92–825–2884–7. Catalogue number CB–33–81–433.

The Economic and social committee on the 26th and 27th May 1982 gave, on its own initiative, opinion on the promotion of small businesses. (*Bulletin of the European Communities* **15** (5) 1982 point 2.4.29).

Further information

Report on competition policy
   Luxembourg: Office for official publications of the European Communities, annual 1970–
Competition law in the European Economic and in the European Coal and Steel, Communities
   Luxembourg: Office for official publications of the European Communities, 1972. 124p. (latest issue 1981. 134p. ISBN 92–825–2389–6. Catalogue number CB–30–80–576–EN–C)
Catalogue of Community legal acts and other texts relating to the elimination of technical barriers to trade for industrial products and nomenclature for iron and steel products (EURONORM)
   Luxembourg: Office for official publications of the European Communities, 1981. 112p. ISBN 92–825–2769–7 Catalogue number CB–33–81–110–EN–C
'Application of the rules of competition to air transport'.
Bulletin of the European Communities **14** (7/8) 1981. points 1.3.1–1.3.8
There is a Competition Policy desk at the Department of Trade, Sanctuary Buildings, Great Smith Street, London SW 1P 3DB. Telephone 01–215 3714. This is a useful starting point for queries on this subject

Stabilization of Export Earnings (STABEX)

Basic information

Export Receipt Stabilization System (STABEX) is an insurance policy against bad years. It is designed to compensate for a shortfall in the export earnings (not prices of products) of ACP countries due to a decline in production as a result of natural or climatic circumstances. It covers those states which signed the Lomé conventions (qv) and concerns certain products arranged in a number of groups. These are agricultural products or minerals.

Products

Initially twelve were covered including certain by-products:

• groundnuts, cocoa, coffee, cotton, coconut, palm, palmnut and kernel products, hides, skins, and leather, wood, fresh bananas, tea, raw sisal and iron ore

The following products and by products have since been added:

- vanilla, cloves, pyrethrum, mohair wool, gum arabic, ylang-ylang and, in 1979, sesame seed

STABEX

STABEX system covers the revenues from the export of these products when they are more than 7½% of the total export receipts of the country concerned, or they approach the threshold of dependence. This threshold is reduced to 2½% in the case of the least developed African, Caribbean and Pacific (ACP) countries. The EC guarantees only receipts from exports to the Community and only if they are consumed or processed in Europe. However, in the cases of Guinea-Bissau, Ethiopia, Rwanda, Burundi and Swaziland which export little to the EC, STABEX applies to all their exports of the products concerned to the Community.

For each product and for each ACP country a reference level is drawn up each year, on the basis of export receipts over the previous four years. When receipts drop below this level by a certain percentage (called the dependence threshold) the country involved calls on the EC to pay it a sum corresponding to the difference or shortfall. The country will repay this amount when its export receipts are expanding except in the case of the least developed countries which are exempt from repayment. Up to 30 April 1979 STABEX payments had been agreed covering a total amount of 172,772 million EUA.

Further information

The European community and the Third World
  Brussels: EC Spokesman's Group and Directorate-General for Information, November 1977. 47p. (Dossier series) Catalogue number CI–22–524–EN–C)
Europe today, state of European integration 1980–1981
  Luxembourg: Office for official publications of the European Communities, 1981. 617p. ISBN 92–823–0037–4. Catalogue number AX–30–80–972–EN–C

Generalized System of Preferences (GSP)

Basic information

In May 1963 at a meeting of the, General agreement on tariffs and trade (GATT), the EC proposed that industrialized countries should grant preferential treatment to imports of manufactures from the developing countries, in order to promote their industrial development. Agreement in principle on this proposal was reached at the second Session of the UN

Conference on trade and development (UNCTAD) in New Delhi, 1968. Implemented by the Community on 1 July 1971 (OJ L287 30.12.71), these generalized preferences mark a new turning point in international trade relations leading to collaboration between developed and developing countries (*Fifth general report on the activities of the European Communities 1971*, points 452–455).

Characteristics of the GSP are outlined in the references at the end of this entry. The value of the GSP offer has increased from 3,250 million ua in 1974 to 7,900 million EUA in 1979. Usually about 65% of the offer is taken up by developing countries.

Current position of GSP

The Community's initial period for GSP was due to expire at the end of 1980. A review of the first ten years operation shows that to attain its objectives no major alteration to the system is necessary (EP Working document 1–67 7.4.80). Proposals for a second ten year period of GSP were adopted by the Council, starting with those for 1981–5 (OJ L354/1–81 29.12.80) (Regulation 3320/80/EEC).

From now on, for industrial and ECSC products, global quotas, ceilings and maximum country amounts are abolished. As a parallel development the scheme aims to limit the imports from highly competitive countries and expand those benefits accruing to the least developed countries. A new scheme was introduced in 1980 under the Multi fibre arrangement (MFA) for textile products.

Further information

General report on the activities of the European Communities
    Luxembourg: Office for official publications of the European Communities, annual
Development of the Community's generalized preferences
    Brussels: EC Spokesman's Group and Director-General for Information, December 1978.
    7p. (Europe Information, Development series, special edition)
    Catalogue number CC–AB–78–025–EN–C
Development of the Community's generalized preferences
    Brussels: EC Spokesman's Group and Director-General for Information, March 1979. 7p.
    (Europe Information, External Relations series no. 18/79) Catalogue Number CC–NA–
    79–R18–EN–C
Europe today, state of European integration 1980–1981
    Luxembourg: Office for official publications of the European Communities, 1981. 617p.
    ISBN 92–823–0037–4. Catalogue number AX–30–80–972–EN–C

Financial Aid from the European Communities

Basic information

Under the Treaty of Rome (1957) founding the EEC, a major aim is to ensure that all the population share in the prosperity generated by the Common Market.

Article 130 of the founding treaty refers to the European Investment Bank and outlines a policy which could be generally applicable '... to contribute ... to the balanced and steady development of the common market in the interests of the Community ...'

The European Coal and Steel Community (ECSC) (1952) treaty states, 'The Community shall progressively bring about conditions which will of themselves ensure the most rational distribution of production at the highest possible level of productivity ...' 2nd paragraph, Article 2 ECSC treaty.

Article 1 of the European Atomic Energy Community (EURATOM) (1957) states 'It shall be the task of the Community to contribute to the raising of the standard of living in member states ...'

Purpose of the distribution of financial aid

As the geographical area covered by member states of the European Community embraces wide differences of climate, resources and industry, the various organizations which form the EC, attempt to redress the balance in the interests of those who live in the least prosperous areas.

Method of Work

Each of the following organizations contribute to this work and details will be found under the headings listed:

- European Agricultural Guidance and Guarantee Fund (EAGGF) – financial assistance
- European Social Fund – financial assistance
- European Regional Development Fund (ERDF) – financial assistance
- European Coal and Steel Community (ECSC) – financial assistance
- European Investment Bank (EIB) – financial assistance
- European Atomic Energy Community (EURATOM) – financial assistance
- Energy objectives – financial assistance
- Environmental research programme – financial assistance
- Waste materials recycling – financial assistance
- European information network
- Data processing scheme – financial assistance

Work undertaken

In 1978, intervention appropriations were running at 10,891.05 million EUAs. In the sections listed above an attempt is made to show the amount which is available to Britain and, by example, to illustrate the wide spread of these grants and loans.

Further information

General report on the activities of the European Communities
    Luxembourg: Office for official publications of the European Communities, annual
Grants and loans from the European Community
    Luxembourg: Office for official publications of the European Communities, 1981. 83p.
    (European documentation series 7–8/1981 ISBN 92–825–2633–X. Catalogue number
    CB–NC–81–008–EN–C
European Communities Commission Press Release series
    London, European Communities London Office. 20 Kensington Palace Gardens W8
    4QQ, irregular. [details of aid to Britain under the various funds are given from time to
    time]
Scott, Gay
Guide to European community grants and loans – 2nd ed
    Biggleswade: Euroinformation Limited, 1981. 111p. ISBN 0–907304–01–X
Official sources of finance and aid for industry in the UK
    London: National Westminster Bank Limited, Commercial information Market intelligence
    department, 1981. 67p.

Regional Policy

Basic information

Article 2 of the treaty establishing the European Economic Community provided for the harmonious development of economic activities and in the Preamble to the Treaty there is a reference to '...strengthen the unity of their economies ... and reduce the differences existing between the various regions ...'.

Development of the Policy

During the 1960s there was considerable discussion of the problems involved in co-ordinating regional development. In October 1972 the Paris Conference of heads of state or government wished to find a community solution to regional problems. They invited institutions to prepare a report on the problem in the enlarged community, to provide for the co-ordination of regional development and to set up a European Regional Development Fund (ERDF) (qv). This was established in 1975

(OJ L73/1–7 21.3.75) (Regulation 724/75/EEC).

In the same year a Regional Policy Committee was established (qv). It was attached to the Council and the Commission and it undertook investigations at their instigation as well as on its own initiative.

Both these organizations aim to work for the correction of imbalances in the Community and in particular those resulting from the preponderance of agriculture, from industrial change and from structural underemployment. It was considered that an effective regional policy was an essential prerequisite to the realization of economic and monetary union.

Supplementary measures in favour of the United Kingdom under the Regional policy programme were running at 1,437,584,000 ECU at the end of 1981 (*Bulletin of the European Communities* **15** (1) 1982 point 2.1.35). See also entry under, Budget of the European Communities – Purpose of the budget.

Tourism is another aspect of Regional Policy. Its main responsibility is with member states and the Community is able to supply assistance from Regional funds, Social funds and from the EAGGF. The Commission has submitted proposals to the Council on a number of aspects of this subject including:

- duty free allowances for travellers
- tourist assistance
- civil liability insurance for motor vehicles
- freedom of establishment in certain services in transport and travel agencies (OJ L73   23.4.66) adopted by the Council on 29.6.82.

On 30.6.82 the Commission submitted a communication covering:

- an extension of the tourist season
- protection of the architectural heritage
- promoting social, cultural and rural tourism

(*Bulletin of the European Communities* **15** (6) 1982 points 1.4.1 – 1.4.4).

Further information

General report on the activities of the European Communities
   Luxembourg: Office for official publications of the European Communities, annual
Report on the regional problems of the enlarged Community
   Bulletin of the European Communities supplement 8/73
Regional policy the start of a new phase
   Brussels: Spokesman's Group and Director-General for Information, July 1978. 7p.
   (Europe Information Regional Policy series no 11/78) Catalogue number CC–AB–78–-
   A11–EN–C
Yuill, Douglas and Allen, Kevin
European regional incentives: 1981
   Glasgow: University of Strathclyde, 1981. 490p. ISBN 0–90–7243–04–5

Hopkins, Michael
Policy formation in the European Communities, Chapter 10
London: Mansell. 1981. 339p. ISBN 0-7201-1597-3. [background bibliographical detail]
Study of the effect on regions of the common agricultural policy
Luxembourg: Office of official publications of the European Communities, 1981. 178p.
ISBN 92-825-2441-8.Catalogue number CB-NS-81-021-EN-C
Keeble, David and others
The influence of peripheral and central locations on the relative development of regions,
final report
London: HMSO for the Department of Industry, 1982. 277p. ISBN 0-11-513575-8

Regional Policy Committee

Basic information

The Committee (OJ L73/47–48 21.3.75) (Decision 75/185/EEC) and updated in 1979 (OJ L35/9 9.2.79) (Decision 79/137/EEC), was set up at the same time as the European Regional Development Fund (ERDF) (qv) in March 1975. It is composed of senior national and Commission officials.

Work of the Committee

Its task is to keep the development of the regions under constant review, to compare and assess national regional policies which should be compatible with each other and with EC aims. It also examines all aspects of Community activity which affect the regions, with particular reference to the Community's Economic policy programmes (qv) to ensure that regional policy keeps in step. It advises the Commission and the Council where Community level action is needed in order to protect regional interests.

Rules of procedure were published in 1975 (OJ L320/17 –18 11.12.75) (Act 75/761/EEC). They were followed by guidelines for Community regional policy (OJ C36/10–11 9.2.79). The guidelines were as follows:

* to develop a comprehensive system of analysis and policy formulation for Community regional policy
* to provide an assessment of the regional impact of Community policies
* to develop the co-ordination of national regional policies

Further information

General report on the activities of the European Communities
Luxembourg: Office for official publications of the European Communities, annual 1975 –

Regional development problems of the Community during the period 1975/77 and the
establishment of a common regional policy
    Luxembourg: Office for official publications of the European Communities, 1976. 11p.
Regional policy the start of a new phase
    Brussels: Spokesman's Group and Director-General for Information, July 1978. 7p.
    (Europe Information, Regional Policy series no. 11/78). Catalogue number CC–AB–78–
    All–EN–C

European Regional Development Fund (ERDF)

Basic information

Under the EEC treaty, preamble paragraph 6, general article 235, and other articles
regarding specific requirements, the ERDF was established in 1975. (OJ L73/1–7 21.3.75)
(Regulation 724/75/EEC), as amended by (OJ L35/1–7 9.2.79) (Regulation 214/79/EEC)
and (OJ L349/10 23.12.80) (Regulation 3325/80/EEC). Proposals for further amendments
were made in 1981 (OJ C336/60–72 23.12.81).
It had a three year budget of 1,300 million EUAs. The 1978 budget was 581 million EUAs,
rising to 1,540 million in 1981. These resources are allocated in part on a member state
quota basis. In 1981 the Commission sent to the Council a proposal amending regulation
724/75 (OJ C336/60–72 23.12.81).

Tasks of the ERDF

- supplement to national regional policies
- support for backward regions
- reduction of concentrations of industry in built-up areas
- co-ordination of existing Community policies and financial instruments
  so that they may be better utilized for purposes of regional policy
- permanent analysis and assessment of regional integration processes in
  the EC

Work undertaken

It makes grants to help industrial and service sector investments as well
as to create new, or safeguard existing, jobs. It is designed to assist
infrastructure investments – roads, water supply, industrial estates, etc. It
is designed to assist less favoured regions. In the period 1975–9 inclusive,
Ireland had 523 investments aided to a total of 152.2 million EUAs, Italy
2,984 investments aided to a total of 916.3 million EUAs and Great Britain
2,669 investments aided to a total of 665.7 million EUAs. On the other
hand Denmark had 248 investments aided to a total of 34.5 million EUAs
and Western Germany 1,086 investments aided to a total of 210.1 million
EUAs. Application for grants are submitted by national governments (q.v.
ERDF, financial assistance).

The Fund regulations provided for its re-examination by the Council before 1 January 1978 (Article 18). Commission, *Guidelines for Community regional policy*, were presented by the Commission to Council in 1977. These amendments were subject to conciliation procedure, and were published later (OJ L35/1–7 9.2.79) (Regulation 214/79/EEC).

By 1981 experience had shown that the ERDF was unable to realize its full potential because of limited resources. This was first outlined in, *Bulletin of the European Communities* supplement 1/81. These ideas were expanded in a subsequent supplement 4/81 under a sub-heading, *New regional policy guidelines and priorities.* Also in 1981 the Economic and Social Committee (ESC) decided to submit an opinion on its own initiative on the ERDF's 6th annual report covering 1980. This included comments on the inadequacy of ERDF resources (OJ C64/1–5 15.3.82).

Further information

General report on the activities of the European Communities
   Luxembourg: Office for official publications of the European Communities, annual 1975–
European regional development fund annual report
   Luxembourg: Office for official publications of the European Communities, annual 1976–
   (The first annual report also published in, *Bulletin of the European Communities,* supplement 7/76)
European regional development fund
Bulletin of the European Communities supplement 7/76
Regional policy, the start of a new phase
   Brussels: Spokesman's Groups and Directorate-General for Information, July 1978. 7p. (European Information, Regional Policy series no. 11/78). Catalogue number CC–AB–78–A11–EN–C
Regional development and the European Community
   Brussels: EC Directorate-General for Information, 1979. 7p. (European, file 10/79). Catalogue number CC–AD–79–010–EN–C
Europe today, state of European integration 1980–1981
   Luxembourg: Office for official publications of the European Communities 1981. 617p. ISBN 92–823–0037–4. Catalogue number AX–30–80–972–EN–C

European Regional Development Fund (ERDF) – Financial Assistance

Basic information

The purpose of the Fund is to ensure that all Community members share in the prosperity and growth as equally as possible. Because of differences in climate, resources, etc the ERDF was set up to correct economic imbalances which have developed in the past.

ERDF provides additional aid for operations and projects mounted by national public authorities for regional development.

Resources allocated

ERDF was set up in March 1975 (OJ L73/1–7 21.3.75) (Regulation 724/75/EEC). Its regulations were amended in late 1978 (OJ L35/1–7 9.2.79) (Regulation 214/79/EEC). It was given resources as follows:

1975 300 million ua
1976 500 million ua
1977 500 million ua   681 million EUA from
1978 581 million EUA   the start of the fund
1979 945 million EUA   to July 1981 has been
1980 1,165 million EUA   allocated to Britain
1981 1,540 million ECU
1982 1,940 million ECU*

*(Preliminary draft, *Bulletin of the European Communities* **14** (5) 1981 point 2.3.52).

Since 1979 the fund is in two sections. The larger section is subject to a national quota system (for the UK this is just over 27% of the total funds). The other, non-quota system, is currently limited to 5% of the total resources of the fund and is designed to work in conjunction with other aid sources to help Community decisions in additional fields.

Projects benefiting under the Fund

Assistance is confined to the regional development areas, so designated by the member states concerned. Investments located in national priority areas, take precedence.

Developments which may benefit member states should be costed. Those valued at 50,000 EUA and upwards are considered. They should be within the development programme of the member state. At least 10 jobs should be created or preserved by each development. Projects in the following fields are eligible:

- investments in industrial activities **A**
- investments in artisan activities **B**

These should be considered economically viable

- investments in service activities are limited to tourism or those which have a variable location **C**
- investments in the infrastructure of an area the cost of which is borne by a public authority or an agency with delegated responsibility for infrastructure projects **D**

One of the current integrated projects (July 1981) which is under preparation is for the Belfast area.

- investments in rural infrastructure, as above, except those which are already receiving an EAGGF grant (OJ L128/1–7 19.5.75) (Directive 75/218/EEC). A list of what are considered less favoured areas in the UK are in subsequent directive (OJ L128/231–266 + map 19.5.75) (Directive 75/276/EEC)**E**

Since the Fund was established up to mid 1982 some 15,363 projects have been financed to a total of 5,692 million ECU.

Rules of grants

Contributions by the ERDF amount to:

- 20% of the cost of the investment in **A**, **B** and **C**. Exceptionally this percentage may be exceeded up to 50% of the cost in the case of **A** and **B**. The number of jobs created or preserved is a factor which is considered when decisions are taken regarding the grant and its size.
- 30% of the cost of the investment in **D** for projects costing less than 10 million ua and 10–30% for other projects. Projects may exceptionally be allocated 40% grant if they are of special value to the Community involved.

Payment

- money is paid to the Government concerned
- for projects **A** and **C**, fund assistance may be held by the local authority as partial reimbursement of aid granted. The money must be used for further aided projects
- for projects **D**, the aid is granted in whole or part to the authority concerned

Submission of applications

Undertaken by the national authorities of the member state concerned to the Commission which then makes a decision whether to approve or not. Local authorities submit applications to the appropriate national authority which will then decide which to forward.

In the UK the Department of Industry is reponsible for private sector appllictions. These should be sent to the local office of the Department **or** the Welsh Office, Scottish Office **or** the Department of Commerce of Northern Ireland.

Public infrastructure project applications are sent to the Department of the Environment **or** its regional office **or** the Welsh office, Scottish office **or** the Department of Commerce of Northern Ireland.

Work undertaken

In Britain the following are examples of support under the ERDF:

- Merthyr Tydfil, Wales, 4.6 million EUA to Hoover Limited for factory expansion
- Kielder reservoir, Northumberland, 45 million EUA for water supply improvements in Newcastle upon Tyne and adjacent industrial towns
- National road building programme – a multi-annual project which received 194.4 million ECU for the period 1981/2.

Further information

Grants and loans from the European Community
   Luxembourg: Office for official publications of the European Communities 1981. 83p. (European documentation series 7–8/1981) ISBN 92–825–2633–X. Catalogue number CB–NC–81–008–EN–C
Scott, Gay
Guide to European Communities grants and loans – 2nd ed
   Biggleswade: Euroinformation Limited, 1981. 111p. ISBN 0–907304–01–X
Yuill, Douglas and Kevin Allen (eds)
European regional incentives: 1981, a survey of regional incentives in the countries of the European Communities, Portugal and Sweden
   Glasgow: University of Strathclyde, 1981. 600p. ISBN 0–907243–04–5

Agriculture
Basic information

Within the European Community, agriculture has held a central position in the process of European integration.

In part 2 of the Treaty establishing the EC, title 2 concerns Agriculture and the establishment of a Common Agricultural Policy (CAP). (qv)

Purpose

It is hoped that the policy will:

- increase agricultural productivity

- ensure a fair standard of living for the agricultural community
- stabilize markets
- ensure the availability of supplies
- ensure supplies reach customers at reasonable prices

Work undertaken

Agriculture is one of the sectors of economic activity which has progressed further in European integration than any other. When the Community was established in 1957 the population was approximately 167.4 million with 16.2 million in agriculture. By 1973 after the first expansion, the population grew to approximately 256.5 million with only 9.4 million in agriculture. By 1978/9 before the second expansion of the Community there were 8 million in agriculture out of a total population of 259.5 million. Thus article 39 (a) of the Treaty of Rome which stated there should be the '... optimum utilization of the factors of [agricultural] production, in particular labour', is being achieved. It should be noted that the tenth member of the EC, Greece, has a higher percentage of its population engaged in agriculture as do the proposed eleventh and twelfth members, Portugal and Spain.

During its first ten years, agricultural policy in the EC has been based mainly on the common organization of the agricultural markets, eliminating its previous fragmentation. The Community's internal markets have been sheltered from excessive fluctuations in world prices and Community farmers given some measure of priority in trade in agricultural products with non-member countries, by being organized on an EC basis.

Land use for agricultural production is decreasing at about 0.3% per annum. The number of individual farms is decreasing at between 2% and 3% per annum. However the productive potential of the average farm continued to expand. On the whole, Community agricultural production had difficult years 1974–6 but, since then up to 1980, the rise in value of farm production has expanded each year.

Agricultural legislation has the most extensive cover within the Community and is still being enlarged. In the veterinary field its aim is to combat outbreaks of disease eg foot and mouth in Denmark (OJ L167/37–8 15.6.82) (Decision 82/259/EEC), to improve the quality of cattle by eradicating brucellosis, tuberculosis and leucosis (OJ C289/4–6 11.11.81) etc. Plant health legislation commenced in 1966 (OJ L125/2289–90 11.7.66) (Directive 66/399/CEE). The maintenance of fair competition in the costs of agricultural production in member states, eg in Guernsey the granting by the UK government of a quality premium on flowers, aid for advertising and a deficiency payment system for tomato growers was agreed by the EEC (*Bulletin of the European Communities* **15** (2) 1982 point 2.1.72).

The common organization of the agricultural market has been based on three principles:

- unity of the market (elimination of both tariff and quantitative internal barriers plus a single price structure throughout the Community)
- Community preference (achieved either by levies or by the external tariff, sometimes in conjunction with supplementary charges)
- financial solidarity (see entry under European Agricultural Guidance and Guarantee Fund (EAGGF) (Covers price support, supplementary aid to products, flat rate financial aid per hectare)

The first of these principles has been seriously undermined by the introduction of monetary compensatory amounts (see entry under 'Green' exchange rates).

Criticisms have developed of market and price policy:

- imbalance on a number of agricultural markets due in large part to the open-ended guarantee system
- high cost of the price support policy which has been worked out in an indiscriminate manner and tended to benefit the richer areas
- rigidity and administrative complexity of the machinery of management

Proposed solutions are:

- the introduction of a new basic principle of co-responsibility or producer participation in the form of levies or other mechanism
- reassessment of Community external trade in agriculture
- readjustment of structural policy and concentrated financial backing on least favoured forms and regions

Each year the Commission sends to the Council a list of, Agricultural price proposals, for consideration both by it and by Parliament. With the 1981/82 price proposals the idea of co-responsibility, previously limited to milk production, was extended. (In the latest price proposal this levy on excessive milk production in 1981/82 is based on production norms of 1979/80 and 1980/81). It is proposed that this principle be extended to other sectors, eg cereals (Agricultural price proposals for 1981/2 in, *Bulletin of the European Communities* **14** (2) 1981. points 1.2.4–9 and 2.1.42–9). See also entries under specific aspects of agriculture eg 'Green' exchange rates and the last item under, Further information, below.

Further information

The agricultural situation in the Community...report
    Luxembourg: Office for official publications of the European Communities, annual
The agricultural policy of the European Community – 2nd ed
    Luxembourg: Office for official publications of the European Communities, 1979. 38p.
    (European documentation 2/79). ISBN 92–825–0775–0. Catalogue number CB–NC–79–002–EN–C

Common agricultural prices 1981/82 – decisions of the Council
Green Europe Newsletter in brief, April 1981. Available from the Agricultural information
service of the Directorate-General for Information, EEC. (For 1982/83 see ... newsletter
... 20/1982)

Standing Committee on Agricultural Research (Scar)

Basic information

The Committee was established under article 43 of the Treaty of Rome (1957) by a 1974
Council regulation (OJ L182/1–3 5.7.74) (Regulation 1728/74/EEC).

SCAR – representation

All member states are represented on SCAR. Voting at meetings is in
accord with article 184 (2) of the EEC treaty (1957). The chairman does
not vote.

The Committee examines and reports on questions submitted by member
states through the chairman of SCAR, those from the Council and the
Commission, or those which members consider important, after these
have been agreed by the chairman.

Purpose of the Standing Committee

The 1974 regulation was concerned with the co-ordination at Community
level of agricultural research in member states and SCAR was set up to
implement the decision. It is concerned with:

- the acquisition of information on agricultural research amongst member
  states and the development of consultation
- the co-ordination of research between member states and the distribution
  to all of research reports
- the production of an annual report on the state of co-operation in
  agricultural research. This report to be sent to the Commission for
  distribution to both Council and Parliament

Work of SCAR

Under a 1978 Council decision a programme of work was outlined (OJ
L316/37–40 10.11.78) (Decision 78/902/EEC). This was for five years

commencing 1 January 1979. A sum of 18.6 million EUA was allocated for the whole programme.

By means of seminars, conferences, study visits, exchanges of research and collecting, analysing and publishing the results of the research, the Committee aims to fulfil its duties.

The 1978 decision also listed a number of aspects of agricultural research which should be the concern of SCAR. These are:

- socio-structural objectives
  - programme for the appropriate use of land and rural development
  - programme of Mediterranean agriculture
  - programmes on agricultural waste and the effluent of intensive stock rearing

- elimination of barriers on the intra-community agricultural markets
  - programme of animal pathology

- production efficiency
  - programme to improve the productivity of Community beef herds
  - programme on integrated and biological pest control
  - programme on ways of improving plant resistance to disease and environmental pressures
  - programme on primary processing of agricultural products
  - programme on elm disease

- alternative products (increase of market value of fodder production)
  - programme for improved production of vegetable proteins

Further information

The agricultural situation in the Community
    Luxembourg: Office for official publications of the European Communities, annual
The organization and management of Community research and development
    Brussels: General secretariat of the European Economic and Social committee, 1980.
    159p. Catalogue number ESC–80–001–EN

Common Agricultural Policy (CAP)
Basic information

In 1979 the average EC consumer was spending 26% of his income on food. Currently this percentage is decreasing as the standard of living rises.

At the present time (1981) there are some 8 million full time agricultural workers in the Community. Through technical progress and productivity increases, their numbers are falling but their earnings have risen, though not always at the pace of other sectors in the economy.

The Treaty of Rome (1957) gives major attention to agriculture though the agricultural condition at the time differed considerably from that of the present day Community. It also differed considerably from country to country amongst the six partners when a CAP was first considered.

Purpose

The potential advantages of a CAP were seen originally as:

- offering farmers a vast market in which to sell existing products and to launch new ones
- increasing specialization and greater complementarity between member states
- offering consumers a wider choice of products at more attractive prices and with greater stability

Article 39 of the Treaty of Rome defines the five fundamental principles given to the CAP, as:

- to increase productivity through technical development, rational production and the optimum use of labour
- to ensure a fair standard of living for the agricultural community
- to stabilize markets
- to ensure the availability of supplies
- to ensure supplies reach consumers at reasonable prices

Work undertaken

Following a single market for agricultural products there is:

- community preference which gives protection for the European market against low priced imports and fluctuations on the world market, and
- joint financial responsibility which formalizes the solidarity between the regions of the Community. This common financial responsibility is embodied in the European Agricultural Guidance and Guarantee Fund (EAGGF) which is an integral part of the Community budget. In 1977 the cost of the CAP as a percentage of the total Community budget was 77%. This had dropped to 70% in 1980 and 67% in 1981 (Bulletin of the European Communities 15 (1) 1982 point 2.1.45).

Protection from outside competition plus a very large home market and aid to farmers has led to growing production levels (an increase of 2.5% every year for the last 20 years) which in some cases has resulted in large surpluses (the 'wine lake', the 'butter mountain', etc). The problem for agricultural administrators is to find larger overseas markets allowing farmers to contribute more to European trading wealth, or to restrict production of certain commodities, or both. Up to 1980 this problem had not been resolved satisfactorily. With broadly agricultural Member states of the Community the problem had not yet become imperative. With industrial countries such as Britain there were considerable payments to European agriculture without compensatory returns. This matter was raised in the Council and a conclusion regarding UK financing proposed up to 1982 (OJ C158/1–2 27.6.80). At the same time it was seen necessary to reconsider CAP policy and whilst maintaining the positive benefits listed in the paragraph above, mechanisms need to be established to hold in check the financial consequences of production surpluses and to concentrate financial resources on the least favoured farms and regions, thus adjusting the CAP structural policy. This problem, which in mid 1981 is in process of being resolved, is outlined in, *Reflections on the common agricultural policy*, see, Further information. A somewhat similar theme was included in, *Report from the Commission of the European Communities to the Council* pursuant to the mandate of 30 May 1980 (*Bulletin of the European Communities* supplement 1/81). This theme was expanded in, 'Guidelines for European agriculture', to be found in *Bulletin of the European Communities* supplement 4/81. In the Agricultural price proposals for 1981/82 a co-responsibility levy, first introduced in 1977 for milk, was continued and extended to cereals in an effort to reduce excessive production. By this means the total production of a particular crop or product was agreed with the producers for the coming year. If the amount was exceeded a levy on the producers was imposed.

With the enlargement of the Community to 12 member states – Greece (1 January 1981, + Portugal and Spain later), the farming population is disproportionately increased, a higher proportion of farms have structural problems, there will be a greater volume of production and keener intra-Community competition, and new rates of self supply will be introduced. See, *European booklet* series, 80/5 issued by the Meat and livestock commission, P.O. Box 44, Bletchley, Bucks.

Further information

The agricultural situation in the Community . . . report
   Luxembourg: Office for official publications of the European Community, annual
Bulletin of the European Communities
   Luxembourg: Office for official publications of the European Communities. 11 issues per year. ISSN 0378 3693
'Improvement of the common agricultural policy'
Bulletin of the European Communities supplement 17/73
'Stocktaking of the common agricultural policy'
Bulletin of the European Communities supplement 2/75
Europe's common agricultural policy
   Brussels: EC Directorate-General for Information, 1979. 7p. (European File 9/79). Catalogue number CC–AD–79–009–EN–C
'Reflections on the common agricultural policy'
Bulletin of the European Communities supplement 6/80

Agricultural Management and Regulatory Committees

Basic information

The treaty establishing the European Communities provided for a limited number of committees to help the Council and Commission in their work.

Subsequently both Council and Commission found it necessary to form other committees to assist them.

After an initial decision in July 1975 defining four research programmes, the Council continued its efforts to co-ordinate agricultural research in the Community by adopting a second decision in October 1978, launching ten research programmes under four main headings:

- socio-structural objectives:
  appropriate use of land and rural development
  Mediterranean agriculture
  utilization of effluent from intensive stock-rearing
- elimination of barriers on intra-Community market:
  animal pathology

- production efficiency:
  improvement of beef and veal quality
  integrated and biological pest control
  gene bank
  agri-foodstuffs
  elm disease
- alternative products:
  vegetable proteins

An eleventh theme, animal welfare, was added later.

These programmes are managed by the Commission with the assistance of the, Standing Committee on Agricultural Research.

Work of the Committees

About a hundred contracts were either already in effect in 1980 or due to take effect in January 1981. Excluded from the following list are working parties and Commission expert groups not set up under a formal act and whose existence may be terminated at any time.

Agricultural management and regulatory committees are:

Agricultural and forestry tractors committee
Agricultural research, standing committee on
Agricultural statistics, standing committee on
Agricultural structure policy, advisory committee on questions of (2)
Agricultural structures, standing committee on
Agriculture, special committee on
Animal feeding stuffs, advisory committee on (1)

Animal nutrition, scientific committee on
Beef and veal, advisory committee (1)
Beef and veal, management committee for
Cereals, advisory committee on
Cereals, management committee for (1)
Dried fodder, management committee for
Eggs, advisory committee on (1)
European Agricultural Guidance and Guarantee Fund (EAGGF)
Farm accountancy data network, community committee on the (FADN)
Feeding stuffs, advisory committee on
Feeding stuffs, standing committee on
Fertilizers committee
Fisheries, scientific and technical committee on
Fishery problems, advisory committee on (2)
Fishery products, advisory committee on (1) (4)
Fishery products, management committee for
Fishing industry, standing committee on the
Flax and hemp, advisory committee on (1)
Flax and hemp joint group, advisory committee on (1)
Flax and hemp, management committee for
Food, scientific committee for (SCF)
Foodstuffs, advisory committee on (3)
Foodstuffs, management committee for
Freshwater suitable to support fish life, committee on the quality of
Fruit and vegetables fresh and processed, advisory committee on (1)
Fruit and vegetables, management committee for
Fruit and vegetables, management committee for processed
Fruit and vegetables, management committee for products processed
    from
Hops, advisory committee on (1)
Hops, joint group advisory committee on (1)
Hops, management committee for (1)
Isoglucose, management committee for
Legislation approximation, special section of the animal foodstuffs advisory
    committee on (3)
Live plants, advisory committee on (1)
Live plants, management committee for
Milk and milk products, advisory committee on (1)
Milk and milk products, management committee for
Oils and fats, advisory committee on (1)
Oils and fats, management committee for
Oilseeds and fruits derived products section, of the advisory committee
    on oils and fats (1)
Olives and derived products section of the advisory committee on oils
    and fats (1)
Pesticides, scientific committee on
Pigmeat, advisory committee on (1)
Pigmeat, management committee for

Plant health, standing committee on
Poultry meat, advisory committee on (1)
Poultry meat and eggs, management committee for
Raw tobacco, advisory committee on (1)
Raw tobacco joint group, advisory committee on (1)
Raw tobacco, management committee for
Rice section of the advisory committee on cereals
Seeds, advisory committee on (1)
Seeds, management committee for
Seeds and propagating material for agriculture, horticulture and forestry,
    standing committee on
Sheep and goats, management committee for
Silk worm section of the advisory committee on flax and hemp (1)
Social problems in sea fishing, joint committee on (4)
Social problems of agricultural workers, joint committee on the (4)
Social questions affecting farmers, advisory committee on (4) (2)
Sugar, advisory committee on (1)
Sugar joint group, advisory committee on (1)
Sugar, management committee for
Veterinary committee, advisory (3)
Veterinary committee, standing
Wine, advisory committee on (1)
Wine, management committee for
Zootechnics, standing committee on

(1) Committees set up to advise on implementation of Community
     policies
(2) Advisory committees on structural problems
(3) Advisory committees on harmonization of legislation
(4) Advisory committees on social, employment and consumer
     protection policies

Further information

Council and Commission committees
  Bulletin of the European Communities supplement 2/80
AGREP, permanent inventory of agricultural research projects in the European Com-munities
  Luxembourg: Office for official publications of the European Communities, 1977. 2 v.
  [updated in the monthly periodical – Euroabstracts]
Community advisory committees for the representation of socio-economic interests
  Farnborough: Saxon House for EC Economic and Social Committee, 1980. 215p. ISBN
  0–566–00328–7

Farm Accountancy Data Network (FADN)

Basic information

A system for the collection of accountancy information on the incomes and business operations of agricultural holdings in the Community, was set up by Council regulation (OJ 109/1859–65 23.6.65) (Regulation 79/65/EEC). It was amended in 1973 (OJ L299/1–3 27.10.73) (Regulation 2910/73/EEC).

Purpose of the network

It is one of the basic sources of information for the common agricultural policy. The first three accountancy results covering 1968, 1969 and 1970 were produced together (in, *Bulletin of the European Communities* 5 (10) 1972. section 101). This first survey is of the technical and economic situation of the principal types of farms in member states and corresponds to a running in period.

Work of the network

The number of farms supplying data rose from 13,600 in 1975 to 28,167 in 1978 and to 30,000 in 1980.

In 1975 a new Community typology for recording agricultural holdings was brought into force. From 1981 the annual results will no longer represent merely the new returns of holdings but all the holdings represented in the surveys, now (1981) over 1,500,000.

Further information

General report on the activities of the European Communities
   Luxembourg: Office for official publications of the European Communities, annual

European Agricultural Guidance and Guarantee Fund (EAGGF)

Basic information

This fund embodies the joint financial responsibility of the Common Agricultural Policy (CAP). In 1981 it represented 67% of the Community budget. Provision was made for the

Fund in the founding treaty (Article 40 of the Treaty of Rome 1957). It was set up in 1962 (OJ L30/991–3 20.4.62) (Regulation 25/62/EEC). In February 1964 the EAGGF was subdivided into two sections (OJ 34/586–94 27.2.64) (Regulation 17/64/EEC).

Purpose of the EAGGF

There are two parts to the Fund – guarantee and guidance:

- Guarantee section finances all public expenditure arising out of the implementation of the common organization regularizing the internal market. It was costing in 1978 some 8,672.7 million EUA, 10,440.7 million EUA in 1979 and 11,315 million EUA in 1980. This covers purchases by intervention bodies and the storage cost resulting. Direct income assistance includes subsidies to facilitate the marketing of products, competition with low priced imports, etc, also export refunds running at 3,000 million EUA in 1978.
- Guidance section contributes to the financing of the common policy by supporting individual farm improvement projects, partially reimbursing general modernization work. This was running at 86.5 million ECU in 1980 giving assistance to farms in the worst-off regions. Note particularly aid for hill farmers which was running at 88.6 million ECU in 1979, and financing action for the re-organization of markets – 82.3 million ECU in 1980. (*Bulletin of the European Communities* **14** (9) 1981 point 2.1.89–2.1.90). 1981 figures showing lower production rates in the Community can be seen in *Bulletin of the European Communities* **15** (4) 1982. point 2.1.72. Common measures to improve the conditions under which agricultural products are processed and marketed were established in 1977 (OJ L51/1–6 23.2.77) (Regulation 355/77/EEC) and updated from time to time. One of the more recent changes will be found in *Bulletin of the European Communities* **15** (6) 1982 point 2.1.125 and table 3.

Common measures for forestry in certain Mediterranean zones of the Community (OJ L38/1–5 14.2.79) (Regulation 269/79/EEC) are also updated periodically, eg (*Bulletin of the European Communities* **15** (6) 1982 point 2.1.126).

Work undertaken

Annual credits from this sector, running at approximately 11,500 million EUA in 1980, showed an 11% rise over the previous year compared with 23% in almost all previous years since 1975.

In an effort to maintain market stability the EAGGF has financed the purchase of butter, milk powder, wine, etc which became difficult to sell or sugar production when it outstrips domestic needs. This policy has led to the 'butter mountain', 'wine lake', etc and to proposals for the reform of this policy.

In, *Reflections on a common agricultural policy* (see, Further information) the Commission put forward the extension of the policy of co-responsibility. This policy considered that producers should bear at least part of the financial responsibility for the disposal of production in excess of an agreed quantity. First brought into force for milk in the 1977 agreed agricultural prices – and extended to other products in 1981/2 (*Bulletin of the European Communities* **14** (3) 1981. points 2.1.64–2.1.104).

Further information

The agricultural situation in the community ... report
   Luxembourg: Office for official publications of the European Communities, annual
Importance and functioning, European agricultural guidance and guarantee fund
   Luxembourg: Office for official publications of the European Communities, 1978. 86p.
   ISBN 92–825–0042–X. Catalogue number CD–22–77–790–EN–C
Europe's common agricultural policy
   Brussels: EC Directorate-General for Information, 1979. 7p. (Europe File 9/79). Catalogue
   number CC–AD–79–009–EN–C
'Reflections on the common agricultural policy'
Bulletin of the European Communities supplement 6/80

European Agricultural Guidance and Guarantee Fund (EAGGF) – Financial Assistance

Basic information

The Guarantee section of the EAGGF is used to support prices whereas the Guidance section is designed to help improve farm structures (OJ 34/599–601 27.2.64) (Regulation 64/127/EEC) and many subsequent legislative items (see, *Guide to EEC Legislation* in Further information).

Beneficiaries under EAGGF

The work of the Guidance section is concerned with:

- the improvement of existing buildings
- the introduction of new systems of farm management
- storage and conservation facilities
- processing and marketing farm products (OJ L51/1–6 23.2.77) (Regulation 355/77/EEC)

Between 1964 and 1977 1,987.7 million u a were granted towards financing individual projects under (OJ L34/586–94 27.2.64) (Regulation 17/64/EEC). A programme of agricultural reform was devised by Sicco Mansholt (*Bulletin of the European Communities* supplement 1/69). He was a vice-president of the Commission with responsibility for agricultural policy 1958–72 (qv). This plan was supported by the EAGGF.

Rates of grants

- in processing and marketing the grant is generally in the order of 25% with the farmer putting up 50% and the government of the member state at least 5%. Fund aid may be paid in several instalments as the work progresses on submission of documentary evidence. Payments are made through agencies designated by the state concerned. Requests for aid go to the Commission to arrive by 1 May each year. The following regulation authorizes this aid up to 1982. (OJ L51/1–6 23.2.77) (Regulation 355/77/EEC)
- for the improvement of buildings (modernization) and guidance premiums (production incentives), the EAGGF will in both cases refund 25% of eligible expenditure. Requests are sent to the member state's national authority (in UK the MAFF) to reach the Commission by 1 July
- cessation of farming. 25% or 65% of the member state's eligible expenses. Applications to member state's national authority are forwarded to EAGGF by 1 July
- farming in less favoured areas such as mountain and hill farming. An annual allowance or aid on special terms for development plans or aid for fodder production, is paid. EAGGF will refund 25–35% of the cost. Aid goes to the farmers in the areas concerned. Submission of plans are made as with previous grants.

Submission of applications

Details of aid for certain categories of products and special premiums granted in certain cases, can be obtained from the government department concerned of the member state. In the UK it would be the MAFF Marketing Policy Division, Great Westminster House, Horseferry Road, London SW1P 2AG from whom the appropriate EEC form may be obtained, as well as advice on these grants and the timing of submissions. Note proposals for the inshore fishing industry (OJ L211/30–33 1.8.78) (Regulation 1852/78/EEC), a scheme for producer groups and related associations (OJ L166/1–8 23.6.78) (Regulation 1360/78/EEC).

Further information

Guide to EEC legislation, Chapter 13.1.1
    Amsterdam: North Holland Publishing Company, 1979. 2 v ISBN 0444-85320-0   3p.
Scott, Gay   ber
Guide to European Community grants and loans - 2nd ed
    Biggleswade: Euroinformation Limited, 1981. 111p. ISBN 0-907304-01-X
Grants and loans from the European Community
    Luxembourg: Office for official publications of the European Communities, 1981. 83p.
    (European documentation series 7-8/1981) ISBN 92-825-2633-X. Catalogue number
    CB-NC-81-008-EN-C

'Green' Exchange Rates

Basic information

The Community introduced 'Green' exchange rates (Representative rates) in 1973 for new member states and March 1975 for the original six member states, as a means of organizing support for agricultural producers affected by fluctuating exchange rates. By these representative rates the producer and the consumer are likely to have more equitable prices.

Purpose

The aim of the 'Green' rate is to translate the Common Market's agricultural prices, expressed in European Currency Units (ECU), into national currencies taking into account fluctuations in the national exchange rate for each particular currency. The current Representative rates ('Green' rates) will be found in each issue of Part 3 of the, *Bulletin of the European Communities*. It will be noted that the rate will differ for particular products, especially those incurring co-responsibility in prices.

To support producers, monetary compensatory amounts (MCA) were introduced as a payment to balance out the fluctuations between the 'Green' rate and the Commercial rate. From 1978 adjustments to the 'Green' rates were favoured in preference to a continued expansion of MCA.

Further information

Europe's common agricultural policy
    Brussels: EC Directorate-General for Information, 1979. 7p. (European File 9/79). Catalogue
    number CC-AD-79-009-EN-C

Europe today – state of European integration, Chapter 3.231
  Luxembourg: Office for official publications of the European Communities, 1980. xlii,
  586p. ISBN 92–823–0021–8. Catalogue number AX–28–79–916–EN–C
ECU
  Bulletin of the European Communities **13** (12) 1980. points 3.1.1–3.1.5

Monetary Compensatory Amounts (MCA)

Basic information

The purpose of the MCA is to maintain the value of agricultural price guarantees. It is especially important during periods of financial instability. It permits the free movement of goods at fixed prices. Fixed MCAs were first introduced in December 1969 following a devaluation of the French franc and a revaluation of the German mark. With the introduction of floating exchange rates in May 1971 a new system of variable MCAs of unlimited duration was introduced (OJ L106/1–2 12.5.71) (Regulation 974/71/EEC).

Extent of MCAs

MCAs apply to trade between countries of the Community as well as to trade with third countries. In 1972 MCAs represented 0.01% of the EAGGF's (European Agricultural Guidance and Guarantee Fund), Guarantee section. By 1978 this percentage had risen to 11.38%. MCAs are based on the difference between the central monetary rate and the agricultural conversion rate for currencies in the 'snake' (qv). In countries having free floating currencies, MCAs are based on the difference between the agricultural conversion rate and the spot market rate for the currency.

Development of the MCAs

As MCAs became permanently established during the 1970s, they had an adverse affect on the unity of the market for agricultural products and had a tendency to ossify the economic structure. By the Commission's proposal for a Council regulation fixing representative exchange rates in the agricultural sector (OJ C274/3–4 19.11.76), a ceiling for MCAs was proposed and a regular adjustment of 'Green' currency rates (qv).

During 1977 the Commission proposed the abolition of MCAs (COM(77) 480 final). A favourable opinion was obtained on dismantling the existing MCAs over a seven year period with new MCAs being of limited duration and having an annual cut off point (European Parliament (EP) working document 390/77 22.11.77).

However, the opinion of the Committee on budgets firmly advocated the introduction of the European Unit of Account (EUA) into the agricultural sector. In place of a regular and direct reduction in MCAs, it suggests this reduction be linked to the annual price review.

In 1978 the European Parliament's working document 104/78 re-addressed the various proposals. Agreement was reached on dismantling MCAs over a period.

At a Council meeting on 5/6 March 1979 eight member states (Denmark is not involved), agreed to the dismantling of the MCAs. Any new MCAs which might be applied within two years following the entry into force of the EMS – European Monetary System (qv) would be dismantled in two stages taking effect from the beginning of the first and second marketing years. (*Thirteenth general report on the activities of the European Communities* points 313–315. Details in Further information).

Monetary fluctuations in early 1981 caused proposals on dismantling the MCAs to be temporarily frozen (*Bulletin of the European Communities* **14** (3) 1981 points 2.1.105–107).

As a direct result of adjustments of 12.6.82 to the ECU (see European monetary system (EMS), comparable adjustments were made to the Monetary Compensatory Amounts (OJ L170/1–31 16.6.82) (Regulation 1528/82/EEC), (OJ L176/1–27 21.6.82) (Regulation 1576/82/EEC) for the UK (OJ L184/19–22 29.6.82) (Regulation 1668/82/EEC) for Denmark, Greece and the Republic of Ireland.

Basic legislation on applying MCAs was agreed in 1975 (OJ L139/37–43 30.5.75) (Regulation 1380/75/EEC). This was amended frequently and these amendments were consolidated in 1981 (OJ L138/1–13 25.5.81) (Regulation 1371/81/EEC) and (OJ L138/14–19 25.5.81) (Regulation 1372/81/EEC).

Further information

The agricultural situation in the Community
   Luxembourg: Office for official publications of the European Communities, annual
General report of the activities of the European Communities
   Luxembourg: Office for official publications of the European Communities, annual
'Restoring balance on the milk market, action programme 1977–80'. *Bulletin of the European Communities* supplement 10/76
'Progressive establishment of balance on the market in wine, action programme 1979–85 and report from the Commission'. *Bulletin of the European Communities* supplement 7/78
How the European Commission is tackling dairy surpluses
   Brussels: EC Directorate-General for Information, 1980. 7p. (European File 4/80) Catalogue number CC–AD–80–004–EN–C

Forestry

Basic information

European Community forests cover over 31 million ha or 21% of the total land area. France alone accounts for 45% of the total forest area of the Community.

Community policy and legislation is a recent growth. The first legislative item concerning common forestry measures was for certain dry Mediterranean zones, approved by Council in 1979 (OJ L38/1–5 14.2.79) (Regulation 269/79/EEC).

Work undertaken

Earlier legislation had covered the genetic quality of forest reproductive material eg seeds and nursery plants (1966–), freedom of establishment and provision of services by self-employed in forestry and logging (1967), classification of wood in the rough (1968), phytosanitary measures (1976).

In 1977 the Commission authorized and commenced publishing studies in forestry subjects. Finally certain forestry statistics are compiled on a Community basis and published within the agricultural series.

A wide ranging survey of European forestry, together with proposals for a Council resolution concerning the objectives and principles of forestry policy, and proposals for a Council decision to set up a forestry committee, appear in, *Bulletin of the European Communities* Supplement 3/79. This publication also includes the text of the Commission submission to the Council on forestry policy in the EC, the amendments to it by the European Parliament and the opinion of the Economic and Social Committee.

Further information

Year book of agricultural statistics
    Luxembourg; Office for official publications of the European Communities, annual. –
    (Forestry accounts tables B9–11)
Forestry policy for the Community
Bulletin of the European Communities 11 (7/8) 1978. points 2.1.97–99
Bulletin of the European Communities 11 (12) 1978. points 1.5.1–5
Forestry statistics 1970–5
    Luxembourg: Office for official publications of the European Communities, 1978. 138p.
    ISBN 92–825–0629–0. Catalogue number CA–24–77–382–60–C

Fisheries

Basic information

Based on article 43 of the Treaty of Rome (1957), a common fisheries policy was adopted in 1970. The main features being the withdrawal price system applied to producers' organizations (OJ L271/14 15.12.70) (Regulation 2517/70/EEC) and price recording and fixing, the list of representative wholesale markets or ports for fishery products (OJ L271/15–18 15.12.70) (Regulation 2518/70/EEC).

Problems within the Industry

The basic principle was that all fishermen should have equal access to the waters of member states. It introduced a market organization with reference prices to control imports. It encouraged the setting up of producer organizations to improve marketing (OJ L20/1–18 28.1.76) (Regulation 100/76/EEC) (OJ L20/19–22 28.1.76) (Regulation 101/76/EEC) etc. When Britain joined the Community the question of equal access to fishery grounds was important to her and special arrangements were made lasting to 1982. The major difficulties to be overcome before an effective common fisheries policy is introduced, are:

- fixing total allowable catches to prevent over fishing
- allocation of catches amongst member states (quotas)
- access by Community fishermen to the inshore waters of member states

Work undertaken

However, on 1 January 1977 member states extended their fishing zones to 200 miles in the North Sea and North Atlantic. As a temporary measure the Council laid down interim regulations for the conservation of fishery resources during 1980. (OJ L258/1–15 1.10.80) (Regulation 2527/80/EEC). As a final agreement was not reached these measures were extended through 1981. Up to March 1981 when four attempts were made to resolve the stalemate, no new Community fisheries policy had been reached. A number of UK and Dutch measures to conserve stocks of fish were approved by the Commission during 1981 as consistent with the implications of a future Community fisheries policy. Gradually other member states submitted their own proposals for approval by the EEC. On 10 February 1982 the Commission sent to the Council a proposal for reintroducing technical and quantitative measures for the conservation of fisheries resources. The Council renewed its interim decision on catch quotas and technical measures (OJ L120/29 1.5.82) (Decision 82/271/EEC). Essential legislation which should form the basis for EEC fisheries policy, is gradually being introduced on a national basis and approved by the Community. One case where this has been done concerns herrings where quotas for 16.6.84–14.2.85 have been fixed (OJ L206/3–5 14.7.82) (Regulation 1866/82/EEC).

In order to prevent misunderstandings regarding the geographical boundaries referred to in common fisheries policy rules, on 7.1.82 the Commission adopted a communication on the, Boundaries of the International Council for the Exploration of the Sea (ICES), divisions and sub-divisions in the North East Atlantic.

A fisheries agreement with the Faroes was published in 1980, destined to last for ten years initially, which came into force provisionally on 1.1.77 when the Faroes decided on a 200 nautical mile fisheries zone (OJ L226/11–15 29.8.80) (Regulation 2211/80/EEC).

An expanded agreement for 1982 which detailed quotas of specific fish, continued an interim agreement (OJ L120/18–26 1.5.82) (Regulation 1042/82/EEC). This was further enlarged by an exchange of letters covering the salmon fishing season 1982/3 (OJ L138/15–17 19.5.82) (Decision 82/311/EEC).

At a diplomatic conference in Reykjavik convened by the Icelandic government on 2.3.82, a, Convention for the conservation of salmon in the North Atlantic ocean, was signed by the Community, Canada, Iceland, Norway and the United States. A, North Atlantic salmon conservation organization was established with its headquarters in Edinburgh.

Further information

General report on the activities of the European Communities
Luxembourg: Office for official publications of the European Community, annual

Insurance

Basic information

The varied aspects of insurance have been the concern of the European Communities over many years and are provided for under articles 52–66 (Right of establishment and services) of the Treaty of Rome (1957) establishing the Community. Whilst legislation has not been restricted to the 1970s and is currently continuing, there was more in this period than earlier. In 1981 the Commission produced a list of authorities in member states responsible for issuing certificates of competency concerning the activities of insurance agents and brokers (OJ C136/3–6 5.6.81).

Extent of the cover

Life insurance in its several forms
The first Council directive was approved in 1978. Its purpose was to achieve in each member state equal conditions of extablishment between local sales staff and those from other Community countries. The directive concerned was published in 1979 (OJ L63/1–17 13.3.79) (Directive 79/267/EEC). A paraphase appeared in, *Bulletin of the European Communities* 11 (12) 1978. points 2.1.47–2.1.50.

Direct insurance other than Life
The earliest directive, in 1973, concerns the taking up and pursuit of direct insurance by undertakings established in a member state or which wishes to be established there (OJ L228/3–19 16.8.73) (Directive 73/239/EEC) and (OJ L228/20–22 16.8.73) (Directive 73/240/EEC). A corrigenda was published in 1978 (OJ L5/27 7.1.78). The 1973 directives were altered in part, and as far as the currency rate was concerned, in 1976 (OJ L189/13–14 13.7.76) (Directive 76/580/EEC). A draft directive to provide more efficient services was first issued in 1975, criticized by the Economic and Social committee (ESC) in 1976 and Parliament in 1978. An amended version appeared as a Commission Document COM (78) 63 final dated 16.2.78.

Co-insurance
Co-insurance, in order to obtain freedom of service for non-life business as a whole, enabled companies to provide cover throughout the Community (OJ L151/25–27 30.5.78) (Directive 78/473/EEC).

Reinsurance and retrocession
Under a 1964 directive restrictions based on nationality in the provision of reinsurance services and retrocession (reassigning all or part of a risk from one reinsurer to another), were abolished. This was approved by Council (OJ 56/878–879 4.4.64) (Directive 64/225/EEC).

Motor insurance
An EC 3rd party cover was designed to eliminate the 'green card' checks at the frontiers of Community countries. The first directive to harmonize the legislation on vehicle civil liability insurance appeared in 1972 (OJ L103/1–3 2.5.72) (Directive 72/166/EEC). There were Commission decisions on this legislation in 1974 (OJ L87/13 30.3.74) (Decision 74/166/EEC) and (OJ L87/14 30.3.74) (Decision 74/167/EEC) and in 1975 (OJ L6/33–4 10.1.75) (Decision 75/23/EEC). A second (draft) directive is under consideration, designed to reduce disparities in the scope of compulsory liability insurance (OJ C214/9–10 21.8.80).

Credit insurance
A draft directive, the purpose of which is to remove the provision in directive 73/239/EEC (see Direct insurance other than life, above) allowing

Germany to maintain its system of compulsory specialization for credit and suretyship insurance, has been published (OJ C245/7–8 29.9.79). Opinions have been given by the ESC (OJ C146/6–7 16.6.80) and by Parliament (OJ C291/70–6 10.11.80). As a result the Commission produced amended proposals with amended references to state export credit insurance operations. These were transmitted to the Council on 17 May 1982. (*Bulletin of the European Communities* **15** (5) 1982 point 2.1.25).

Health insurance

A working paper has been produced by the Commission dealing with the harmonization of this form of insurance. For example in Germany, there is a system of compulsory specialization in health insurance. One alternative is to bring these specialist companies into the life insurance orbit. The working paper was issued in June 1980 and is numbered XV/174/80.

Direct insurance undertakings

A working paper has been produced by the Commission on the liquidation of such undertakings. It is related to the draft bankruptcy convention and insurance companies are likely to be included once the current procedures have been harmonized. The paper is number XV/203/79.

Insurance contracts

The purpose of the final directive will be to harmonize contract law, excluding marine, aviation and transport as well as credit and suretyship. Opinions on a draft directive (OJ C190/2–6 28.7.79) have been presented by the ESC (OJ C146/1–5 16.6.80) and Parliament (OJ C265/80–9 13.10.80).

Insurance companies, annual accounts

So far, only a Commission working paper has been drawn up by an EC Accountants Study Group. This has been necessary as insurance companies are exempt from the 4th company law directive. The paper is numbered XV/201/79.

Legal expenses insurance

The proposed directive aims to correct the present rather anomalous position whereby Germany is allowed to maintain its system of compulsory specialization for legal expenses insurance (OJ C198/2–4 7.8.79).

Further information

EEC checklist of Community legislation and legislative proposals of concern to financial institutions and markets
London: British Bankers Association, 1981 (looseleaf)

Statistics

Basic information

A statistical cover of the EC is available from a number of sources. Generally, the broader the cover the less detailed are the statistics. Thus one would not expect to find in a United Nations (UN) *Statistical Yearbook* the same depth of information on say The Netherlands as one would find in that country's own Departmental Statistics. The biggest problem as far as Eurostat is concerned is to harmonize the various series of statistics from member states. This is of course an on-going process.

Statistical information

UN statistics which include in reasonable detail those of member states of the Community will be found in the UN's *Statistical Yearbook,* which is brought up to date by their, *Monthly bulletin of statistics.* This is obviously useful for comparisons. A somewhat similar cover is produced by most of the UN agencies on their own subject eg Food and Agriculture Organization, or regions, eg Economic Commission for Europe. However, naturally this information is rather slow in production. Rather more prompt production will be found in Eurostat publications available from Luxembourg such as the, *Basic statistics of the community,* annual, *Eurostatistics,* monthly; Monthly *External trade bulletin;* Quarterly *Bulletin of industrial statistics; Yearbook of agricultural statistics; Coal statistics,* annual; *National accounts,* annual; and many other series (for details see under, Further information).

The most up to date statistics will be found in the statistical offices of individual countries in the EC. A free guide to these, their telephone and telex numbers as well as their full postal address is produced by The Department of Trade, Statistics and Market Intelligence Library, 1 Victoria Street, London SW1H 0ET. This listing is regularly updated and issued under the title, *National Statistical Offices of overseas countries.*

Eurostat periodical publications are colour coded eg grey covers series of general statistics, yellow is for population and social statistics, green – agricultural statistics, red – foreign trade statistics, etc. There are also a number of internal publications intended for the service of the Commission, etc. In certain cases these are made available to national administrations and professional bodies. They may be consulted at the EC Information Office in each country. A list is included periodically in Eurostat News.

The computerized economic data bank of the statistical office of the Community (CRONOS) has been incorporated in Euronet/Diane through the Paris based Compagnie internationale de services ent informatique (CISI). Diane users now have the latest Eurostat information on immediate call. Details of the statistics available through this service will be found in, *Eurostat News* 4/80.

Mention should also be made of the value of statistics from the Organization for Economic Co-operation and Development (OECD) which produces its foreign trade statistics (quarterly) very promptly in fiche format by computer output in microform (COM).

Trade classifications and statistical classifications are summarized in Foreman's chapter (see Further information below) and a little more fully in *Statistics and market research sources – use and acquisition* by Frank Cockrane (see Further information). The EC's commodity classification NIMEXE (qv) as well as others to which it is related will be found in, 'Trade statistics the EECs and other commodity classification', in *Trade and Industry* (now *British Business*) 17 September 1976 p 726–8.

Further information

Department of Trade and Industry, Statistics and Market Intelligence Library. 'Sources of statistics' 2. *The European Economic Community*
   London: Department of Trade and Industry Library. 1971
Publications of the statistical office of the European Communities
   Luxembourg: Office for official publications of the European Communities, annual (Offprint from the first quarterly issue of *Eurostat News* each year) (A very brief title list)
Eurostat review
   Luxembourg: Office for official publications of the European Communities, annual (a ten year run of all major statistics for Europe as a whole, individual member states, countries likely to join the EC, the USA and Japan)
Harvey, Joan M
Statistics Europe – sources for social, economic and market research. 3rd ed. Beckenham
   Kent: CBD Research Ltd, 1976. 467p. ISBN 0–900241–18–9
Palmer, Doris M (ed)
Sources of information on the European Communities, Chapter p. 129
Sources of statistics on the European Economic Community: the Statistics and Market Intelligence library by, Lewis Foreman
   London: Mansell, 1979. x 230p. ISBN 0–7201–0724–5
Campbell, Malcolm J (ed)
Manual of business library practice, 2nd ed, chapter on, 'Statistics and market research sources' by Frank Cochrane
   London: Clive Bingley, 1981. ISBN 0–208–01359–8
Ramsay, Anne
Eurostat index
   Edinburgh: Capital Planning Information, 1981. 152p. ISBN 0–906011–15–9. (A detailed and most useful keyword subject index with notes on the series)
Ramsay, Anne
How to find out about the statistics of the European Communities
   Newcastle upon Tyne: Polytechnic Library, Newcastle upon Tyne for the, Association of EDC Libraries, 1982. 4p. ('How to' leaflets)

4 Common Industrial and Energy Policies

The first of the broad subject chapters dealt with economics and agriculture (Chapter 3). This chapter delves more deeply into Community harmonization of both policy and practice in Industry and Energy and outlines plans for the future.

Prior to the introduction of the European Communities there was considerable competition between industries of the member states. There was also the fear that the industries which made the second world war possible could be used again for the same purpose. In the early 1950s this was a major fear which led directly to support for the first of the Communities, the ECSC .

The growing economic problems of the 1970s – the 1973 and 1979 oil crises – the need for a unified and long term energy policy, led to considerable debate and planning in the institutions of the Communities.

To assist British industry in Europe the Department of Trade in London, in its weekly publication *British Business* produces a number of useful lists. One of these is:

- **Industry and trade organizations in Europe** (pages 154–160)

Individual industries covered in this chapter include:

- **Steel** (pages 161–3)
  Steel industry safety and health commission (pages 163–4)
- **Coal** (pages 164–5)
  Working conditions in the coal industry, mixed committee on harmonization (page 166)
  Mines safety and health commission (pages 166–7)
- **Automobile** (pages 168–9)
- **Shipbuilding** (pages 169–171)
- **Aerospace** (pages 171–2)

Transport systems which overlap country boundaries have an obvious need for the harmonization of regulations, conditions of work, etc:

- **Transport policy** (pages 172–4)
  Advisory committee on transport (pages 174–5)
  Transport infrastructure committee (pages 175–6)

FOR A DETAILED INDEX SEE THE YELLOW PAGES.

- **Air transport** (pages 176–7)
  Schwartzenburg report (pages 177–8)
- **Inland waterway transport** (pages 178–9)
  Joint advisory committee on social questions arising on inland water transport (pages 179–180)
- **Rail transport** (pages 180–1)
  Joint advisory committee on social questions arising on the railway industry (pages 181–2)
- **Road transport** (pages 182–4)
  Joint advisory committee on social questions on road transport (page 184)
  Driving licence for the Community (page 185)
- **Sea transport** (pages 185–6)
- **Channel tunnel** (page 187)

Energy policy is a comparatively recent need though the initial guidelines were submitted in 1968:

- **Energy policy** (pages 188–190)
- **Energy objectives** (pages 190–1)
  Energy objectives – financial assistance (pages 192–4)
- **Alternative energy sources** (pages 194–7)
  Solar energy (pages 197–8)

It will be realized that the section on Coal, ECSC, Water resources, etc, all contribute to information on Energy.

Industry and Trade Organizations in Europe

The following list of industrial and manufacturers' organizations in Europe was compiled by the UK Department of Trade. Each UK trade association should be in touch with its European counterpart. A guide to British commercial representatives overseas is also prepared by the Department of Trade and appears every six months in *British Business,* a weekly publication issued by HMSO. Inquiries about either list should be made to the British Overseas Trade Board, Export Services and Promotions Division, Department of Trade, 1, Victoria Street, London SW1H OET

Contacts

Selected Industrial and trade representation in the common market

General

UNICE
Union of Industries of the European
  Community (see also separate entry)
rue de Loxum 6 (bte 21)
1000 Brussels
tel 010 322 512 67 80
telex 26013

UK Confederation of British Industry
rue de Loxum 6 1000 Brussels
tel 010 322 512 99 80
telex 25654

EUROPMI
EEC Committee of Small and Medium
  Sized Industries
avenue de l'Emeraude 63
1040 Brussels
tel 010 322 736 14 14

Business Co-operation Centre
17 rue Archimede (3me étage)
1040 Brussels
tel 010 322 735 59 13/48
telex 616558

Permanent Conference of Chambers of
  Commerce and Industry of the EEC
Sq. Ambiorix 30 (bte 57)
1040 Brussels
tel 010 322 736 28 58
telex 25315

CEEP
European Centre of Public Enterprises
rue de la Charité 15 1040 Brussels
tel 010 322 219 15 65

Advertising

EAAA
European Association of Advertising
  Agencies
av du Barbeau 28 3 eme étage
Brussels
tel 010 322 672 45 60

Agriculture

COPA
Committee of Agricultural Organizations
  in the EEC (Farmers Union)
rue de la Science 23–25 1040
Brussels
tel 010 322 230 39 45
telex 25816

CIBE
EEC Committee for the International
  Confederation of European Sugar Beet
  Growers
29 rue General Foy
75008 Paris
tel 010 331 292 42 11

CIAA–UNICE
Agricultural and Food Industries
  Commission of UNICE
rue de Loxum 6 1000 Brussels
tel 010 322 513 45 62
telex 26013

FEFAC
European Feed Manufacturers
  Association
rue de la Loi 223
1040 Brussels
tel 010 322 734 39 70
telex 23993

GEFAP
European Group of National Associations
  of Pesticide Manufacturers
Common Market Section
av Hamoir 12 1180 Brussels
tel 010 322 374 59 81
telex 62120

Chemicals

ECCMF
European Council of Chemical
  Manufacturers Federation
ave Louise 250
1050 Brussels
tel 010 322 640 20 95
telex 62444

Clothing and Footwear

AEIH
European Association of EEC Clothing
  Industries
rue Montoyer 24
B–1040 Brussels
tel 010 322 230 42 07
telex 61055

CEC
European Footwear Industry
  Confederation
rue de Luxembourg 19 (bte 14)
B–1040 Brussels
tel 010 322 513 06 20
telex 26885

CECG
European Wholesale Footwear Trade
  Confederation
av de Afsneelaan 6
B–9000 Ghent
tel 010 32 91 82 33 58

Construction

CECE
European Construction Equipment
  Committee
c/o the Federation of Manufacturers of
  Construction Equipment and Cranes
8 St Bride St
London EC4A 4DA
01 353 3020

International European Construction
  Federation
33 av Kléber
F–75016 Paris
tel 010 331 720 10 20

Electrical

CAPIEL
Co-ordinating Committee for Common
  Market Associations of Manufacturers
  of Industrial Electrical Switchgear and
  Control Gear
rue des Drapiers 21
B–1050 Brussels
tel 010 322 511 23 70
telex 21078

CENELEC
European Electrotechnical
  Standardization Committee
rue Brederode 2
B–1000 Brussels
tel 010 322 511 79 32

EECA
European Electronics Components
  Manufacturers Association
7/8 Savile Row
London W1X 1AF
tel 01 437 4127
telex 895 4834

CEN
European Committee for Standardization
rue Brederode 2
1000 Brussels
tel 010 322 513 55 64
telex 26 257 b

Engineering

ORGALIME
European Engineering and Metal
  Industries Liaison Body

rue de Stassant 99
B–1050 Brussels
tel 010 322 511 34 97
telex (02) 2 1078

CECT
European Committee of Boiler, Vessel
  and Pipework manufacturers
c/o Fachverband
Dampfkessel-Behalter und
  Rohrleitungsbau ev.
Sternstrasse 36
D–4000 Dusseldorf 30
tel 010 49 211 48 50 06
telex 8584966

Food and drink

CLITRAVI
Liaison Centre of Meat Processing
  Industries of the EEC
av Cortenbergh 172
1040 Brussels
tel 010 322 735 81 70
telex 26246

and at the same address:

European Federation of Quick Frozen
  Foodstuff Manufacturers in the EEC

AEEF
European Association of Refrigeration
  Enterprises

CIMCEE
Committee of EEC Mustard Industries

FEDIAF
European Petfood Federation
Square Marie-Louise
18, B–1040 Brussels
tel 010 322 230 62 46
telex 64393

FEDIOL
EEC Seed Crushers and Oil Processors
  Federation
rue de la Loi 74
1040 Brussels
tel 010 322 230 31 25
telex 23628

IMACE
Association of EEC Margarine Industries
rue de la Loi 74
1040 Brussels
tel 010 322 230 48 10
telex 23628

EEC Flour Milling Associations Group
rue de l'Orme 19
1040 Brussels
tel 010 322 733 12 64
telex 61473

CBMC
Working Group of Common Market
Brewers
chee de la Hulpe 178
1170 Brussels
tel 0 10 322 672 23 9 l

UNESDA
Union of Aerated Drinks Associations
of the EEC
av General de Gaulle 5 l
1050 Brussels
tel 0 10 322 649 12 86

European Union for Alcohol Brandy and
Spirits
av de Tervueren 192
1150 Brussels
tel 0 10 322 771 77 35

AFCASOLE
Association of Soluble Coffee
Manufacturers in the EEC
12 rue de 4-Septembre
F 750092 Paris
tel 0 10 331 742 50 78

EEC Liaison Bureau of the European
Association of the Flavour Industry
Maison des Industries Chimiques
Sq Marie Louise 49
1040 Brussels
tel 0 10 322 230 40 90

EUROGLACES
Association of the Ice Cream Industries of
the EEC
194 rue de Rivoli
75001 Paris
tel 0 10 331 260 30 12
telex 680553

AVEC
Association of Poultry Processors and
Poultry Import and Export Trade in the
EEC
Vester Farimagsgade l
1606 Copenhagen
tel 0 10 451 11 56 70
telex 27101

ASFALEC
Association of EEC Concentrated and
Powdered Milk Manufacturers
140 bld Haussmann
75008 Paris
tel 0 10 331 622 40 63
telex 280050

ASSILEC
Association of EEC Dairy Industries (as
above)
tel 0 10 331 227 12 51

Association of National Federation of
Bakers and Pastry Makers of the EEC
bld Louis Mettwie 83
1080 Brussels
tel 0 10 322 465 20 00

UNECOLAIT
European Federation of Dairy Trade
Retailers
19 Cornwall Terrace
London NW1 4QP
tel 01-486 7244
telex 262027

UGAL
Association of Food Wholesalers
av Gribaumont 3
1150 Brussels
tel 0 10 322 770 22 07
telex 24268

GEMAS
European Group of Food and Grocery
Chains (as above)
tel 0 10 322 770 66 42

FRUCOM
European Federation of Importers of
Dried Fruits, Preserves, Spices and
Honey
John West Foods Ltd
PO Box 122
54 Stanley Street
Liverpool L69 1AG
tel 051 236 8771
telex 627188

CAOBISCO
EEC Association of the Sugar Products
Industries
194 rue de Rivoli
75001 Paris
tel 0 10 331 260 30 12
telex 680553

Finance
EEC Banking Federation
av de Tervueren 168 (bte 5)
B-1150 Brussels
tel 0 10 322 771 00 94
telex 23516

GCECEE
EEC Savings Banks Group
sq Eugene Plasky 92-94
B-1040 Brussels
tel 0 10 322 736 80 47

EEC Mortgage Federation
av de la Joyeuse Entrée 12
B-1040 Brussels
tel 0 10 322 736 12 50

EUROFINAS
EEC Liaison Committee of the European
   Federation of Finance House
   Associations
av de Tervueren 267
B-1150 Brussels
tel 010 322 771 21 07/8

BIPAR
International Association of Insurance and
   Re-insurance Intermediaries
rue d'Amsterdam, 31
F 75008 Paris
tel 010 331 874 19 12

CEA
European Insurance Committee
rue Meyerbeer 3
F-75009 Paris
tel 010 331 770 50 77
telex 641901

GEEC
EEC Accountants Study Group
rue Caroly 17
B-1040 Brussels
tel 010 322 513 42 65

EEC Confederation of Tax Consultant
   Associations
9 rue Richepanse
F-75008 Paris
tel 010 331 260 10 18

Furniture

UEA
European Furniture Federation
rue de l'Association 15
B-1000 Brussels
tel 010 322 218 18 89
telex 61933

UTMM
European Metal Furniture Group
rue des Drapiers 21
B-1050 Brussels
tel 010 322 511 23 70

Glass and ceramics

EEC Glass Industry Standing
   Committee
rue du Commerce 20 (bte 3)
B-1040 Brussels
tel 010 322 511 21 70

CERAMIE-UNI
Common Market Ceramic Industries
   Liaison Office
rue des Colonies 18-24
B-1000 Brussels
tel 010 322 511 30 12

CMC
EEC Ceramic Tile Producers Group
(as above)

FEPF
Common Market Committee of the
   European Federation of Porcelain,
   Tableware and Ornaments Industries
(as above)

Leather

COTANCE
EEC Confederation of National
   Association of Tanners and Leather-
   Dressers
av Albert-Elisabeth 40
B-1200 Brussels
tel 010 322 734 56 65

CEDIM
Common Market Committee of National
   Federations of Leather Goods and
   Travel Articles Trade and Allied
   Industries
6 rue Beranger
75003 Paris
tel 010 331 272 10 05

Machinery

EMPA
European Metalworking Plantmakers
   Association
7 Ludgate Broadway
London EC4V 6DX
tel 01-248 1543
telex 8812908

COCEMA
European Committee of Food Machinery
   Manufacturers
Lyoner Strasse 18
D-6000 Frankfurt Main 71 FDR
tel 0 611 6603 431
telex 21078

EUROMAP
European Committee of Plastic and
   Rubber Machinery Manufacturers
2 av Hoche
F-75008 Paris
tel 010 331 267 20 07
telex 280900

CEMA
EEC European Committee of
   Associations of Manufacturers of
   Agriculture Machinery
19 rue Jacques Bingen
F-75017 Paris
tel 010 331 766 02 20
telex 640362

Mechanical Handling

FEM
European Federation of Lifting,
    Conveying and Handling Equipment
    Manufacturers
Kirchenweg 4
Case Postale 179
CH–8032 Zurich, Switzerland
tel 010 411 47 84 00
telex 54924

Metal

EEC Liaison Committee for Non-Ferrous
    Metal Industry
Pl. du Samedi 13
B–1000 Brussels

Paper

CEPAC
European Confederation of the Pulp and
    Paperboard Industry
rue de Crayer 14
B–1050 Brussels
tel 010 322 649 67 09
telex 227 13

Pharmaceuticals and cosmetics

EFPIA
European Pharmaceutical Industries
    Association Federation
ave Louise 250 (bte 91)
B–1050 Brussels
tel 010 322 640 68 15

COLIPA
European Associations of the Perfume,
    Cosmetic and Toilet Industry Liaison
    Committee
av de Tervueren 34 (bte 45)
B–1040 Brussels
tel 010 322 736 20 64
telex 21908

Plastics

APME
European Plastic Manufacturers
    Association
ave Louise 250 (bte 73)
B–1050 Brussels
tel 010 322 640 28 50
telex 62444

GPRMC
Common Market Reinforced Plastic
    Industry Group
c/o Fabrimetal
Groupe 18 Fabriplast
rue des Drapiers 21

B–1050 Brussels
tel 010 322 511 23 70
telex 210 78

EUTRAPLAST
European Plastics Converters
    Federations Committee
(as above)

Printing, publishing

CAEJ
EEC Union of Newspaper Publishers
    Associations
rue Belliard 20 (bte 5)
B–1040 Brussels
tel 010 322 512 17 31
telex 26854

CELC
EEC Book Publishers Group
av du Parc 111
B–1060 Brussels
tel 010 322 538 21 67

EUROGRAF
EEC Group of Federations of Graphic
    Industries
sq Marie-Louise 18
B–1040 Brussels
tel 010 322 230 86 46
telex 64 393

Rubber

BLIC
Liaison Office of the EEC Rubber
    Industries
av des Arts 19
B–1040 Brussels
tel 010 322 218 49 40

Textiles

COMITEXTIL
Co-ordination Committee of EEC Textile
    Industries
rue Montoyer 24
B–1040 Brussels
tel 010 322 511 18 77
telex (02) 22 380

EUROCOTON
Committee of EEC Cotton and Allied
    Textile Industries
rue Montoyer 24
B–1040 Brussels
tel 010 322 230 32 39

MAILLEUROP
EEC Committee of Knitwear Industries
Frere Orbanlaan 236
B–9000 Ghent
tel 010 091 234051
telex 11256

INTERLAINE
EEC Association of Wool Textile
    Industries
rue de Luxembourg 19
B–1040 Brussels
tel 010 322 513 06 20
telex 26885

AIFUAS
Common Market Working Group of the
    International Association of Users of
    Yarn/Man Made Fibre
12 rue d'Anjou
75008 Paris
tel 010 331 266 11 11

CITTA
International Confederation of Carpet and
    Furnishing Fabric Manufacturers
Domagkweg 8
5600 Wuppertal-Elberfeld
Germany
tel 01 49 202 75 00 35
telex 08591789

Toys

European Federation of Toy
    Manufacturers' Associations
Sand Strasse 29 IV
D85 Nuremberg
Germany, FR

Transport

Automobile Constructers Liaison
    Committee of the EEC
Sq de Meeus 5
B–1040 Brussels
tel 010 322 513 58 48
telex 26308

CLEPA
Automobile Parts and Equipment
    Manufacturers Liaison Committee
112 av Ch de Gaulle
F–92522 Neuilly-sur-Seine
tel 010 33 637 06 36

EEC Shipbuilders Linking Committee
243 Knightsbridge
London SW7 1DG
tel 01 589 3488
telex 917060

ICOMIA
International Council of Marine Industry
    Associations
Boating Industry House
Vale Rd
Oatlands
Weybridge KT13 9NS
tel 97 54511
telex 885471

IOMTR
International Organization for Motor
    Trades and Repairs
Veraartlaan 12
NL–2280 ak Rijswijk (Zrl)
tel 010 31 90 72 22
telex 31296

Wood

AGNIB
EEC Wood Dealers Organization
rue Royale 109–111
B–1000 Brussels
tel 010 322 219 28 32

OES
European Sawmills Organization
1 Place du Thêátre Français
F–75001 Paris
tel 010 331 260 30 27

FEFPEB
European Federation of Pallets and
    Packing Cases Manufacturers
5 Greenfield Crescent
Edgbaston
Birmingham B15 3BE
tel 021–454 2177
telex 338 396

FESYP
European Federation of Associations of
    Particle Board Manufacturers
Wilhelmstrasse 25
D–Giessen
tel 010 45 641 733 57

CEI–Bois
European Confederation of Woodworking
    Industries
rue Royale 109–111
B–1000 Brussels
tel 01 322 217 63 65
telex 61 933 meubel b

Steel

Basic information

The European Coal and Steel Community (ECSC) was inaugurated with the Treaty of Paris, 1952. Its purpose to remove the traditional rivalry of the European nations. In the first five years there was an increase in the trade of the six by 129% and this assisted in the economic recovery of Europe. The reason for its importance is that in all countries of the EC except for Denmark and Ireland, it occupies a central role in the national economies.

Position in the 1970s

During the period 1946–74 there was a sixfold increase in crude steel production throughout the world. The rise was from 112 million to 708 million, tonnes. Community steel accounted for 22% of world production, it employed close on 800,000 workers and was responsible for 7% of industrial production of the community.

From the beginning of 1975 there has been a crisis in the industry. In that year there being a 9% drop in world crude steel production. By 1977 the European steel industry was running at 60% capacity. This has meant in the EC:

1   Cutbacks in production. 1977 output was 126 million tonnes against 155 million in 1974. In 1978 it rose to 134 million tonnes. Productive capacity in the EC ran at 200 million tonnes and it would have needed to sell between 160 and 170 million tonnes to be a viable industry.
2   Slump in prices. Between 1974 and 1977 these dropped 50%. Subsequently they rallied 20% to 25% as a result of measures taken by the community. However, production costs remained high.
3   Between 1974 and June 1978 there were 95,000 redundancies (12% of the payroll) and more than 100,000 put onto short-time working. It is aimed to cut the workforce to 600,000 by 1980.
4   Financially the loss amounted to 3,000 million EUAs for the whole industry in 1977.

Proposals for the improvement of the industry

A number of solutions were proposed for the crisis and the one adopted was known as the DAVIGNON PLAN (Commissioner in charge of industrial questions). Plan has two approaches – internal and external and two phases short term and medium term.

Short Term Plan will:
1   Put a ceiling on production in the Community. Establish compulsory

minimum prices for sensitive sectors of production and recommended prices for the rest.

2   Discipline EC/world trade. Introduce anti-dumping measures. This has reduced imports from 12.4 million tonnes in 1976 to 11 million tonnes in 1978. Exports rose from 21.5 million tonnes to 30 million tonnes in the same period.

Medium Term Plan will:

1   Prohibit National aids which increase production capacity.
2   Community Loans to modernize and rationalize plant.

In 1980 there was a worsening of the situation. The Commission adopted Community rules for specific aids to the steel industry (OJ L29/5–8 6.2.80) (Decision 257/80/ECSC), in operation until 31 December 1981. On 30 October 1980 the Council gave its assent to a series of production quotas (less certain special steels) under article 59 of the ECSC treaty (OJ L291/1–29 31.10.80) (Decision 2794/80/ECSC). Details of voluntary reductions for the first quarter of 1982 appeared in the *Official Journal* (OJ C337/3–5 24.12.81). This covered the production of reversing mill plate and heavy sections. For high alloy steels in categories V and VI, production and marketing guidelines for the first half of 1982 appeared in OJ C19/4 26.1.82. Future guides to production quotas will also be found in the *Official Journal.*

In 1981 (on 23 February) the Commission sent to Council a paper setting out objectives and measures proposed in the light of an overall assessment of the situation and based on the experience gained since its 1980 decision mentioned above. Details are summarized in, *Bulletin of the European Communities* **14** (2) 1981 points 1.4.1–11 and 2.1.19. The Council's proposals at their meeting on 26/27 March are recorded in *Bulletin of the European Communities* **14** (3) 1981 point 3.4.1. which included a request to the Commission to replace their L29 of 1980. At meetings on the 4th and 24th June 1981 the Council approved a package of measures to improve the steel industry. These are summarized in, *Bulletin of the European Communities* **14** (6) 1981. points 1.4.1 to 1.4.3 and detailed in (OJ L180/1–8 1.7.81) (Decision 1831/81/ECSC), amended by (OJ L184/1–5 4.7.81) (Decision 1832/81/ECSC).

Early in June 1982 at the Western Economic Summit meeting at Versailles, the growth of world trade was deemed a necessary element in, and a consequence of, the growth of each individual country (*Bulletin of the European Communities* **15** (6) 1982 point 3.4.1). Within a week the US Department of Commerce announced countervailing duties on imports of steel from Community countries because of subsidies. On the 18th June the US President decided to extend the scope of sanctions against the export of oil and gas equipment to the USSR much of which is made from Community manufactured steel (*Bulletin of the European Communities* **15** (6) 1982 points 2.2.41–2.2.46). At the European Council meeting in Brussels on 28 and 29.6.82 it was considered important to adhere to the Versailles summit, to defend the legitimate interest of the Community at

GATT, and that a dialogue between those in the Community and the USA responsible for policy, should commence without delay.

Further information

General report on the activities of the European Communities
    Luxembourg: Office for official publications of the European Communities, annual
Iron and steel year book
    Luxembourg: Office for official publications of the European Communities, annual
Financial report, European coal and steel community
    Luxembourg: Office for official publications of the European Community, annual
'Steel: manifest crisis'. *Bulletin of the European Communities,* **13** (10) 1980. points 1.1.1–1.1.9
Catalogue of Community legal acts and other texts relating to the elimination of technical barriers to trade for industrial products and nomenclature for iron and steel products (EURONORM)
    Luxembourg: Office for official publications of the European Communities, 1981. 112p. ISBN 92–825–2769–7. Catalogue number CB–33–81–110–EN–C

Steel Industry Safety and Health Commission

Basic information

The High Authority of the ECSC set up in 1964 a Commission on safety and health in the steel industry under article 46 of the Treaty of Paris in 1952, in response to a proposal by the European Parliament. This safety and health commission was included in the minutes of the 802nd meeting of the High Authority dated 24 September 1964.

Safety and Health Commission – representation

The Commission consists of four representatives from each member state, excluding Denmark, a representative of the steel producers' association, a representative of a leading steel company, two trade union representatives from the steel industry and has two observers from Sweden.

Work of the Safety and Health Commission

The work of the Commission is to exchange information between member states on health and safety in the industry, to produce reports, hold discussions and lectures, arrange visits.

It has working parties on:

• health in rolling mills

- organization of accident prevention
- electric furnaces
- safety training
- use of explosives
- first aid and rescue
- tapping of metal from blast furnaces, safety measures
- overhead cranes, safety measures
- gas pipes, safety measures
- oxygen pipes, safety measures

Further information

Community advisory committees for the representation of socio-economic interests
  Farnborough: Saxon House for EC Economic and Social Committee, 1980. 215p. ISBN
  0–566–00328–7

Coal

Basic information

Under the Treaty of Paris (1952) which set up the, European Coal and Steel Community
(ECSC), there are provisions for an energy policy on coal. Research and development in the
coal industry and welfare amongst workers in that industry have developed. However,
harmonization of laws in the industry and co-ordination of commercial policy has not yet
made much progress.

Investment

The ECSC loaned to the coal industry in Britain some 226.85 million EUA
in 1980 alone, together with a further 135.85 million EUA for conversion
programmes in both the coal and steel industries for the same year.

Investment in the coal industry of the Communities is expected to be in
the region of 1,360 million EUA in 1980.

Energy policy

With the energy crises in the 1970s there has been a change in Electricity
generation from oil fired stations to coal. However, there have been
considerable savings in the use of energy which has meant that by 1980
the use of coal was approximately equivalent to that in 1979. It was noted,

however, that the 1979 demand had shown a considerable increase over that for the previous years.

In its communication, Medium term guidelines for coal 1975–1985, the Commission stressed the need to stabilize coal production whilst increasing productivity (OJ C22/1–18 30.1.75).

Under the long term Energy objectives for 1990, coal mining is seen as an expanding industry and the aim that coal and nuclear energy would provide 70–75% of the electricity produced by 1990 (*Bulletin of the European Communities* **12** (6) 1979 point 2.1.109). The Energy programme also included research projects for the more efficient use of fuel in the hydrocarbon sector. Details of the award of these research contracts and their results are notified in the *Bulletin*, for example *Bulletin of the European Communities* **15** (6) 1982 points 2.1.160–2.

The 1981 Commission report on the coal market for 1980 and outlook for 1981 (OJ C123/1–46 25.5.81) concludes that the demand in 1981 will be slightly down on the previous year due to the economic recession. The 1982 report (OJ C131/1–47 24.5.82) forecast a small rise in consumption in 1982.

The 1976 decision on measures to be taken by member states to improve the coal mining industry (OJ L63/1–10 11.3.76) (Decision 528/76/ECSC) were reassessed on 11 November 1981 for the period 1976–80. As a result it has been decided that the proposals should remain in force until 1985 (*Bulletin of the European Communities* **14** (11) 1981 point 2.1.123).

Imports

Imports of coal from third countries rose in the late 1970s but the 1981 imports showed a slowing of this growth and were running at 71 million tonnes, somewhat lower than in 1980. (*Bulletin of the European Communities* **14** (5) 1981 point 2.1.108 and **15** (5) 1982 point 2.1.39.)

Further information

General report on the activities of the European Communities, section 12 'Energy'
   Luxembourg: Office for official publications of the European Communities, annual
Europe today, state of European integration, 1980–1981
   Luxembourg: Office for official publications of the European Communities, 1981. 617p.
   ISBN 92–823–0037–4. Catalogue number AX–30–80–972–EN–C

Working Conditions in the Coal Industry, Mixed Committee on Harmonization

Basic information

Set up in 1975 (OJ L329/35–6 23.12.75) (Decision 75/782/ECSC).

Mixed Committee – representation

Its membership consists of representatives of the two sides of the industry not more than twenty from each side. Governments of member states may participate in an advisory capacity or as observers.

Work of the Mixed Committee

The aim of the Committee is to assist the Commission with advice on improving the working conditions and standard of living within the ECSC. It arranges discussions, exchanges information and carries out studies as necessary.

Further information

Community advisory committees for the representation of socio-economic interests
   Farnborough: Saxon House for EC Economic and Social Committee, 1980. 215p. ISBN 0–566–00328–7

Mines Safety and Health Commission

Basic information

The Commission was established under a 1957 Council decision (OJ/ECSC 28 487–9/57 31.8.57) amended by (OJ 46 698–9/65 22.3.65) and (OJ L185/18–19 9.7.74) (Decision 74/326/EEC).

Commission – representation

Membership of the Commission consists of four delegates from each

Community member state (two Government, one employer, one worker). The ILO may be invited to attend specific meetings. Governments may appoint up to two additional specialists for specific meetings. There is a Restricted committee consisting of representatives from member state governments. The Restricted committee has been charged with implementing certain sections of Community legislation. For example, Council directive on the approximation of the laws of the member states concerning electrical equipment for use in potentially explosive atmospheres in mines susceptible to fire damp (OJ L59/10–28 2.3.82) (Directive 82/130/EEC).

Work of the Commission

The duties of the Commission – terms of reference and rules of procedure – were laid down in a 1957 notice establishing the Commission, as amended (see first paragraph above).

Working parties cover:

- Roof control
- Rescue arrangements, fires and underground combustion
- Electrification
- Winding engines, winches, ropes and shaft guides
- Combustible dusts
- Mining accident statistics
- Health in coal mines
- Mechanization
- Effects of working time on safety at work
- Psychological and sociological factors
- Ventilation and mine gas

Further information

General report on the activities of the European Communities
Luxembourg: Office for official publications of the European Communities, annual
Community advisory committees for the representation of socio-economic interests
Farnborough: Saxon House for EC Economic and Social Committee, 1980. 215p. ISBN 0–566–00328–7

Automobile Industry

Basic information

Under Community primary legislation article 100 of the Treaty of Rome (1957), the Council may work towards an approximation of laws in member states. This industry tends to fall under article 100.

Interest in improving the safety and efficiency of motor vehicles started in the late 1960s and continued, in a small way, until by the mid-1970s some 28 directives had been adopted by the Council. These covered road traffic, carriage of people and goods by road, vehicle lighting, safety in vehicles, noise levels of vehicle engines, etc. The very large number of directives, communications, etc is recorded in, *Guide to EEC legislation,* chapter 24.4.1 (see under Further information).

Parallel to this was the development of a common transport policy 1972 onwards (qv Road transport).

Work undertaken

By December 1975 the Commission organized a Motor Vehicle Symposium, which also recommended the technical updating of a 1970 directive on the pollution of the environment by automobiles (qv Environment and Pollution control).

The following year one of the directives adopted by the Council included an attempt to reduce the barriers within the Community on marketing of community produced cars.

The Commission completed its work on updating a 1970 directive (OJ L42/1–15 23.2.70) (Directive 70/156/EEC), on Community type approval procedure for motor vehicles and their trailers. The proposed new law covered both technical and legal aspects. It has been submitted in draft form (OJ C25/2–16 2.2.77) and parts have become law.

By the early 1980s interest was also developing in the automobile industry because of its decline. On 6 October 1980 the Commission transmitted to Parliament a document containing background information on the current situation of the motor industry. Parliament debated this in December 1980 and January 1981, passing a resolution on the European Automobile Industry (OJ C28/12, 13, 17–23 9.2.81) The larger 1981 debate instructed its President to forward this resolution and the report of its committee, to both the Council and the Commission.

Developments and changes in automobile insurance have also taken place (qv. Insurance).

The problem of imports into the Community of foreign cars and, in particular, those from Japan, has caused increasing concern. Statistics of imports have been started (OJ L54/61 28.2.81) (Regulation 535/81/EEC). Statements from the Council have expressed concern recently during

18/19 May 1980 and 25 November 1980 (*Bulletin of the European Communities* **13** (11) 1980 point 1.2.4), on 17 February 1981 (*Bulletin of the European Communities* **14** (2) 1981 points 2.2.30) and at the Council meeting on 18/19 May 1981. Restrictions on car imports from Japan have been applied by the UK, France and Italy. Parliament has urged the Commission to submit to Council a proposal that exports of Japanese cars to the Community should be subject to a limitation analogous to the one decided by Japan vis-à-vis the United States (*Bulletin of the European Communities* **14** (5) 1981 points 1.3.1–1.3.8).

Further information

General report on the activities of the European Communities
  Luxembourg: Office for official publications of the European Communities, annual
Guide to EEC legislation
  Amsterdam: North Holland Publishing Company, 1979. 2 v. ISBN 0–444–85320–0
Future of the car industry
  Luxembourg: Office for official publications of the European Communities, 1982. 7p.
  (European file 1/82) ISSN 0379–3133.Catalogue number CC–AD–82–001–EN–C

Shipbuilding Industry

Basic information

With the post-war growth in world economy, orders for new ships continued increasing, particularly between the years 1960 and 1973. The result was an overcapacity of building reaching 33 million gross registered tons (grt) between the periods 1974–6.

Following the deepening economic problems in the second half of the 1970s, the oil crisis affecting the building of new tankers, and the fact that Community shipbuilding is handicapped by unsuitable building facilities which have high operating costs, a crisis in the industry was inevitable.

Extent of the change

By 1979 new orders fell to 2.5 million c grt (compensated grt) and subsequent years may show still further falls. The Association of West European Shipbuilders (AWES) forecast a fall of 46% between 1975 and 1980 compared with a world production fall of 40% for the same period.

The firms involved tended to introduce short term palliatives eg cutting out overtime, encouraging early retirement, restricting recruitment, etc.

Under the auspices of the OECD the European Community countries, AWES and Japan, signed *General guidelines for government policies in the shipbuilding industry*, on 12 May 1976. This agreement aimed to reduce production in order to restore the balance between supply and demand. It is noted however that Japanese percentage of the market rose from 41% in 1979 to 50% in 1980 (14th general report on the activities of the European Communities in 1980, point 146).

Work undertaken

Community intervention has two aspects, the co-ordination of aids to shipbuilders, and through the European regional development fund, financial aid to ship builders.

The objectives of Community intervention are:

● to make EC shipbuilding yards competitive
● to concentrate on seagoing non-naval ships
● the attainment of general production geared to foreseeable demand
● adjustment of building capacity to future needs
● labour needs to be redeployed in part to other industries; a retraining programme initiated
● demand for ships needs to be restimulated.
    Substandard ships sailing under flags of convenience are presenting both operating hazards and a threat to the marine environment.

The Commission sent a fourth directive on aid to shipbuilding to the Council on 4 November 1977 (OJ L98/19–25 11.4.78) (Directive 78/338/EEC). This is an essential element of an industrial approach to the problem. It also covers member state's aids to shipowners and provides that such aids must not discriminate against the shipyards of other Community states. On 9 December 1977 a communication was sent from the Commission to the Council – (Bulletin of the European Communities supplement 7/77). This led to a 1978 Council resolution reorganizing the industry (OJ C229/1–2 27.9.78). It was agreed that six monthly reports should be produced on the industry and submitted to Council. The first of these is mentioned under, Further information.

Between 1976 and 1979 the level of new orders represents only 50–60% of completions. Shipyard output in the Community has been reduced by 25–30%. Between 1975 and 1978 the workforce has been reduced by some 50,000. Market forecasts are expecting the crisis to extend well into the 1980s. A substantial market upswing cannot be expected before 1982/3.

A reassessment of demand has led to a communication from the Commission to the Council of 4 April 1978 concerning a proposal for a scrap and build programme which has been submitted to Council. This was included in, Shipbuilding – state of the industry and crisis measures, mentioned under, Further information. On this subject see also House of Lords, Select Committee on the European Communities. Shipbuilding London: HMSO House of Lords paper 155 Session 1979/80. 14p.

Further restructuring measures were thought necessary to build a healthy and competitive industry. The fifth directive on aid to shipbuilding has now been issued (OJ L137/39–43 23.5.81) (Directive 81/363/EEC). This directive provides a framework for continuing aid to reorganize the industry, and covers the period up to 31 December 1982.

Further information

Shipbuilding – state of the industry and crisis measures and first half yearly report on ... *shipbuilding* ... *Bulletin of the European Communities* supplement 7/79
Report on competition policy
   Luxembourg: Office for official publications of the European Communities, annual (Published in conjunction with General report on the activities of the European Communities). 1970–
Second half yearly report on the state of the shipbuilding industry in the Community (situation as at 1 January 1980). *Bulletin of the European Communities* **13** (9) 1980. point 2.1.12.

Aerospace Industry

Basic information

Community interest in this industry commenced in the mid 1970s when under a Council resolution of 4 March 1975 a report from the Commission on the state of the industry and proposals, was requested (OJ C59/1–2 13.3.75). This was published later in the year (OJ C265/2–4 19.11.75) and also published as, 'Action programme for the European aeronautical sector' (*Bulletin of the European Communities* supplement 11/75).

Progress towards an aviation industry policy

The Commission's 1975 proposals were followed by a Council statement in 1977 determining criteria for the establishment of a joint programme for the construction of large civil aircraft (OJ C69/6 19.3.77). These criteria included:

- a strategy for the introduction of new programmes to avoid duplication
- new forms of co-operation with comparable sectors of the American industry
- co-operation between European airlines and manufacturers regarding the design of new aircraft
- political pressure to ensure that the European market buys European manufactured planes
- co-operation to produce the basic research information for the next generation of aircraft

The Commission produced proposals on short-term projects and long term strategy regarding aeronautical research (OJ C210/8–9 2.9.77). These were based on discussion with the, European association of aerospace manufacturers.

In 1978 negotiations took place between European aerospace manufacturers outside the Communities. These resulted in a joint programme for a large civil aircraft. In the case of medium-haul models the British BA146 and the Dutch F29 remained in competition. The major 1979 activity of the Community was the conclusion of a trade agreement in civil aircraft removing tariff and non-tariff barriers. Signatories were the EC, USA, Japan, Canada, Sweden, Norway and Switzerland. This was within the framework of GATT.

Little seems to have taken place on a Community basis since 1978 though much in various member states.

Further information

General report on the activities of the European Communities
    Luxembourg: Office for official publications of the European Communities, annual
European aerospace industry trading position and figures
    Brussels: Commission of the European Communities, 1981. 114p. (Commisssion staff working paper 111/1146/81(E)).

Transport Policy

Basic information

The European Community was founded on the principal of a common market in which goods and services move freely (Treaty of Rome, articles 75–83).

Development of transport policy

Since 1955 uniform international tariffs (OJ L9/701–711 19.4.55) were introduced for transporting coal and steel in the Community.

In 1958, just after the European Economic Community was formed, the Transport Committee rules were formulated by the Council (OJ L25/509–510 27.11.58) and amended subsequently.

Between 1958 and 1979 the volume of trade between member states of the Community has quadrupled.

Under a Council decision (OJ L23/720 3.4.62) a procedure was instituted of prior examination by the Community and consultation in respect of certain laws, regulations and administrative provisions concerning transport, which member states were considering.

Several regulations on the elimination of discrimination (OJ L52/1121–1125 16.8.60) (Regulation 11/60/EEC), on competition (OJ L88/1500–1502 24.5.65) (Decision 65/271/EEC) were issued. Two-yearly reports on the implementation of Decision 271 are published. These were general provisions covering rail, or road, or inland waterways. In addition a number of specialized regulations for example the duty free admission of fuel for commercial vehicles, were issued to aid the development of a transport policy.

In 1969 regulations were introduced concerning the obligations inherent in the concept of a public service in transport by road, rail and waterway (OJ L156/1–7 28.6.69) (Regulation 1191/69/EEC) supplemented on 20 January 1981 by a criteria for the concept of a public service *(Bulletin of the European Communities* **14** (1) 1981 point 2.1.54).

1973 saw a major communication from the Commission to the Council on the development of a common transport policy *(Bulletin of the European Communities* supplement 16/73).

The principal objective of the EC policy on transport, that of creating a European transport infrastructure, to meet user needs at the least cost to the taxpayer, was being developed particularly during the period 1978–80 *(Eleventh general report on the activities of the European Communities,* point 362. See under Further information).

The Commission has been making proposals for the better financing of inland transport infrastructure since 1976 (OJ C207/9-10 2.9.76). On 15 February 1980 proposals were made to extend this aid to certain non EC countries. These proposals are being considered by Council (OJ C89/4–5 10.4.80).

In October 1980 in response to a Parliamentary request, the Commission sent the Council a communication concerning priorities and a timetable for decisions to be taken in the transport sector up to the end of 1983 (OJ C294/6–8 13.11.80). This was linked to the list of main topics to be given priority, produced at the Council meeting of Transport Ministers in Brussels on 26 March 1980. At this meeting the Council adopted the topics. One concerned frontier formalities and a proposed directive on this was sent by the Commission to the Council in April 1982 (OJ C127/6–8 18.5.82).

See also entries under specific types of transport e.g. *Road Transport*, etc.

Further information

General report on the activities of the European Communities
Luxembourg: Office for official publications of the European Communities, annual
Statistical yearbook transport, communications tourism
Luxembourg: Office for official publications of the European Communities, annual
1962/3–
Transport in the European Community
London: Departments of the Environment and Transport Library Services, 1974. 42p.
(Biography series no 169)
A transport network for Europe outline of a policy
Bulletin of the European Communities supplement 8/79
The common transport policy
Brussels: EC Directorate-General for Information, 1979. 7p. (European File 20/79).
Catalogue number CC–AD–79–020–EN–C
The European Communities transport policy
Luxembourg: Office for official publications of the European Communities, 1981. 37p.
(European Documentation series 2/1981). ISBN 92–827–2170–2

Advisory Committee on Transport

Basic information

Created under the Treaty of Rome, article 83. Its rules were formulated in 1958 (OJ 25/509–10 27.11.58) amended by (OJ 102/1602 29.6.64) (Decison 64/390/EEC).

Advisory Committee – representation

The Committee members are experts on transport questions and have been nominated by member states. They are usually one or two senior civil servants concerned with transport together with up to three experts in one or more aspects of the subject. Alternative membership is on a similar basis. The term of office is two years and reappointments may be made.

Work of the Advisory Committee

The purpose of the Committee is to assist the Commission in matters affecting its subject. Care is taken not to overlap with the work of the, Section for transport of the Economic and Social Committee. Whilst the Committee is asked for its comments on technical matters, it may not be asked for its comments on questions concerning the interpretation of relevant Community law (article 83 of the Treaty of Rome (1957)). Opinions are usually given in writing in report form though the Commission may ask for an oral report. Working parties may be established by the

Committee for specific purposes.

An example of one of its opinions is the, *Report on energy and transport* (*Bulletin of the European Communities* **14** (1) 1981. point 2.1.56), which was adopted by the Commission.

On 15 December 1981 the Council requested the Commission, with the advice of the Committee, to apply on an experimental basis a limited number of specific transport infrastructure projects. A report on these projects was requested by 1.10.82 (*Bulletin of the European Communities* **14** (12) 1981 point 2.1.47).

Further information

General report on the activities of the European Communities
    Luxembourg: Office for official publications of the European Communities, annual
Community advisory committees for the representation of socio-economic interests
    Farnborough: Saxon House for EC Economic and Social Committee, 1980. 115p. ISBN 0-566-00328-7

Transport Infrastructure Committee

Basic information

The Committee was set up under the Commission in 1978 (OJ L54/16-17 25.2.78) (Decison 78/74/EEC). It takes the place of the 1966 procedure for consultation in respect of transport infrastructure investment (OJ 583/66 8.3.66) (Decision 66/161/EEC).

Committee – representation

Each of the member states to be represented with a Commission representative as chairman.

Work of the Committee

- provide a forum for consultation with member states on transport infrastructure
- at the request of the Commission it organizes exchanges of information between member states regarding the proposed development of their transport infrastructure and on any question on transport infrastructure of interest to the Community as a whole
- it is to be consulted on the three yearly, Report on transport infrastructure, submitted to Council and Parliament

Further information

General report on the activities of the European Communities
Luxembourg: Office for official publications of the European Communities, annual

Air Transport

Basic information

Article 84 (2) of the Treaty of Rome (1957) makes provision for the improvement of the market structure of air transport within the Community. Article 3e mentions 'the institution of a common policy in the sphere of transport'.

In the Community, air transport is dominated by government organizations and influence and inevitably by the international organization IATA (International Air Transport Association).

Purpose

In 1972 the Commission submitted a proposal on initial measures for air transport (OJ C110/6 18.10.72). Four operational objectives were set by the Commission:

- total network unhampered by national barriers, efficient services at low cost to users
- financial soundness with a diminution of their present costs and an increase in their productivity
- safeguards of the interests of air transport workers
- improvements in the condition of life for the general public and respect for the wider interests of the economy and society

Some three years later a report and proposed decision on a programme of action for the European aeronautical sector was produced (OJ C265/2–4 19.11.75). In 1977 the Council asked the Committee of Permanent Representatives to establish a working party to study air transport questions.

In June 1978 the Council approved a list of nine priority matters which offered a good basis for a number of practical Community initiatives:

- common standards restricting nuisances due to aircraft (Air traffic control, *Bulletin of the European Communities* **13** (7/8) 1980 point 2.3.13)
- simplification of formalities with particular reference to air freight
- implementation of technical standards
- provisions regarding aids and competition (Air fares, *Bulletin of the European Communities* **13** (6) 1980 point 2.1.138)
- mutual recognition of licences

- working conditions
- right of establishment
- possible improvements to inter-regional services (Commission proposal of 22 October 1980, *Bulletin of the European Communities* **13** (10) 1980 point 2.1.87)
- search, rescue and recovery operations. Accident enquiries (Council directive 16 December 1980)

Proposals for a Council resolution concerning priorities and the time table for decisions to be taken by the Council in the transport sector during the period up to the end of 1983, have been submitted by the Commission (OJ C294/6–8 13.11.80). These have been examined by Parliament and amendments proposed (OJ C77/82–4 6.4.81).

Further information

'Air transport: a Community approach' – Memorandum of the Commission (adopted on 4 July 1979). *Bulletin of the European Communities* supplement 5/79
The European Community's transport policy
   Luxembourg: Office for official publications of the European Communities, 1981. 37p.
   (European Documentation Series 2 – 1981). ISBN 92–825–2170–2

Schwartzenberg Report

Basic information

R G Schwartzenberg was rapporteur of a Parliamentary committee on transport which considered the problem of restrictions on competition in the air transport sector (EP working document 1–724/79 11.2.80).

Though article 84 (2) of the Treaty of Rome (1957) excludes both air and sea transport from the common transport policy, yet in a judgement of 4.4.74 case 167/73, the European Court of Justice decided they remain on the same basis as other modes of transport and are subject to the general rules of the EEC treaty. Therefore articles 85–90 of the Treaty of Rome governing competition are applicable.

Purpose

The unsatisfactory operation of air transport services in the EC has been debated more than once in Parliament (6.7.78 and 13.10.78 etc).

The Commission submitted a memorandum on the development of air traffic services (COM (79) 311 Final 6.7.79) and (*Bulletin of the European Communities* Supplement 5/79) covering:

- competition

- industrial policy
- transport policy
- regional economic development
- commercial policy

The problems amongst European air transport authorities in 1979 were:

- lack of flexibility in market terms
- lack of flexibility in their system of tariffs

It was thought that these were caused by the Chicago Convention on air transport which was concerned with intergovernmental co-operation rather than private competition. With the USA airline deregulation of 1978, American airlines were given greater freedom of competition.

EP Document 1–724/79 outlined means of stimulating competition and put forward procedures for implementing competition rules in a changing air transport sector.

Further information

General report on the activities of the European Communities
   Luxembourg: Office for official publications of the European Communities, annual
'Air transport: a Community approach' *Bulletin of the European Communities* supplement 5/79

Inland Waterway Transport

Basic information

During 1976 some 680 million tons of goods were transported by waterways. The major inland waterways are in Germany, Holland and Belgium and Northern France. Under articles 74 and 75 of the Treaty of Rome (1957), proposals have been made for the extension of these waterways in, *A transport network for Europe*, mentioned in Further information. The real problem, however, is their infrastructure.

Most of the undertakings are small family firms usually with one boat and under-capitalized. It is difficult for them to keep up to date with technical developments. Further there is at the moment (1980) a degree of over capacity.

Individual EC member states have taken action to scrap old, uneconomic vessels. Negotiations have taken place with Switzerland on the temporary laying up of inland waterway vessels in order to ease the current Rhine navigation problem.

Work undertaken

A series of proposals for restoring the inland shipping market to health, were put up by the Commission in 1967 (OJ C95 21.9.68), but were not adopted. New proposals are being formulated – see under Further information.

However agreements have been reached on reciprocal recognition of navigability licences (OJ L21/10–12 29.1.76) (Directive 76/135/EEC).

Proposals for a Council resolution concerning priorities and the time table for decisions to be taken by the Council in the transport sector during the period up to the end of 1983, have been submitted by the Commission (OJ C294/6–8 13.11.80). These have been examined by Parliament and amendments proposed (OJ C77/82–4 6.4.81).

Further information

A transport network for Europe, outline of a policy,
   Bulletin of the European Communities supplement 8/79
The European Community's transport policy
   Luxembourg: Office for official publications of the European Communities, 1981. 37p. (European Documentation Series 2–1981). ISBN 92–825–2170–2

Joint Advisory Committee on Social Questions arising on Inland Water Transport

Basic information

The Commission decided to set up this Committee in 1967 (OJ 297/13–15 7.12.67) (Decison 67/745/EEC). This was amended by a Commission decision (OJ L140/24 27.6.70) (Decision 70/326/EEC).

Joint Advisory Committee – representation

Whilst at the moment there are seventeen full places and eleven alternative places for each side (carriers and workers) the scope of this Committee is being reconsidered and it may be that the responsibilities as well as the size of the Committee may be altered. Members are appointed for three years. These appointments may be renewed.

Work of the Joint Advisory Committee

The work of the committee is to assist the Commission by opinions on subjects of concern to it. It may also initiate action through the Commission and it may set up working parties.

Further information

General report on the activities of the European Communities
  Luxembourg: Office for official publications of the European Communities, annual
Community advisory committees for the representation of socio-economic interest
  Farnborough: Saxon House for EC Economic and Social Committee, 1980. 115p. ISBN
  0–566–00328–7

Rail Transport

Basic information

In 1978 Community railways carried 3,300 million passengers and some 900 million tonnes
of goods. About 1 million people were employed on the railways whose fixed assets were
worth some 35,000 million EUA. Between 1965 and 1976 their share of inland goods
transport fell from 31% to 19%.

Railway policy within the Community is based on a 1965 Council decision (OJ 88/1500–2
24.5.65) (Decision 65/271/EEC) with amendments including the major decision of 1975 (OJ
L152/3–712.6.75) (Decision 75/327/EEC). However, progress was slow with rising costs
and ever greater government interference.

Work was completed in 1977 on proposals for railways accounting systems (OJ L334/13–21
24.12.77) (Regulation 2830/77/EEC) and in the following year on uniform costing principles
(OJ L258/1–6 21.9.78) (Regulation 2183/78/EEC).

Work undertaken

By the 1980s it was decided that a series of new measures had become
appropriate and these were developed by the Commission and sent to
the Council on 17 December 1980. Action was proposed as follows:

- development and full application of existing Community legislation
- series of new measures including:
  - attainment of a financial balance through improved planning of
    financing and activities. The Commission sent the Council a proposal
    on this subject (OJ C37/7–12 20.2.81). Parliament's opinion
    recommended changes and these were incorporated in Commission
    amendments to its proposal submitted on 15 and 17 March 1982
    (*Bulletin of the European Communities* **15** (3) 1982 point 2.1.102).
        The Commission submitted proposals on 20 January 1981, (*Bulletin
    of the European Communities* **14** (1) 1981 point 2.1.54), to the
    Council to supplement previous regulations (OJ L156/1–7 28.6.69)
    (Regulation 1191/69/EEC).
  - financial restructuring to provide adequate funds
  - infrastructure alterations to aim towards a Community wide ap-
    propriate rail network

o improved co-operation between rail systems

On 7 April 1981 the Commission called a meeting of experts of the Group of ten railways to prepare, on the basis of a working paper, a Commission report to the Council on co-operation. This proposal was agreed by the Council and on 11 May 1982 the Commission submitted an action programme for international railway co-operation (*Bulletin of the European Communities* **15** (5) 1982 point 2.1.137). It was concerned with the:

o effective use of all forms of transport in the ways most appropriate to each. Use of combined transport.

The Council meeting of Transport Ministers, Brussels 26 March 1981, requested priority for this development and the extension of the Community's system of combined transport (OJ L48/31–2 22.2.75) (Directive 75/130/EEC) to neighbouring countries.

Proposals for a Council resolution concerning priorities and the timetable for decisions to be taken by the Council in the transport sector during the period up to the end of 1983, have been submitted by the Commission (OJ C294/6–8 13.11.80). These have been examined by Parliament and amendments proposed (OJ C77/82–4 6.4.81).

Further information

'Community railway policy'. *Bulletin of the European Communities* **13** (12) 1980 points 1.6.1–4
'A transport network for Europe, outline of a policy'. *Bulletin of the European Communities* supplement 8/79

Joint Advisory Committee on Social Questions arising in the Railway Industry

Basic information

In 1972 the Commission decided to set up this Committee (OJ L104/9–11 3.5.72) (Decision 72/172/EEC). The previous (1971) Commission decision to set up a similar committee was revoked (OJ L57/22–4 10.3.71) (Decision 71/122/EEC).

Joint Advisory Committee – representation

Whilst the Committee consisted of 28 full and 28 alternative members in its original form, the rules are being revised to widen its terms of reference and possibly alter the number of members.

Both employees and employers organizations make recommendations to the Commission for filling these places. The appointments are for a period of three years which may be renewed.

Work of the Joint Advisory Committee

The work of the Committee is to assist the Commission by opinions on subjects of concern to it. It may also initiate action through the Commission. The Committee may set up working parties.

Further information

General report on the activities of the European Communities
   Luxembourg: Office for official publications of the European Communities, annual
Community advisory committees for the representation of socio-economic interests
   Farnborough: Saxon House for EC Economics and Social Committee, 1980. 115p. ISBN 0-566-00328-7

Road Transport

Basic information

Legislation on this subject in any one of the member states of the Community is complex. Bringing together ten sets of legislation is a difficult task. The Community decided to undertake this formidable project in a pragmatic way whereby the emphasis is laid on finding practical solutions to Community problems. Legislation started in a small way in the early 1960s. Policy was summarized in 1973 (*Bulletin of the European Communities* supplement 16/73).

Work undertaken

One of the earlier aspects of the subject which was tackled by a Council directive concerned the carriage of goods (OJ 70/2005-6 6.8.62). This dealt with the establishment of certain common rules for international transport. As with most other regulations in this section, it has been amended extensively. For example, rates for carriage of goods (OJ 194/1-5 6.8.68) (Regulation 1174/68/EEC) which concerned bracket tariffs, was supplemented by a regulation (OJ L334/22-8 24/12/77) (Regulation 2831/77/EEC) which fixed rates for the carriage of goods by road between member states.

Passenger transport by coach or bus has its own set of regulations, the basic one in 1966 (OJ 147/2688–91 9.8.66) (Regulation 117/66/EEC). Regular services between member states are covered by (OJ L67/19–24 20.3.72) (Regulation 517/72/EEC). Combined road/rail transport of goods was initiated (OJ L48/31–2 22.2.75) (Directive 75/130/EEC). These provisions were simplified in 1982 (OJ L161/11–12 12.6.82) (Regulation 1499/82/EEC). The international carriage of passengers by means of occasional coach and bus services (ASOR) is concerned with West European countries. The value of the ASOR agreement, signed in Dublin on 26.5.82, is to rationalize legislation and documentation on this subject (*Bulletin of the European Communities* 15 (5) 1982 point 2.1.136 and (6) 1982 points 2.1.154–5). The agreement was endorsed by Parliament (OJ C 182/27–8 19.7.82) and approved by Council on 12.7.82.

Vehicle insurance (OJ L103/1–3 2.5.72) (Directive 72/166/EEC). A Community style driving licence is to be issued by member states with effect from 1983 (OJ C119 16.11.72) (See entry, Driving Licence for the Community.) Limitation of driving hours by heavy goods vehicle drivers (Introduction of Tachograph) (OJ L164/1–15 27.7.70) (Regulation 1463/70/EEC). The harmonization of certain social legislation relating to road transport (OJ L77/49–60 29.3.69) (Regulation 543/69/EEC) article 17 of which called for annual reports to Council on the implementation of this regulation.

Harmonization of equipment in vehicles has been extensively covered and legislation is still being produced on various aspects of this subject eg strength of seats (OJ L221/1–9 12.8.74) (Directive 74/408/EEC) anchorages for safety belts (OJ L24/6–20 30.1.76) (Directive 76/115/EEC).

So much legislation has been produced on this subject that readers are referred to the European Community's own indexes to secondary legislation:

Annual alphabetical and methodological index to the Official Journal of the European Communities.

The last annual index can be brought up to date by appropriate monthly indexes. Earlier secondary legislation will be found in English under:

Official Journal. Special Edition. English (1952–72) London: HMSO, 1973. 31 volumes.

There is a subject index and numerical list to the 31 volumes, also produced by HMSO in 1973.

Alternative sources of information are:

Halsbury's Statutes of England – 3rd ed. v 42A European continuation volume 1952–72 updated by the latest year's cumulative supplement – volume containing European supplement.

Further information

General report on the activities of the European Communities
   Luxembourg: Office for official publications of the European Communities, annual
'A transport network for Europe, outline of a policy' in, *Bulletin of the European Communities*
supplement 8/79
Europe today, state of European integration 1980–1981
   Luxembourg: Office for official publications of the European Communities, 1981. 617p.
   ISBN 92–823–0037–4. Catalogue number AX–30–80–972–EN–C

Joint Advisory Committee on Social Questions on Road Transport

Basic information

The Commission decided to set up a Committee in 1965 (OJ 2184–2186/65 16.7.65)
(Decision 65/362/EEC).

Joint Advisory Committee – representation

Whilst at the moment there are twelve full places and twelve alternative
places for each side (carriers and wage-earners), the scope of this Committee
is being reconsidered and it may be that the responsibilities as well as the
size of the Committee may be altered. Members are appointed for three
years. This appointment may be renewed.

Work of the Joint Advisory Committee

The work of the Committee is to assist the Commission by opinions on
subjects which are of concern to it. It may also initiate action through the
Commission and it may set up working parties.

Further information

General report on the activities of the European Communities
   Luxembourg: Office for official publications of the European Communities, annual
Community advisory committees for the representation of socio-economic interests
   Farnborough: Saxon House for the EC Economic and Social Committee, 1980. 215p.
   ISBN 0–566–00328–7

Driving Licence for the Community

Basic information

Under proposals for the harmonization of aspects of Community work, was included a Community driving licence. This proposal had been considered periodically over a long period.

On 4 December 1980 the Council adopted its first directive on this subject (OJ C119 16.11.72) also commented on in *Bulletin of the European Communities* **5**(9) 1972 point 80.

Proposal

A Community style driving licence will be issued by each member state with effect from 1983 and will have mutual recognition (OJ L375/1–15 31.12.80). (Directive 80/1263/EEC)

This means that a citizen of one member country, moving to another will be able to apply to his new licencing authority for a driving licence of that country in exchange for his existing one. Further problems regarding the period of validity of driving licences, standards for driving tests, vehicle catagories, etc are being considered (*Bulletin of the European Communities* **14**(10) 1981 point 2.1.136).

Further information

Fourteenth report on the activities of the European Communities, 1980 point 421
   Luxembourg: Office for official publications of the European Communities 1981. 360p.
   ISBN 92–825–2197–4. Catalogue number CB–31–80–102–EN–C

Sea Transport

Basic information

In the late 1970s EC interest in sea transport developed considerably. Particularly was this so after the European Court of Justice laid down in a 1974 judgement, that sea transport was not exempt from the provisions of the Treaty of Rome (1957) (Case 167/73 Commission of the European Communities v. French Republic (1974) ECR p. 371/judgement and p. 380/opinion).

Purpose

The aims of the Community with regard to sea transport are to:

- promote safety on a worldwide basis through agreements issued by the international organizations
- ensure universal ratification and stringent and uniform application of these agreements including:
  safety of life at sea
  prevention of pollution by ships
  standards for merchant ships
  training of seafarers
  certificates of competence for seafarers
  rest periods aboard ship

Work undertaken

Where international agreements are not applicable or contain loopholes, they have been corrected by the Community. For example:

- directive on the use of qualified high-seas pilots in the North Sea (OJ L33/32 8.2.79) (Directive 79/115/EEC)
- minimum requirements for tankers using Community ports (OJ L33/33–5 8.2.79) (Directive 79/116/EEC)
- working conditions aboard vessels

Consultation procedure on shipping matters, between Community members and third countries has been laid down by Council decision (OJ L239/23–4 17.9.77) (Decision 77/587/EEC).

Competition from certain state-trading countries is another large problem outlined in the European Community's transport policy (see Further information) (OJ L258/35–6 21.9.78) (Decision 78/774/EEC).

Proposals for a Council resolution concerning priorities and the time table for decisions to be taken by the Council in the transport sector, during the period up to the end of 1983, have been submitted by the Commission (OJ C294/6–8 13.11.80). These have been examined by Parliament and amendments proposed (OJ C77/82–4 6.4.81).

Further information

The European Community's transport policy
   Luxembourg: Office for official publications of the European Communities, 1981. 37p.
   (European Documentation series 2–1981). ISBN 92–825–2170–2

Channel Tunnel

Basic information

There are many reports and summaries regarding the Channel Tunnel as it has been discussed since the early 19th century. One of the earliest of these was Mathieu's project in 1802. Proposals for both bridges and tunnels were submitted up to the middle 1950s when the English and French governments examined the proposition and in 1964 announced their agreement in principle to the construction of a rail tunnel. (*Proposals for a fixed Channel link*, London: HMSO, 1963. Cmnd 2137)

Current developments

A report was presented to the European Parliament (EP) on 7 and 8 May 1981 by Mr De Keersmaeker. This was the latest of many reports on this subject. Many Parliamentary questions have also been submitted. This called for the implementation of a Channel Tunnel which was thought to be of benefit to Europe as a whole and not just to England and France.

There was general agreement with the proposal in the EP debate, most speakers highlighting not only the psychological aspect but the many other benefits accruing.

The resolution in the report was passed by a very large majority (OJ C 144/48, 98–100 15.6.81) Parliamentary resolutions have been passed concerning the financing of this link (OJ C 125/81 17.5.82). Britain and France have set up a joint study group which is expected to report in the second half of 1982.

Further information

The nature and extent of possible Community interest in a fixed link across the Channel
    London: Coopers and Lybrand Associates, 1979.
Channel Tunnel Bulletin of the European Communities **14** (5) 1981 point 2.3.8
Report drawn up on behalf of the Committee on Transport on the construction of a Channel Tunnel
Rapporteur P de Keersmaeker. EP Working document 1–93/81 15.4.81.30p.

Energy Policy.

Basic information

The European treaties do not formally place on the member states responsibility for a common energy policy. However, the first of these treaties was for a Coal and steel community (ECSC). The sudden surge in oil prices in 1973/4 led to a revision of existing thoughts on energy and the development of policies to meet the new situation.

Problems of the 1970s

In 1968 the Commission submitted its initial guidelines for a Community energy policy. These had been amended before the, First summit conference of the enlarged community, 19–20 October 1972 (*Bulletin of the European Communities*, 5 (10) 1972 points 9–26) which in its final communique emphasized the need for a current policy to be worked out 'as soon as possible'. This, plus the Commission's, Problems and resources of the energy policy 1975–85, led to the first of the main, Guidelines and priority actions for the Community energy policy, issued by the Commission in 1973 (*Bulletin of the European Communities* supplement 6/73). It was concerned with relations with other consumer countries, relations with producing countries and the organization of the market. In the following year, after a Council resolution concerning a, European Community programme in science and technology (OJ C7/2–4 29.1.74), the Commission issued another communication to the Council – Energy for Europe, research and development (*Bulletin of the European Communities* supplement 5/74).

The rises in oil prices in 1973/4 were so far reaching that Community energy policy had to be revised. The Commission produced, Towards a new energy policy strategy for the European Community (*Bulletin of the European Communities*, supplement 4/74). The main change was the reduction of oil consumption from 61.4% in 1973 to a proposed 41% in 1985. The difference between these two percentages being made up in more efficient use of oil consumption and larger percentages of natural gas and nuclear energy.

Up to 1974 the measures taken were forced on the Community by the pressure of the oil crisis. Thereafter whilst the aim of the Community was to develop a long term strategy, the slowness of the administrative machine meant that there were tendencies to react to crisis situations rather than prepare for them beforehand.

Basic regulations concerning energy saving and the rational use of energy, were produced in 1978 (OJ L158/6–9 16.6.78) (Regulation 303/78/EEC). On 16.6.82 the Commission issued an evaluation of the demonstration programmes and is proposing amendments to the 1978 basic regulations.

Proposed solutions to the energy problems

In 1979, the year of the second major surge in oil prices, the Commission took stock of the situation in a communication to the Council, Energy objectives of the Community for 1990 and convergence of policies of the member states. (Stencilled document no. COM (79) 316 of 14.6.79). New objectives were specified in, Energy programme of the European Communities. (Stencilled document no. COM (79) 527 of 4.10.79), and printed as (OJ C149/1–2 18.6.80). The group of experts examining the implications of a more rapid progress towards an energy efficient society saw the problems of dependence on fluctuating outside sources, the near monopoly of any one energy source, and the disassociation of economic growth and growth in energy consumption, whilst at the same time appreciating the right of any country to exploit its natural resources. The medium term aim was a rearrangement of the percentage reliance on existing sources of energy with oil falling and all other resources growing by 1985. The longer term 1990 objectives, as seen in 1980, were:

- development of energy saving techniques to alter the ratio between economic development and energy consumption from 1 to 0.7
- reduction to 50% of Community's dependence on energy imports
- restriction of oil imports to 1978 level of 470 million tonnes
- increase in the use of solid fuels and nuclear energy
- coal production to increase to 1973 level
- increase in nuclear power station construction and a solution to the safety problem
- establishment of rational price policies
- new energy sources to be developed

Progress towards these objectives is outlined in, *Bulletin of the European Communities* **14** (2) 1981 points 1.5.1–1.5.7. On 16.6.82 the Commission commented on the effectiveness of the programme and submitted possible improvements which could be made. (*Bulletin of the European Communities* **15** (6) 1982 point 2.1.157).

The Council, in its Mandate of 30 May 1980, decided that structural changes to the community budget were required from 1982 onwards. In, *Bulletin of the European Communities* Supplement 1/81, the Commission submitted proposals to the Council on this mandate. One of these concerned energy strategy and a more detailed statement appeared in a subsequent supplement 4/81.

An energy strategy for the Community was proposed in a Commission communication of 30.9.81. On 10.2.82 the Commission sent four further communications to the Council.

These were on:

- investment in the rational use of energy.
- the nuclear aspects of the energy policy
- the role of coal

- the security of natural gas supplies (Parliament also passed a resolution on Soviet exports of natural gas to the Community (OJ C66/59-61 15.3.82) (*Bulletin of the European Communities* **15** (2) 1982 points 1.2.1-1.2.14).

See also, Alternative energy sources and Energy objectives.

Further information

'Towards a new energy policy strategy for the European Community'. *Bulletin of the European Communities* supplement 4/74
Towards a European energy policy
   Brussels: EC Directorate-General for Information, 1979. 7p. (European file 8/79). Catalogue number CC-AD-79-008-EN-C
The European Community and the energy problem
   Luxembourg: Office for official publications of the European Communities, 1980. 51p. (European documentation series 2-1980). ISBN 92-825-1695-4
An energy strategy for the Community *Bulletin of the European Communities* **14** (9) 1981 points 1.1.1-1.1.8

'A new impetus for the common policies [section 1]. The development of an energy strategy for the Community'. *Bulletin of the European Communities* supplement 4/81
European Community's energy strategy
   Luxembourg: Office for official publications of the European Communities, 1982. 7p. (European file 8/82) ISSN 0379-3133 Catalogue number CC-AD-80-008-EN-C

Energy Objectives

Basic information

As early as 5 June 1974 in a communication to the Council, the Commission forecast energy objectives. The communication had the title, 'Towards a new energy policy strategy for the European Community' (R/1472/74/(ENER28)), (*Bulletin of the European Communities* supplement 4/74). Council resolutions followed:

- on a new energy policy strategy (OJ C153/1-4 9.7.75) (qv)
- on the rational utilization of energy (OJ C153/5 9.7.75)
- on measures to be implemented to achieve this policy (OJ C153/6-8 9.7.75)
- on the reduction of oil consumption (OJ C153/9 9.7.75)

Repeated increases in the price of oil have led to energy savings which in turn have given rise to, Community energy objectives for 1990. These are based on the converging policies of member states and also the formulation of new lines of action by the Community in energy savings. They formed the basis of a resolution adopted by the Council in Luxembourg in 1980 (OJ C149/1-2 18.6.80).

A Council resolution also of 1980 submitted new lines of action by the Community in the fields of energy saving. (OJ C149/3-5 18.6.80). A series of guidelines for a basic energy-saving programme was included.

Purpose

Guidelines for a basic energy saving programme recommended to every member state includes:

- energy saving in the home for example labelling household appliances with their energy consumption (OJ C149/7–18 18.6.80)
- energy saving in industry
- energy saving in transport
- energy saving in agriculture
- energy saving in office and in commerce
- energy production
- information and education in energy savings
- sustained efforts in research, development and demonstration

Work undertaken

Energy objectives for 1990 are:

- the Community to increase its efforts to save energy and reduce oil consumption and consequently imports
- member states should submit to the Commission, on an annual basis, their energy policy programmes up to 1990
- the national energy policy programmes to be assessed by the Commission in relation to the Community's energy policy

For further details of the 1990 objectives see section, ENERGY POLICY.

Further information

Fourteenth general report on the activities of the European Communities in 1980 section 12
  Luxembourg: Office for official publications of the European Communities, 1981. 360p.
  ISBN 92–825–2197–4. Catalogue number CB–31–80–102–EN–C
Formulating and implementing a Community energy policy
Bulletin of the European Communities **14** (2) 1981 points 1.5.1–1.5.7 and **14** (3) 1981 points
2.1.150–2.1.155
Energy objectives for 1990, where does the Community stand?
  Luxembourg: Office for official publications of the European Communities, 1981. 7p.
  (European file 12/81 ISSN 0379–3133. Catalogue number CC–AD–81–012–EN–C
Bibliography on energy
  Luxembourg: Office for official publications of the European Communities, 1981. 123p.
  (Documentation Bulletin 1981. B2/1) ISSN 0378–4428

Energy Objectives – Financial Assistance

Basic information

The development of an energy policy is appropriate under articles 2 and 3 of the Treaty of Rome (1957).

In 1974 the Council adopted energy policy objectives for 1985 (OJ C153/1–4 9.7.75).

Projects benefiting under energy objectives

The first energy research programme (OJ L231/1–5 2.9.75) (Decision 75/510/EEC) covered the period 1975–9 and with a budget of 59 million ua started the pattern of aid which has been followed subsequently.

The first programme covered the following aspects:

- energy conservation   (1979–83 grant 27 million EUA)
- production and
  utilization of hydrogen   (1979–83 grant 8 million EUA)
- solar energy   (1979–83 grant 46 million EUA)
- geothermal energy   (1979–83 grant 18 million EUA)
- systems analysis   (1979–83 grant 6 million EUA)

The programme was continued by a second energy research programme covering the period 1979–83 with a budget of 105 million EUA (OJ L231/30–3 13.9.77) (Decision 79/785/EEC). In view of the proposals incorporated in the Mandate of 30 May 1980 a review of the Energy research programmes took place in 1981. It was agreed that the existing programme should be completed and that the new energy R & D programme should be integrated in the proposed Community R & D framework programme (*Bulletin of the European Communities* 15 (3) 1982 point 2.1.125).

Rules of grants

In order to develop energy research, the Community contributes towards shared cost projects as they are required to fulfil the programme outlined above.

The Commission would normally contribute up to 50% of the total cost of the project.

Financial support may also be given for demonstration projects in the field of energy savings and some 55 million EUA has been set aside for this work up to the middle of 1983. Normally a grant of between 25% and 49% is awarded (OJ L158/6–9 16.6.78) (Regulation 1303/78/EEC) the amount being authorized under (OJ L93/1 12.4.79) (Regulation 725/79/EEC). Each year saw a list of energy saving demonstration projects, for example 1982 included 18 projects with a sum of 6.8 million ECUs (*Bulletin of the European Communities* **15** (2) 1982 point 2.1.96).

Financial support is also available for demonstration projects to exploit alternative energy sources. Support may not in general exceed 40% of the cost of the project. For this aspect of the work a sum of 95 million EUA has been allocated covering aid for the whole of a 5 year programme to 1984 (OJ L158/3–5 16.6.78) (Regulation 1302/78/EEC). Authority for financial aid is under a 1979 regulation (OJ L93/2 12.4.79) (Regulation 726/79/EEC).

Similar support covering research into liquifaction and gasification of solid fuels, is available with the same financial authority (OJ L158/3–5 16.6.78) (Regulation 1302/78/EEC) (OJ L95/5–6 12.4.79) (Regulation 728/79/EEC). A sum of 50 million EUA has been allocated for this purpose. Grants for this work are normally up to 40% of the total cost.

In the case of solar energy, projects are covered and financed by the 1978 regulation mentioned above (OJ L93/3–4 12.4.79) (Regulation 727/79/-EEC). A sum of 22.5 million EUA has been allocated for demonstration projects in this field of research under regulation 726/79 quoted above. Support is up to 40% of the total project cost where projects are not less than 100,000 EUA.

With geothermal energy projects the 1978 regulation 1302 (see above) covers this work which is financed by (OJ L93/7–8 12.4.79) (Regulation 729/79/EEC). A similar sum of 22.5 million EUA has been allocated to the project with support grants of up to 40% (see regulation 726/79 quoted above).

Submission of applications

Calls for tender are usually published in the, *Official Journal*. Applications are submitted to the Commission in Brussels on the form provided by them. In the UK the Department of Energy, Thames House South, London, SW1 is willing to give advice and assistance to those interested in the projects.

For demonstration projects a similar procedure is carried out for those interested, with the Department of Energy giving advice when requested.

Work undertaken

Under the first tranche of funds in the solar energy sector, one of the many grants included a sum of 44,370 EUA towards the cost of solar heating at Tidscombe First School, Tiverton. The award was to Devon County Council.

Further information

General report on the activities of the European Communities
  Luxembourg: Office for official publications of the European Communities, annual
Scott, Gay
A guide to European Community grants and loans – 2nd ed
  Biggleswade: Euroinformation Limited, 1981. 111p. ISBN 0-907304-01-X
Grants and loans from the European Community
  Luxembourg: Office for official publications of the European Communities, 1981. 83p. (European documentation series 7-8/1981). ISBN 92-825-2633-X. Catalogue number CB-NC-81-008-EN-C
Official sources of finance and aid for industry in the UK
  London: National Westminster Bank Limited, Commercial information market intelligence department, 1981. 67p.
European Community demonstration scheme for energy saving projects, Fourth round April 1982. Notes for applicants.
  London: Department of Energy, 1982. (ETSU/DEn)

Alternate Energy Sources

Basic information

Since the start of the current oil problem in 1973 the Community has been examining the situation with increasing urgency. In 1978 finance was granted to projects exploiting alternative energy resources and to demonstration projects in the field of energy saving (OJ L158/6-9 16.6.78) (Regulation 1303/78/EEC) and (OJ L93/1 12.4.79) (Regulation 725/79/EEC) See also last item under, Further information, below.

Purpose

New energy sources for the Community are important as in 1978, 57% of all energy consumed (mostly oil) was imported. Currently the ten are making strenuous efforts to save energy resources by:

- conserving supplies. A Council meeting in March 1979 decided that for the year, oil consumption should not exceed 500 million tonnes (*Bulletin of the European Communities* 13 (3) 1979 points 1.1.6 and 2.1.108). In 1980 a recommendation was sent by the Commission to member states on the rational use of energy in industry (OJ L239/26-38 12.9.80) (Recommendation 80/823/EEC)
- greater utilization of coal. A forecast of coal supply and demand within the Community up to the year 2,000 was contained in a report from the

Commission to the Council of 21.3.80 (OJ C174/1–49 14.7.80)
- developing nuclear power. In 1979 the Council increased the amount of EURATOM loans to help finance the building of nuclear power stations from 500 million EUA to 1,000 million EUA. However, by 1980 total Community nuclear generating capacity was only approximately 33 GWe.
- developing new energy sources, solar, geothermal, etc. In 1978 a call for the submission of projects on new energy sources was made (OJ L158/3–9 16.6.78) (Regulations 1302–3/78/EEC). In 1981 the Commission decided to support 58 of the replies (*Bulletin of the European Communities* **14** (6) 1981. point 2.1.132)
- undertaking research into long term solutions. These include thermonuclear fusion and a, Fusion review panel was set up in 1980. A research programme covering 1982–6 has been sent to the Council (*Bulletin of the European Communities* **13** (11) point 2.1.112 and **14** (7/8) points 2.1.149–2.1.152).

Work undertaken

To date the EC has:
- extended its R and D programmes into new energy sources through the Community's Joint Research Centre (JRC) at Ispra in Italy, whose programme for new energies 1980–3 proposes more than 200 researchers and 85.7 million EUAs. This sum includes 25.8 m EUA for solar energy research, for hydrogen research 15.5 m EUA, for thermonuclear fusion technology 28.5 m EUA. Subsequently a proposed 5 year development programme, mentioned above, was thought likely to cost ECU 1,504.3 million, etc
- other research has been undertaken on the basis of shared cost contracts where the Community had allocated 59 m EUA during the period 1975–9 and 105 m EUA for the period 1979–83

Solar energy, according to Community experts, will supply 5–10% of our energy supplies by the year 2000. Community research is concerned with investigations on:
- evaluation of solar rays. Monthly solar radiation map for Europe, 1980 –
- use of solar energy in the home
- development of solar power stations. First to come into operation, 'Eurelios', is at Adrano in Sicily 1981. It is currently adding 1 MVe to the national electricy grid (Bulletin of the European Communities **10** (11) 1977 point 2.1.105 and **14** (5) 1981, point 2.1.120)
- photovoltaic power generation. Research is being undertaken at the European solar testing installation (ESTI) based with the JRC establishment at Ispra, Italy (*Bulletin of the European Communities* **14** (9) points 2.1.136–2.1.137)
- photoelectrochemicals

- biomass of organic matter ('green fuel') (*Bulletin of the European Communities* **13** (11)point 2.1.116)

Geothermal energy researched by a 4 year programme 1975–9 (OJ L231/1–5 2.9.75) (Decision 75/510/EEC) and continued in a second programme 1979–83 (OJ L231/30–3 13.9.79) (Decision 79/785/EEC), is being investigated by 13 projects and in three ways:

- high energy geothermics providing water at over 150°C. First project at Lardarello in Tuscany which has been in operation since 1904
- low energy geothermics has a potential of supplying direct heat in houses, etc through a heat exchanger
- hot rock geothermics by the use of rock fractures and the injection of water under pressure. A project is currently being conducted in Cornwall

A proposed Community geothermal resource atlas was discussed by the Geothermal Resources and Reserves Working Party, in February 1982.

Controlled thermonuclear fusion is being examined by researchers, on an inertia and also a magnetic confinement system. Research is integrated at the Joint Research Centre, and covers the member states, Sweden and Switzerland. Expenditure 1979–83 is 190 million ECU. Europe is jointly building, at Culham near Oxford, a Joint European Torus (JET) which is after the pattern of the Russian Tokamak (1958), a most advanced experiment on fusion research, utilizing a magnetic confinement system. The Community is also to participate in financing a general fusion programme designed to promote research on smaller tokamaks. A budget of 301 million ECU has been allocated (*Bulletin of the European Communities* **15** (5) 1982 point 2.1.148).

Hydrogen as a means of transporting energy is being developed. In 1978 for the first time hydrogen was produced in a continuous fashion by thermochemical means by the Community's Joint Research Centre.

In March 1982 Parliament adopted a resolution on research into the use of wind energy, the Commission being asked to submit a proposal (OJ C87/107–8 5.4.82).

Further information

Solar energy for development, proceedings of the international conference held at Varese, Italy, March 26–29, 1979 by the Commission of the European Communities
    The Hague: Martinus Nijhoff for the Commission of the European Communities, 1979. 240p. ISBN 90–247–2239–X
Community action in nuclear safety
    Brussels: EC Directorate-General for Information, 1979. 7p. (European File 15/79). Catalogue number CC–AD–80–002–EN–C
New energy sources for the Community
    Brussels: EC Directorate-General for Information, 1980. 7p. (European File 1980/2). Catalogue number CC–AD–80–002–EN–C

Environmental Resources Limited. *Environmental impact of energy stratiegies within the EEC*
   Oxford: Pergamon Press for the Commission of the European Communities, 1980. 155p. ISBN 0–08–025681–3
European Community demonstration scheme for energy saving projects, third round January–April 1981. Notes for applicants
   London: Department of Energy, 1980. not paged. (ETSU/DEn)

Solar Energy

Basic information

It is expected that by the year 2000 solar energy will account for some 5–10% of energy requirements in industrial countries and 4% in developing countries. With the energy problems of 1973 and 1979 the development of alternative sources of energy have been researched with greater intensity. One of the most useful is solar energy.

Work undertaken

Under the Lomé convention, co-operation began between the ACP and the EC on solar energy. On 15 March 1977 the Commission approved the financing by the European Development Fund (EDF) of the very first project involving the use of solar energy – a solar pump to irrigate a 20 hectare rice growing area in the Senegal river valley in Mauritania. Since then many other solar developments have taken place as examples of ACP/EEC co-operation.

The European Economic Commission organized an international conference on solar energy in Italy, 26–29 March 1979, at which some 300 delegates were invited to exchange experiences in solar energy development. Previously, in September and October 1978, five preparatory regional seminars were held in Nairobi, East Africa; Bamoko, West Africa; Amman for the Arab countries; Caracas for Latin America and New Delhi for South and South East Asia. Subsequent international conferences have been held, the fourth being at Stresa in Italy from 10–14.5.82. (*Bulletin of the European Communities* 15 (5) 1982 point 2.1.149).

The Joint Research Centre (JRC) at Ispra in Italy, Geel in Belgium, Karlsruhe in the Federal Republic of Germany and Petten in the Netherlands, have produced a multiannual research programme running from 1977–80. This new programme includes new forms of energy production including solar energy. The JRC will pursue a number of its own projects on this subject including the European Solar Test Installation (ESTI) project, the Habitat project and basic research on new conversion and storage processes.

In 1981 the EC was represented at the UN Conference on, New and renewable sources of energy, held in Nairobi, Kenya in August of that year. Solar energy was one of the major themes (*Bulletin of the European Communities* **14** (7/8) 1981 points 2.2.15–2.2.17).

The first solar power station – Eurelios – came into force in 1981 (qv Alternate energy sources).

Further information

General report on the European Communities
    Luxembourg: Office for official publications of the European Communities, annual
Solar energy; a new area of ACP–EEC co-operation
    Brussels: EC Spokesman's Group and Director-General for Information, 1979. 15p.
    (Europe Information, Development series.) Catalogue number CC–NA–79–DO4–EN–C
Solar energy for development, proceedings of the International Conference held at Varese Italy, 26–29 March 1979, by the Commission of the European Communities
    The Hague: Martinus Nijhoff for the Commission of the European Communities, 1979. 240p. ISBN 90–247–2239–X

5 Common Social and Environmental Development

Many of the subjects in this chapter though considered in the founding treaties, have been developed and the legislation of member states harmonized, only comparatively recently. These are extremely broad subject fields having extensive legislation in practically all member states. Bringing together the many and varied strands of this legislation takes time and it is likely to be many years yet before the bulk of the law has a degree of uniformity throughout the Community.

As with the two previous chapters on economic development and industrial and energy policies, this chapter treats its subject in a broad way, as will be seen by the inclusion of education leading on to aspects of technical training.

The first few sections are concerned with social development and the social services:

Labour and employment problems, whilst always of concern to the Communities as will be seen from the ECSC treaty articles, have become of very much greater importance during the latter half of the 1970s and the 1980s:

FOR A DETAILED INDEX SEE THE YELLOW PAGES.

- **Advisory committee on safety, hygiene and health protection at work** (pages 221–2)

A subject linked to employment and of special importance in a Europe divided into so many comparatively small countries is the right to move freely from one country to another and retain social security benefits and other advantages:

- **Mobility of labour** (pages 222–3)
  Advisory committee on freedom of movement for workers (pages 223–4)
  Technical committee on freedom of movement for workers (pages 224–5)
  Administrative commission on social security for migrant workers (page 226)
  Advisory committee on social security for migrant workers (page 227)

Equal opportunities and consumer affairs are related subjects of importance throughout the member states. Harmonization of existing legislation and the development of new laws to benefit the disadvantaged, have grown apace during the 1970s and 1980s:

- **Women in the Community** (pages 228–9)
- **Standing liaison group for equal opportunities** (pages 229–30)
- **Consumer affairs** (pages 231–3)   or
  Consumers' consultative committee (pages 233–4)
- **Handicapped persons** (pages 234–5)
- **European foundation for the improvement of living and working conditions** (page 235–6)

The protection and improvement of the environment and the conservation of both areas of interest and beauty and records of past work and history are of value in a community which has such a large industrial growth, and areas of dense population:

- **Environment** (pages 236–9)
  Environmental research programme – financial assistance (pages 239–242)
- **Natural heritage conservation** (pages 242–3)
- **Pollution control** (pages 243–6)
  Advisory committee on the control and reduction of pollution caused by hydrocarbons discharged at sea (pages 276–7)

Within the Community the co-ordination of education and training are subjects which have become of growing interest to the Communities since the 1970s. Special attention has been paid to technical training:

- **Education** (pages 277–9)
  Eurydice network (pages 249–250)
- **European Documentation Centres** (EDCs) (pages 250–6)
- **European Foundation** (pages 256–7)
- **Paul Finet Foundation** (page 257)

- **Diplomas and professional qualifications, mutual recognition** (pages 258–261)
- **Advisory committee for vocational training** (pages 261–2)
- **European centre for the development of vocational training** (CEDEFOP) (pages 263–4)
- **Advisory committee on medical training** (pages 264–5)
  Advisory committee on training in nursing (pages 265–6)
  Advisory committee on the training of midwives (pages 266–7)
- **Advisory committee on the training of dental practitioners** (page 267)
- **Public health** (page 268)
  Committee of senior officials on public health (pages 268–9)
- **Pharmacy** (pages 269–270)
  Committee for proprietary medical products (pages 270–271)

Social Development

Basic information

The Commission in accordance with article 122 of the Treaty establishing the European Economic Community (1957) (for details see under Further information), produces a, *Report on social development,* Luxembourg: Office for official publications of the European Communities, annual.

The reports include a survey of the political situation, a summary of the social actions of the community in the year reviewed, an outline of activities by the institutions of the EC in the social field, and a description by aspect of social development (eg housing, family affairs, etc). There are also a number of statistical tables in each report.

Work undertaken

Up to 1971 development was by sector only. In 1974 as a result of the publication of a Community social policy (OJ C13/1–4 12.2.74) there was given impetus to a wider action programme covering employment protection, migrant workers, living and working conditions, equality of men and women, measures to combat poverty, etc (qv).

Related summaries will be found under the following headings, Economic and Social committee, Women in the community, European social fund, Social security, Employment, Mobility of labour and a number of related advisory committees.

Further information

European information service
London: International union of local authorities, British section and Council of European municipalities, British section, 10 issues per year, 1979–. ISSN 0261-2747 [Designed to inform local authorities of developments in the EC likely to have an impact on the services they provide]
Report on social developments
Luxembourg: Office for official publications of the European Communities, annual
Treaties establishing the European Communities
Luxembourg: Office for official publications of the European Communities, 1973. 1502p.
The European social budget
Luxembourg: Office for official publications of the European Communities, quinquennial (1970–5)
The Common Market and the common good
Brussels: Commission of the European Communities, nd. 33p.
Social indicators for the European Community 1960–75
Luxembourg: Office for official publications of the European Communities, 1977. 488p. Catalogue number CA-22-77-766-6A-C
Community advisory committees for the representation of socio-economic interests, the machinery for the consultation and participation of socio-economic interest in Community decision making
Farnborough: Saxon House for EC Economic and Social Committee, 1980. 215p. ISBN 0-566-00328-7
Social policy of the European Community 2nd ed
Luxembourg: Office for official publications of the European Communities, 1981. 51p. (Documentation series 3/1981) ISBN 92-825-2411-6. Catalogue number CB-NC-81-003-EN-C

European Social Fund

Basic information

In part 3, concerning social policy, of the Treaty establishing the European Economic Community (1957) chapter 2 makes provision for the establishment of a European social fund (articles 123, 124, 153). Council, Rules of the Fund, made the necessary arrangements for its entry into force (OJ 56/1201–2 31.8.60).

The Fund underwent a substantial reform in 1971 (OJ L28/15–17 4.2.71) (Decision 71/66/EEC).

Extent of the cover

The purpose of these changes was to transform the Fund into an instrument for a more active employment policy and to link it more effectively with Community policy objectives (Regulation 858/72/EEC). It was decided that a series of reports on the European social fund should be produced. The first was issued in 1973 and covered the period May to December 1972. Subsequent reports are on an annual basis. The work of the Fund was reviewed and the 1971 reforms implemented in 1977 (OJ

L337/1–4 27.12.77) (Regulation 2893/77/EEC). The 1972 administrative and financial procedures were also amended in 1977 (OJ L337/5–6 27.12.77) (Regulation 2894/77/EEC). A new regulation on operations qualifying for a higher rate of intervention was issued (OJ L337/7 27.12.77) (Regulation 2895/77/EEC).

The 1971 reforms were again reformed (OJ L337/8–9 27.12.77) (Decision 77/801/EEC) and article 4 of the earlier Decision was separately amended (OJ L337/10–11 27.12.77) (Decision 77/802/EEC) as was action for migrant workers (OJ 337/12–13 27.12.77) (Decision 77/803/EEC) and action for women (OJ 337/14 27.12.77) (Decision 77/804/EEC).

Those wishing to make applications under the Fund are advised to see the last item but one under, Further information – a *Guide for possible applicants*, and also, *Guidelines for the management of the European social fund for the period 1981–1983* (OJ C119/2–8 14.5.80). These were extended and enlarged for 1983 (OJ C133/13 25.5.82).

Immediately prior to the publication of these guidelines, the Fund's list of priority regions based on youth unemployment had been amended (OJ C42/3–4 27.2.81). In the UK the regions included are North, North West, Wales, Scotland, Northern Ireland.

New rules of the European social fund came into force on 1 January 1983. (*Bulletin of the European Communities* **14** (12) 1981 point 2.1.58 and **15** (1) 1982 point 2.1.27).

Further information

General report on the activities of the European Communities
   Luxembourg: Office for official publications of the European Communities, annual
Report on social development
   Luxembourg: Office for official publications of the European Communities, annual
The European social budget
   Luxembourg: Office for official publications of the European Communities, quinquennially (1970–5)
Treaties establishing the European Communities
   Luxembourg: Office for official publications of the European Communities, 1973. 1502p.
Practical handbook of social security for employed persons and their families moving within the Community
   Luxembourg: Office for official publications of the European Communities for the Commission of the European Communities, 1973. (loose-leaf). Catalogue number CE–28–79–035–EN–C
Social indicators for the European Community, 1960–1975
   Luxembourg: Office for official publications of the European Communities, 1977. 488p.
The European social fund, what it does, who can apply, how to apply
   London: Department of Employment, Jan 1981. 28p.
Social policy of the European Community 2nd ed
   Luxembourg: Office for official publications of the European Communities, 1981. 51p. (Documentation series 3/1981) ISBN 92–825–2411–6. Catalogue number CB–NC–81–003–EN–C

European Social Fund – Financial Assistance

Basic information

The fund was set up in 1958 to assist in, 'Rendering the employment of workers easier and increasing their geographical and occupational mobility within the Community' (article 123 of the Treaty of Rome, 1957).

This was extended in 1971 and 1977 to participate more fully in the private sector and also to assist the socially disadvantaged (OJ L28/15–17 4.2.71) (Decision 71/66/EEC) and (OJ L337/8–9 27.12.77) (Decision 77/801/EEC).

Current guidelines for the management of the Fund during the period 1981–3 were published in 1980 (OJ C119/2–8 14.5.80).

Beneficiaries under the Fund

- those leaving agriculture who require retraining
- those working in the textile or clothing sector or leaving it
- migrant workers
- handicapped persons requiring entry or re-entry into full or part time work
- women 25 or over who have lost their job or are seeking work for the first time
- unemployed young people, 25 or under
- persons unemployed threatened with loss of work, underemployed, or forced to give up a self-employed job or those from areas of high unemployment
- workers who need their qualifications upgraded

Support which can be provided

Aid can be given for:

- training courses, including the training of instructors
- financial support for trainees
- support for those having to change their residence to follow their trade and costs involved in their reintegration in a new location
- aid to handicapped persons to facilitate the adaptation of jobs to their needs and abilities or to facilitate their change, adaptation or re-adaptation
- aid to those of 50 or over to maintain their salary levels during the first six months of their vocational retraining or change
- aid to undertakings to make up the salary of inexperienced staff whose output is lower than that expected from the qualifications held or those workers undergoing retraining

- aid to promote the recruitment of staff under 25 years old
- aid to those providing work experience for unemployed under 25 (with certain exceptions)

Rates of grants

- for operations undertaken by the public sector, the Fund supplies 50% of eligible expenditure
- for operations undertaken by the private sector the Fund contributes an amount equal to any expenditure borne by the public authority
- the Fund's contributions can be increased by 10% in areas with particularly serious and prolonged unemployment
- for pilot schemes the Fund may not contribute more than 50% of the cost
- for studies the contribution is usually 50% but may be higher

Payment

- an amount equal to 30% of the assistance is paid as an advance, as soon as the member state certifies that the operation has begun
- a second advance of not more than the first is paid once half the project has been completed
- the balance is paid as soon as a claim for payment of the completed project has been received from the member state

Submission of applications

- to the employment authorities (Dept of Employment, Division B 2 Marsham Street, London, SW1) of the member state before the project is carried out

Work undertaken

Two examples from many available are:

- in 1980 the Commission proposed to launch an integrated operation to assist Belfast. The total sum involved was £432 million made up from the various aid support agencies of the Community. Of this sum £50 million was for improving social and industrial infrastructure. The plan has been submitted by the UK and Northern Ireland authorities and in August 1981 it is being considered in the Community (see, Europe 81,

issues for August/September, October and November 1981)
- from the Social fund statistics for 1978, during that year some 198,000 people in the UK benefitted from retraining schemes, Youth employment programmes, etc which were supported by the Fund.

Further information

Guidelines for the management of the European social fund for the period 1981–1983 (OJ C119/2–8 14.5.80)
Scott, Gay
Guide to European Community grants and loans – 2nd ed
   Biggleswade: Euroinformation Limited, 1981. 111p. ISBN 0–907304–01–X
The European social fund, what it does, who can apply, how to apply
   London: Department of Employment, January 1981. 28p.
Grants and loans from the European Community
   Luxembourg: Office for official publications of the European Communities, 1981. 83p. (European documentation series 7–8/1981). ISBN 92–825–2633–X. Catalogue number CB–NC–81–008–EN–C
European Community textile industry
   Luxembourg: Office for official publications of the European Communities, 1982. 7p. (European file 7/82) ISSN 0379–3133. Catalogue number, CC–AD–82–007–EN–C

Advisory Committee on the European Social Fund

Basic information

Established under article 124 of the Treaty of Rome (1957). The rules governing the Committee were laid down in 1960 by the Council (OJ 1201/60 31.8.60) now extensively changed, including (OJ L91/25 12.4.68) amending rules of the Committee and (OJ L249/54–8 10.11.71) (Regulation 2396/71/EEC) on the reform of the European Social Fund.

Advisory Committee – representation

The Committee consists of two full government members, two trade union members and two employers' association members from each member state. In addition there are single alternative members from each of these groups, also from every member state. Appointments are made by the Council. The alternative member automatically takes part in committee discussions when either or both of the full members are absent. He may also attend meetings when the full members are present, but may only participate with the agreement of the chairman and full members. Outside experts may be invited by the chairman when the committee agrees. Several organizations represented on the Standing committee on employment have also been invited to attend meetings as observers.

Work of the Advisory Committee

The Committee's duties include the following:

- produce opinions regarding questions on, or support from, the Fund when requested by Community organizations
- produce opinions regarding the work of the Fund when it considers these necessary
- consult the Standing committee on employment on a number of subjects including:
  matters concerning the Fund, proposals to Council regarding subjects which fall under its purview, applications for assistance from the Fund, the possibility of amending Regulation 2396/71/EEC (OJ L249/54 10.11.71), matters concerned with implementing the Council decision of 1 February 1971 on the reform of the European Social Fund, the desirability of reinserting article 126 into the Treaty of Rome (deleted on the accession of the three new members in 1973).
  Establishment of working groups as appropriate

A working group has been established to examine applications made to the Fund.

Further information

General report on the activities of the European Communities
  Luxembourg: Office for official publications of the European Communities, annual
Community advisory committees for the representation of socio-economic interests
  Farnborough: Saxon House for EC Economic and Social Committee, 1980. 115p. ISBN 0–566–00328–7

Social Action Programme

Basic information

Under article 2 of the Treaty of Rome (1957) the EEC has the duty 'to promote throughout the Community a harmonious development of economic activities . . . an accelerated raising of the standard of living, . . .'.

The Council adopted its, Social action programme by a 1974 resolution (OJ C13/1–4. 12.2.74).

Purpose of the Programme

Council objectives under this Programme during the years 1974–6 were outlined under the following headings:

- attainment of full and better employment in the Community
- improvement of living and working conditions throughout the member states of the Community
- increased involvement of management and labour in the economic and social decisions of the Community and of workers in the life of undertakings

The Council laid great emphasis on all concerned with Community development having the Social action programme in mind whilst making their own proposals and carrying out their duties.

Work undertaken

- one of the earlier actions within this programme was a study of poverty within the Community (qv)
- the problem of harmonizing legislation on equal pay for men and women received a boost through proposals in this programme (qv Women in the Community)
- the harmonization of legislation on social security amongst member states (qv and also European social fund)
- protection of workers threatened with unemployment (qv Employment and Tripartite conferences on employment)
- housing for the socially deprived (qv Social security)
- migrant workers housing, living conditions, voting rights, etc (qv Administrative commission on social security of migrant workers)
- promotion of full employment (qv Tripartite conferences)
- vocational training programme (qv Advisory committee for vocation training)

Further information

General report on the activities of the European Communities
    Luxembourg: Office for official publications of the European Communities, annual
Report on social development (prior to 1979, Report on the development of the social situation in the European Community)
    Luxembourg: Office for official publication of the European Communities, annual
Social policy of the Euopean Community, 2nd ed
    Luxembourg: Office for official publications of the European Communities, 1981. 51p. (Documentation series 3/1981) ISBN 92–825–2411–6. Catalogue number CB–NC–81–003–EN–C
Social policy of the European Community
    Luxembourg: Office for official publications of the European Community, 1982. 7p. (European file 13/82) ISSN 0379–3133. Catalogue number CC–AD–812–013–EN–C

Poverty in the European Communities

Basic information

Article 2 of the Treaty of Rome (1957) mentions the need for a rising standard of living. Whilst most will agree that over the last quarter century this has been taking place, yet few would pretend that poverty has been eliminated even if rags and hunger are rare.

Under the Social action programme (OJ C13/1-4 12.2.74) a major change in policy was initiated which has continued and developed in subsequent years as may be seen from the annual, Report on social development (see, Further information).

Purpose of the Social Action Programme on poverty

The first five year European programme of pilot schemes and studies to combat poverty, usually known as the, European anti-poverty programme, covers the period to 1981. A first report from the Commission to the Council was produced in 1977 and a detailed second report in 1979 (COM (79) 537 final).

The definition of poverty on page 5 of the second report mentioned above is a relative one. The programme is an attempt to lift action and research above the national level so that workers in the programme may pool their experiences and learn from each other.

Whilst the majority of schemes are national ones to understand local conditions and problems and provide practical solutions, a certain number of cross-national studies, which are comparative studies, have also been initiated.

The national projects were supported on a shared cost basis, 50% by the national group or authority and 50% by the EC. The cross-national projects were funded wholly by the EC.

The projects tested and developed new methods of helping the poor or those likely to fall into this category.

Work of the Programme

The cross-national projects covered:

- poverty and social policy in Europe. An examination of social security in Bristol, Reims and Saarbrucken
- perception of poverty in Europe when some 8,600 people throughout the member states were interviewed to understand how they perceived poverty. In Britain the survey covered Waltham Forest (London) and the Fenland

- transmission of poverty, an examination of the extent to which poverty was transmitted from one generation to the next
- poverty amongst gypsies and nomads. Organized by the Catholic University of Louvain

The national projects varied considerably according to local needs. In Britain the projects were:

- joint family day-centres project. Six schemes in London and one in Liverpool. The London centres include one run by ATD (Aide à toute détresse, an international organization sometimes referred to as the Fourth World); Downtown family centre, Rotherhithe; Camden, Family service unit 'drop in' centre; Croydon, Gingerbread play centre for single parent families; Defoe day care centre; and the London, Voluntary service council – Family groups project. In Liverpool there is the, Personal service society, family clubhouse project
- area resource centres in South Wales, Glasgow and London. The first supported by the Commission was the, South Wales anti-poverty action centre limited; the Govan, Area resource centre; the London, Voluntary service council – community work service
- Craigmillar festival society – Edinburgh
- Edinburgh, social and community development programme
- Wolverhampton, tribunal representation unit
- Northern Ireland, voluntary organizations, areas of special need and welfare rights

Further information

Report on social developments
   Luxembourg: Office for official publications of the European Communities, annual
Second report of the European programme of pilot schemes and studies to combat poverty
   Luxembourg: Office for official publications of the European Communities, for the Commission, 1979. 124p. (COM(79) 537 final)
Combating poverty
   London: European Communities Commission, London office, 1979. 3p. (ISEC/B51/79)
Scott, Gay
Guide to European Community grants and loans – 2nd ed
   Biggleswade: Euroinformation Limited, 1981. 111p. ISBN 0–907304–01–X

Social Security

Basic information

Social security is covered by article 51 of the Treaty of Rome (1957) establishing the European Economic Community. Under a Council regulation of 25 October 1958 wage earners became entitled to social security benefit irrespective of the country in which they are working within the EC.

The major regulation was in 1971 (OJ L149/2–49 5.7.71) (Regulation 1408/71/EEC) on the application of social security schemes to employed persons and their families moving within the Community. In the following year the procedure for implementing regulation 1408 mentioned above, was published (OJ L74/1–75 27.3.72) (Regulation 574/72/EEC) and again in the following year was amended (OJ L86/1–25 31.3.73) (Regulation 878/73/EEC). This legislation replaced previous bilateral or multilateral agreements between member states.

Purpose

By 1979 some two million persons per year were estimated to be benefiting from these regulations. They cover most aspects of social security including sickness and maternity benefits, invalidity, old age and death, accidents at work, occupational diseases, death grants, unemployment, family benefits and allowances. Social security was extended to self-employed workers moving within the Community on 27 November 1980 by the Council approving 1977 and 1978 Commission regulations (*Bulletin of the European Communities* **13** (11) 1980 point 2.1.34).

Work undertaken

An, Administrative commission was set up under the 1971 regulation. It was formed from a government representative from each of the member states assisted where necessary by expert advisers. A representative of the Commission is to attend meetings. The Administrative commission is also assisted in technical matters by the International Labour Office (ILO). Its work is to deal with queries concerning the interpretation of the 1971 regulation (Regulation 1408) and subsequent amendments, translate appropriate documents, foster co-operation between member states in social security matters, draw up details of the accounts of the social security schemes and to submit proposals to the Commission for the improvement of the service. An, Advisory committee on social security for migrant workers, was also set up under Regulation 1408 of 1971. See entry under title for details.

European social budgets. (*Bulletin of the European Communities* **11** (7/8) 1978. point 2.1.59). On 9 November 1972 the Council instructed the Commission to prepare a social budget based on the social accounts of the Community in order to obtain a fuller picture of social protection within the EC. The first social budget was forwarded to the Council in December 1974 and covered 1970–5. Guidelines for a second social budget were adopted by the Council on 30 April 1976 (*Bulletin of the European Communities* **9** (4) 1976. point 2221). This second budget covering the years 1976–80 was forwarded by the Commission to the Council, Parliament and the Economic and Social Committee on 28 July 1978. Parliament passed a resolution on it (OJ C127/20–21 21.5.79) and the ESC an opinion (*Bulletin of the European Communities* **12** (10) 1979, point 2.3.93).

Further information

General report on the activities of the European Communities
   Luxembourg: Office for official publications of the European Communities, annual
Working in the EEC, a guide to your rights
   Luxembourg: Office for official publications of the European Communities, 1980. 30p.
   ISBN 92-825-1835-3 Catalogue number CB-30-80-277-EN-C
Comparative tables of the social security systems in the member states of the European Communities, 11th ed.
   Luxembourg: Office for official publications of the European Communities, 1981 (biennial)
   119p ISBN 92-825-2334-9.Catalogue number CB-31-80-376-EN-C

Employment

Basic information

In the Treaty of Rome (1957) a number of articles are concerned directly with employment and rather more have an indirect association. Article 117 deals with improved working conditions and standard of living. Article 118 deals with close co-operation between member states particularly in employment. Articles 119, 120 and 121 are concerned with equal pay, holidays with pay and social security for migrant workers, all related to employment. Articles 123-8 concern the social fund and a common vocational training policy. On all of these articles there is a growing body of legislation.

Community responsibilities

The Economic Communities traditional responsibilities concerning the labour force are rooted in improved employment opportunities, free movement of workers (qv mobility of labour), eradication of discrimination between Community nationals (qv diplomas and professional qualifications, mutual recognition), social security entitlement (qv) and European social fund and Social development (qv), rising living and working conditions, and employment of the disabled (qv Handicapped persons).

Through the, Standing committee on employment (qv), contacts have been made between both sides in industry, the governments of member states and the Community. Through a series of Tripartite conferences on employment (qv), efforts were made to try and resolve problems relating to employment with special reference to the current fundamental difficulties over the economic situation (see, *Bulletin of the European Communities* **14** (4) 1981 points 1.1.1-1.1.11 and **14** (5) 1981 point 2.1.34).

Work undertaken

Community policy concerning a social action programme has been outlined (OJ C13/1–4 12.2.74). Policy on stability of growth and full employment in the Community is recorded (OJ L63/19–20 5.3.74) (Directive 74/121/EEC), vocational rehabilitation of handicapped persons (OJ C80/30–2 9.7.74) action by the Social fund for handicapped persons (OJ L185/22–3 9.7.74) (Decision 74/328/EEC), programme on social security for migrant workers (OJ 28/561 and 28/597 16.12.58), action by the Social fund for persons affected by employment difficulties (OJ L199/36 30.7.75) (Decison 75/459/EEC), productive re-employment of workers through the Social fund (OJ 1189 31.8.60) (Regulation 9/60/EEC), guidelines for a Community labour market policy (OJ C168/1–4 8.7.80). All of this basic legislation has been amended considerably (see under, Further information).

At the request of Council, the Commission (June 1977) undertook a detailed review of youth unemployment and produced a booklet on its findings (Youth employment, mentioned in Further information, below).

Through the European system for the international clearing of vacancies (SEDOC) (qv), existing placement schemes have been widened. Use has been made of employment offices and job centres. A training programme for those in the offices and centres has been started, to improve the service.

In October 1980 Henk Vredeling, the EC Commissioner for Social Affairs, submitted proposals for maintaining the information flow to workers of details of their organization or firm and the introduction of a type of collective bargaining to areas of company policy. These were known as the Vredeling proposals and carried the title, Proposal for a directive on procedures for informing and consulting the employees of undertakings with complex structures, in particular transnational [Multinational] undertakings (OJ C297/3–8 15.11.80) and (*Bulletin of the European Communities* supplement 3/80). It followed a directive relating to the protection of employees in the event of the insolvency of their employer (OJ L283/23–7 28.10.80) (Directive 80/987/EEC). They supplement a series of directives on Company law which included disclosure requirements on employers (*Bulletin of the European Communities* **13** (10) 1980 points 1.3.1–1.3.4) and last item under Further information below.

Current problems on employment were discussed on 16 March 1982 at meetings of Directors-General for Employment. These problems were considered at a meeting of the European Council on the 29th and 30th of the same month (*Bulletin of the European Communities* **15** (3) 1982 points 1.3.2, 1.3.5, 1.3.7–1.3.8). It was agreed that the situation called for quick-acting measures. Vocational training and work experience for young people was again emphasized. The Council was asked to convene a special meeting to study specific measures to promote employment and would report back to the European Council meeting at the end of 1982.

Further information

'Youth employment', *Bulletin of the European Communities* supplement 4/77
'From the tripartite conference to the European Council'. *Bulletin of the European Communities* **10** (6) 1977 points 1.1.1–1.1.7
'The fourth tripartite conference'. *Bulletin of the European Communities* **11** (11) 1978 points 1.3.1–1.3.6
Guide to EEC legislation – Chapters 28 and 29
   Amsterdam: North Holland Publishing Company, 1979. 2v. ISBN 0–444–85320–0. [In English, French and German. Particularly useful for minor and supplementary regulations]
Hutchinson, E A S and Thomas, R C H.
Company law in Europe; the Vth directive and the harmonization programme
   London: Institute of Directors, 1982. 69p. ISBN 0–900–939–00–21
'Protection of the rights of temporary workers'. (*Bulletin of the European Communities* **15** (4) 1982 points 1.2.1–1.2.8

Standing Committee on Employment

Basic information

Under article 104 of the Treaty of Rome (1957) and as a result of proposals at the first, Tripartite conference (qv) the Council under article 145 established a, Standing committee on employment, in 1970 (OJ L273/25–6 17.12.70) (Decision 70/532/EEC). It ceased work in 1973 and resumed its activities again in December 1975 (OJ L21/17–18 28.1.75) (Decision 75/62/EEC) after amendments to the 1970 constitution.

Standing Committee on Employment – representation

- ministers of labour from member states
- representatives of the employers' organization (UNICE) (qv)
- representatives of the workers' organization (ETUC) (qv)
- representatives from the Commission

Work of the Standing Committee on Employment

Its work consists of analysing employment prospects in the future. For example in 1977 it was looking at prospects up to 1980.

It is considering especially:

- young people in employment
- work sharing
- employment premiums
- revision of the European social fund (qv)

- the co-ordination of the Communities financial instruments
- employment of women
- migrant workers
- co-ordination of employment policies
- development of meetings between branches of industry

It produces reports, studies, films (eg 'Equal chances equal opportunities' (on the employment of women)).

It has regular meetings on employment eg 17th meeting in Brussels on 26 February 1980 discussed amongst other things:

- employment in the light of the development of micro-electronic technology (*Bulletin of the European Communities* **13** (2) 1980 points 2.1.33 to 2.1.35)

It undertakes work sent to it from other organizations in the Community eg the Commission sent to the Council for the attention of the Standing committee on employment, a series of communications covering temporary employment, part time work and flexible retirement. The Committee was asked to advise on these proposals.

During 1981 the Commission submitted discussion papers in April with the title, 'Problems of employment – points for examination' (*Bulletin of the European Communities* **14** (4) 1981 points 1.1.1–1.1.11). These papers set out guidelines for a concerted response to employment problems in the Community. They were designed for discussion at the 19 May meeting of the Committee in Brussels. The conclusions have been recorded (*Bulletin of the European Communities* **14** (5) 1981 point 2.1.34) and form the basis of further discussions at the 707th Council meeting on 10 June in Luxembourg and the 714th meeting on 20 June also in Luxembourg. Both these discussions were led by Mr Ivor Richard for the Commission. The 23rd meeting of this committee held on 27 April 1982 (*Bulletin of the European Communities* **15** (4) 1982 point 2.1.27) advocated:

- a joint meeting with the Council on economic, financial and social affairs to discuss Community solutions to this problem
- emphasis be placed on the need to increase productive public and private investment
- a range of priority areas for public investment
- investment for the development of less favoured regions
- the Commission to prepare a package of proposals to relieve the situation on unemployment
- existing restructuring programmes should also give attention to employment
- post school employment training for young people (*Bulletin of the European Communities* **15** (3) 1982 points 1.3.2 and 1.3.5)
- attention be paid to the long term unemployed, adjustment of working hours for the employed
- improvement of public employment services

- small firms, local initiatives and co-operatives should be able to receive financial assistance from the EEC to enhance their competitiveness

These points were reflected in a Council resolution of 27 May 1982.

Further information

General report on the activites of the European Communities
   Luxembourg: Office for official publications of the European Communities, annual
As this subject is changing rapidly it is useful to refer to its cover in the monthly, *Bulletin of the European Communities* and the current information sheets issued by the EEC Office in London and similar offices elsewhere
Community advisory committees for the representation of socio-economic interests
   Farnborough: Saxon House for EC Economic and Social Committee, 1980. 215p. ISBN 0-566-00328-7

Tripartite Conferences [on Employment]

Basic information

Conferences held so far include the following:

1st	27/28 April	1970 at Luxembourg
2nd	16 December	1974 at Brussels
3rd	18 November	1975 at Brussels
4th	24 June	1976 at Luxembourg
5th	27 June	1977 at Luxembourg
6th	9 November	1978 at Brussels

They have not been put on an official basis (OJ C148/38-9 23.6.77). There is a steering group which prepares future conference programmes.

Tripartite Conference – representation

They bring together representatives of the governments of member states together with representatives from the Council and Commission, the employers' association – the Union of industries of the European Communities (UNICE) and the workers' association of the European Trade Union Confederation (ETUC).

Work of the Tripartite Conferences:

- 1st: development of the employment situation
- 2nd: prospects of a European social policy

- 3rd: economic and social situation in the Community and its outlook
- 4th: full details of proposals for this conference are outlined at point 219 in the Tenth general report on the activities of the European Communities. Details in Further information
- 5th: requested the, Standing committee on employment to study specific measures as a follow-up to the conclusions of previous conferences, notably that social operations should form an integral part of the industrial restructuring policy
- 6th: which was also attended by ministers of finance, economic affairs and employment, as well as the usual two sides of industry. The paper discussed was concerned with work sharing, a greater role for the services sector, structural re-adaptation measures, and the stimulation of growth. The Commission was requested to undertake further research, in particular on:
    stimulating investment
    reducing working time
    access of young people and women to training and employment
    opportunities for expanding part-time work

As a result of the 6th conference, the Commission submitted to Council a communication for the improvement of relations with the social Committees in the context of the Tripartite conferences (COM (79) 224 final). This was debated by Parliament (OJ C 140/48–51 5.6.79) which thought that Tripartite conferences in their present form were unable to meet the demands made on them and proposed sectoral conferences instead in future.

Further information

General report on the activities of the European Commission
    Luxembourg: Office for official publications of the European Commission, annual
Community advisory committees for the representation of socio-economic interests
    Farnborough: Saxon House for EC Economic and Social Committee, 1980. 215p. ISBN 0–566–00328–7

European System for the International Clearing of Vacancies (SEDOC)

Basic information

Established in 1968 (OJ L257 (Part II)/5–7 19.10.68) (Regulation 1612/68) as part of a wider regulation on the freedom of movement for workers.

SEDOC works through the European office for co-ordinating the clearance of vacancies and applications for employment (The European co-ordination office) which was set up under the Commission. It meets representatives of member states twice a year to discuss problems.

Work of SEDOC.

Using an audiovisual programme prepared in 1974, SEDOC has run seminars to train national users from member states. Exchanges of employment service officials have been undertaken.

The organization relies on the work and opinions of the Technical Committee as well as the Advisory Committee on freedom of movement for workers (qv).

Further information

General report on the activities of the European Communities
    Luxembourg: Office for official publications of the European Communities, annual

Trade Unions

Basic information

Because of their historic development and the political and economic conditions under which they have grown, trade union organization varies considerably from country to country.

In Brussels, union officials from EC countries have the opportunity of giving their opinions to the Consultative Committee of the ECSC as well as to the Economic and Social Committee. On three occasions each year they have the opportunity to meet the Chairman of the Council and the Commission.

Though having a much wider cover than Europe, the International Confederation of Free Trade Unions (ICFTU) and the European Trade Union Conference (ETUC) are but two of a number of trade union organizations which have an interest in the progress of unionism in the Community.

Work of the trade unions

The major objectives of the ETUC include full employment, security of employment, security of income, stability of prices, safety at work, equal rights for women, availability of training, high level of education, care of the migrant worker, collective bargaining, workers' participation in management. The Commission organizes a large number of briefing and consultation meetings. During the 1980s these have been dealing in particular with the crisis industries and growth industries.

Further information

General report on the activities of the European Communities, section 2. 'Institutions and other bodies'
 Luxembourg: Office for official publications of the European Communities, annual
Williams, Michael (ed)
Directory of trades unions in the European Economic Community
 London: Graham, Trotman, Dudley Publishers Ltd, 1978. 124p. ISBN 0–86010–118–5

European Trade Union Confederation (ETUC)

Basic information

The organization representing workers within the Community was founded on 9 February 1973.

It is the successor to the, European confederation of free trade unions for the EEC and to the, Trade Union committee of EFTA. Its address is rue Montagne-aux-Herberes, Potagères 37–41, B 1000 Bruxelles, Belgium. Telephone Bruxelles 219 1090. Its single representation is of 18 national trade unions from 15 European countries.

The first president of the ETUC was the late Victor Feather, previously general secretary of the Trades Union Congress in London.

The confederation has an executive committee and officers. It represents one third of Europe's working population. It arranges congresses (three yearly) conferences, symposia, etc.

Purpose

Its aims are to work for full employment, security of income, stability of prices, safety at work, equal rights for women, a high level of training and education, migrants, collective bargaining and participation in decision making.

Work undertaken

It works closely with the, Standing committee on employment. It is called upon to participate in Community activities with particular reference to employment. It presents its case, provides papers for discussion at joint meetings. Possibly the most important of the joint meetings in which it participated have been the, Tripartite conferences on employment (qv).

Further information

Williams, Michael (ed)
Directory of trade unions in the European Economic Community
   London: Graham, Trotman, Dudley Publishers Ltd 1978. 124p. ISBN 086010–118–5
Economic and social committee of the European Communities
   Luxembourg: Office for official publications of the European Communities, annual

Union of Industries of the European Community (UNICE)

Basic information

The organization representing employers within the Community. When it was founded in November 1952 it was known as the Union des industries des six pays de la Communauté Européenne. Its first headquarters was in Paris but it is now in Brussels at rue de Loxum 6 (1 te 21)B 1000 Bruxelles, Belgium. Telephone: Bruxelles 512 6780. Telex: 26 013. UNICE organization consists of a Council of presidents, an Executive committee, a Committee of permanent delegates and a Secretariat-General. Its languages are usually English and French. Meetings of the organization are normally closed. It is financed by member organizations. So far eleven national organizations are represented by it covering nine countries.

Purpose

UNICE represents European industry and puts forward both its own ideas and the ideas of its member federations. It aims to inform the Commission and other organizations of the European Community.

Work undertaken

It works closely with the, Standing committee on employment, where it presents its case and provides papers for discussion. Possibly the most important of the joint meetings in which it participated have been the, Tripartite conferences on employment (qv).

It stimulates a policy for industry in a European context. It undertakes research on problems of European integration.

Further information

Yearbook of international organizations 5th ed
   Brussels: Union of international associations, 1981. ISBN 92-834-1241-9
Economic and social committee of the European Communities (Chapter IV)
   Luxembourg: Office for official publications of the European Communities, annual

Advisory Committee on Safety, Hygiene and Health Protection at Work

Basic information

The Committee was set up under a decision of the Council in 1974 (OJ L185/15-17 9.7.74) (Decision 74/325/EEC).

Advisory Committee – representation

It consists of two representatives of the Government, two from trade unions and two from employers' organizations, from each member state. There is an alternative member for each full member, who shall attend meetings only when the full members are absent.

Work of the Advisory Committee.

The main purpose of the Committee is to assist the Commission with problems within its subjects. It covers all aspects of these subjects except those which fall under the purview of the, Mines safety and health commission. Ionizing radiations are the responsibility of EURATOM. In its subjects it:

- reviews existing or planned legislation
- works towards a common Community approach, spotlighting priorities and their solutions
- brings to the attention of the Commission areas where further study is required
- initiates and plans safety campaigns
- provides an information service of good practice and an annual report

Working parties to forward the work of the Committee are based on article 6 (4) of the 1974 Decision.

- Group 1   Defining procedures for keeping the Commission informed. Suggesting priorities for action by consultation

- Group 2　Co-ordination of the collection of information on research and critical analysis and to propose subjects of importance which have not been covered
- Group 3　Participation in surveys of the situation and formulation of proposals for improvements

Further information

Community advisory committees for the representation of socio-economic interests
　Farnborough: Saxon House for EC Economic and Social Committee, 1980. 215p. ISBN 0-566-00328-7

Mobility of Labour

Basic information

The treaty establishing the European Economic Community (1957) states in article 3(c) the principles that the activities of the Community shall include '... the abolition, as between member states, of obstacles to freedom of movement for persons, services and capital.' This was expanded in Title III of part two of the treaty, articles 48–73.

Restrictions on the movement of Community workers within the EC were abolished under a Council regulation of 1968 (OJ L257/2–11 19.10.68) (Regulation 1612/68/EEC). This was extended to residence within the Community for workers of member states and their families (OJ L257/13–16 19.10.68) (Directive 68/360/EEC).

The Advisory committee on freedom of movement for workers was established under regulation 1612/68 (articles 24–31), mentioned above (qv).

The Technical committee on freedom of movement for workers (qv) was established under the same regulation (articles 32–37).

Purpose

Freedom of movement constitutes one of the fundamental rights of members of the Community.

Mobility of labour within the Community is one of the means whereby the worker is guaranteed the possibility of improving his working and living conditions and promoting his social advancement. It is also a method of satisfying the requirements of the economies of member states.

It is a means of affirming the rights of all workers in member states to pursue the activity of their choice.

Work undertaken

This subject obviously includes general movement of workers under the term migrant labour, diplomas and professional qualifications and their mutual recognition (qv), exchanges of young workers, social security (qv), women in the community (qv), European system for the international clearing of vacancies (qv), etc.

Both of the committees mentioned above (qv) set up under regulation 1612/68 have considered the employment of migrant workers, including second generation migrant workers (*Thirteenth general report on the activities of the European Communities* point 223. For details see, Further information).

The Commission increased its efforts to eliminate discrimination against migrant workers. The Court of Justice has dealt with a number of cases on this subject (*Fourteenth general report on the activities of European Communities* points 737–9. For details see, Further information).

Further information

Freedom of movement for workers within the Community, official texts
    Luxembourg: Office for official publications of the European Communities, 1975. 26p.
Hasse, H M J M
Mobility of cultural workers within the Community
    Luxembourg: Office for official publications of the European Communities, 1976. 98p.
    (Collection studies, cultural matters series No. 1.)
General report on the activities of the European Communities
    Luxembourg: Office for official publications of the European Communities, annual

Advisory Committee on Freedom of Movement for Workers

Basic information

The Committee was established by the Council in 1968 (OJ L257/2–11 19.10.68) (Regulation 1612/68/EEC).

Advisory Committee – representation

Each member state has two government representatives, two trade union representatives and two employers' organization representatives. The appointments are made by the Council which tries to strike a balance between the various economic sectors represented. A single alternative member is appointed for each of the categories listed above. Appointments in all cases are for two years and are renewable. The Committee may invite observers or experts and the Chairman may be assisted by technical advisers.

Work of the Advisory Committee

Its duties are:

- to endeavour to obtain a co-ordination of national employment policies with regard to free movement of workers, employment, etc
- to maintain a watching brief on the impact of Regulations 1612/68 on freedom of movement for workers within the Community
- submit to the Commission any proposals thought necessary to amend Regulation 1612/68
- at the request of the Commission, or on its own initiative, to draft opinions within the subject responsibilities of the Committee
- the working groups may be established when considered approprate by the Committee

It will be noted that this Committee deals with matters relating to migration policy and not the Standing committee on employment.

Further information

General report on the activities of the European Communities
   Luxembourg: Office for official publications of the European Communities, annual
Community advisory committees for the representation of socio-economic interests
   Farnborough: Saxon House for EC Economic and Social Committee, 1980, 215p. ISBN 0-566-00328-7

Technical Committee on Freedom of Movement for Workers

Basic information

The Treaty of Rome (1957) established the principle of freedom of movement for workers in article 3(c).

Restrictions on movement of Community workers within the EC were abolished in 1968 (OJ L257/2-11 19.10.68) (Regulation 1612/68/EEC). Articles 32-7 of Regulation 1612/68 established the Technical committee on freedom of movement for workers.

Technical Committee – representation

- one representative from each member state. This should be one of the government representatives appointed to the Advisory committee on freedom of movement for workers (qv)
- one alternative from each member state. This should be one of the government representatives or alternative government representative, appointed to the, Advisory committee on freedom of movement for workers
- the chairman shall be from the Commission and shall not vote
- the chairman and members of the Committee may be assisted by expert advisers

Work of the Technical Committee

The committee to be responsible for:

- assisting the Commission prepare, promote and follow up technical work giving effect to regulation 1612/68
- promoting and advancing co-operation between public authorities in member states on freedom of movement by workers
- formulating procedures for implementing the purpose of the committee
- facilitating the acquisition of information likely to be of use to the Commission
- investigating at a technical level the harmonization of the criteria by which member states assess the state of their labour markets.

Currently the committee is holding discussions on the guidelines for the establishment of Community provisions in the fields of:

- temporary work
- fixed-term contracts

(in, *Bulletin of the European Communities* **14** (6) 1981. point 2.1.48).

Further information

General report on the activities of the European Communities
Luxembourg: Office for official publications of the European Communities, annual

Administrative Commission on Social Security for Migrant Workers

Basic information

The Administrative Commission was established by a Council regulation in 1971. Articles 80 and 81 of this regulation refer to the Administrative Commission (OJ L149/2–49 5.7.71) (Regulation 71/1408/EEC). Other references to the work of this Commission will be found in the original outline of the procedure for providing Social Security for migrant workers (OJ L74/1–49 27.3.72) (Regulation 574/72/EEC).

Administrative Commission – representation

One government representative from each of the member states assisted where necessary by expert advisers. A representative of the Commission shall attend meetings in an advisory capacity.

The Administrative Commission shall be assisted in technical matters by the International Labour Office (ILO).

Work of the Administrative Commission

The duties allocated are:

- responsibility for administrative questions, questions of interpretation of the regulations in force
- responsibility for translations of documents relating to the implementation of these regulations at the request of the competent authorities of the member states and of claims of beneficiaries
- fostering co-operation between member states in social security matters
- fostering co-operation between member states with a view to expediting awards
- assembling details of accounts relating to costs to be borne by member states under these regulations
- undertaking other duties considered within its competence
- submitting proposals to the Commission for subsequent regulations or amendments

Further information

General report on the activities of the European Communities
   Luxembourg: Office for official publications of the European Communities, annual

Advisory Committee on Social Security for Migrant Workers

Basic information

The Committee was established in 1971 under a Council regulation, articles 82 and 83 of which are solely concerned with its establishment (OJ L149/2–49 5.7.71) (Regulation 71/1408/EEC). Details of the many communications and rather fewer regulations on the subject covered by this advisory committee, will be found in the OJ Annual alphabetical and methodological indexes. Before 1973 these references will be found under the heading, Workers, migrant, social security and in 1974 and later these references are transferred to Social Security, social security for migrant workers. The Committee is appointed by the Council.

Advisory Committee – representation

Each member state is permitted the following representation:

- two government representatives plus an alternative member
- two employers' representatives plus an alternative member
- two trade union representatives plus an alternative member

They are appointed for a period of two years after which they may be re-appointed. Outside experts may be appointed to attend meetings if proposed by the Chairman and approved by the Committee.

Work of the Advisory Committee

The Committee's main tasks are:

- to consider issues and problems raised under article 51 of the Treaty of Rome (1957)
- to provide the Administrative commission on social security for migrant workers (qv), with opinions and recommendations for the amendment of Community law on social security.

Further information

General report on the activities of the European Communities
   Luxembourg: Office for official publications of the European Communities, annual
Community advisory committees for the representation of socio-economic interests
   Farnborough: Saxon House for EC Economic and Social Committee, 1980. 215p. ISBN 0–566–00328–7

Women in the Community

Basic information

In 1980 four women out of ten between the ages of 14 and 59 either had a job or were actively engaged in the search for one. 65% were in the service sector, 28% in industry and 7% in agriculture.

Article 119 of the Treaty of Rome which founded the European Economic Community stipulated that, 'Each member state ... maintain the application to the principle that men and women should receive equal pay for equal work'.

Work undertaken

At regular intervals and in various forms this principle has been reiterated:

- October 1972 at the Paris summit
- January 1974 at the meeting of the Ministers of the Nine
- February 1975 the Commission sent to the Ministers of the Nine a Community programme to benefit women workers
- February 1976 Council directive on equal treatment of men and women on access to employment, vocational training, promotion and working conditions (OJ L39/40–2 14.2.76) (Directive 76/207/EEC)
- December 1978 the Nine adopted a directive on the gradual implementation of the principle of equal treatment for men and women as regards social security
- January 1979 the Commission stated that the principle of equal pay has not been completely realized in any Community country
- May 1980 on the Commission's initiative, delegates from member states attended a conference on, Equal treatment for women: assessment, problems and perspectives – a Manchester approach. Held from 28–30 May (*Bulletin of the European Communities* 13 (5) 1980. point 2.1.24). The Commission then set up a Standing Liaison group for equal opportunities (qv)

Equal pay cases have also come before the Court of Justice eg 1974 Case 43 Defrenne v. Sabena, (1976) ECR 455 and 1979 Case 129 Macarthys Ltd v. Smith, (1980) ECR 1275.

A Bureau for questions affecting women's employment has been set up within the Directorate-General for Social Affairs. It utilizes the legal means available to the Community as well as striving for the optimum utilization of the financial resources.

The European Social Fund (OJ L337/14 27.12.77) (Decision 77/804/EEC) grants assistance to women to promote their access to skilled jobs, particularly in areas not traditionally open to them.

The European Commission has prepared and circulated a film and accompanying folder on 'Equal chances, equal opportunities'.

A brochure with the title 'Women and The European Community' has been circulated.

A bi-monthly journal, 'Women of Europe' is published by the Commission and is available from the Directorate-General of Information, rue de la loi 200, B–1049–Brussels.

In October 1979 the European Parliament decided to set up an ad hoc, Committee on women's rights (OJ C289/56–7 19.11.79). Its task is to prepare for a debate in Parliament on the position of women in the European Community using an outline report drawn up by the Commission. It has undertaken surveys and one of its findings 'European women in paid employment, their perception of discrimination at work' has been published as Supplement No. 5 December 1980 to 'Women of Europe'. The conclusion reached in a 1981 report of the Commission to the Council is that no improvement of the situation of women in working life has been made since the 1976 Directive (*Bulletin of the European Communities* **14** (6) 1981.point 2.1.60). The report of this ad hoc committee was presented to Parliament on 10/11 February 1981, debated and the resolution in the report was passed after it had been amended (OJ C50/21, 22, 35 9.3.81). The ad hoc committee was then discharged and will be reconstituted in two years time for a further debate. (*Bulletin of the European Communities* **14** (2) 1981. point 2.3.7).

In view of this lack of progress within the Community over womens' rights, a plan for changing the situation has been evolved. This was issued under the title, 'A new Community action programme on the promotion of equal opportunities for women 1982–1985'. It was published as *Bulletin of the European Communities* supplement 1.82.

Further information

Equal opportunity for working women
  Brussels: EC Directorate-General for Information, 1980. 7p. (European File 5/80) ISSN 0379–3133. Catalogue number CC–AD–80–005–EN–C
The position of women in the European Community
  Luxembourg: European Parliament, 1981. (Working documents 1–829/80–1 (Motion for a resolution) 1–829/80–11 (Explanatory statement) and 1–829/80 addendum).

Standing Liaison Group for Equal Opportunities

Basic information

Established by the Commission in 1981 as a result of a conference held in Manchester from 28–30 May 1980 under the title, 'Equal treatment for women: assessment, problems and perspectives – a Manchester approach'. The conference was held as a result of a Commission initiative. At the same time the European Parliament's ad hoc committee on women's rights was reporting and recommendations 49 and 50 call on a strengthening of Community offices concerned with women's rights (European Parliament working documents 1–829/80–I, 1–829/80–II and 1–829/80 addendum).

Standing Liaison Group – representation

Each member state is represented by delegates from local committees or commissions for the employment of women or for equal opportunities or for equivalent bodies.

Work of the Standing Liaison Group

First meeting of the Group was held on 21 and 22 May 1981. It took action on the following:

- the preparation of a new action programme for women. To be submitted to the Commission by the end of 1981.
- an examination of Community work on employment, the new technologies and the reorganization of working time, particularly in regard to their effects on women.

Advisory committee on equal opportunities

The Commission in December 1981 decided to give a formal status to the Standing liaison group ... and it became the, Advisory committee on equal opportunities, on 1 January 1982 (OJ L20/35–7 28.1.82). Its first chairperson was Baroness Lockwood and its 1982 programme was to make preparations to assist the Commission's action programme on the promotion of equal opportunities for women 1982–5 (see last item under, Further information, below).

Further information

'Equal treatment for men and women'. *Bulletin of the European Communities* **14** (5). 1981 point 2.1.45
'A new Community action programme on the promotion of equal opportunities for women 1982–5'. *Bulletin of the European Communities* supplement 1/82

Consumer Affairs

Basic information

With the establishment of a, Consumers' consultative committee in 1973 (qv) the work of the Commission on this subject field increased considerably.

A programme for consumer protection and its related information policy has been produced (OJ C92/1–16 25.4.75). Appendix 2 of the Annex to this programme, pages 13–16, give a selection of Community directives of interest to the consumer – a useful basic list which can be updated when necessary by references in the annual reports on Consumer protection and information policy commencing in 1977.

Purpose

In his programme address to the European Parliament on 8 February 1977 the President, Roy Jenkins, stated 'We must make the Community a practical reality in terms of everyday life'. Richard Burke, the member of the Commission responsible for consumer affairs, stated 'The key to that ultimate accomplishment lies in the recognition by all interests, of the consumer dimension as a natural and indispensable one in the achievement of [a] balanced development of the Common Market'. (*Consumer protection and information policy second report*, page 3 see under Further information).

Work undertaken

Consumer product protection is one of the major aspects of this subject. Work has been progressing on the harmonization of regulations already in force in member states. Article 100 of the Treaty of Rome makes provision for this. For example:

- binary textile fibre mixtures, quantitative analysis (OJ L173/1–27 31.7.72) (Directive 72/276/EEC) together with amending directive (OJ L57/23–6 4.3.81) (Directive 81/75/EEC)
- cosmetic products (OJ L262/169–200 27.9.76) (Directive 76/768/EEC) amended by (OJ L192/35 31.7.79) (Directive 79/661/EEC), (OJ L63/26 6.3.82) (Directive 82/147/EEC) and (OJ L167/1–32 15.6.82) (Directive 82/368/EEC). As a result of a Commission decision of 19 December 1977 a, Scientific committee on cosmetology was formed (*Consumer protection and information policy second report*, page 55 see under Further information).
- food:
    Advisory committee on foodstuffs (OJ L182/35–6 12.7.75) (Decision 75/420/EEC)

individual foodstuffs are the subject of a large number of legislative acts

labelling, presentation and advertising (OJ L33/1–14 8.2.79) (Directive 79/112/EEC) (Bulletin of the European Communities **14** (4) 1981 point 2.1.41)

materials and articles intended to come in contact with foodstuffs (OJ L340/19–24 9.12.76) (Directive 76/893/EEC) and (OJ L44/15–17 15.2.78) (Directive 78/142/EEC)

removal of technical barriers to trade (OJ C117/1–14 31.12.73) Scientific committee for food (OJ L136/1–2 20.5.74) (Decision 74/234/EEC)

- home study courses (OJ C208/12–15 31.8.77)
- motor vehicles, technical harmonization of motor vehicle parts (OJ L42/1–15 23.2.70). A large number of further directives dealing with specific parts of motor vehicles have appeared subsequently. Sound levels for motor cycles (OJ L349/21–30 13.12.78) (Directive 78/1015/EEC) whole vehicle, type approval for passenger cars (OJ C177/1 26.7.77)
- textile names (OJ L185/16–26 16.8.71) and proposed amendment (OJ C63/3–10 13.3.80)
- toys, protection of children (OJ C228/10–42 8.9.80)

As harmonization develops it is hoped that the best aspects of each country's legislation are extended to the Community as a whole. On agricultural crops there are a series of advisory committees (qv) for individual products (see *Annual report on consumer protection* ...).

Consumer purchasing protection is yet another aspect of consumer affairs and aims to provide the purchaser with as much information as he needs to make his choice. Examples are:

- advertising with special reference to misleading advertisements (OJ C70/4–6 21.3.78)
- Community trade mark. (New trade mark system... *Bulletin of the European Communities* supplement 5/80)
- domestic appliances, their energy consumption (OJ C149/7–18 18.6.80)
- non-food household products, unit price (OJ C163/1–2 30.6.79)
- prices of foodstuffs, marking and display (OJ L158/19–21 26.6.79)

Economic and legal interests have also been part of the work of the Committee:

- on 27 February 1979 the Council received a proposal concerning minimum standards of protection for credit transactions (OJ C80/4–8 27.3.79)
- unfair advertising was covered by an amended Commission directive (OJ C194/3–6 1.8.79)
- small claims courts. A pilot scheme was started in Scotland to facilitate consumer access to the courts in minor cases. This had Commission backing
- 'small print' in contracts. Unfair clauses in contracts (so called 'small print') (*11th General report on the activities of the European Communities*

point 301, Luxembourg: Office for official publications of the European Communities, 1978. 336p. ISBN 92–825–0014–4)

Interest in consumer education has been shown through working parties in the fields of:

- teacher training
- pilot school courses

Basic programmes have been produced for 1979–82. Work on curriculum development and teaching methods is being undertaken. (*Consumer protection and information policy second report* see under Further information).

Further information

General report of the activities of the European Communities
   Luxembourg: Office for official publications of the European Communities, annual
The European consumer – his preoccupations – his aspirations – his information
   Luxembourg: Office for official publications of the European Communities, 1976. 41p.
Consumer protection and information policy
   Luxembourg: Office for official publications of the European Communities, annual 1977–
   (2nd report published 1979)
The consumer organizations and the public authorities
   Luxembourg: Office for official publications of the European Communities, 1977. 60p.
   Catalogue number CG–22–76–140–EN–C
Proceedings of the symposium of consumer organizations on 2 and 3 December 1976
   Luxembourg: Office for official publications of the European Communities. 1977 reprinted
   1979. 126p.
'Bibliography on the promotion of consumer interests' in, *Documentation bulletin* B10 (v.1 Selection of publications, v.2 Community legislation and publications, selected articles) 1978
The second Community programme of consumers. *Bulletin of the European Communities* supplement 4/79

Consumers' Consultative Committee

Basic information

This committee was established by a Commission decision of 25 September 1973 (OJ L283/18–19 10.10.73) (Decision 73/306/EEC) amended by (OJ L341/42 10.12.76) (Decision 76/906/EEC).

Committee – representation

The Committee consists of representatives of European consumer organizations, trade unions and individuals experienced in consumer affairs.

Membership since 16 October 1980 (OJ C 43/4–5 28.2.81) is 33. The term of office is three years and is renewable. Appointments are made by the Commission.

Work of the Committee

The major tasks of the Committee are to accept consumer problems and pass these to the Commission with possible solutions, to develop a consumer policy and to make recommendations to the Commission regarding this, and to give opinions on draft Council directives when requested.

The Commission's Environment and consumer protection service administrative unit 9 on specialized information and education, is particularly concerned with the work of the Committee.

Further information

Community advisory committees for the representation of socio-economic interests
   Farnborough: Saxon House for EC Economic and Social Committee, 1980. 215p. ISBN
   0–566–00328–7

Handicapped Persons

Basic information

Reports on social development (prior to 1973, *Reports on the development of the social situation in the Community*) issued annually, have a section or sections on handicapped persons.

On 27 June 1974 a Council resolution was issued on the need for vocational rehabilitation of handicapped persons (OJ C80/30–2 9.7.74).

In the early days of the Community the main aim was to codify action being taken by member states. Later came a move to harmonize services throughout all constituent countries. This was followed by reports and surveys to improve conditions on a Community basis.

Work undertaken

On the financial side the, European social budget 1980–1975–1970 (details in Further information), includes projections of costs for supporting handicapped persons.

In March 1979 (21st to 23rd) the Commission organized study and information meetings in Luxembourg on the subject of vocational rehabilitation of the handicapped. These were used to highlight problems over training instructors and the financing of this aid.

By 30 October 1979, the Commission had forwarded to the Council a report on an initial Community action programme for the vocational rehabilitation of handicapped persons, based on a series of projects between 1974 and 1979 which had been aided by the Social Fund. (*Bulletin of the European Communities* **12** (10) 1979. point 2.1.61).

During 1981 (International year for disabled persons), Parliament adopted a resolution on the economic, social and occupational integration of handicapped persons (OJ C77/18 6.4.81). This was the result of a report submitted to it by the Committee on social affairs ('Disabled people in employment', *Bulletin of the European Communities* **14** (3) 1981. point 2.3.10).

Further information

Report on social development
   Luxembourg: Office for official publications of the European Communities, annual
The European social budget 1980–1975–1970
   Luxembourg: Office for official publications of the European Communities, 1978. 183p.
   ISBN 92–825–0913–3. Catalogue number CB–25–78–704–EN–C
Social policy of the European Communities 2nd ed
   Luxembourg: Office for official publications of the European Communities, 1981. 51p.
   (European Documentation series 3/1981). ISBN 92–825–2411–6. Catalogue number
   CB–NC–81–003–EN–C

European Foundation for the Improvement of Living and Working Conditions

Basic information

Under a general article no. 235 of the Treaty of Rome (1957), the Council adopted a regulation establishing the Foundation in 1975 (OJ L139/1–4 30.5.75) (Regulation 1365/75/EEC). Financial and staffing provisions for the Foundation were made in the following year under (OJ L164/16–30 24.6.76) (Regulation 1417/76/EEC) and (OJ L214/24–46 6.8.76) (Regulation 1860/76/EEC).

Foundation – representation

Its members are drawn from EC member states, the employers'

organizations, the trade unions and the Commission. There is also a Committee of experts (12) selected from scientific and other groups which are concerned with the work of the Foundation.

Work of the Foundation

Its headquarters is in Dublin in the Republic of Ireland.

Under Council decision of 22 July 1975 a programme of pilot schemes and studies to combat poverty was started (OJ L199/34–5 30.7.75) (Decision 75/458/EEC). Investigations were made into shiftwork, and a seminar held in Dublin 24–26 October 1979. Papers given were produced as, *Cases of innovations in shiftwork,* Dublin: European foundation for the improvement of living and working conditions, 1980(?) various paginations.

Further information

General report on the activities of the European Communities
   Luxembourg: Office for official publications of the European Communities, annual
Community advisory committees for the representation of socio-economic interests
   Farnborough: Saxon House for EC Economic and Social Committee, 1980. 215p. ISBN 0–566–00328–7

Environment

Basic information

In Europe both the natural and the man-made environments are at risk.

The major risk to the natural environment is pollution as a result of mismanagement.

The European Community is one of the most densely populated areas in the world and the city population rose from 61% in 1950 to 69% in 1970. Living and working conditions deteriorate through noise, poor air quality, dirt, congestion and the ugliness of the urban industrial sprawl.

Under article 235 of the Treaty of Rome (1957) provision is made for action concerning those subjects which are considered important but not included in the basic text of the treaty. Environment falls under this article.

The need for a Community environment policy was recognized at the Paris summit conference 19–20 October 1972. The EC adopted the first joint action programme in 1973 (OJ C112/1–53 20.12.73). A second programme was drawn up for the period 1977–81. (OJ C139/1–46 13.6.77) in Title 1 of the action programme included in this Council resolution, is a restatement of the objectives and principles of a Community environment policy.

A draft third action programme on the environment was discussed at the Council meeting of 24 June 1982 and a resolution on the programme was adopted.

This third programme made provision for a continuation of the protection projects based on the 1973 guidelines which were updated in 1977. Thus a continuity in the programme for the period 1982–6 is being assured (OJ C305/2–16 25.11.81).

Work undertaken

The second programme aimed:

- to continue work started by the first programme
- to lay special emphasis on setting up machinery for preventive action on pollution, careful land use, etc
- to give special attention to the protection of space
- to reduce existing pollution and noise (qv Pollution control)
- to add an environmental dimension to the policy of co-operation between the EEC and developing countries

It is the work of the Commission to submit proposals to the Council on all of these subjects. Examples of these include:

- preventing and reducing water pollution. For instance Community countries have been invited to draw up and introduce by 1 July 1987, programmes for the progressive reduction of pollution from the titanium dioxide industry. In December 1980 (OJ C356/32–40 31.12.80) the Commission drew up detailed rules regarding the control of pollution from this industry and the first comments on these rules came from Parliament in 1982 (OJ C149/99–102 14.6.82)
- fighting atmospheric pollution. A directive in 1974 on pollution from motor vehicles was strengthened in 1977. Lead content of petrol to be reduced to 0.4 grammes per litre after 1 January 1981. (OJ L159/61–9 15.6.74) (Directive 70/220/EEC)
- noise reduction directives have been introduced and adopted. For instance pneumatic drills are covered in the following proposal (OJ C82/112–21 14.4.75)
- waste disposal directives have been adopted and a joint programme accepted on the management and storage of radioactive waste (OJ L178/28–9 9.7.75)
- impact of chemicals on the environment. Two directives have been adopted one covering detergents and the other their biodegradability. Other directives cover dangerous substances, the fluorocarbon problems and a screening system covering all chemicals has been examined. (OJ L194/5–21 25.7.75) (Decision 75/437/EEC). The Commission was required to draw up a, European inventory of existing commercial chemical substances (EINECS). This was under Council directive (OJ L196/1 16.8.67) (67/548/EEC) which was frequently amended in particular by (OJ L259/10–28 15.10.79) (Directive 79/831/EEC). EINECS consists of a European Core inventory (ECOIN) which was compiled from existing lists of chemicals, and a, Compendium of known substances (about 15,000) placed on the Community market between 1.1.71 and 18.9.81, excluding items in ECOIN. Each item recorded is given a,

Chemical abstract service (CAS) number for identification. In future new substances not in EINECS and for which no CAS number can be traced, have to be notified to national centres. In the UK this is:

> The Health and Safety Executive
> CEC Inventory contact point (HSD C3)
> Room 11.8
> 25 Chapel Street
> London NW1 5DT
>
> Telephone 01–262 3277 ext. 535 **or** 523
> Telex 299950

(OJ L167/31–8 24.6.81) (Decision 81/437/EEC).

This legislation concerning the approximation of laws, regulations and administrative provisions relating to the classification, purchasing and labelling of dangerous substances, is designed to protect man and the environment against potential risks arising from marketing new substances. It is necessary in the future to ensure that new substances (with certain exceptions) are subject to prior study by manufacturer/importer and the competent authorities informed of the result. To ensure a satisfactory cover of chemical substances, existing ones have to be listed. This has been done in:

Compendium of known substances, and European core inventory (ECOIN)
   Luxembourg: Office for official publications of the European Communities, 1981. 2 v.
   ISBNs 92–825–2463–9 and 92–825–2455–8 (I), (II), (III) and (IV).

In 1975 the EC adopted a 'Polluter pays' principle. (OJ L194/1 25.7.75) (Recommendation 75/436/EURATOM, ECSC, EEC).

A programme of scientific research against pollution is being developed, having been started in 1973 at the Joint Research Centre (qv) at Ispra, Italy. The 1973–5 total programme was financed by 15.9 million ua, and this was continued to 1980 (OJ L200/4–9 8.8.77) (Decision 77/488/EEC, EURATOM) covering atmosphere, water, chemical products and renewable resources to a total of 35.18 million ECU. Other programmes cover improvement of the environment and co-operation with non-Community countries. By February 1981, when an exchange of letters was concluded with Norway, there were seven countries with environmental agreements with the EC – Austria, Canada, Japan, Sweden, Switzerland and the United States. Notification to the Council of the second environment, action programme (OJ C139/1–46 13.6.77) and selective legislation based on it and on the first programme of 1973, enabled the Community to notify member states where they are lapsing from agreed environmental harmonization programmes.

The Community's, Environment and consumer protection service commissioned a report on future energy strategies and their effect on the environment up to the year 2000 (see, Further information).

Further information

Programme of environmental action of the European Communities. *Bulletin of the European Communities* supplement 3/73
Slype, G Van
Information management. Conferences on the environment – a study on information sources
    Luxembourg: Office for official publications of the European Communities, 1976. 44p. (EUR 5554 ef)
Environment programme 1977–81. *Bulletin of the European Communities* supplement 6/76
The European Community's environmental policy
    Luxembourg: Office for official publications of the European Communities, 1977. 32p. (European documentation series 6/77). Catalogue number CC–AA–77–006–EN–C
State of the environment
    Luxembourg: Office for official publications of the European Communities, annual 1977 –
European Community and the environment
    Brussels: Office for official publications of the European Communities, 1979. 7p. (European File 4/79). Catalogue number CC–AD–79–004–EN–C
Environmental Resources Limited. *Environmental impact of energy strategies within the EEC*
    Oxford: Pergamon Press for the Commission of the European Communities, 1980. 155p. ISBN 0–08–025681–3

Environmental Research Programme – Financial Assistance

Basic information

These programmes have been instituted under article 235 of the Treaty of Rome (1957). So far there have been three research programmes:

- first programme 1973–5 (OJ L189/43–4 11.7.73) (Decision 73/180/EEC). This was an indirect project and it worked on a shared cost basis with organizations in the member states. It covered six research areas. The programme was costed at 6.3 million ua.
- second programme 1976–80 (OJ L74/36–7 20.3.76) (Decision 76/311/EEC) also on a shared cost basis with organizations in member states. The programme was divided into two phases and covered four research areas. It was costed at 16 million ua.
- third programme 1981–5 (OJ L101/1–8 11.4.81) (Decision 81/213/EEC). The programme is due to be carried out by indirect action (contracts with organizations in member states) and by concerted action (co-ordination at Community level of existing programmes in member states or in the Community). This programme has been costed at 42 million ECU. It is not only a continuation of the second programme outlined above but it consolidates in one research development the three COST programmes mentioned below as well as research on climatology. Previously there had been separate programmes.

Project benefiting under the third Environmental Research Programme

Many of the programmes listed below started under the second or the first programme and are due for continuation (or conclusion) in the 1981-5 period:

Environmental protection
Research area 1:

- sources, pathways and effects of pollutants
  heavy metal (contracts)
  organic micro pollutants ... (COST programme) 18.12.79–31.12.83.
  See also concerted action, table 1 of Decision 81/213
  asbestos and other fibres (contracts)
  air quality (COST programme) 9.10.78–31.12.83. See also concerted action, table 2 of Decision 81/213
  surface and underground fresh water quality (contracts)
  thermal pollution (contracts)
  marine environment quality (COST programme)
  noise pollution (contracts)

Research area 2:

- reduction and prevention of pollution and nuisances
  sewage and sludge (COST programme) 27.9.77–31.12.83. See also concerted action table 3 of Decision 81/213. This programme of research has now been extended to non-Community countries of Europe including Austria, Finland, Norway, Sweden and Switzerland under a COST project
  pollution abatement technologies (contracts)
  clean technologies (contracts)
  ecological effects of solid waste disposal (contracts)
  oil pollution cleaning techniques (contracts) (concerted action)
  impact of new technologies (contracts) (concerted action)

Research area 3:

- protection, conservation and management of natural environments
  ecosystem studies (contracts)
  biogeochemical cycles (contracts)
  ecosystems conservation (contracts)
  bird protection (contracts) (concerted action)
  reclamation of damaged ecosystems (contracts)

Research area 4:

- environment information management
  databank on environmental chemicals (contracts)
  evaluation, storage and exploration of data (contracts)
  ecological cartography (contracts)

Research area 5:

- complex interactive systems: man environment interactions (contracts) (concerted action)

Climatology
Research area 1:

- understanding climate
    reconstruction of past climates (contracts)
    climate modelling and prediction (contracts)

Research area 2:

- man-climate interactions
    climate variability and European resources (contracts)
    man's influence on the climate (contracts)

Service activities:

- inter-disciplinary studies re research area 2
- inventory, co-ordination and enrichment of European data sets

Rates of grants

The total resources of the, Environmental research programme 1981–5 were 42 million ECU, allocated as follows:

- Environmental protection
    33 million ECU indirect action (contracts)
    1 million ECU concerted action
    Research area 1
        50–55% of total funds
        800,000 ECU for concerted action
        400,000 ECU for each of the COST programmes
    Research area 2
        20–25% of total funds
        200,000 ECU for COST programme
    Research area 3
        15–20% of total funds
    Research area 4
        5–10% of total funds
    Research area 5
        1–5% of total funds
        Climatology
        8 million ECU

Further information

Environment and quality of life, second environmental research programme (indirect

action) 1976–80, reports on research sponsored under the first phase 1976–8
   Luxembourg: Office for official publications of the European Communities, 1980. 850p.
   ISBN 92-825-0496-4. Catalogue number CD-NO-79-003-EN-C
Scott, Gay
Guide to European Community grants and loans – 2nd ed
   Biggleswade: Euroinformation Limited, 1981. 111p. ISBN 0-907304-01-X
Grants and loans from the European Community
   Luxembourg: Office for official publications of the European Communities, 1981. 83p.
   (European documentation series 7–8/81) ISBN 92-825-2633-X. Catalogue number
   CB-NC-81-008-EN-C
Official sources of finance and aid for industry in the UK
   London: National Westminster Bank Limited, Commercial information market intelligence
   department, 1981. 67p.

Natural Heritage Conservation

Basic information

A programme of action on the environment of the European Communities as laid down in
1973 (OJ C112/1–53 20.12.73) stated that the aim was 'to improve the setting and quality of
life and the surroundings and living conditions of the peoples of the Community' (*7th
General report on the activities of the European Communities* Luxembourg: Office for
official publications of the European Communities, 1973. 527p.).

This aim was, of course, concerned with the full range of community living and the built
environment, but included in it was the natural heritage.

The classification of Community territory on the basis of its environmental characteristics
was carried out by the Scientific and technical research committee (CREST) (qv).

Work undertaken

A European foundation for the improvement of living and working
conditions was proposed in 1973 (OJ C112/45 20.12.73) and it was set up
in Dublin. The Council provided it with funds, appointed its Director and
Deputy Director in 1976 and met to discuss its programme of work due to
start at the beginning of 1977.

As early as the 1973 programme of action, the EC gave importance to the
protection of birds, particularly migrants and set out to harmonize legislation
in member states. A directive on bird conservation received the Council's
approval. (OJ C24/3–15 1.2.77). This was approved at a Council meeting
in Brussels on 18/19 December 1978 (*Bulletin of the European
Communities* 11 (12) 1978. point 2.1.83).

Land development and the assessment of its environmental impact was
the subject of an opinion by the Economic and Social Committee at the
EC plenary session on 29/30 April 1981. This was based on a proposal
sent by the Commission to the Council in the previous year (OJ C169/14–22
9.7.80).

Endangered species of wild fauna and flora are listed in a Commission proposal (OJ (C243/16–66 22.9.80) approved by Council on 24.6.82. This implements the Washington Convention within the Community. Rules were laid down to govern trade in these species. Similar regulations were sent by the Commission to the Council in 1980 regarding common rules for the imports of whale products. These were adopted on 20 January 1981 (OJ L39/1–3 12.2.81) (Regulation 348/81/EEC).

The Council of the Communities signed the, Berne convention on the Conservation of European wildlife and natural habitats, in December 1981 (OJ L38/1–32 10.2.82) (Decision 82/72/EEC) and it came into force throughout the EEC on 1.9.82.

Further information

Publications on the environment for the use of teachers, have been issued through the Luxembourg Office for official publications of the European Communities. To inform and educate young people about the environment a network of pilot courses was started in 1977. Annual seminars are held in Luxembourg
General report on the activities of the European Communities
   Luxembourg: Office for official publications of the European Communities, annual
Cramp, Stanley
Bird conservation in Europe, a report prepared for the, Environment and consumer protection service of the Commission of the European Communities
   London: HMSO, 1977. 58p. ISBN 0–11–700258–5
Environmental impact of energy strategies within the EEC
   Oxford: Pergamon Press for the Commission of the European Communities, 1980. 155p. ISBN 0–08–025681–3

Pollution Control

Basic information

A programme of action concerning the environment was outlined in a 1973 Council declaration and included as part II title I, 'measures to reduce pollution and nuisances' (OJ C112/1–53 20.12.73). Subsequently the Commission submitted a large number of proposals, details of which can be found under the 'Environment' heading in the 1974 and later, Annual alphabetical and methodological indexes, which are issued as supplements to the, *Official Journal of the European Communities.* During the middle 1970s research programmes had been initiated. By 1981, the Commission had expanded considerably its interest in pollution control and this is recorded in numerous COM documents of the late 1970s and early 1980s. In 1975, the Council made recommendations regarding the cost allocation and action by public authorities on environmental matters (OJ L194/1–4 25.7.75) (Recommendation 75/436/EURATOM, ECSC, EEC).

Application

The following references have been selected to show the range of EC Legislation on pollution control:

- Air pollution:
  air pollution caused by gases from motor vehicles (OJ L76 6.4.70) (Directive 70/220/EEC) and (OJ L159/61–9 15.6.74) (Directive 74/290/EEC)
  air pollution, joint project in the field of physico-chemical behaviour of atmospheric pollutants (OJ L311/10–12 4.11.78) (Decision 78/889/EEC)
  air pollution caused by chlorofluorocarbons (aerosols and the ozone layer) (OJ L90/45 3.4.80) (Decision 80/372/EEC)
  air quality standard covering lead were proposed in 1979 (OJ C324/3–9 28.12.79) and approved by the Council on 24.6.82
- Biological care:
  biological screening of the population for lead (OJ L105/10–12 28.4.77) (Directive 77/312/EEC)
- Chemical pollution:
  titanium dioxide industrial waste (OJ L54/19–24 25.2.78) (Directive 78/176/EEC)
- Industrial pollution:
  waste disposal (OJ L194/39–41 25.7.75) (Directive 75/442/EEC)
  waste oils disposal (OJ L194/23–5 25.7.75) (Directive 75/439/EEC)
  Major accident hazards of certain industrial activities (OJ L230/1–18 5.8.82) (Directives 82/501/EEC)
- Noise pollution:
  noise of subsonic aircraft (OJ L18/26–8 24.1.80) (Directive 80/51/EEC) updated by (OJ C276.5–6 28.10.81) which was approved by Council on 10.6.82. Currently (1982) the Commission is seeking opinions on a proposed directive to control the noise of household electrical appliances (*Bulletin of the European Communities* **15** (1) point 2.1.39 and **15** (5) point 2.4.31).
- Nuclear pollution:
  ionizing radiation, safety standards for health and the general public (OJ L187/1–44 12.7.76) (Directive 76/579/EURATOM) and (OJ L83/18 3.4.79) (Directive 79/343/EURATOM)
  nuclear safety experts (OJ L141/26–7 9.6.79) (Decision 79/520/EEC) and (OJ L251/26 5.10.79) (Decision 79/828/EURATOM)
- Water pollution, general:
  bathing water, quality of (OJ L31/1–7 5.2.76) (Directive 76/160/EEC)
- Water pollution, freshwater:
  surface water, drinking quality required (OJ 194/26–31 25.7.75) (Directive 75/440/EEC)
  surface water, sampling and analysis (OJ L271/44–53 29.10.79) (Directive 79/869/EEC)

surface water, protection against pollution (OJ L20/43–8 26.1.80) (Directive 80/68/EEC)

water analysis, micropollutants (OJ L311/6–9 4.11.78) (Decision 78/888/EEC)

- Water pollution, seawater:

  marine pollution from the land (OJ 194/5–21 25.7.75) (Decisions 75/437/EEC and 75/438/EEC)

Research

A research programme was agreed by Council decision (OJ L153/11–12 9.6.73) (Decision 73/126/EEC) and (OJ L189/43–4 11.7.73) (Decision 73/180/EEC). Some fifty shared cost contracts in environmental research, mostly in pollution problems, have been concluded with specialized organizations in member states. These have been approved by the, Advisory committee on programme management (ACPM) (*Bulletin of the European Communities* **8** (2) 1975. point 2248, **8** (3) 1975. point 2245 and **8** (6) 1975. point 2270). A sectoral research and development programme in the environment was approved (OJ L101/1–9 11.4.81) (Decision 81/213/EEC).

Co-operation

The Community has been represented at many international meetings on the environment, including three on marine pollution. (One of the more immediate concerns the Mediterranean). In 1976 the Barcelona Convention was signed. It concerned specially protected areas of the Mediterranean sea. In 1982 a fourth protocol was agreed, which is leading towards the protection of the whole area. This was signed in Geneva in April 1982 by EEC representatives (*Bulletin of the European Communities* **15** (2) 1982 point 2.1.44).

Another example of co-operation was the, International commission for the protection of the Rhine against pollution. At its meeting in Dusseldorf on 9.3.82 it was concerned with pollution by the discharge of chlorides (*Bulletin of the European Communities* **15** (3) 1982 point 2.1.52).

Further information

General report on the activities of the European Communities
   Luxembourg: Office for official publications of the European Communities, annual
First European congress on waste oils, proceedings
   Luxembourg: Office for official publications of the European Communities, 1976. 367p.

Radioactive waste management and storage, first annual report
   Luxembourg: Office for official publications of the European Communities, annual. 1977–
   (Nuclear science and technology EUR series)
Social and economic implications of controlling the use of chlorofluorocarbons in the EEC
   London: Metra Consulting Group Limited for the Commission of the European
   Communities, 1978. 287p.
Ecological and economic necessity of waste recycling
   Luxembourg: Office for official publications of the European Communities, 1979. 7p.
Johnson, Stanley P
Pollution control policy of the European Communities
   London: Graham and Trotman, 1979. 157p. ISBN 0-86010-136-3

Advisory Committee on the Control and Reduction of Pollution Caused by Hydrocarbons Discharged at Sea

Basic information

Following the Amoco Cadiz oil tanker disaster (1978) the Commission submitted a communication to the Council in 1978 to combat oil pollution at sea. This was adopted by the Council (OJ C162/1–4 8.7.78). The annex to this communication outlined an action programme.

Advisory Committee – representation

This Committee was set up by the Commission in 1980 (OJ L188/11–12 22.7.80) (Decision 80/686/EEC). It consists of three representatives per member state who are experts in the subject. Representatives of those departments of the Commission which are concerned, are allowed to participate in the meetings of the Committee. Alternative members should be appointed who will participate in meetings only when the original member is absent.

Work of the Advisory Committee

The tasks of the Committee are:
- the compilation of a record of the views of member states on controlling and reducing oil pollution at sea
- gathering information on methods of carrying out their tasks
- co-ordination of measures taken

The first meeting was held in Brussels on 21 April 1981. It started on the first of the tasks listed above.

Further information

Oil spills at sea
Bulletin of the European Communities **13** (6) 1980. point 2.1.75
Environment, 3rd action programme
Bulletin of the European Communities **14** (11) 1981. point 2.1.34

Education.

Basic information

In EC countries education absorbs about 12% of public expenditure and historically occupies a strategic position in the process of economic and social development.

Community co-operation in the educational field started in 1971 with the meeting of education ministers from member states. In 1973 education appeared in the portfolio of a commissioner (Professor Ralph Dahrendorf).

Purpose

On 6 June 1974 the education ministers of the nine member states agreed on the need to maintain local educational traditions whilst stressing the value of developing educational co-operation across Europe in the following sectors:

- improved facilities for training nationals as well as migrant workers and their families
- closer relations between educational systems within the EC
- provision of up-to-date information on documents and on education statistics at Community level
- improvement of language teaching, especially of EC languages. Co-operation with this problem between institutes of higher learning
- encouragement of mobility amongst students and researchers. Mutual recognition of diplomas and periods of study
- equal opportunity for access to all forms of education throughout the Community

Work undertaken

Based on the points listed above the first programme of educational co-operation appeared in February 1976 (OJ C38/1 19.2.76). On 13 December of that year (OJ C308/1–3 30.12.76) specific initiatives were adopted regarding education for the transition from school to work. These were monitored and co-ordinated by an education committee composed of representatives from each of the nine countries and from the European Commission. The programmes of educational co-operation which started in 1976 continued on a regular basis. In 1982, for example, the Commission decided to award grants totalling 218,000 ECU to 73 teachers to give them the opportunity to extend their knowledge and experience of higher edcation amongst member states. At the same time 216 local and regional government officers were enabled to study the organization of secondary general and technical education (*Bulletin of the European Communities* **15** (1) 1982. point 2.1.30).

A European university was set up in Florence in 1976. In 1978 the EC put forward proposals to encourage the study of European languages and the European Community, in schools. A common admissions policy for students attending higher educational establishments, grants for higher education students wishing to work in another EC country and equal opportunities for girls, formed other aspects of these proposals. Both the European university and the European university institute, produce annual reports of their activities.

In order to encourage study of the work of the Community and to spread knowledge of its activities, European Documentation Centres are established in member states as they join the Community. Support has been given to studies on facets of European educational problems and a number of these have been published by the Commission in an Education series of Studies. All are available from Luxembourg: Office for official publications of the European Communities.

For the sixth time the Council and Ministers of education of member states met in Luxembourg on 22 June 1981. At the close of this meeting the President of the Council made the following points:

- education and training in relation to employment. The rigidity of the educational system will need to give way to a more flexible approach for those concerned with employment. It was thought that the Community pilot projects programme aimed at ensuring the easy transition from school to working life should become part of the system in member states (original proposal OJ C308/1-3 30.12.76). For details of the project in Britain see under, Further information. Linked work and training pilot projects based on a Council resolution of December 1979 (OJ C1/1-2 3.1.80) were evaluated and the support of the European social fund, assessed by the Education committee on 11.3.82 (*Bulletin of the European Communities* **15** (3) 1982 points 2.1.42-2.1.43). The report prepared by the Education committee was examined at the seventh meeting of Ministers of Education from member states with the Council on 24 May 1982. A resolution regarding a second series of pilot schemes for 1983-6, is given in *Bulletin of the European Communities* **15** (5) 1982 points 2.1.34-2.1.38
- impact of demographic changes on education systems in the European Community. In all member states a decline in numbers of students was

expected over the next five years. Attention was focused on the rise in numbers of immigrant children, implication of rationalization measures on the size of institutions, equipment in schools, pupil/teacher ratio, and finance. The education committee was instructed to examine these points with particular reference to the Eurydice network (qv)
- mutual recognition of diplomas and certificates and periods of study (qv). Discussion was based on a report prepared by the Education committee. It was proposed that this committee should prepare another report in 1982.

A summary of this meeting can be found in, *Bulletin of the European Communities* **14** (6) 1981. points 2.1.50–2.1.52.

In higher education an academic selection panel for the, Joint programmes of study, meets regularly to select candidates for financial support by the Community. In the 1982/3 academic year 93 projects were selected and awarded grants totalling 315.000 ECU.

Further information

'Education in the European Community'. *Bulletin of the European Communities* supplement 3/74
Economic and Social Committee.
Systems of education and vocational training in the member countries of the European Communities
     Luxembourg: Office for official publications of the European Communities, 1976. 114p.
Education statistics 1970–5
     Luxembourg: Office for official publications of the European Communities, 1977. 198p.
     Catalogue number CA–22–76–043–6A–C
Towards a European education policy.
European documentation 1977/2
Higher education in the European Community, a handbook for students
     Brussels: Directorate-General for research, science and education, 1979. 251p. ISBN 92–825–1307–6. Catalogue number CG–28–79–762–EN–C
European Community and education
     Brussels: EC Directorate-General for Information, October 1979. 7p. (European File 18/79). Catalogue number CC–AD–79–018–EN–C
EEC project, transition from school to working life
     Sheffield: EEC Project Director, Chief Education Officer, City of Sheffield Metropolitan District Education Department, 1979 – (Bulletin series)

Eurydice Network

Basic information

The decision to establish this educational information network was taken in 1976 (OJ C38/1–5 19.2.76).

The headquarters was established in Brussels in 1979 and is connected to one or two national centres in each member state. This facilitates the rapid exchange of information needed by those responsible for policy decision on education in the Community.

Purpose

Initially Eurydice will concentrate on the following:

- transition from school to working life
- modern language teaching
- education for migrant workers and their families
- policy and conditions for the admission of students to higher education establishments

A proposal for extending this cover is in, *Bulletin of the European Communities* **14** (5) 1981. point 2.1.39.

Work undertaken

EUDISED, the automated multilingual thesaurus, is being developed (in 1981) to cover the main subject fields of EURYDICE. This thesaurus is jointly financed by the Commission and the Council of Europe.

Seminars on Eurydice are being held in each member state in turn, to foster mutual understanding of education systems in the Community (*Bulletin of the European Communities* **14** (6) 1981. point 2.1.54).

Further information

General report on the activities of the European Communities
  Luxembourg: Office for official publications of the European Communities, annual
'Inauguration of the Eurydice information network'. *Bulletin of the European Communities*
13 (9) 1980. point 2.1.92

European Documentation Centres (EDCs)

Basic information

It wasn't until 1964 that European Documentation Centres in the UK began to be established. This resulted from an earlier, rather expensive policy of personal distribution of documents to individuals which failed to be successful in providing a wide distribution of EC information. This personal distribution was undertaken by the Commission mainly to individual lecturers and professors in Universities who were considered likely to influence national and local thought and policy.

EDC collections

The total number of Centres is 316 – the UK having 49, a figure which includes 4 depository libraries. The distinction between EDCs and depository libraries has become blurred owing to the failure of the Commission to specify precisely the types of documents it is distributing, and its staff to adhere strictly to the rules laid down. However, depository libraries should be fuller collections of material than they are, for the Community tends to be selective in its despatch of some serials and documents. If the librarian is not alert to check the range of material received and take positive action to keep his collection updated his EDC will be only of limited value. In Britain only a few public libraries are EDCs. As will be seen from the following list the majority are Universities and Polytechnics, not all of which are as centrally located as the Public Library. The public in Britain, unlike other European countries, are not so familiar with using academic libraries for reference purposes. Additionally 8 reference centres provide smaller collections of documents.

Work of the EDC

Problems encountered by the EDCs are, the variety of sources for EC publications, the rather erratic nature of the distribution, the category of publications known as Limited Distribution Documents as well as the formally published material, the changes in references used, the slowness in the production of lists of documents issued, as well as the fact that many in the EC show surprise that these things are considered important.

Action taken to resolve these problems includes the formation of Library Association/European Community Working Party 1979 – to co-ordinate on a national basis efforts to improve the production and flow of EC documents. Librarians and others in various parts of the United Kingdom have formed groups to exchange information and press for improved services. One of the most active of these is the Northern Group centred on Newcastle-upon-Tyne Polytechnic Library. In Germany too EDC Librarians have met to express dissatisfaction with the receipt of documents.

Further information

Jeffries, John
'European Documentation Centres in the United Kingdom' *Government Publication Review*. 1977. v. 4 no. 2 p. 127–9
Palmer, Doris M (ed)
Sources of information on the European Economic Community, Chapter p. 81. 'European Communities material in … documentation centres in the United Kingdom', by J P Chillag
  London: Mansell Publishing, 1979. 230p. ISBN 0–7201–0724–5

Ramsay, Anne
'European Communities information – how to track it down and keep pace with it'

Refer **1** (3) Spring 1981 p.4–7 (Part 1)
       1 (4) Autumn 1981 p.3–5 (Part 2)

A number of leaflets have been published by the EDC Librarians in their 'How to' series eg 'How to find out about the Court of Justice of the European Communities'. All are dated 1982 and vary between four and five pages. Available from any EDC Librarian

EDC – European Documentation Centres in United Kingdom

Aberdeen
University of Aberdeen
University Library
European Documentation Centre
New Library
Meston Walk
Aberdeen AB9 2UB
Tel: 0224 40241
Librarian: Miss H Greer

Bath
University of Bath
University Library
Claverton Down
Bath BA2 7AY
Tel: 0225 6941
Librarian: Mrs M Cramp

Belfast
Queen's University
Government Publications Department
The Library
Belfast BT7 1LS
Northern Ireland
Tel: 0232 45133
Librarian: Miss F Brown

Birmingham
Birmingham Polytechnic
Commerce Centre Library
European Documentation Centre
Main Library
Perry Barr
Birmingham B42 7HA
Tel: 021 356 6911
Librarian: Miss J M Thomas

University of Birmingham
Main Library
PO Box 363
Birmingham B15 2TT
Tel: 021 4721301
Librarian: Mr St Hewett

Bradford
University of Bradford
The Library
Richmond Road
Bradford BD7 1DP
Tel: 0274 33466
Librarian: Mr J J Horton

Brighton
University of Sussex Library
Documents Section
Falmer
Brighton BN1 9QL
Tel: 0273 66755
Librarian: Mr D V Kennelly

Bristol
University of Bristol
Law Library
Wills Memorial Bldg
Queens Road
Bristol BS8 1RJ
Tel: 0272 24161
Librarian: Mr C A Ward

Cambridge
University of Cambridge
University Library
West Road
Cambridge CB3 9DR
Tel: 0223 61441
Librarian: Mr R C G Vickery

Canterbury
University of Kent at Canterbury
The Library
Canterbury CT2 7NU
Kent
Tel: 0227 66822
Librarian: Mr J Jeffries

Cardiff
Arts and Social Studies Library
University College
PO Box 78
Cardiff CF1 1XL
Tel: 0222 44211
Librarian: Mr Andrew Green

Coleraine
New University of Ulster
European Documentation Centre
The Library
Coleraine BT52 1SA
Londonderry
Northern Ireland
Tel: 0265 4141
Librarian: Miss P J Compton

Coventry
Lanchester Polytechnic Library
Priory Street
Coventry CV1 5FB
Tel: 0203 24011
Librarian: Mr A G Owens

University of Warwick
The Library
Coventry CV4 7AL
Tel: 0203 417417
Librarian: Mr J D S Hall

Dundee
University of Dundee
Law Library
Scrymgeour Building
Park Place
Dundee DD1 4HN
Tel: 0382 23181
Librarian: Mr D R Hart

Durham
University of Durham
University Library
Palace Green
Durham DH1 3RN
Tel: 0385 61262
Librarian: Dr C D Watkinson

Edinburgh
University of Edinburgh
Centre of European Governmental
Studies
Old College
South Bridge
Edinburgh EH8 9YL
Tel: 031 667 1011
Librarian: Mrs C L Kelly

Colchester
University of Essex
Library
PO Box 24
Colchester CO4 3UA
Tel: 0206 862286
Librarian: Mr A J Baines

Exeter
University of Exeter
Faculty of Law
Centre for European Legal Studies
Amory Building, Rennes Drive
Exeter EX4 4RJ
Tel: 0392 77911
Librarian: Miss A Pyrah

Glasgow
University of Glasgow
The University Library
European Documentation Centre
Hillhead Street
Glasgow G12 8QE
Tel: 041 334 2122
Librarian: Mr G K Anderson

Guildford
University of Surrey
The Library
Guildford GU2 5XH
Tel: 0483 71281
Librarian: Miss S E Telfer

Hull
University of Hull
European Documentation Centre
Brynmor Jones Library
Cottingham Road
Hull HU6 7RX
Yorkshire
Tel: 0482 46311
Librarian: Mrs W M Carroll

Keele
University of Keele
University Library
European Documentation Centre
Keele ST5 5BG
Tel: 078 2 621111
Librarian: Mr B G Finnemore

Lancaster
University of Lancaster
University Library
Lancaster LA1 4YH
Tel: 0524 65201
Librarian: Mr J L Illingworth

Leeds
University of Leeds
Faculty of Law
European Documentation Centre
Leeds LS 9JT
Tel: 0532 31751
Librarian: Mr J Porter

Leeds Polytechnic Library
European Documentation Centre
Calverley Street
Leeds LS1 3HE
Tel: 0532 462925
Librarian: Miss B Downing

Leicester
University of Leicester
University Library
University Road
Leicester LE1 7RH
Tel: 0533 50000
Librarian: Mr A R Siddiqui

London
British Library of Political and Economic
Science
(London School of Economics and
Political Science)
10 Portugal Street
London WC2A 2HD
Tel: 01-405 7686
Librarian: Mr D F Ross

University of London
Queen Mary College
The Library
Mile End Road
London E1 4NS
Tel: 01-980 4811
Librarian: Miss J Neilson

The Polytechnic of Central London –
EEC Unit
309 Regent Street
London W1R 8AL
Tel: 01-580 2020
Librarian: Miss B E Williams

Polytechnic of North London
The Library
Kentish Town
Prince of Wales Road
London NW5 3LB
Tel: 01-607 2789
Librarian: Mr C J Andrew

Royal Institute of International Affairs
The Library
10 St James Square
London SW1Y 4LE
Tel: 01-930 2233
Librarian: Mr N M Gallimore

University of London
Centre for European Agricultural Studies
Wye College
Wye
Ashford
Kent TN25 5AH
Tel: 0233 812401
Librarian: Miss W Pryce

Loughborough
Loughborough University of Technology
The Library
Loughborough
Leicestershire LE11 3TU
Tel: 0509 63171
Librarian: Mr M Hopkins

Manchester
University of Manchester
Library of Manchester
John Rylands University
Oxford Road
Manchester M13 9PP
Tel: 061 273 3333
Librarian: Mr K J McVeigh

Newcastle upon Tyne
Newcastle upon Tyne Polytechnic
Library
Ellison Place
Newcastle upon Tyne NE1 8ST
Tel: 0632 326002
Librarian: Mrs E A Ramsay

Norwich
University of East Anglia
University Plain
Library
Norwich NR4 7TJ
Tel: 0603 56161
Librarian: Miss J M Kinsey

Nottingham
University of Nottingham
University Library
Nottingham NG7 2RD
Tel: 0602 56101
Librarian: Mr M J Kirby

Oxford
University of Oxford
Official Papers
Radcliffe Camera
Bodleian Library
Oxford OX1 3BG
Tel: 0865 44675
Librarian: Mr S Richard

Portsmouth
Portsmouth Polytechnic
Frewen Library
Cambridge Road
Portsmouth PO1 2ST
Tel: 0705 27681
Librarian: Mr T Hanson

Reading
University of Reading
University Library
European Documentation Centre
Whiteknights
Reading RG6 2AA
Tel: 0734 84331
Librarian: Mr I M Sainsbury

Salford
University of Salford
The Library
Salford M5 4WT
Tel: 061 7365843
Librarian: Miss M Carruthers

Sheffield
Sheffield City Polytechnic
The Library
Pond Street
Sheffield S1 1WB
Tel: 0742 20911
Librarian: Mr G H Wills

Southampton
University of Southampton
Faculty of Law
Highfield
Southampton SO9 5NH
Tel: 0703 559122
Librarian: Mr J L M Hoyle

Wolverhampton
Polytechnic of Wolverhampton
The Robert Scott Library
St Peter's Square
Wolverhampton WV1 1RH
Tel: 0902 27371
Librarian: Mr J S Nockels

DL – Depositary Libraries

Boston Spa
European Communities Liaison Officer
British Library Lending Division
Boston Spa – Wetherby – W Yorkshire
LS23 7BQ
Tel: 0937 843434
Librarian: Mr J P Chillag

Liverpool
Liverpool and District Scientific,
Industrial and Research Library
Advisory Council (LADSIRLAC)
William Brown Street
Liverpool L3 8EW
Tel: 051 2071937
Librarian: Mr E Fleming

London
British Library – Reference Division
Department of Printed Books
Overseas English Section
Great Russel Street
London WC1B 3DG
Tel: 01–636 1544
Librarian: Miss I Sternberg

City of Westminster Libraries
Central Library
St Martin's Street
London WC2H 7HP
Tel: 01–930 3274
Librarian: Miss P M Chamberlain

European Reference Centres

Aberystwyth
Wales – University College
PO Box 2
Old College
Aberystwyth
Dyfed

Brighton
Brighton Reference Library
Church Street
Brighton
Sussex BN1 1UE

Ealing
Ealing College of Higher Education
St Mary's Road
Rm 215 Tutor Libn/Archive/Research
Rm
London W5 5RF

Edinburgh
National Library of Scotland
Official Papers Section
George IV Bridge
Edinburgh EH1 1EW

Preston
The Library
Preston Polytechnic
St Peter's Square
Preston PR1 7BB

Stirling
Stirling University Library
Stirling FK9 4LA

Swansea
University College of Swansea
Singleton Park
Swansea SA2 8PP

Teesside
Teesside Polytechnic Library
Middlesbrough
Cleveland TS1 3BA

Dublin (Republic of Ireland)
The Library
University College of Dublin
Earlsfort Terrace
Dublin 4
Tel: 0001 01 693244

The Library
Trinity College
College Street,
Dublin 2
Tel: 0001 01 772941

European Foundation

Basic information

In December 1975 in the report to the Council on European Union, the idea of a European Foundation was presented by Mr Leo Tindermans.

At the European Council meeting in Copenhagen 7–8.4 1978 decisions were taken on its objectives, framework and financing. It was to be located in Paris.

The agreement setting up the Foundation was signed on 29.3.82.

Purpose of the Foundation

- to increase mutual understanding
- to cultivate Europe's cultural heritage
- to foster a deeper perception of European integration
- to foster the study of European languages
- to encourage exchanges of persons
- to foster the cultural influence of the Community

Foundation representation

The authorities will be:

- a Board – responsible for policy and consisting of 40 members serving for four years and with their term of office renewable once
- an Executive committee consisting of ten members
- a Secretariat

Finance

The foundation to have 4 million ECU for the first three years.

Further information

European Union
Bulletin of the European Communities supplement 1/79
Bulletin of the European Communities **14** (11) 1981 point 3.5.1
Setting up the European Foundation
Bulletin of the European Communities **15** (3) points 1.2.1–1.2.3

Paul Finet Foundation

Basic information

Founded in 1965 by the High Authority of the European Coal and Steel Community, the Foundation grants scholarships to the dependents of workers, employed during their lifetime in the industries of the ECSC, who died as a result of accidents at work or occupational illness since 30 June 1965 (for British, Irish and Danish nationals, since 1 January 1973).

Work undertaken

The Foundation made 3,242 grants totalling B frs 25,398,358 up to the end of 1973. Subsequently the annual allocation of funds is between 7 and 9 millions of Belgium francs.

The Board is composed of nineteen members representing the Commission of the European Communities, the employers' organizations and the trade union organizations.

(Paul Finet was a Belgian steel worker and trade unionist, born 1897 at Montignies-sur-Sambre; became national secretary of the Fédération générale des travailleurs belges in 1936; helped form the International confederation of free unions in 1949 and became its president in 1951. In 1958 he became president of the European Coal and Steel Community, following René Mayer).

Further information

Report on social developments
  Luxembourg: Office for official publications of the European Communities, annual

Diplomas and Professional Qualifications, Mutual Recognition

Basic information

The Treaty of Rome (1957) upon which the European Community is based, included as part of its policy the free movement of people and services.

In many cases an individual's ability to carry out specific trades or professions is recorded by a qualification. If it is possible for workers to move from one member state to another it is important that their qualifications have a Community wide recognition.

This criterion is of economic importance to both the individual and the Community. It is politically important also as the Community is moving towards closer unity and ultimately a single entity.

A Council resolution on the mutual recognition of diplomas was issued in 1974 (OJ C98/1–2 20.8.74). This resolution also established an Education committee to further this aim.

Extent of the cover

Since the early 1960s over seventy-five directives have been adopted to facilitate, on a Community wide basis, the practice of duties and professions which need a qualification.

On 5 May 1981 the Commission sent to the Council a communication on the academic recognition of diplomas and periods of study. The aim was to resolve the lack of information on this subject at Community level. The proposal is for an information network which would form part of Eurydice (*Bulletin of the European Communities* 14 (5) 1981. point 2.1.39) (qv).

Work undertaken

- Education

  A report by the Education committee on problems associated with the mutual recognition of diplomas and certificates and periods of study was discussed at the sixth meeting of the Council and Ministers of Education of member states. At their seventh meeting on 24 May 1982 (*Bulletin of the European Communities* 15 (5) 1982. point 2.1.36) they agreed the following proposals:

  - bilateral agreement should be made between member states
  - students in higher education to be encouraged to study in another member state with appropriate courses
  - information regarding existing bilaterial agreements should be disseminated
  - Eurydice network should be utilized for the exchange of information

- member states should draw up biennial reports on bilateral agreements

- Medicine

  As in many professional subjects, the mutual recognition of national medical qualifications has to be based on the extent and standard of training. In order to work in other member states in many cases a further ability in the language of the new state has to be obtained. From December 1976 some 500,000 Community doctors can practice anywhere in the EC (OJ L167/1–13 30.6.75) (Directive 75/362/EEC). This directive includes lists of equivalent qualifications. Further recommendations concern the duties and the clinical training of doctors (OJ L167/14–16 30.6.75) (Recommendation 75/363/EEC). On 26 January 1982 this Recommendation was amended in particular the provisions relating to the part-time training of specialists. The original proposed was in February 1981 (OJ C121/3–7 23.5.81). An, Advisory committee on medical training was set up (qv) (OJ L167/21 30.6.75) (Recommendation 75/367/EEC). The numbers of doctors who are nationals of one member state but obtained their qualification in another is given in, *Bulletin of the European Communities* **12** (12) 1979. point 2.1.13.

- Dentistry

  Currently, to ensure the mutual recognition of diplomas, certificates and other evidence of the formal qualifications of practitioners in dentistry as well as to facilitate the right to set up as a dentist in member states, the Council approved a directive (OJ L233/1–9 24.8.78) (Directive 78/686/EEC). This item gives lists of the titles of professional staff in the various member states. It also lists the diplomas, etc appropriate to dental practitioners, by country. It includes details of academic titles which may be used within the profession and finally mentions that disputes and queries on the mutual recognition of qualifications should be settled by the Committee of senior officials of public health. A further directive lays down the future training of dentists in order to ensure a greater degree of uniformity (OJ L233/10–14 24.8.78) (Directive 78/687/EEC). This includes details of the work to be practiced by dentists. Member states were asked to comply with this directive within eighteen months of the date of publication or in the case of Italy, within 6 years of the same date.

- Nurses responsible for general care

  In 1971 the Commission presented proposals to the Council covering:
  mutual recognition of diplomas, etc
  rights of establishment of nurses and freedom to provide services

  (OJ L176/1–7 15.7.77) (Directive 77/452/EEC).

  An, Advisory committee on training in nursing was set up in 1977 (OJ L176/11–12 15.7.77) (Decision 77/454/EEC). Its purpose was to establish a high standard of training throughout the Community, and to maintain a watching brief on medical, social science and teaching methods (qv).

- Veterinary science

  A number of directives cover veterinary surgeons but one of the first was for the mutual recognition of diplomas (OJ L362/1–6 23.12.78) (Directive 78/1026/EEC).

  An, Advisory committee on veterinary training has been established with the tasks of:

  maintaining a high standard of training throughout the Community arranging for the exchange of information
  holding a watching brief on developments in veterinary science and teaching methods

  (OJ L 362/10–11 23.12.78) (Decision 78/1028/EEC).

- Pharmacy

  In 1981 the Commission presented Council with proposals covering:

  right of establishment of pharmacy graduates in the Community
  mutual recognition of diplomas and mention of examining bodies of each member state
  establishment of an advisory committee on training

  (OJ C35/3–10 18.2.81)

- Midwifery

  In member states there are two schools of thought on the work and responsibilities of midwives. In the first directive on this subject the EC established regulations for:

  mutual recognition of diplomas, certificates, etc
  the right of establishment
  freedom to provide services

  These have been agreed amongst member states of the EC (OJ L33/17 11.2.80) (Directive 80/154/EEC). An, Advisory committee on the training of midwives (qv) to ensure future uniformity of training within the EC, has been established (OJ L33/13–14 11.2.80) (Decision 80/156/EEC).

- Architecture

  One of the earliest proposals concerned architects. In 1968 the Commission submitted to Council draft proposals for mutual recognition of qualifications and facilities to provide services anywhere in the Community (OJ C72/3 19.7.68). Many proposals and amendments have been made. In an effort to speed action, the European Parliament which was consulted over the 1968 draft, received a proposed resolution on the subject (EP working document 1–810/79).

  A debate took place in Parliament (OJ C291/95 10.11.80) and a resolution passed which calls on the Council to consult Parliament as there have been so many changes made to the 1968 proposals in the past twelve years.

- Legal profession

  Whilst no directive has been agreed on the mutual recognition of qualifications of lawyers in member states up to 1980, yet a 1977 directive has some slight bearing on the matter (OJ L78/17–18 26.3.77) (Directive 77/249/EEC).

  This directive is to facilitate the effective exercise by lawyers of the provision of services. In this directive the distinctive title of lawyers in each member state has been listed and it was agreed that the lawyer working in another part of the EC should be entitled to use the appropriate local designation.

- Insurance, agents and brokers

  A directive to facilitate the effective exercise of freedom of establishment and freedom to provide services in respect of the activities of Insurance agents and brokers was issued in 1976 (OJ L26/14–19 31.1.77) (Directive 77/92/EEC). This transitional directive defines the professions, lists their titles in member states and details their qualifications.

- Road haulage operators, Road passenger transport operators

  In 1974 details of the qualifications and proof of honesty and, in some countries, financial standing, which were required by such drivers on national or international operations, were listed (OJ L308/18–22 19.11.74) (Directive 74/561/EEC) and (OJ L308/23–5 19.11.74) (Directive 74/562/EEC). It was noted that the road haulage operator also has a list of subjects, details of which are required for his transport operation. In 1977 these two sets of qualifications were combined in one directive (OJ L334/37 24.12.77) (Directive 77/796/EEC). Measures to comply with this directive were brought into force in member states by 1.1.79.

Further information

General report on the activities of the European Communities
Luxembourg: Office for official publications of the European Communities, annual

Advisory Committee for Vocational Training

Basic information

Under article 128 of the Treaty of Rome (1957) a Council decision of 1963 established general principles for implementing a common vocational training programme (OJ 63/1338–41 20.4.63) (Decision 63/266/EEC). The fourth principle (last sentence) made provision for the establishment of this Committee. Entry into force was 1.1.75.

In the same year the rules of the Advisory committee ... were recorded (OJ 190/3090–1 30.12.63) (Decision 63/688/EEC) and subsequently amended. These came into force on 1.1.73.

Advisory Committee – representation

- two Government members from each member state plus one alternative member
- two trade union members from each member state plus one alternative member
- two employers' association members from each member state plus one alternative member
- one non-voting representative from ECSC
- one non-voting representative from EURATOM
- appointments are for two years and they may be renewed
- a non-voting chairman and vice-chairman are provided by the Commission

Work of the Advisory Committee

In May 1977 the Advisory committee ... adopted guidelines for the implementation of a common vocational training policy (OJ L180/18–23 20.7.77) (Recommendation 77/467/EEC). Its programme included:

- training and employment of young people
- vocational training for women
- a documentation and information service
- a research programme

Further information

General report on the activities of the European Communities
   Luxembourg: Office for official publications of the European Communities, annual

The Commission of the European Communities has also sponsored a series of reports on vocational guidance, including:

- *The evaluation of vocational training*, Report of a seminar held in the University of Manchester, United Kingdom January 1975
- *Report on vocation guidance activities in the Community 1975*
- *Vocational guidance and training for women workers*, European seminar 24–28 November 1975 Paris

These are available from Luxembourg: Office for official publications of the European Communities

European Centre for the Development of Vocational Training (CEDEFOP)

Basic information

Under article 128 of the Treaty of Rome (1957) the Council adopted a regulation establishing this Centre in 1975 (OJ L39/1–4 13.2.75) (Regulation 337/75/EEC). Financial and staffing provisions for the Centre were made in the following year under (OJ L164/1–15 24.6.76) (Regulation 1416/76/EEC) and (OJ L214/1–23 6.8.76) (Regulation 1859/76/ECSC, EEC, EURATOM).

European Centre – representation

Members of the Centre are drawn from all EC member states, the employers' organizations, the trade union organizations and the Commission.

The management board adopted its own rules of procedure and submitted to the Commission names for its director. An annual report is submitted to the Commission by 31 March each year.

The annual budget of the European Communities includes a subsidy for the Centre.

Work of the Centre

Working parties have been set up on vocational guidance, apprenticeship, etc.

Its aims are:

- to assist the Commission in the promotion and development of vocational and in-service training
- to contribute to a common vocational training policy
- to encourage the exchange of information and experience on vocational training
- to compile selected documentation on its subject field and contribute to research; disseminate information; support initiatives concerned with the development of vocational training and provide a forum for those concerned where these matters may be debated
- to organize courses, conclude study contracts, commission projects, publish and distribute. Examples of its publishing are:

  Comparative study of the financing of training systems for professional workers – legislation and regulations in the Federal Republic of Germany, France, Italy, UK,
  Berlin: CEDEFOP, 1981. 360p. ISBN 92–825–1783–7.

Publications include a Community vocational training bulletin, *Vocational training*, now published three times a year (commenced in 1974, published by the Commission and taken over by CEDEFOP in 1977) and a number of reports including, *Youth employment and vocational training; the material and social standing of young people during transition from school to work in the United Kingdom*, Berlin: CEDEFOP, 1980. 75p. ISBN 92–825–1975–9 and, *Legislative and regulatory structure of vocational training systems*, Berlin: CEDEFOP, 1980. 224p. ISBN 92–825–1782–9.

The Centre is independent of Departments of the EC but must fully co-operate with them and implement Council decision of 2 April 1963 (OJ 63/1338–41 20.4.63) (Decision 63/266/EEC). This laid down principles for a common vocational training programme.

Its headquarters is in West Berlin and the Centre was opened on 9 March 1977.

Further information

General report on the activities of the European Communities
Luxembourg: Office for official publications of the European Communities, annual
Community advisory committees for the representation of socio-economic interests
Farnborough: Saxon House for EC Economic and Social Committee, 1980. 215p. ISBN 0–566–00328–7

Advisory Committee on Medical Training

Basic information

The Council decided to set up a Committee in 1975 (OJ L167/17–18 30.6.75) (Decision 75/364/EEC).

Advisory Committee – representation

The Committee consists of three experts from each member state consisting of one from the profession, one from the University medical school and one from the State Medical department or ministry. Alternative members for each full member should be appointed and these may attend meetings. All appointments are made by the Council for a period of three years. Observers and experts may be invited by the Committee to attend its meetings.

Work of the Advisory Committee

The Committee's duties are:

- to maintain a comparable high level of training throughout the Community, by the exchange of information, discussion and consultation, maintaining training standards in line with developments within the profession
- working parties may be established
- to suggest amendments to those articles which relate to medical training
- to advise the Commission on matters which it considers need investigation and which relate to medical training

Further information

Community advisory committees for the representation of socio-economic interests
Farnborough: Saxon House for the EC Economic and Social Committee, 1980. 215p.
ISBN 0-566-00328-7

Advisory Committee on Training in Nursing

Basic information

The Council decided to set up this Committee in 1977 (OJ L176/11-12 15.7.77) (Decision 77/454/EEC).

Advisory Committee – representation

The Committee consists of three experts from each member state, one from the profession, one from a nursing training organization and one from the authority in the member state. An alternative should be nominated for each full member. Members and alternates may attend the meeting of the Committee. Nominations are made by member states and appointments are made by the Council.

Duties of the Advisory Committee

The Committee's duties are:

- to ensure a comparable high standard of training throughout the

Community by the exchange of information, discussion, developing a common approach to standards and keeping under review training methods in the light of developments in practical medicine, social service and teaching methods
- to set up working parties
- to submit proposals for Commission action

Further information

Community advisory committees for the representation of socio-economic interests
   Farnborough: Saxon House for the EC Economic and Social Committee, 1980. 215p.
   ISBN 0–566–00328–7

Advisory Committee on the Training of Midwives

Basic information

In 1980 the Council issued a decision setting up this Committee (OJ L33/13–14 11.2.80) (Decision 80/156/EEC).

Advisory Committee – representation

Three experts are required from each member state together with a similar number of observers.

A chairman and two deputy chairmen are to be selected by the Committee from its members. All are to serve for a three year term. They are entitled to call upon or allow, observers or experts to assist but not to vote.

Work of the Advisory Committee

Its purpose is to ensure a future uniformity of training for midwives within the Community.

Directive 80/155/EEC includes as an annex a training programme for midwives. It also covers the extent of the training thought necessary and a full list of subjects to be covered. (OJ L33/8–12 11.2.80) (Directive 80/155/EEC).

Further information

General report on the work of the European Communities
Luxembourg: Office for official publications of the European Communities, annual

Advisory Committee on the Training of Dental Practitioners

Basic information

In 1978 the Council issued a directive setting up this Committee (OJ L233/15–16 24.8.78) (Directive 78/688/EEC), which is attached to the Commission.

Advisory Committee – representation

Three experts are required from each member state. One of these should be from the department of the government responsible for dentistry, one from a university dental school and one should be a senior practising dentist.

The Committee should elect its own chairman and two deputy chairmen.

The term of office of all members is three years. Working parties may be set up.

Observers and experts may be called upon to attend meetings and assist the Committee over special aspects of their work.

Work of the Advisory Committee

The purpose of this Committee is to ensure comparable standards of training for its members throughout the Community.

It is empowered to arrange for the exchange of information on dentistry.

It has to maintain a watching brief on developments in dental science and teaching methods.

Further information

General report on the activities of the European Communities
Luxembourg: Office for official publications of the European Communities, annual

Public Health

Basic information

Social security is available in all member states but is not identical in each. Bilateral agreements of long standing allow the nationals of one country living or working in another to come within the orbit of the host country's social security services. Article 118 of the Treaty of Rome makes provision for the public health aspect of social security. Under the European Atomic Energy Community agreement (EURATOM) 1957, Chapter III and the European Coal and Steel Community (ECSC) 1952, considerable safeguards have been brought into force, medical aid introduced and research on medical problems undertaken.

Work undertaken

To date a number of aspects of public health have been dealt with. For example approximation of the law relating to cosmetic products (Directive 76/768/EEC), biological screening of the population for lead (Directive 77/312/EEC), approximation of the laws relating to detergents (Directive 73/404/EEC). Under medicine and pharmacy there is a directive on the approximation of provisions laid down by law, regulation or administrative action relating to proprietary medical products (Directive 75/319/EEC). A somewhat similar directive deals with colouring matters which may be added to medical products (Directive 78/25/EEC).

See also entries on, Diplomas. . . mutual recognition, Advisory Committee on medical training, Social development, etc.

Further information

General report on the activities of the European Communities
   Luxembourg: Office for official publications of the European Communities, annual
National health security systems in the European Economic Community
   Luxembourg: Office for official publications of the European Communities, 1977. 159p.
   (EUR 5747e) Catalogue number CK–SJ–77–001–EN–C
Hospitals in the EEC, organization and terminology
   Copenhagen: Gyldendalske Boghandel Nordisk Forlay AS, 1978. 464p. ISBN 87–01–59851–1 [in English, French, German, Italian, Dutch and Danish]

Committee of Senior Officials on Public Health

Basic information

When first established in 1975 this committee was concerned with doctors only (OJ L 167/19 30.6.75) (Decision 75/365/EEC). During 1977 and 1978 amendments were made bringing in other classes of professionals. In 1980 the secondary legislation was consolidated (OJ L33/15–16 11.2.80) (Decision 80/157/EEC).

Committee – representation

The committee consists of one senior representative from each member state plus an alternative for each member. The chairman to be a Commission representative.

Work of the Committee

Its purpose is to discover and analyse all the difficulties which may arise over the implementation of the directives associated with the mutual recognition of diplomas as professional qualifications (qv) of:

- doctors
- dentists
- nurses
- midwives

It should also collect relevant information. This includes information on doctors and nurses trained in one EC country but working in another (*Bulletin of the European Communities* **14** (3) 1981. point 2.1.13).

On 24–25 April 1979 the committee considered proposals submitted to it on the training of general practitioners (*Bulletin of the European Communities* **12** (4) 1979 point 2.1.14).

Further information

General report on the activities of the European Communities
   Luxembourg: Office for official publications of the European Communities, annual

Pharmacy

Basic information

Article 100 of the Treaty of Rome (1957) concerning the approximation of existing laws in member states is the appropriate primary legislation for pharmacy.

In 1965 a directive was issued on the approximation of provisions laid down by law, regulation or administrative action relating to proprietary medical products (OJ 22/369–71 9.2.65) (Directive 65/65/EEC). This directive was amended in the following year (OJ 144/2658 5.8.66) (Directive 66/454/EEC). In 1975 a directive was issued on the approximation of laws of member states relating to analytical pharmacotoxicological and clinical standards as well as protocols for the testing of medical products (OJ L147/1–12 9.6.75) (Directive 75/318/EEC). A further directive in 1977 relates to the colouring matter which may be added to medical products (OJ L11/18–20 14.1.78) (Directive 78/25/EEC).

A Pharmaceutical committee (qv) was established in 1975 (OJ L147/23 9.6.75) (Decision 75/320/EEC).

A Committee for proprietary medical products (qv) was also set up in 1975 (OJ L147/13–22 9.6.75) (Directive 75/319/EEC).

In 1981 the Commission presented to Council a draft of two directives. The first on the right of establishment of pharmacy graduates, and the second the mutual recognition of diplomas, etc (qv) (OJ C35/3– 10 18.2.81).

Extent of cover

Whilst the co-ordination of legislation regarding drugs is well established in the Community, the training and qualifications of pharmacists is currently being approximated in member states.

Further information

General report on the activities of the European Communities
  Luxembourg: Office for official publications of the European Communities, annual

Committee for Proprietary Medical Products

Basic information

Article 100 of the Treaty of Rome on the approximation of provision within member states is the basis of this Committee. The secondary legislation is to be found in Chapter III of the directive relating to proprietary medical products (OJ L147/13–22 9.6.75) (Decision 75/319/EEC).

Under decision 75/320/EEC the fields of work of this Committee and the Pharmaceutical Committee are mutually exclusive.

Committee representation

The Committee shall consist of representatives of the member states and the Commission.

Work of the Committee

Member states having issued a marketing authorization for such a product have to forward to the Committee details of the product and authorization as well as the names of the other member states involved. These states to be notified by the Committee and objections are required within 120 days. The decision mentioned above gives details for dealing with objections and the part to be played by the Committee.

Further information

General report on the activities of the European Communities
Luxembourg: Office for official publications of the European Communities, annual

⑥ Common Technology and Research

In the Community, each member state and many of the major industries have their own research organizations. A part at least of this very large research effort was duplicated in more than one state. Some co-ordination between member states began before the Community was established. Similarly as the largest national firms grew into multinationals, their research effort was co-ordinated.

With the start of the Communities, and particularly ECSC and EURATOM, it was realized that the elimination of duplication would enable more projects to be allocated funds for investigation and development. The largest research projects previously only undertaken by the USA and USSR could now be carried out within the Communities for the benefit of all the member states. Facilities such as laboratories, equipment etc which previously were used for the needs and interests of a single country, could now undertake investigations to benefit and improve the knowledge of every one of the 10 member states.

Through European wide co-operation under the 'COST' projects, other countries outside the Communities, could participate in investigations, share the benefits and share the expenses. The majority of these projects are with EFTA countries.

The co-ordination of research is through a series of committees:

FOR A DETAILED INDEX SEE THE YELLOW PAGES.

From the commencement of EURATOM, existing research establishments amongst member states were used for Community projects:

- **Nuclear energy** (pages 292–4)

Chemical research:

- **Scientific advisory committee on the toxicity and ecotoxicity of chemical compounds** (pages 294–5)
- **Scientific committee on cosmetology** (page 295)

Information and documentation:

- **Scientific and technical information and documentation committee** (STIDC) (pages 296–7)
- **European information network** (pages 297–9)
- **Data processing scheme – financial assistance** (pages 300–301)

Patents and trademarks:

- **Patent law** (pages 301–2)
- **Trademarks** (pages 302–3)

Waste:

- **Waste materials recycling – financial assistance** (pages 303–5)

Research and the Community

Basic information

As this is a wide subject, various aspects of research have been dealt with under separate headings. These will carry a qv reference in the following text.

The Communities treaties do not themselves include comprehensive research tasks or powers. Research is authorized by individual treaties and limited to specific sectors. Article 235 of the EEC treaty (1957) is a comprehensive article to make provision for subjects omitted from the original treaty and some research falls within this article.

Organization and Purpose of Research

A number of committees have been set up to guide and initiate research at various levels and within differing fields of interest.

At policy level there is a twin task of harmonizing the research policies of member states and developing a joint Community policy. These twin developments should coalesce when these tasks reach conclusion.

In a 1974 resolution, the Council decided to develop a common policy in the field of science and technology (OJ C7/2–4 29.1.74). One of the major planks in the fulfilment of this task was the multiannual programme

1980–3 for the Joint Research Centre (qv) which emphasized a common research policy for Europe, developed in the intervening years (OJ L72/11–17 18.3.80) (Decision 80/317/EEC, EURATOM).

The means of progress between the 1974 decision and its implementation in 1980 was the, Scientific and technical research committee (CREST) (qv). This was set up in 1975 and co-ordinates a large number of specialized research and development organizations within the Community in order to advise both the Council and the Commission.

The European committee for research and development (CERD) (qv) is a small committee of top experts whose job is to advise the Commission on research decisions.

The principal scientific and technological programmes of the Community are:

- energy resources with its five aspects:
  fossil energy research
  nuclear fission
  nuclear fusion
  non-nuclear energy sources
  energy conservation
- raw materials, both primary and secondary
- agriculture and food reserves
- water resources
- environment
- social policy relating to life in society
- town and country planning
- medical research
- radiation protection
- molecular biology and genetics
- co-operation in the area of reference materials and methods (standards)
- co-operation in the area of information

The last two items are support services for the rest of the programme.

Work undertaken

Under the ECSC treaty 1952 research is encouraged on:

- production
- increased consumption of coal and steel (Annex 1 of the 1952 treaty)
- industrial safety

A series of multi-annual programmes on scientific development have been organized covering aspects of the subjects listed above. Coal research programme for 1975–80 is continuing. For steel there are 16 million EUA involving 140 contracts covering production methods, product improvement etc which were in operation in 1979 (qv Steel industry).

Adoption of R & D programmes
ROLE OF THE EC ORGANS AND THEIR ADVISORY BODIES

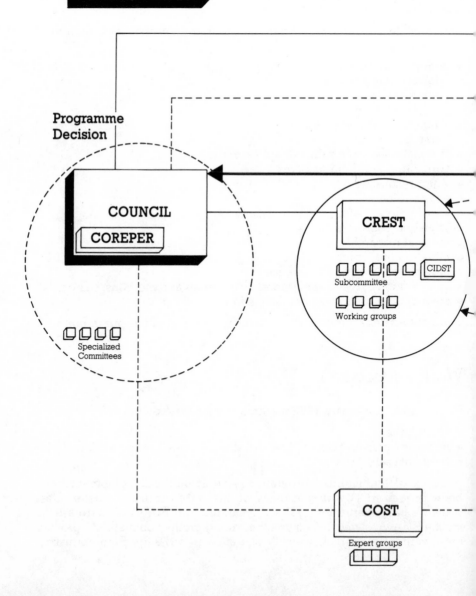

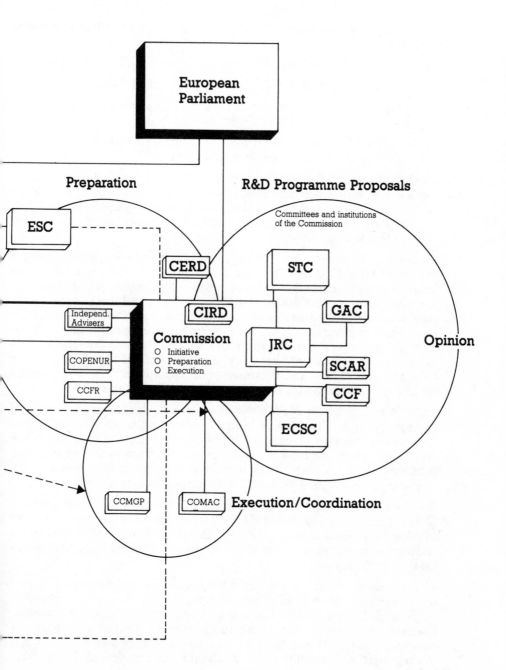

The, Consultative committee of the European Coal and Steel Community (qv) ensures that progress in development throughout the Community is co-ordinated.

In the textiles and clothing industry the Community has adopted R and D programmes

1974–6 (OJ L/111/34–6 30.4.75) (Decision 75/266/EEC)

1981–3 (OJ L367/29–30 23.12.81) (Decision 81/1014/EEC)

From time to time shared cost contracts are awarded (*Bulletin of the European Communities* **15** (4) 1982. point 2.1.103).

Under the EAEC treaty (1957) the, Scientific and technical committee (STC) advises the Commission on nuclear energy.

The Joint Research Centre (JRC) (qv) which was originally set up solely to serve EAEC is now serving all the Communities needs. The development of Nuclear energy (qv) and its Community wide organization has been arranged so that Europe can act jointly, even over the purchase and storage of fission material.

Under the EEC treaty (1957) energy objectives (qv) became increasingly important after 1973 and the first of the series of oil price rises. Large research programmes were initiated in the environment (qv). This became increasingly important during the 1970s as was social development (qv). Both were obtaining sizeable research incomes until the recession of the early 1980s affected the Community. A big effort in co-ordinating national R & D plans was made during the second half of the 1970s. The development of Euronet Diane (qv) and the work of the Scientific and technical information and documentation committee (STIDC) (qv) both act as support services for research within the Community.

In its Mandate of 30 May 1980, the Council decided that structural changes to the Community budget were required by 1982. The Commission's response concerned fundamental changes in the Community and these were outlined in *Bulletin of the European Communities* supplement 1/81. Research and development co-ordination was detailed in a later supplement, 4/81 which gave proposals for the 1980s.

A statistical assessment of research in the Community has been published, *Government financing of R and D in the Community countries – analysis by objectives, detailed report 1975–81*. This showed that in 1981 (excluding Greece) there was an increase of 18% in the finances available, over those for the previous year.

With the development of a series of long term research programmes, and their widening scope, the Council meeting of 30.6.82 was a policy debate on R & D for the 1980s. There was under discussion a Commission, Framework programme for Community scientific and technical activities covering 1984–7. It was thought that the Joint Research Centre's (qv) multiannual programme 1984–7 should be incorporated into this

Framework programme. Finally it was noted that there was need for a Community programme for R & D in information technology co-ordinated with national programmes (qv) European information network (*Bulletin of the European Communities* **15** (6) 1982. points 2.1.164–6).

Further information

General report on the activities of the European Communities
   Luxembourg: Office for official publications of the European Communities, annual
'Common policy for science and technology'. *Bulletin of the European Communities* supplement 3/77
The organization and management of Community research and development
   Brussels: General secretariat of the European Economic and Social committee, 1980. 159p. Catalogue number ESC–80–001–EN
'A new impetus for the common policies [section 2] Scientific and technical research and the European Community – proposals for the 1980s.' *Bulletin of the European Communities* supplement 4/81
Vade-mecum of contract research (indirect action)
   Luxembourg: Commission of the EEC, 1981. 46p.
Aims and priorities of a common research and development policy
   Brussels: General Secretariat of the Economic and Social Committee, 1982. 59p.

Joint Research Centre (JRC)

Basic information

Originally set up under the Euratom treaty articles 4–11 (1957), research was limited to nuclear and related subjects of concern to that Community. The first reorganization of the JRC took place in 1970 (OJ L16/14–16 20.1.71) (Decision 71/57/EURATOM). Only since 1974 (OJ C7/2–4 29.1.74) when the Community decided on a common policy on science and technology, has the JRC undertaken other research. This was under article 235 of the EEC treaty (1957). During the period 1967–72 the JRC was going through a period of crisis. With the four year development programmes of 1973 (OJ L153/9–14 9.6.73) (Decision 73/125–7/EEC) and (OJ L189/34–5 11.7.73) (Decision 73/176/EEC) the inclusion of non nuclear projects was made. All these programmes, which were the responsibility of the Commission, were phrased '... and shall avail itself of the facilities of the JRC'. New impetus was given to the Centre by the inclusion of these non nuclear research projects. This meant that once again it had to reorganize and redefine its activities – a difficult task for such a large and highly specialized organization. In 1977 a new four year programme to 1980, made the future of the JRC secure (OJ L200/4–9 8.8.77) (Decision 77/488/EEC, EURATOM). As is seen the single decision was for both Euratom and the EEC and applied singly to the JRC.

Purpose of the JRC

To undertake work along the guidelines provided by the Commission to the Director-General of the JRC. The Director-General to provide detailed plans of work to be approved by the Commission. The Director-General to be responsible for the effective implementation of these approved plans. He is assisted by a, General advisory committee. See last item under 'Further information'.

The JRC has four research establishments:

- at Ispra, Italy where considerable research is being undertaken in the fields of nuclear reactor safety and nuclear waste management. The latest of these the Super-Sara project, has been approved by the Council at its meeting of 18/19 May 1981. It is concerned with the behaviour of nuclear fuels in the event of loss of coolant. This is the problem which occurred in the USA at the Three Mile Island accident (28 March 1979) (*Bulletin of the European Communities* **14** (5) 1981, point 2.1.118). Research on the use of solar energy and on underground seasonal heat is in progress.

  The establishment is undertaking studies on the Next European Torus (NET). Environmental research includes an inventory of dangerous chemical substances, the human intake of lead from petrol, coastline pollution, pollution of the Mediterranean (Archimedes project), microwave applications, etc

- at Petten, Netherlands where a programme is underway to develop high temperature materials for future energy technology. Its high flux reactor is mainly concerned with irradiation projects in the field of nuclear safety. Measurement of the corrosion of special steels and the prevention of such corrosion is another project, a part of the 1980–3 programme
- at Geel, Belgium where there is a Central bureau for nuclear measurements
- at Karlsruhe, Federal Republic of Germany where a study on actinide fuels and their safe handling is in process. Behavioural studies on the operating limits of plutonium fuels is one of the other research projects

Work undertaken

A major landmark in Community scientific research was the adoption by the Council of a multiannual programme (1980–3) for the JRC costing 511 million EUA (OJ L72/11–17 18.3.80) (Decision 80/317/EEC, EURATOM). This emphasizes the importance to the future of Europe of a common research policy. The key areas are nuclear safety, new energy sources and the environment. It repeated Decision 77/488/EEC, EURATOM and outlined a research programme for the full period.

July 1981 saw the inauguration of a 40 MeV cyclotron accelerator at Ispra. This makes it possible to investigate irradiation damage in materials intended for the next generation of fusion technology plant.

A, Fusion review panel set up on 26.11.80 submitted its final report on

6 July 1981 (*Bulletin of the European Communities* **13** (11) 1980 point 2.1.112 and **14** (7/8) 1981. point 2.1.149). It recommended that the average annual budget be increased to 300 million ECU during the period up to the end of 1985. It thought that priority should be given to the Joint European Torus (JET) which is the sole means whereby European fusion research can hope to compete with that of the USA or the USSR. The project is based at Culham, Oxfordshire. Research on solar energy has been doubled by the 1980–3 multiannual programme and this will also involve technical assistance to developing countries.

The JRC is co-ordinating work on thermochemical processes concerned with hydrogen. Its purpose being to develop a new source of energy.

In June 1981 in conjunction with the, European Space agency (ESA), JRC commenced the SAR 580 remote sensing campaign. This is a preliminary experiment to check the results sent in by the European satellite ERS–1. It covers mapping of icebergs, sea ice, agricultural field types, a proposed motorway, geological mapping, mineral prospecting, sea traffic through the Straits of Dover, pollution in the Mediterranean etc (*Bulletin of the European Communities* **14** (2) 1981. point 2.1.83 and **14** (6) 1981. point 2.1.135).

The environment has also been of concern to the JRC. Special reference has been paid to air and water pollution, to teledetection in the field of renewable resources especially in the Agricultural sector.

In May 1982 the Commission sent to the Council guidelines for the JRC's 1984–7 programme.

They are intended to:

- strengthen and rationalize the nuclear safety programme
- develop remote-sensing and data processing techniques
- assist other Community departments with special reference to agriculture and development

(*Bulletin of the European Communities* **15** (5) 1982 point 2.1.143).

In a policy debate on these guidelines held in June 1982, the Council took note of the Commission's intention of incorporating the JRC programme in the proposed framework programme (qv Research and the Community).

The address of the JRC is:

- rue de la Loi 200
  1049 Brussels, Belgium.

Further information

General report on the activities of the European Communities, Chapter II Section 14
Luxembourg: Office for official publications of the European Communities, annual

'Common policy for science and technology' (in particular section 3). *Bulletin of the European Communities* supplement 3/77
The organization and management of Community research and development
    Brussels: General secretariat of the European Economic and Social committe, 1980. 159p. Catalogue number ESC–80–001–EN
Willson, Denis
A European experiment, the launching of the JET project
    Bristol: Adam Hilger, 1981. 181p. ISBN 0–85274–543–5

Interdepartmental Committee on Research and Development (CIRD)

Basic information

CIRD was set up by the Commission to assist in co-ordinating its research and development (R & D) activities. It reports to Directorate B of Directorate-General XII Research, Science and Education of the Commission.

Work of CIRD

Besides co-ordinating the R & D activities of the Commission it is also available as an organization for consultation on these activities.

Further information

'Common policy for science and technology'. *Bulletin of the European Communities* supplement 3/77
The organization and management of Community research and development
    Brussels: General Secretariat of the Economic and social committee, 1980. 159p. Catalogue number ESC–80–001–EN

Scientific and Technical Research Committee (CREST) (STRC)

Basic information

Usually known under the initials of the French form of its title as CREST.

In order to assist both the Council and the Commission in developing a Community scientific and technological expanding policy, the Council decided in a 1974 resolution:

- firstly to co-ordinate national policies in science and technology and define projects of interest to the Community

- secondly to participate in the European science foundation
- thirdly to develop a Community action programme for science and technology
- fourthly to develop a programme of forecasting, evaluation and methodology (the first stage in a Europe + 30 feasibility study)

The Council decided to set up a central body (CREST) to undertake the first of these four proposals. The importance ascribed to CREST is shown in its organizational position, for it stands between the Council and the Commission (OJ C7/2–4 29.1.74.).

When CREST was set up relevant sections of the, Working party on scientific and technical research policy (PREST), were transferred to it. These concerned the third point of the 1974 resolution outlined above.

Purpose of CREST

The first of the 1974 Council decisions outlined above, obviously have a considerable influence on all the others.

In the case of the second decision, whilst the Council thought that Community interests should have priority yet it would obviously be helpful to participate under the, European co-operation on scientific and technical research (COST) programme.

The third decision was with the aid of sections from PREST (qv).

The fourth decision was entrusted to a Project board and team under Lord Kennett.

CREST is assisted by sub-committees on:

General standing sub-committees

- R & D statistics
- Scientific and technical information and documentation committee (STIDC) (CIDST). See entry under this heading

Specialized standing sub-committees

- energy
- medical research committee (These cover a range of subjects from epidemiology to road accidents)

Planning sub-committees

- oceanology
- town planning
- raw materials
- materials for chemical plant

Scientific and technical information and documentation committees (STIDC) (qv).

- technical aspects of information systems
- economic and financial aspects of information systems
- training specialists

- agriculture
- biology and medicine
- environment
- energy
- documentation and patents
- metallurgy

Data processing including training in data processing.

The Committee consists of representatives of member states and the Commission.

Work undertaken

It has developed a system of working closely with appropriate national bodies in order to discover the current scientific and technical research programmes and be appraised of future policies and trends. In an annex to the 1974 Council resolution, a three year programme of establishing the Committee's procedure was outlined.

The plan of working in the Community could be considered as follows:

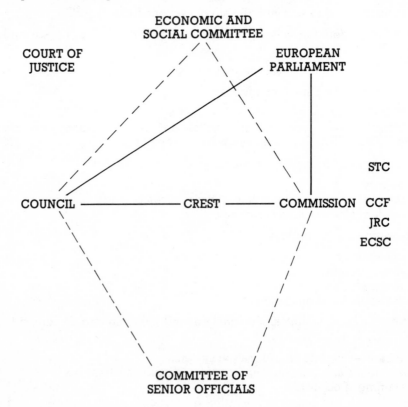

The organization of CREST is generally as follows:

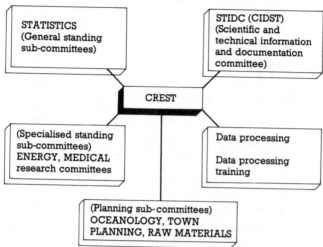

Work on the 1974 Council Resolution mentioned above and the development of an outline Plan for a common science and technology policy from 1980–90, continued throughout the rest of the 1970s. The Council stressed the importance for this work, of the regular comparisons between national and Community research programmes which are being undertaken by CREST (*Bulletin of the European Communities* **12** (12) 1979. point 2.1.153).

In June 1981 CREST examined and approved the proposed multiannual (1982–5) R & D programme in the raw materials sector (*Bulletin of the European Communities* **14** (6) 1981. point 2.1.133). In April 1981 the Commission approved for transmission to the Council, a proposed four year (1982–5) Community programme concerning scientific and technological development with special reference to shared research with developing countries. This is not intended to be a separate EEC programme but is designed to reinforce suitable existing programmes of member states (*Bulletin of the European Communities* **14** (4) 1981 point 2.1.91) CREST gave a favourable opinion to this proposal in February 1982. In October 1981 the Commission submitted a proposal for a Council decision adopting a sectoral research and development programme in the field of medical and public health research during the period 1982–6. Co-ordination of the Community institutions involved would be the responsibility of CREST (OJ C291/13–20 12.11.81). Examination of this proposal continued during 1981 and into 1982. Whilst the total cost would be in the region of 300 million ECUs, there was also an original proposal of 20 million for co-ordination. However, CREST thought that this latter sum might be reduced considerably and submitted its general agreement and particular amendments during February 1982. Also in 1981 it recommended inter alia that the, European advanced machine translation system (EUROTRA) programme be extended to five and a half years (*Bulletin of the European Communities* **14** (4) 1981. point 2.1.82).

Further information

General report on the activities of the European Communities
   Luxembourg: Office for official publications of the European Communities, annual
'Scientific and technological policy programme'. *Bulletin of the European Communities* supplement 14/73
'Scientific and technological policy: adoption of an action programme'. *Bulletin of the European Communities* **7** (1) 1974. points 1401–6
The scientific and technical research committee (CREST), its origin, role and function
   Luxembourg: Office for official publications of the European Communities, 1975. 24p. (EUR series 5393e)
Committees attached to the Community institutions active in the field of scientific and technical policy
   Luxembourg: Office for official publications of the European Communities, 1976. 22p. (EUR 5437 series)
'Common policy for science and technology'. *Bulletin of the European Communities* supplement 3/77
The organization and management of Community research and development
   Brussels: General Secretariat of the Economic and Social committee, 1980. 159p. Catalogue number ESC–80–001–EN

European Co-operation in the Field of Scientific and Technical Research (COST)

Basic information

In a 6 March 1970 resolution the Council set up groups of experts in the scientific and technical research field to speed co-operation with non-member countries.

Later in 1970 a steering committee was set up to co-ordinate this work. At a Ministerial conference 22–23 November 1971 the Committee was made responsible for implementing draft projects and known as COST.

Purpose of COST

To assist the Council and Commission by assessing the needs for research in the following areas and to answer questions in these subjects which are put to them by these two committees

- data processing
- telecommunications
- transport development
- metallurgy

- meteorology and oceanography
- work applicable to a European meteorological computer centre

Many western European countries co-operate with EC countries in scientific and technological research through COST. This is also a useful way of enabling potential members of the Community to participate in some Community work before they become full members.

Work of COST

Details of some current COST programmes and advice can be found in the section on the Environmental research programme – financial assistance. Others include the following, where the name of the co-operating country is in brackets:

- physical properties of foodstuffs (OJ L54/25–8 25.1.78) (Decision 78/177/EEC) (Sweden)
- effect of thermal processing on food (OJ L270/53–7 27.10.79) (Decision 79/878/EEC) (Sweden)
- physico chemistry of atmospheric pollutants (OJ L39/18–23 15.2.80) (Decision 80/177/EEC) (Austria, Sweden)
- analysis of organic micropollutants in water (OJ L39/24–9 15.2.80) (Decision 80/178/EEC) (Norway, Portugal, Switzerland and Sweden)
- effects of processing on the physical properties of foodstuffs (OJ L39/30–5 15.2.80) (Decision 80/179/EEC) (Switzerland and Sweden)
- on remote data processing. Continuation of a 1971 agreement (*Bulletin of the European Communities* 14 (1) 1981 point 2.1.65) (Finland and Sweden)
- on substitute motor fuels (*Bulletin of the European Communities* 14 (7/8) 1981 point 2.1.145 and 15 (5) 1982 point 2.1.147) (Denmark, Finland, Norway and Sweden)
- on the treatment and utilization of sewage sludge (*Bulletin of the European Communities* 15 (2) 1982 point 2.1.108) (Finland and Norway) and 15 (4) 1982 point 2.1.99) (Austria, Sweden and Switzerland)
- on coastal centhic ecosystems (*Bulletin of the European Communities* 15 (4) 1982 point 2.1.98) (Portugal)
- on recycling urban and industrial waste (*Bulletin of the European Communities* 15 (5) 1982 point 2.1.146) (Sweden)
- on electric road vehicles (*Bulletin of the European Communities* 15 (6) 1982 point 2.2.171) (UK, Federal Republic of Germany, Denmark and Sweden)

Further information

General report on the activities of the European Communities
  Luxembourg: Office for official publications of the European Communities, annual

'Objectives and instruments of a common policy, for scientific research and technological development' *Bulletin of the European Communities* supplement 6/72
'Scientific and technological policy programme'. *Bulletin of the European Communities* supplement 14/73
Committees attached to the Community institutions active in the field of scientific and technical policy
   Luxembourg: Office for official publications of the European Communities, 1976. 22p. (EUR 5437)
'Common policy for science and technology'. *Bulletin of the European Communities* supplement 3/77
The organization and management of Community research and development
   Brussels: General secretariat of the European Economic and social committee, 1980. 159p. Catalogue number ESC-80-001-EN

Committee for Medical Research (CRM)

Basic information

Set up by the Scientific and technical research policy (PREST) committee (now, Scientific and technical research committee (CREST)) on 15.6.72.

It has ad hoc working parties to assist it:

- toxic and psychological factors in road accidents
- congenital and environmental factors in deafness
- monitoring the seriously ill

It has standing working parties on:

- epidemiology
- medical biology
- bioengineering

Purpose of CRM

It was established to help CREST in the medical field by:

- assisting in the co-ordination of research undertaken by member states in medical subjects.
- relating member states medical research to that undertaken by the Community
- pointing out those areas where future research could usefully be undertaken for the benefit of the Community
- assisting Council, Commission and CREST with answers to enquiries concerned with medical research

Further information

General report on the activities of the European Communities, section on 'Research and Education'
   Luxembourg: Office for official publications of the European Communities, annual

European Committee for Research and Development (CERD)

Basic information

Under articles 2 and 116 of the Treaty of Rome (1957) and as a result of a report from the Commission to the Council (see, Objectives and instruments of a common policy for scientific research and technological development, *Bulletin of the European Communities* supplement 6/72) presented on 14 June 1972, CERD was established.

Purpose

Most European countries have a high ranking science policy committee to advise the government. In Britain this is the, Advisory council for applied research and development. There is also the Department of Education and Sciences, Science research council, one of five research councils.

In a similar way the European Community needs objective scientific advice to assist in formulating many of its policies. Since 1974 the Community has had an explicit mandate on this subject (OJ C7/2–4 29.1.74). It established CERD in 1972 as an independent advisory committee which assists the Commission.

Work undertaken

In the Community, Directorate B of the Directorate-General XII on Research, Science and Education is responsible for liaison with this independent Committee. It is the means whereby the Commission maintain contact with well known figures in research, science and technology.

In the 1970s it gave effective support in the development of an energy R & D policy, the, Europe + 30 project and the committee of experts on long term research – outlook and methodology (*Bulletin of the European Communities* supplement 3/77 page 11 and supplement 14/73 page 19).

At its June 1981 meeting at Culham, Oxfordshire it was rather critical of a Community R & D proposal in the field of development. This proposal was concerned with agriculture and tropical medicine and CERD considered greater emphasis should be placed on training.

In the early 1980s the Committee set up a team to discover ways of involving industry more closely with R & D and in taking up research results (*Bulletin of the European Communities* **15** (3) 1982 point 2.1.121). This, Forecasting and assessment in the field of science and technology

(FAST) committee is producing a report on its three major areas of activity – the biosociety, the information society and work and employment.

On 18.6.82 the Commission sent to the Council a proposed plan for industrial innovation and technology transfer, covering the period 1983–5. It proposed:

● improvement of contacts on a European basis, to provide the interface between industry, research, financial sources and others
● development of a Community market perspective in these organizations
● the optimization of measures in these organizations and the harmonization of relevant national policies
● the promotion of a rapid penetration of the European economy and industry (particularly small and medium sized businesses) by the new technologies

(*Bulletin of the European Communities* **15** (6) 1982 point 2.1.30 and 2.1.167).

Further information

General report on the activities of the European Communities
   Luxembourg: Office for official publications of the European Communities, annual
Common policy for science and technology. *Bulletin of the European Communities* supplement 3/77
Europe plus thirty report
   Luxembourg: Commission of the European Communities, 1975. various pagings
Danzin, A
Science and the second renaissance of Europe
   Oxford: Pergamon Press for the Commission of the European Communities, 1979. 125p.
   ISBN 0–08–022442–3
The organization and management of Community research and development
   Brussels: General Secretariat of the European Economic and Social Committee, 1980.
   159p. Catalogue number ESC–80–001–EN

Advisory Committees on Programme Management (ACPM)

Basic information

First set up by the Council on 30 June 1969 to assist Community institutions in the task of co-ordination of Community and national research activities. Subsequent resolutions were dated 22.7.72, 19.11.73, 10.12.73, 17.12.74, 26.6.75 and 22.8.75.

ACPMs – representation

Each committee shall consist of not more than:

- 3 officials from the Commission
- 3 experts from each of the member states participating
- Chairman to be appointed for one year on a proposal from the Commission delegation

Purpose of the ACPMs

Their duties according to a Council resolution dated 18 July 1977 (OJ C192/1–2 11.8.77) were additional to co-ordination of research and were to:

- plan for the successful implementation of the programmes for which it is competent
- provide a detailed description of the project
- provide an evaluation of the results
- work towards the progressive co-ordination of all Community and national research activities

They were divided into direct action committees and the following proposals adopted (OJ L200/4–9 8.8.77) (Decision 77/488/EEC, EURATOM) covering:

- reactor safety
- plutonium fuels
- measurements, etc – nuclear
- operation and utilization of the HFR reactor
- high temperature materials
- informatics
- fissile material control

Indirect action (Programme adopted as above) committees (These are shared cost research programmes usually between the Commission and other bodies within the Community):

- plutonium recycling
- energy conservation
- geothermal energy
- systems analysis
- biology – health protection.

Direct and indirect action committees:

- solar energy
- production and utilization of hydrogen
- environment and resources
- reference materials and methods

- management and storage of radioactive waste (The first contract-based radioactive waste programme covered the period 1980–4 (OJ L78/22–3 25.3.80) (Decision 80/343/EURATOM). In 1982 it was found to be working effectively (*Bulletin of the European Communities* **15** (2) 1982 point 2.1.112).
- fusion and plasma physics

Under the Commission's efforts in 1980 to map out guidelines for the Community's continuing rationalization of research and development, it was proposed that the links between direct action projects and indirect action projects should be strengthened.

Mention should also be made of the, Committees on concerted action (COMACs) where the Community simply provides co-ordinating services. These are referred to and listed in the last item under 'Further information'.

Further information

General report on the activities of the European Communities
  Luxembourg: Office for official publications of the European Communities, annual
The organization and management of Community research and development
  Brussels: General Secretariat of the European Economic and Social committee, 1980.
  159p. Catalogue number ESC–80–001–EN

Nuclear Energy

Basic information

The organization in the EEC responsible for nuclear energy is EURATOM (1957). The text of the European Atomic Energy Community (EURATOM) can be found in, *Treaties establishing the European Communities*. Luxembourg: Office for official publications of the European Communities, 1973. 1502p.

EURATOM's main aim is to create the conditions necessary for the speedy establishment and growth of nuclear industries, in order to raise the standard of living of member states.

Work undertaken

To reach this aim it was thought necessary to promote research. In 1980 the Council adopted the latest in a series of decisions furthering a Community research programme on controlled thermonuclear fusion for 1979–83 costing ECU 66.4 m (OJ L72/11–21 18.3.80) (Decision 80/317/ EEC EURATOM) (Decision 80/318/EURATOM). The latter decision is specifically concerned with this subject. On 25 May 1982 the Council adopted an R & D programme in the field of controlled thermonuclear fusion. It covers the period 1982–6 at a cost of 620 million ECUs. Its purpose is to discover a fusion based energy source using hydrogen isotopes, deuterium and tritium. Sweden and Switzerland are participants in the programme.

One of the many research projects is the Joint European Torus (JET) which studies plasma behaviour in conditions and dimensions approaching those required in a fusion reactor. (*The JET project*, Luxembourg: Office for official publications of the European Communities, 1976. 613p.) The Community's Office for official publications produce a number of research reports in their Nuclear science and technology EUR series, as part of their policy of disseminating information.

The treaty also included a clause (article 2(b)) to establish uniform safety standards. An example of this is Radioactive waste management and storage. This is an annual report which started in 1977 and is issued in the EUR series mentioned above. See also Further information.

The treaty aims to facilitate investment. One way this is achieved is to grant loans towards nuclear power station building and development (*Bulletin of the European Communities* 13 (12) 1980. point 2.1.131). It tries to ensure that all users receive a regular and equitable supply of ores and nuclear fuels. Under the 1978 R & D programme on uranium exploration and extraction (OJ L72/12–13 14.3.78) (Decision 78/264/EUR-ATOM) resources are being built up. As a result of the report of the, Ad hoc advisory committee on the reprocessing of irradiated nuclear fuels (OJ L52/9–10 26.2.80) (Decision 80/237/Euratom) and the views of the Commission which were sent to the Council in 1982 (OJ L37/36 10.2.82) (Recommendation 82/74/Euratom), it was recommended that member states take measures to promote the industrial development of these fuels. It is proposed that this programme should be continued during 1982–5 under an R & D programme in the raw material sector. See under, Waste materials recycling.

Care is taken to prevent the misuse of nuclear materials, to ensure that special fissile materials are reserved for the exclusive use of the Community and, at the same time, to build up a Common market in fissile material for the Community.

Whilst pursuing these aims the EC wishes to establish with other countries and international organizations, such relations as will further the peaceful uses of nuclear energy.

Further information

General report on the activities of the European Communities
   Luxembourg: Office for official publications of the European Communities, annual
Operation of nuclear power stations
   Luxembourg: Office for official publications of the European Communities, annual

Towards fusion energy: the European programme
   Luxembourg: Directorate-General Scientific and Technical Information and Information
   Management, 1976. 39p
Community action in nuclear safety
   Luxembourg: EC Directorate-General for Information, 1979. 7p. (European File 15/79).
   Catalogue number CC-AD-79-015-EN-C
*Risks, regulation responsibilities and costs in nuclear waste management: a preliminary
survey in the European Community*
   Luxembourg: Office for official publications of the European Communities 1980. 37p.
   (EUR 6893) ISBN 92-825-2082-X
Fichtner, N and others
Nuclear standards catalogue and classification
   Berlin: Beuth Verlag for the Commission of the European Communities 1981. 230p. ISBN
   3-410-58002-6

Scientific Advisory Committee on the Toxicity and Ecotoxicity of Chemical Compounds

Basic information

A Committee on the environmental control of chemical products was set up in 1978 (OJ L198/17-18 22.7.78) (Decision 78/618/EEC) and held its first meeting on 24/25 October 1979.

Scientific Advisory Committee – representation

The Committee consists of 24 members, 20 of whom are senior experts of member states (2 from each state) together with 4 from the Commission.

Work of the Scientific Advisory Committee

At a meeting on 2 April 1981 the Committee:

• drew up a future work programme
• defined in the Community languages certain terms
• adopted opinions concerning cadmium
• drew up definitions in the Community languages for carcinogenic, multagenic and teratogenic substances (Bulletin of the European Communities **14** (4) 1981. point 2.1.37)

The work of the Committee during its sixth meeting in Luxembourg 18-19 May 1982 is outlined in *Bulletin of the European Communities* **15** (5) 1982 point 2.1.64.

Further information

General report on the activities of the European Communities
Luxembourg: Office for official publications of the European Communities, annual (see also section on Environment)

Scientific Committee on Cosmetology

Basic information

On 19 December 1977 the Commission agreed on establishing this scientific committee (OJ L 13/24-5 17.1.78) (Decision 78/45/EEC).

Scientific Committee – representation

Members are appointed by the Commission and consist of scientists in the subject. The term of office of a member is three years after which his appointment may be renewed. Members are not paid. Relevant members of the Commission may attend meetings.

Work of the Scientific Committee

The bulk of the work of this Committee is concerned with drawing up and amending Community rules governing the composition, manufacturing characteristics, packaging and labelling of cosmetic products, and involves scientific and technical problems. It includes:

- requests for opinions by the Commission which form the bulk of the work of this Committee. The Committee produces reports on its findings
- instructions by the Commission as to which of its requests are to remain confidential
- permission for the Committee to set up working parties as appropriate

Further information

General report on the activities of the European Communities
Luxembourg: Office for official publications of the European Communities, annual

Scientific and Technical Information and Documentation Committee (STIDC) (CIDST)

Basic information

The Committee was set up by a Council resolution of 24.6.71 (OJ C122/7–8 10.12.71) and at that time it was under the, Medium term economic policy committee (qv). It is frequently referred to by the initials of the French form of its title, CIDST.

With the establishment of the, Scientific and technical research committee (CREST) (qv) in 1974 and the outline of its responsibilities under a Council resolution (OJ C7/2–4 29.1.74), STIDC was transferred to assist with the work of harmonizing scientific and technical research and development projects from member states with those undertaken by the Community. The aim is to produce a Community research and development policy.

It is responsible for assisting CREST as well as its own duties.

Committee representation

This Committee includes in its membership a selection from those responsible for drawing up policy on scientific and technical information and documentation in each of the member states, plus representatives from the Commission.

Purpose

Dates and methods of operation of STIDC were outlined in 1978 (OJ L311/1–5 4.11.78) (Decision 78/887/EEC).

CREST (qv) is concerned with a broad approach to the co-ordination of scientific and technological research and development programmes between member states and the Community.

STIDC on the other hand is concerned with the more detailed subject parts of these programmes. With these more limited fields of research, the comparison is carried out in greater detail by the specialized sub-committees of the STIDC (see, Common policy for science and technology, diagram 2 in, *Bulletin of the European Communities* supplement 3/77).

Specialized standing working parties cover:

- technical aspects of information systems
- economic and financial aspects of information systems
- training of specialists
- agriculture
- biology and medicine
- environment
- energy

- documentation and patents
- metallurgy (SMDI)

Further information

'Scientific and technological policy programme' *Bulletin of the European Communities* supplement 14/73
Committees attached to the Community institutions active in the field of scientific policy
   Luxembourg: Office for official publications of the European Communities, 1976. 22p.
   (EUR 5437)

European Information Network

Basic information

Under the Treaty of Rome (1957) article 235 Community members are encouraged to organize an information network.

Many European organizations developed their own information systems, similar to EURA-TOM with its, Information and documentation centre. These showed the way to the importance of having a central information service. This led to a Council resolution on 24 June 1971 (OJ C122/7 10.12.71), providing for the co-ordination of member states' actions on scientific and technical information and documentation and later to EURONET. Under this resolution a Scientific and technical information and documentation committee (STIDC) was proposed.

By a Council resolution (OJ C7/6 29 1.74) section 2 of which concerned information in the scientific and technological field, action was taken to prepare for the first, Three year plan of action in the field of scientific and technical information and documentation (STIDC) (OJ L100/18–19 24.4.75) (Decision 75/200/EEC). A second three year plan appeared in 1978 with an allocation of 9.5 million EUA (OJ L311/1–5 4.11.78) (Decision 78/887/EEC). This decision also outlined the duties and method of operation of STIDC (qv).

EURONET was inaugurated in 1979 as a European telecommunications network in the scientific and technical information field.

On 13 February 1980, EURONET-DIANE (Direct information access network for Europe) was officially inaugurated at the European Parliament at Strasbourg. There were 23 host centres (computerized information and documentation services) providing on-line access to some 150 data bases (February 1980). Some 200 are proposed by 1981. The system works through entry points in every member state. It started commercial operations on 1 April 1980.

Purpose

On the subject of information organization within the European Community, STIDC became responsible for providing the Commission with proposals on the second Three year plan as follows:

- the Commission to consult STIDC on measures it intends to take:

  the transfer of EURONET into a public on-line information network to develop the market in information within the Community
  to improve the information service through the promotion of its technology and methods of operation

- the Commission shall seek the opinion of STIDC on certain measures it intends to take:

  in preparation for future work
  in co-ordination of the 2nd plan of action with related multi-lingual programmes
  on negotiations with non-community institutions including those in 3rd countries and with responsible telecommunication authorities

- the STIDC should be asked to give opinions on:

  policy details and priorities
  annual preparation of budgets
  aims and budgets for projects
  work to be undertaken and selection of contractors
  supervision of development

- the Commission shall periodically submit a report to STIDC on measures taken and results obtained

STIDC to consist of two representatives from each member state. An alternative member for each full member is to be appointed. Appointment is for three years. The Committee to provide its own rules of procedure.

It should have an advisory relationship with CREST (Scientific and technical research committee) (qv).

The EURONET-DIANE network, supported financially by the Community has:

- created the first consortium of nine posts and telecommunications administrations who acted together to build EURONET
- adopted a standard international tariff for EURONET irrespective of distance
- through the host centres has adopted a standardized interface for connection to EURONET and future national networks
- extended the services to Switzerland by the end of 1980. This proposal was approved by the Council and signed on 28 September 1979 (OJ L214/18–25 22.8.79) (Decision 79/721/EEC) includes the exhange of letters and a declaration of intent
- developed a number of aids to users including:

  a standard command language in host centres
  an automated enquiry and referral service
  a central launch team
  multi-lingual tools including terminology data banks and thesauri

In November 1979 the Commission announced that funds were available for selected projects on a shared funding basis. Community contribution would be 25% rising in certain cases to 49%. The maximum Community support for each project was 200,000 EUA (OJ C298/4 29.11.79).

Under the third three year plan of action. 1981-3, in the field of information and documentation (OJ L220/29-33 6.8.81) (Decision 81/599/EEC) the Commission called for proposals for new information services or the improvement of existing services (OJ C169/2-3 7.7.82). The funding of these proposals continued on lines similar to those announced in November 1979 and 15 million ECU have been allocated for the period.

The Community is also currently examining in conjunction with other organizations, the development and use of new information technology. This project, of an Inter-institutional information system (INSIS), is being designed to assist European industry amongst others (OJ C291/2-3 12.11.81) and (*Bulletin of the European Communities* supplement 4/81, page 54). On 25 May 1982 the Commission sent to the Council a proposal entitled, Towards a European strategic programme for research and development in information technologies. This was for a meeting of Ministers of Research held on 30.6.82.

Further information

General report on the activities of the European Communities
    Luxembourg: Office for official publications of the European Communities, annual [up to and including 1976 see chapter III section 13. From 1977 onwards, chapter II section 15]
First European congress on information systems and networks
    Munich: Verlag Dokumentation for the Commission of the European Communities, 1974
Second European congress on information systems and networks, Luxembourg 27-30 May 1975
    Munich: Verlag Dokumentation for the Commission of the European Communities, 1976. 231p. ISBN 3-7940-5164-5
Third European congress on information systems and networks, Luxembourg 3-6 May 1977
    Munich: Verlag Dokumentation for the Commission of the European Communities, 1977. 2 v. ISBN 3-7940-5184-X
EURONET Guidelines for co-operation between data base suppliers and host organizations
    Luxembourg: Office for official publications of the European Communities, 1977. 10p. Catalogue number CK-22-77-427-EN-C
Gillespie, Paul D and others
Problems of document delivery for the EURONET user
    London: Bingley and Saur for the European Communities Directorate-General for scientific and technical information and information management. 1979. 228p. ISBN 3-598-10069-8
Scott, Gay
*Guide to European Community grants and loans,*2nd ed
    Biggleswade: Euroinformation Limited, 1981. 111p. ISBN 0-907304-01-X
Transfer and exploitation of scientific and technical information, proceedings of the symposium ...
    Luxembourg: Office for official publications of the European Communities, 1982. 363p. ISBN 92-825-2837-5

Data Processing Scheme – Financial Assistance

Basic information

Article 235 of the Treaty of Rome makes provision for an information network (qv European Information network) and the development of data processing.

Schemes aided

Financial support is awarded for any scheme fulfilling the following conditions:

- a scheme with supporting projects in two or more member states
- an aim to develop new or improved software
- an aim to develop new or improved applications
- both software and applications to forward EEC objectives

A multiannual programme (1979–83) in data processing was agreed (OJ L231/1–4 13.9.79) (Regulation 1996/79/EEC) and (OJ L231/23–8 13.9.79) (Decision 79/783/EEC) and a Commission proposal on 9 June 1982 aimed to extend this programme to 1986 with an increase in funds and a broadening of its scope.

Finance available

Grants or loans are provided, with loans being the usual form of support.

50% of the project cost can be obtained. This is interest free during the development phase and for two years thereafter whilst the development is being exploited.

Repayment of loan and interest is expected over the following four years.

For feasibility studies grants are available for 50% of the total cost. Where studies cost less than £60,000 100% of this cost may be obtained as a grant.

Details may be obtained from:

- European Communities Commission, Information Office, 20 Kensington Palace Gardens, London W8 4QQ.
- Computers, Systems and Electronics Division, Department of Industry, Dean Bradley House 52 Horseferry Road, London SW1P 2AG

Further information

Scott, Gay
Guide to European Community grants and loans – 2nd ed
   Biggleswade: Euroinformation Limited, 1981. 111p. ISBN 0–907304–01–X
Official sources of finance and aid for industry in the UK
   London: National Westminster Bank Limited, Commercial information market intelligence department, 1981. 67p.

Patent Law

Basic information

Harmonization of British with European patent law was brought about mainly by the 1977 UK Patents act.

This act aligned British patent legislation with the decision of the European patent convention.

The convention proposed the, European patent office in Munich, Germany, which opened for the receipt of patents on 4 June 1978. Member countries at present are the United Kingdom, Austria, Belgium, France, Germany (FDR), Italy, Lichtenstein, Luxembourg, Netherlands, Sweden and Switzerland.

Patent registration

Under article 75 of the European patent convention any European application may be filed at the Patent Office London and UK residents filing patent applications must do so.

A patent court has been set up in Britain to deal with cases under the 1977 act as well as the earlier 1949 Patents act.

Patent guide

A continuing guide to this legislation will be found in:

White, T A Blanco and others
Encyclopaedia of UK and European patent law
   London: Sweet and Maxwell, 1980 (updating service) ISBN 0421–23350–8

Further information

Convention on the grant of European patents (European patents convention) Industrial property misc. no. 24 (1974)
    London: HMSO, 1974, 152p. (Cmnd. 6553)
Convention for the patent of the Common Market (Community patent convention)
    London: HMSO, 1976. 56p. (Cmnd 5656)
Patent information and documentation, an inventory of services available to the public in the European Community
    Munich: Verlag Dokumentation for the Commission of the European Community, 1976. 173p. ISBN 3-7940-5167-X
Bowen, R
The Patents Act 1977
    London: Sweet and Maxwell, 1978. ISBN 0-421-24750-9
European patents abstracts
    London: Derwent Publications Limited, 1979 – fortnightly
    (also available on-line in a number of libraries through Infoline (London) and SDC (California))
For the United Kingdom location list. see, *Patent information and documentation* p. 107–38, listed above
Thomsen, E
Parameters for the establishment or extension of regional public patent information and documentation centres
    Luxembourg; Directorate-General Information market and innovation. 1981. 52p. + 51p. of Appendix: (Mimeographed document)

Trademarks

Basic information

Work on trademarks in the Community falls under articles 100 and 235 of the Treaty of Rome (1957). Preliminary discussions were held as long ago as the 1960s on the idea of an EC trademark. In 1973 a, Preliminary draft of a convention on European trademark law was mentioned in a reply to a Parliamentary written question number 543/73 (OJ C39/11 6.4.74).

Trademarks in the Community

On 25.11.80 the Commission sent to the Council a first directive to approximate the Trademark law of member states. It also sent a draft regulation creating a Community trademark and a Community trademark office. Their purpose is to ensure that facilities are available throughout the Community similar to those in individual member states (*Bulletin of the European Communities* supplement 5/80) Pleas for the Community trademark office had been published in 1976 (*Bulletin of the European Communities* supplement 8/76).

The draft regulation concerning the Community trade mark contains:

• the substantiative law on the subject

- rules regarding the extension and conclusion of trademarks
- procedure, collective trademarks, etc

Work on a Community trademark law was inevitable in view of the Community's aim for a single EC market and the free transfer of goods within the Community.

Further information

'EEC trademark law' by Rudolph du Mesnil de Rochemont. *International Business Lawyer* **7** (1) February 1979
A Community system of trademark law. *Bulletin of the European Communities* **13** (11) 1980 point 1.5.1–1.5.4

Waste Materials Recycling – Financial Assistance

Basic information

Under article 2 of the Treaty of Rome (1957) the Community has taken some corrective measures under a series of directives which set out rates and principles for the control as well as the re-use of waste products
(OJ L194/39–41 25.7.75) (Directive 75/442/EEC) waste;
(OJ L194/23–5 25.7.75) (Directive 75/439/EEC) waste oils;
(OJ L54/19–24 25.2.78) (Directive 78/176/EEC) waste titanium dioxide;
(OJ L84/43–8 31.3.78) (Directive 78/319/EEC) toxic and dangerous wastes.

The Council agreed to a long term (1979–82) research and development programme concerned with industrial and urban (municipal) waste or secondary raw materials (OJ L293/19–22 20.11.79) (Decision 79/968/EEC).

Projects under Waste Materials Recycling

The Commission is responsible for the co-ordination of activities and is helped by an, Advisory committee on a multiannual management programme for research and development in urban and industrial waste recycling. This Committee was also made responsible for paper and board recycling under a multiannual (1978–80) Council programme. (OJ L107/12–13 17.4.78) (Decision 78/384/EEC). The cost of this programme was 2.9 million ECU. The research for it is being carried out under contract. In 1981 the Commission sent the Council a proposal for an R & D programme (1982–5) in the raw materials sector (OJ C170/5–12 10.7.81). This was later amended (OJ C57/13–14 5.3.82). It was approved by Council on 17 May 1982 (OJ C137/12–16 29.5.82) which includes invitations to participate. The research areas 1–4 below would become sub-programme V of the proposed R & D programme.

The sub-programmes were listed as:

I   Metals and mineral substances
II   Uranium exploration and extraction
III   Ceramics
IV   Wood
V   Recycling of urban and industrial waste
VI   Recycling of non-ferrous metals
VII   Substitution

Thus individual research programmes were integrated into a single framework programme.

Under the, Waste materials recycling programme the following areas of research are being examined on a country basis:

- Research area 1, sorting of household waste:

  assessment of waste sorting projects (co-ordination of activities in member states)
  methods of sampling and analysis of household waste (co-ordination of activities in member states)
  evaluation of health hazards (co-ordination of activities in member states)
  technology for the sorting of bulk waste (co-ordination of activities in member states) + (contracts)
  materials recovery
  paper (co-ordination of activities in member states) (contracts)
  plastics (co-ordination of activities in member states) (contracts)
  non-ferrous metals (co-ordination of activities in member states)
  energy recovery (co-ordination of activities in member states) (contracts)
  new collection and transport system (co-ordination of activities in member states)

- Research area 2, thermal treatment of waste

  firing of waste derived fuel (as in Research area 1 – energy recovery)
  pyrolysis and gasification (co-ordination of activities in member states) (contracts)
  recovery of metal and glass from residue (co-ordination of activities of member states)

- Research area 3, fermentation and hydrolysis

  anaerobic digestion (co-ordination of activities in member states) (contracts)
  carbohydrate hydrolysis (co-ordination of activities in member states) (contracts)
  composting (co-ordination of activities in member states)

- Research area 4, recovery of rubber waste

  retreading (co-ordination of activities in member states)

size reduction (co-ordination of activities in member states)
reclaiming and recycling of rubber powder (co-ordination of activities in member states)
pyrolysis (co-ordination of activities in member states)

Rates of grants

A sum of 9 million ECU for the 3 year programme has been allocated. The allocation of these funds is as follows:

- area 1 45–50%
- area 2 15–25%
- area 3 20–40%
- area 4 5–15%

Further information

Environmental Resources Limited
Economics of recycling, a report on the potential for further recovery of materials from waste in Europe, prepared for the, Environment and consumer protection service of the Commission of the European Communities
    London: Graham and Trotman, 1978. 167p. ISBN 0–86010–123–1
Bridgewater, A V and K Lidgren
Household waste management in Europe, economics and techniques
    London: Van Nostrand, 1981. 249p. ISBN 0–442–30464–1
Scott, Gay
Guide to European Community grants and loans – 2nd ed
    Biggleswade: Euroinformation Limited, 1981. 111p. ISBN 0–907304–01X

7 Community External Affairs

At international meetings, member states whilst putting forward their own point of view, frequently have a Community spokesman – usually a Minister for external affairs from one of the Community countries – to put forward an agreed opinion from all member states.

Similarly whilst countries have their own aid programme, they also contribute to the Community aid and development projects which are extensive, are increasing year by year, and are encouraging both developing nations and the UN designated, 'Least developed countries' to utilize their own resource for progress.

In the following country sections the emphasis is on each nation's relations with the Communities:

FOR A DETAILED INDEX SEE THE YELLOW PAGES.

- **Japan** (pages 327–8)
- **New Zealand** (page 329)
- **Turkey** (pages 330–1)
- **USA** (pages 331–2)

State Trading nations:

- **China** (pages 333–4)
- **CMEA/COMECON** (pages 334–6)

South East Asia:

- **Association of South East Asian Nations** (ASEAN) (pages 336–7)
  ASEAN, inter-regional meetings (page 338)
  Indonesia (pages 338–340)
  Malaysia (pages 340–1)
  Philippines (pages 341–2)
  Singapore (pages 342–3)
  Thailand (pages 343–4)

African, Caribbean and Pacific (ACP) states:

- **African, Caribbean and Pacific states (ACP) and OCT, trade agreements** (pages 344–6)
- **Lomé conventions** (pages 347–350)
  Mauritius and the ACP states (pages 350–1)
  Sudan (pages 351–2)

South America

- **Latin America** (pages 352–5)

Middle East, etc

- **Maghreb states** (pages 355–6)
- **Mashreq states** (pages 357–8)
- **Israel** (pages 358–9)

Developing Nations:

- **Third world** (pages 359–360)

Agreements between the EC and Third Countries

In the External relations series of the publication, *Europe Information,* there is published a regularly updated list of main agreements. This list, with effect from the issue noted below, gives the main references to where details of each agreement can be found in the, *Official Journal of the European Communities.*

It should be noted that this listing covers the main agreements only and is not exhaustive. For each agreement is given date of entry into force, its duration, the OJ reference, and notes. The arrangement is by geographical grouping with an additional section covering State Trading Countries. See also detailed index on yellow pages, under Agreements.

Further information

List of Main EEC Agreements with other Countries
  Brussels: EC Spokesman's Group and Directorate-General for Information, 1980. 10p. (Europe Information, External Relations series, no 37/80)

Greece

Basic information

The first European country to become an Associate of the EC under the terms of Article 238 of the Treaty of Rome was Greece. The Association Agreement was signed in Athens on 9 July 1961. It came into force on 1 November 1962 (OJ 26/343–9 18.2.63) (Acte Final 63/108/EEC). It was extended to cover the nine EC countries on 28 April 1975 and was of unlimited duration. On 1 January 1981 Greece became the tenth member of the Community (OJ L291/1–192 19.11.79).

Association

The Association provided for the establishment of a customs union, the development of common action and the harmonization of Greek and Community policies in a range of areas such as agricultural policy, the right of establishment and the free movement of workers, transport, fiscal policy, rules of competition and economic policy; it also made available to Greece resources intended to facilitate the speedy development of its economy.

Membership

The Community of ten is broadly comparable to the nine except in shipping. The inclusion of the Greek merchant fleet of 34 million gross tonnes gives the Community the world's leading merchant fleet of 110 million gross tonnes. With the entry of Greece the population of the Community rose to 270 million and the surface area to 1,658,000 km^2.

Since the 1961 Association agreement, Greece has made great economic progress and the gap between its average productivity and income and that of the nine member states has been narrowed considerably. The new membership has necessitated large scale structural change if Greece is to withstand the greatly increased pressure of international competition. The major problems are the disproportionate importance of agriculture, a low level of concentration and specialization in trade and industry, heavy external protection and a closely regulated financial system.

The EC has decided that from the date of its accession Greece should participate in full payment of agricultural levies including compensatory amounts. Up to the end of 1985 there should be full payment of customs duties on the basis of a notional CCT and from 1 January 1986 the full payment on customs duties levied. VAT or financial contribution, calculated on the basis of GNP was due in full from 1 January 1981 with refunds on an annual declining rate basis up to 1985.

Under the Treaty of accession, there is a transitional period until 1 January 1988 before freedom of movement of workers comes into force.

Further information

General report on the activities of the European Communities
   Luxembourg: Office for official publications of the European Communities, annual
Tsatsos, Constantine
Greece and Europe
   Athens: General Secretariat for Press and Information, 1977. 58p.
Greece and European Community
   Brussels: Spokesman's Group and Director-General for Information, September 1978. 7p.
   (Europe Information, External Relations series no. 14/78). Catalogue Number CC–AB–78–014–EN–C
'Europe of ten'. *Bulletin of the European Communities* **14** (1) 1981 points 1.1.1–1.2.5
Europe today, state of European integration 1980–1
   Luxembourg: Office for official publications of the European Communities, 1981, 617p.
   ISBN 92–823–0037–4. Catalogue number AX–30–80–972–EN–C

Portugal

Basic information

Between 1969 and 1972 a Free Trade agreement was prepared and signed on 22 July 1972. It entered into force as part of a series of EFTA agreements on 1 January 1973 (OJ L301/165–367 31.12.72) and it is of indefinite duration.

A financial protocol and an additional protocol were added later (OJ L274/2–42 29.9.78). The EIB were authorized to make grants to Portugal of up to 200 million EUA for a period of up to five years.

History of events concerning the negotiations

After the establishment of democracy in Portugal and between 1974 and 1976, both the Community and Portugal wished to draw closer.

General and specific discussions are now taking place at a number of levels. These are regular ministerial meetings, meetings at deputy level and meetings of the EEC – Portugal Joint Committee set up to administer the Free Trade agreement.

In view of the special position Portugal has had regarding imports into the United Kingdom and Danish markets, partly from historical reasons and partly because all three were EFTA countries, special consideration has been given to the large agricultural sector of the Portuguese economy.

Objectives of the Portuguese – EEC association

- to further the harmonious development of economic relations between Portugal and the Communities
- to further the expansion of reciprocal trade
- to ensure that fair conditions for trade competition are reached
- to work towards the abolition of trade barriers

A timetable for EEC tariff dismantling was proposed. Originally this was to run from 1973–7, however this period was entended to 1 January 1984 for imports into the EEC and 1 January 1985 for exports from the EEC. For customs union and the ECSC and external relations, the period of application of the transitional tariff measures was set at seven years by the Conference at ministerial level held at Luxembourg on 22.6.82. It was agreed that VAT should be introduced into Portugal three years after accession. Direct investment in Portugal by nationals from other member states is to be limited for a four year period (*Bulletin of the European Communities* **15** (6) 1982 point 2.2.1).

1977 saw the start of a third phase, in bringing Portugal closer to the Community. A formal request was submitted by Portugal on 28 March 1977 and the Council instructed the Commission to prepare its opinion on this matter (COM (78) 220).

Aid has also been given to a growing industrial sector in Portugal principally by limiting imports of Community manufactured goods.

It was expected that greater financial support would be provided by Europe. Negotiations took place leading to an agreement on pre-accession aid (OJ L349/2–7 23.12.80). The agreement came into force in January 1981 (OJ L367/88 31.12.80). The amount involved is 275 million EUA. Two further financing agreements were signed on 15.6.82 (rebuilding of three sections of the National highway 16) and 24.6.82 (provision of a Farm accountancy data network (qv) in Portugal).

Further information

General report on the activities of the European Communities
   Luxembourg: Office for official publications of the European Communities, annual
Portugal and the European Community
   Brussels: EC Spokesman's Group and Directorate-General for Information, May 1978.
   11p (Europe Information, External Relations series no 7/78). Catalogue number CC–
   AB–78–007–EN–C
Spain, Portugal and the European Community
   London: University Association for Contemporary European Studies, 1978. 62p. ISBN
   0–906384–01–X
Portugal and the European Community
   Brussels: EC Spokesman's Group and Directorate-General for Information, June 1980.
   18p. (Europe Information, External Relations series, no 34/80)

Spain

Basic information

From 1962 the Spanish government made approaches regarding an association with the Community leading eventually to membership.

During the period 1964–6 discussions took place over negotiating a purely commercial agreement. More positive talks from 1967 led to a trade agrement between the EEC and Spain in 1970 (OJ L182/4 16.8.70). It came into force on 1 October 1970. With the enlargement of the Community in 1973, a protocol was signed providing for the non-application of the 1970 agreement to the new Community members (OJ L66/2 13.3.73). After the death of General Franco, on 17 February 1976, Mr de Aveilza, the Spanish Minister of Foreign Affairs visited Brussels to inform Mr Ortoli, then President of the EC and Sir Christopher Soames (now Lord Soames), then Vice-President responsible for external affairs, that Spain would wish to request accession to the Community once the gradual process of reintroducing democracy had been completed.

Association of Spain with the Communities

On 28 July 1977, Mr Oreja Aguirre, the Spanish Minister of Foreign Affairs at that time, presented President Suarez's letter requesting Spain's accession to the EC.

Following the customary procedure the Commission presented an opinion on Spain's proposed membership. This was communicated to the Council on 29 November 1978. It welcomed the inclusion of Spain, outlining the benefits and the difficulties involved. It was thought that Spain should be a complete member from the time of its first accession. A transitional period of ten years was considered appropriate with these negotiations, commencing in February 1979. During 1980 and 1981 the negotiations proceeded smoothly with meetings between officials and delegations from both sides. In October 1980 Spain requested financial co-operation, in the run up to accession, through the EIB (qv). On 16th March 1981 the Council agreed and thought that priority should be given to finance for projects assisting Spain's entry into the Community.

As there was no protocol signed by 1 July 1977 to the 1970 trade agreement, certain trade arrangements were introduced unilaterally by each of the parties concerned. These were designed to expand trade and develop relations between the Community and Mediterranean states. On industrial goods there have been large reductions in customs duties on items originating in Spain and smaller on EEC goods imported. In agriculture, rather smaller reductions in customs tariffs plus quotas on some Spanish products imported and special regulations for the import of Community butter and milk. In fisheries, a framework agreement concerning access to fishery resources and control measures was signed in 1980 (OJ L322/3 28.11.80).

Further information

General report on the activities of the European Communities
    Luxembourg: Office for official publications of the European Communities, annual
Opinion on Spain's application for membership Bulletin of the European Communities supplement 9/78
Spain, Portugal and the European Community
    London: University Association for Contemporary European Studies, 1978. 62p. ISBN 0–906384–01–X
Noelke, Michael and Robert Taylor
Spanish industry and the impact of membership of the European Community
    Brussels: European Research Associates, 1980. 559p.
Spain and the European Community
    Brussels: Spokesman's Group and Director-General for Information, May 1980, 16p.
    (Europe Information External Relations series no 29/80). [historic account of negotiations]
Europe today, state of European integration 1980–1
    Luxembourg: Office for official publications of the European Communities, 1981. 617p. ISBN 92–823–0037–4. Catalogue number AX–30–80–972–EN–C

Mediterranean

Basic information

In the 1960s a policy was devised to give an overall approach to all non-Community countries of this area. The aim was to link these countries in trade and technical, economic and financial matters. By 1972, when the first of the world economic problems were about to beset the Community a more comprehensive approach to a Mediterranean policy was attempted.

Current events

In, *Bulletin of the European Communities* **12** (6) 1979 point 2.2.1 the Commission agreed to put forward proposed solutions for continuing and expanding its Mediterranean policies in the light of Spanish and Portuguese membership, as soon as it thought this appropriate. These proposals formed a communication on Mediterranean policy sent to the Council on 22 June 1982. They covered both agriculture and industry (*Bulletin of the European Communities* **15** (6) 1982 points 1.2.1–1.2.4) and dealt with both internal and external aspects. On 9.6.82 the Commission adopted an, *Interim report on possible Community operations for the Mediterranean regions* for discussion by member states. Concrete proposals are expected to be presented to the Council by the end of 1982.

Further information

Baklanoff, Eric N (ed)
Mediterranean Europe and the Common Market: studies of economic growth and integration
    Alabama: University of Alabama Press for the Office for International Studies and programs. 1976. 244p. ISBN 0–8173–4605–8
Tsoukalis, Loukas
The European Community and its Mediterranean enlargement
    London: Allen and Unwin, 1981. 273p. ISBN 0–04–382030–1

European Free Trade Association (EFTA)

Basic information

In February 1959 representatives of the Austrian, British, Danish, Norwegian, Portuguese, Swedish and Swiss Governments, met in Oslo to lay the foundations of a freetrade zone for industrial products. The Stockholm Convention establishing the foundations of EFTA was signed on 2 January 1960 and entered into force on 3 May of that year. Iceland joined in 1970 and Finland was associated with it from 1961. The Convention provided for the abolition of customs duties and quantitative restrictions on trade. This was reached in 1966. The Convention did not imply the creation of a common customs tariff towards the rest of the world nor the harmonization of legislation.

On 2nd December 1969 a conference of the Heads of States and Governments of the Community approved the principle of opening negotiations aimed at enlarging the Community by the accession of the Republic of Ireland, The United Kingdom, Norway and Denmark. Paragraph 14 of the communiqué of this meeting stated that as soon as negotiations with the candidate countries had been opened, discussions would be started with the other EFTA countries on their position regarding the EC. All the applicant countries except Norway, acceded to the Community on 1 January 1973.

Exploratory talks between the EC and the remaining countries of EFTA took place in 1970 and 1971. Negotiations were started 3rd December, 1971 and ended on 20 July 1972, that with Finland was initialled in July and signed on 5 October 1973. The agreement with

Norway was signed on 14 May 1973. These agreements established a free trade system amongst the remaining partners and Community members referring essentially to industrial products. An evolutionary clause was included in the agreements between the EC and EFTA countries (except Finland) allowing ad hoc co-operation to develop but avoiding binding institutional links. The agreements with Austria, Switzerland and Sweden were published in 1972 (OJ L300/2–92 31.12.72), (OJ L300/189–280 31.12.72) and (OJ L300/97–184 31.12.72) respectively. It is noted that the Principality of Liechtenstein as part of the Swiss Confederation was also included (OJ L300/281–2 31.12.72). The agreement for Iceland also in 1972 (OJ L301/2–160 31.12.72) and those for Norway and Finland in, respectively (OJ L171/2–102 29.6.73) and (OJ L328/2–106 28.11.73).

Portugal, which has applied to join the EC, also applied to join the free trade area linked to the EC (OJ L301/165–367 31.12.72). This agreement came into force on 1 January 1973.

Objectives of EFTA

- to further the harmonious development of economic relations between countries of the two groups
- to further the expansion of reciprocal trade
- to ensure that fair conditions for trade competition are reached
- to work towards the abolition of trade barriers
- to forward the idea of the expansion of world trade

Scope of the agreements

- to apply to industrial produce
- to apply to processed or manufactured agricultural products

By July 1977 a free trade area for a wide range of industrial products covered a very large percentage of Europe. Subsequently new products were introduced into the agreement.

It was agreed that:

- there should be non-discrimination in the field of taxation
- there should be non-discrimination regarding trade payments and credits
- some exceptional clauses should be introduced on security and law and order
- some safeguards on sectoral and regional problems, tariff disparities, dumping, balance of payments problems, etc

ECSC

Under the treaty establishing this Community, individual agreements had to be made between this Community and each country of EFTA.

These include:

- separate agreements lasting for one year with Austria, Finland, Norway, Portugal and Sweden, all dated between 8 and 15 March 1978 on trade in iron and steel products. Agreements renewed in 1979, renewed with a slightly more flexible wording in 1980 and the 1981 renewal took note of Community production cutbacks
- a somewhat similar agreement, confined to reinforcing rods, was concluded with Switzerland on 28 February 1978 and similarly reviewed
- an agreement with Iceland was concluded to secure preferential access to the Icelandic market

Further information

General report on the activities of the European Communities
    Luxembourg: Office for official publications of the European Communities, annual
The European Community and the EFTA Countries
    Brussels: EC Spokesman's Group and Directorate-General for Information, June 1980
    19p. (Europe Information External Relations series no. 35/80) [See also leaflets on individual members of EFTA in this series]
Europe today, state of European integration 1980-1
    Luxembourg: Office for official publications of the European Communities, 1981. 617p.
    ISBN 92-823-0037-4. Catalogue number AX-30-80-972-EN-C

Austria

Basic information

As a member of the European Free Trade Association (EFTA) Austria concluded a number of agreements with the EEC and ECSC.

Co-operation with the Community

Trade between Austria and the Community is governed by the 1972 agreements with the EEC and ECSC (OJ L300/2-92 31.12.72) and (OJ L350/33-52 19.12.73) respectively which came into force in 1973.

Trade expanded between 1973 and 1978, imports of Austrian goods and services by 146% and exports of EEC goods and services during the same period, by 62%. This imbalance continued in 1979, and by May 1981 Austria was having discussions with the Community on how it should be resolved.

The time limit for dismantling EEC tariffs on Austrian paper and paper products was extended to 1 January 1984. At the same time the limit for Austrian tariffs was extended also to 1 January 1984.

Transit agreements for goods passing through Austria on their way from one EEC country to another, came into force on 1 March 1958 (OJ L6/78–82 20.2.58) and covered rail transport of coal and steel. Another agreement was implemented on 1 January 1974 (OJ L294/87 29.12.72) and amended subsequently. It covers the general transit of goods. A further agreement (OJ L276/2–6 30.9.78) (Regulation 2302/78/EEC) regulates the conditions of passage through Austria and warehousing in Austria of goods travelling between the Community and Greece and Turkey.

Agreements were signed which Austria regarded as an exchange of information on environmental matters. A financial contribution was requested from the EEC for the building of a new motorway through Austria linking the North West of Europe with the Balkans, Greece and the Middle East. In a 1980 communication the Commission put forward proposals agreeing to this.

Austria participates in several COST (European co-operation in scientific and technical research) (qv), schemes. It also participates in the 1973 Community Patent Convention of 15 December 1975.

Further information

General report on the activities of the European Communities
  Luxembourg: Office for official publications of the European Communities, annual
European Communities and the EFTA countries
  Brussels: EC Spokesman's Group and Directorate-General for Information, June 1980.
  19p. Europe Information, External Relations series no. 35/80)
Europe today, state of European integration 1980–1
  Luxembourg: Office for official publications of the European Communities, 1981. 617p.
  ISBN 92–823–0037–4. Catalogue number AX–30–80–972–EN–C

Iceland

Basic information

A country of a quarter of a million inhabitants. Originally part of Norway, later part of Denmark, from 1918 an independent country under the Danish crown, and from 1946 an independent republic.

There is no joint committee between Iceland and the ECSC as Iceland has no appreciable coal or steel industries.

Trade with Iceland

As a member of the European free trade association (EFTA), Iceland signed free trade agreements with the EEC and ECSC in 1972. In the case of the EEC (OJ L301/4–163 31.12.72) it entered into force on 1 April 1973 and with the ECSC (OJ L350/2–12 19.12.73) the entry into force was on 1 January 1974 and is mainly for Community exports to Iceland.

Icelandic imports from the EC rose just on 100% between 1973 and 1978, exporting, however, increased by 81% during the same period. Whilst the long standing budget deficit continues, there is a growing approach to equilibrium in trade.

Further information

General report on the activities of the European Communities
   Luxembourg: Office for official publications of the European Communities, annual
The European Communities and the EFTA countries
   Brussels: EC Spokesman's Group and Director-General for Information, June 1980. 19p.
   (Europe Information, External Relations, series no. 35/80)
Europe today, state of European integration 1980–1
   Luxembourg: Office for official publications of the European Communities, 1981. 617p.
   ISBN 92–823–0037–4. Catalogue number AX–30–80–972–EN–C

Finland

Basic information

A country of 4.7 million inhabitants, originally a part of Sweden then part of Russia up to the time of the revolution. It was independent between the two world wars, but some of its territory was lost to the USSR after the second world war. It is independent with a treaty of friendship, co-operation and mutual assistance with the USSR which is its largest trading partner for both imports and exports. As part of the agreements between Finland and the EC, joint committees were set up to ensure their efficient functioning.

Trade with Finland

As a member of the, European free trade association (EFTA), Finland as with other members signed free trade agreements with the EEC and ECSC in 1972 and 1974 respectively. In the case of the EEC (OJ L328/2–106 28.11.73) this agreement came into force on 1 January 1974 and for the ECSC (OJ L348/1–16 27.12.74) with the agreement coming into force on 1 January 1975. Both agreements are of indefinite duration.

In order to extend the free trade area of EFTA to the EEC, provision was made for mutually dismantling tariffs. The Community abolished tariffs on most industrial goods on 1 July 1977, for some textiles, aluminium and certain other non-ferrous metals on 1 January 1980 and for paper imports on 1 January 1984. Finland will abolish tariffs on a range of industrial goods on 1 January 1984. In 1978 an agreement on the management of common fish stocks was initialled. Trade between the EC and Finland has risen since the agreements were signed. Finnish exports have increased by 85% between 1973 and 1978 and were then running at 38% of total Finnish exports. Finnish imports from the EC rose by 59% during the same period.

Additional areas of co-operation

- Finland participates in a series of joint scientific and technological research projects with the COST programme (qv)
- exchanges of information have taken place on matters of economic and currency developments
- similar exchange cover environmental protection
- similar exchanges cover the situation in the timber and paper industries

Further information

General report on the activities of the European Communities
    Luxembourg: Office for official publications of the European Communities, annual
The European Communities and the EFTA countries
    Brussels: EC Spokesman's Group and Director-General for Information. June 1980. 19p.
    (Europe Information, External Relations series no, 35/80)
Europe today, state of European integration 1980-1
    Luxembourg: Office for official publications of the European Communities, 1981. 617p.
    ISBN 92-823-0037-4. Catalogue number AX-30-80-972-EN-C

Norway

Basic information

The history of this country's relations with the Communities differs somewhat from that of other EFTA countries, for in 1970 it participated in the negotiations which led to the first enlargement of the Community in 1973. Whilst the UK, Denmark and Ireland joined the EC, Norway in a referendum of 26 September 1972, rejected entry. It is a country of 4 millions, characterized by a high degree of economic development and like the other Scandinavian countries has a long democratic history and shares most of the aims and ideals supported by member states of the Community.

As part of the free trade agreements, joint committees were set up for the EEC and ECSC, to ensure the efficient functioning of the agreements. In 1981 it was agreed that one of the two annual sessions, normally attended by officials, should be replaced by a meeting of high-ranking representatives and ministers. The first of these restyled meetings took place on 26 June 1981.

Trade with Norway

As a member of the European Free Trade Association (EFTA) it has concluded a free trade agreement with the EEC which came into force on 1 July 1973 and is of indefinite duration (OJ L171/2–102 27.6.73). An agreement with the ECSC signed in 1973 entered into force on 1 July 1975. It is also of indefinite duration (OJ L348/17–35 27.12.74).

A framework agreement on fisheries was signed in 1980 and has a duration of 6 years which is renewable (OJ L226/48–50 29.8.80). It provides reciprocal fishing rights with an annual agreement over quotas. These have been agreed and are issued in the Official journal 'L' series each year. The Agreement is based on the, Law of the sea.

The 1973 and 1975 agreements arranged for a gradual elimination of tariff barriers. By mid 1977 free trade in the industrial field had been largely achieved. Community import controls on aluminium and certain other metals ended on 31 December 1979.

Community import duties and restrictions on paper will be eliminated by 31 December 1983. Norwegian duties on certain textile products will also be finished with by the end of 1983.

Between 1973 and 1980 Community purchases from Norway increased by 450% whilst sales to Norway increased 228%. The major cause of this change being Norwegian exports of oil. Before 1978 there was usually a budget deficit. In 1978 and afterwards this became a considerable surplus. Norway's exports to the Community rose from 47% of its total exports in 1974 to 71% in 1980. Community imports into Norway for the same period rose from 42 to 51% in 1980.

In the steel industry which has been undergoing crisis restrictions within the EC, it was thought necessary for producers in third countries to adopt similar proposals. Arrangements were made with Norway to that end, as was done with other EFTA countries with a steel industry.

Additional areas of co-operation

- the Co-operation in scientific and technical research programme (COST) has been extended to Norway which participates in data processing projects, telecommunications, meteorology, oceanography, transport and metallurgy

- twice annual meetings have been arranged to exchange information in the field of sea transport
- similar arrangements have been made concerning air transport
- similar arrangements have been made in the area of environmental studies
- contacts take place regularly on issues of energy policy and economic and monetary policy
- political links between the two partners have escalated over recent years. These are likely to lead to even closer co-operation in the future

Further information

General report on the activities of the European Communities
    Luxembourg: Office for official publications of the European Communities, annual
The European Community and Norway
    Brussels: EC Spokesman's Group and Director-General for Information, June 1981. 9p.
    (Europe Information, External Relations series no 49/81)
Europe today, state of European integration 1980–1
    Luxembourg: Office for official publications of the European Communities, 1981. 617p.
    ISBN 92–823–0037–4. Catalogue number AX–30–80–972–EN–C

Sweden

Basic information

A country of 8.3 million inhabitants, an advanced industrial community with a developed social welfare system and a deeply rooted democracy, Sweden has more affinities with the ten countries of the Community than differences.

As a member of the European Free Trade Association (EFTA) since its inception in 1960, Swedish links with the Community have developed.

When Denmark joined the EC and Norway considered this move, Sweden never requested negotiations thinking that this link might well be incompatible with its self-chosen policy of neutrality.

Trade with Sweden

As part of the free trade agreements, joint committees were set up for the EEC and ECSC to ensure the efficient functioning of the agreements. In 1981 it was agreed that one of the two annual sessions, normally attended by officials, should be replaced by a meeting of high-ranking representatives and ministers. The first of these restyled meetings took place on 29 June 1981.

The agreement with all EFTA countries applies to Sweden. The arrangement is an individual preferential agreement for each country (OJ

L300/99–186 31.12.72) which came into force on 1 January 1973 and is of indefinite duration. The agreement with the ECSC was signed in 1973 (OJ L350/76–94 19.12.73) but did not come into force until 1 January 1974 and was of indefinite duration.

A framework agreement on fisheries was negotiated, initialled and signed in 1977. However it entered into force provisionally in 1977 (OJ C182/55 31.7.78) and was concluded in 1980 (OJ L226/1–6 29.8.80) (Regulation 2209/80/EEC). It was finally brought into force on 7 April 1981 (OJ L111/41 23.4.81). Its duration is for ten years. It provides reciprocal fishing rights with an annual agreement over quotas. The annual quotas were concluded for 1978–80, but some difficulty occurred over the 1981 agreement which was not concluded until 29 September 1981 (*Bulletin of the European Communities* **14** (9) 1981. points 2.1.91– 2.1.102).

The 1972 agreements were for free trade with a gradual elimination of tariff barriers. These were completed in the main by 1977, for aluminium and some other metals by 1979 and it is expected that pulp and paper restriction will go by 31 December 1983.

In 1980 Swedish imports from the EC were over 49% of its total and it exported to the Community member states just over 50% of its total exports. The balance of trade between the two parties has been more or less in equilibrium since the trading treaty was signed in 1972. In 1980 for both imports and exports this was approximately 11½ billion ECUs.

Additional areas of co-operation

- under the COST programme (qv) Sweden has participated in a number of Community projects in the field of scientific and technical research. Examples are data processing, telecommunications meteorology, oceanography, transport and metallurgy.
- Sweden has an agreement for interconnection with the EC's Euronet/Diane project (qv)
- co-operation takes place over sea and air transport (qv) through regular meetings
- by a 1976 agreement Sweden participates in the JET (qv) programme, etc
- political links between the two partners has escalated over recent years. They are likely to lead to even closer co-operation in the future

Further information

General report on the activities of the European Communities
Luxembourg: Office for official publications of the European Communities, annual

The European Community and Sweden
    Brussels: EC Spokesman's Group and Director-General for Information, June 1981. 9p.
    (Europe Information, External Relations series no 48/81)
Europe today, state of European integration 1980–1
    Luxembourg: Office for official publications of the European Communities, 1981. 617p.
    ISBN 92–823–0037–4. Catalogue number AX–30–80–972–EN–C

Switzerland

Basic information

A country of 4.6 million inhabitants, an advanced industrial community with a developed social welfare system and a strong democratic constitution, Switzerland has very many affinities with the ten countries of the Community.

In order to assist in easing the trade and other associations between the two communities, a Joint committee was set up. This meets regularly, at least once a year, in either a Community country or Switzerland.

Trade with Switzerland

As a member of the European free trade asssociation (EFTA), Switzerland along with other members signed free trade agreements with the EEC and ECSC in 1972. In the case of the EEC (OJ L300/191–282 31.12.72) this agreement came into force on 1 January 1973 and for the ECSC (OJ L350/13–28 19.12.73) this agreement came into force on 1 January 1974. Both are of indefinite duration. An additional agreement including the principality of Liechtenstein in the Swiss agreement follows the main resolutions. In the case of the EEC (OJ L300/283–5 31.12.72) and the ECSC (OJ L350/29–32 19.12.73).

In view of the geographical position of Switzerland (as with Austria), transit agreements have been signed to facilitate the easy passage of goods between one part of the Community and another. The first of these was with the ECSC in 1956 and entered into force on 1 June 1957. The second was signed in 1972 (OJ L294 of 1972) and came into force on 1 January 1974. Several amendments have been made. Customs procedures have been simplified thus facilitating inter-Community trade.

The 1973 and 1974 agreements resulted in a considerably expanded trade. Swiss exports to the Community rose by 158% between 1973 and 1978 and consisted of approximately 52% of total Swiss exports. Switzerland's imports of Community goods increased by 100% during the same period.

For the Community, Switzerland is second to the United States as the biggest importer of EC products.

Additional areas of co-operation

- since autumn 1977 experts on transport problems and policies have been meeting regularly
- similar exchanges of information have been made concerning economic and monetary matters
- agreement in 1967 concerned watchmaking products amended by a 1972 clock and watch agreement (*Bulletin of the European Communities* **14** (10) 1981 point 2.2.33)
- agreement in 1969 on textiles
- agreement on 12 December 1975 on research and the exchange of information on the environment (qv)
- a co-operation agreement in the field of controlled thermonuclear fusion (JET) (qv) in 1978
- negotiations opened in 1976 and have now been concluded in the field of non-life direct insurance with special regard to subsidiary companies (qv Diplomas and qualifications, mutual recognition). The agreement was initialled on 25.6.82 and was largely based on Directive 73/239/EEC (qv Insurance). It will enter into force as soon as appropriate procedures have been completed by the contracting parties
- the Co-operation in scientific and technical research programme (COST) has been extended to Switzerland
- in telecommunications, Switzerland has an agreement (exchange of letters) for interconnection with the EC's Euronet/Diane project (qv)
- Switzerland has acceded to the European patents convention and participates in the work of the European patent office
- in 1976 it signed the Convention on the protection of the Rhine against chemical pollution

Further information

General report on the activities of the European Communities
    Luxembourg: Office for official publications of the European Communities, annual
The European Community and the EFTA countries
    Brussels: EC Spokesman's Group and Director-General for Information, June 1980. 19p. (Europe Information, External Relations series no. 35/80)
Europe today, state of European integration 1980–1
    Luxembourg: Office for official publications of the European Communications, 1981. 617p. ISBN 92–823–0037–4. Catalogue number AX–30–80–972–EN–C.

Australia

Basic information

Australian comparisons with the EC are most striking when it is remembered that it has an area of 7.7 million sq. km. compared with the EC's 1.5 million sq. km. and a 1976 population of 13.6 millions compared to the EC's 258.8 millions for the same year. Its gross domestic product (GDP) also in 1976 was in US $ 6,252 per capita compared with the EC's US $ 6,039 (1976/7).

Agriculture accounts for 46% of Australia's exports. In 1948/9 61.5% of Australian exports went to the nine countries now making up the EC, whereas in 1976/7 this had dropped to 16%. For imports comparable figures are 54.6% dropping to 24.8%. The biggest changes were with the United Kingdom.

Links with Australia

Australia accredited a diplomatic mission to the Community in 1959. Following British accession to the EC in 1973 the need for closer contacts was appreciated by both sides. In 1974 the Commission's Vice-President Sir Christopher Soames (now Lord Soames) proposed regular informal consultations and the first round at official level took place in Brussels in July 1976 followed by a second round in Canberra in March 1977, etc. The first of a series of ministerial consultations was held in Canberra from 21–23 April 1980. EEC representation in Canberra was raised to a delegation in April 1981.

There are no trade agreements between Australia and the Community but contacts are maintained as outlined above.

Community's interests

The EC wishes to obtain as unrestricted access as possible to Australian natural resources. To this end it has:

- uranium – a 30 year agreement with Australia was signed on 21 September 1981
- noted the protectionist measures imposed by Australia
- undertaken investment in Australia
- limited the imports from Australia of sheepmeat to 17,500 tonnes and beef to 60,000 tonnes both for 1981

Further information

General report on the activities of the European Communities
   Luxembourg: Office for official publications of the European Communities, annual
Australia and the European Community
   Brussels: EC Spokesman's Group and Directorate-General for Information, June 1978. 7p.
   (Europe Information, External Relations series no 8/78). Catalogue number CG–AB–78–
   008–EN–C
European Community and Australia
   Brussels: EC Spokesman's Group and Directorate-General for Information, April 1980.
   15p. (Europe Information, External Relations series, no 32/80)
Europe today, state of European integration 1980–1
   Luxembourg: Office for official publications of the European Communities, 1981. 617p.
   ISBN 92–823–0037–4. Catalogue number AX–30–80–972–EN–C

Canada

Basic information

The Canadian GNP in 1977 was estimated at US $ 7400 compared with the Community's
US $ 6039 for the same year. Canada's trade with the EC has shown a surplus in Canada's
favour every year since 1958. EC exports consists largely of manufactured goods, industrial
machinery, transport equipment, chemicals, clothing, footwear, textiles, consumer durables
and manufactured foodstuffs. 80% of Canadian exports to the EC consist of crude and semi-
manufactured materials including minerals, timeber, wood pulp and foodstuffs, particularly
wheat. Overall, the Community is Canada's second biggest trading partner taking 11% of
her exports and accounting for 9% of her imports. It should be noted that both figures are
falling in recent years.

At the end of 1975 the EC had a book investment in Canada of Canadian $ 6 billion or 15%
of Canada's foreign investment. Canada had invested the same percentage in the EC but
this amounted to Canadian $ 1.6 billion.

EEC – Canada relations

A framework Agreement for Commercial and Economic Co-operation
was signed with Canada in July 1976. It was the first of its type to be
concluded by the Community with an advanced industrial nation. Both
partners were members of the Atlantic Alliance.

The start of the Framework Agreement could be considered as a resolution
in October 1972 at the Community Summit Conference of Heads of State
and Government, calling for a constructive dialogue between Canada
and the EC. In November of the same year Canada addressed an aide-
memoire to the Community on the question of a general agreement.
Canadian thinking was taken a step further by a second aide-memoire of
20 April 1974 proposing the negotiation of an Agreement which would
establish a 'direct contractual link between Canada and the Community'.

In a communication to the Council of 16 September 1974, the Commission showed its preference for an agreement which would constitute a broad Community framework for economic and commercial co-operation. In February 1976 the Council adopted the Commission's negotiating mandate and the agreement was initialled on 2 June 1976 and signed on 6 July 1976. This has developed considerably with missions visiting the EEC countries and vice versa. For example, on urban transportation (*Bulletin of the European Communities* **14** (9) 1981. point 2.2.30).

Details of the main features of the agreement for commercial and economic co-operation covered – most favoured nation treatment, development and diversification of trade, economic co-operation and a joint co-operation committee. The agreement is of indefinite duration. One of the more recent in a series of fisheries agreements with Canada, was signed in 1981 (OJ L379/53–57 31.12.81) (Decision 81/1053/EEC). At the same time there was an exchange of letters on fisheries relations (OJ L379/58–63 31.12.81) (Decision 81/1054/EEC). Somewhat similar exchanges of letters cover salmon fishing.

In addition to the Framework Agreement outlined above, the EC and Canada co-operate in the Euratom/Canada agreement on Nuclear Co-operation. Since 1972 there have been twice yearly meetings between the Commission and the Canadian Government. Since 1974 members of the European Parliament and the Canadian Parliament have been meeting annually, a Community Delegation was established in Ottawa on 19 February 1976, and there is co-operation on a number of international and multinational agreements.

Further information

General report on the activities of the European Communities
  Luxembourg: Office for official publications of the European Communities, annual
The European Community and Canada
  Brussels: EC Spokesman's Group and Directorate-General for Information, March 1978.
  10p. (Europe Information, External Relations series, no 1/78)

Japan.

Basic information

Relations between the EEC and Japan were practically non-existent until the early 1970s. Now the major problem between the Community and Japan is concerned with the low volume of EEC imports into that country resulting in unfavourable trade balances.

In 1978 a meeting was held in Tokyo on this subject between the Japanese Minister of State for Economic Relations and Wilhelm Haferkamp, a vice-president of the Commission. Similar meetings at Community and member state levels took place during 1979 and 1980.

Further high level consultations took place in Tokyo on 28/29 January 1981 but with poor results (*Bulletin of the European Communities* 14 (2) 1981. point 2.2.30). Between 1977 and 1980 Japan's surplus of trade with the Community rose form $5,000 million to $10,000 million per annum.

From June 1973 regular half yearly, high level, consultations have been held with the Japanese dealing with bilateral and multilateral problems (*Bulletin of the European Communities* 6 (6) 1973 point 2324).

Since November 1974 the Community has a delegation in Tokyo (*Bulletin of the European Communities* 7 (11) 1974 point 2330).

Every year since 1975 there have been talks on Japanese trade surpluses.

As the President of the EEC – Roy Jenkins – stated in a speech he made at the Foreign Correspondents Club in Tokyo in October 1977, the problem lies in a very limited range of products – iron and steel, shipbuilding, ballbearings, cars and certain electronic products.

On the 24th February 1981 the Commission decided to introduce Community surveillance of certain imports from Japan – motor vehicles, colour television receivers and tubes and certain machine tools. This came into force on 1 March 1981 (OJ L54/61–3 28.1.81) (Regulations 535–7/81/EEC) and was valid until the end of the year.

France, Italy and the UK applied restrictions on the import of Japanese cars. On 6 May 1981 the Commission decided to request that a limitation of car exports to the Community be signed similar to the three year agreement between Japan and the USA announced on 1 May 1981.

On 28.5.82 the Japanese announced a second set of measures intended to open up their markets to manufactures of foreign origin. The Commission thought that:

- these proposals were a further step in the right direction
- they proved that the Japanese government were aware of the problem
- the new decisions were not, however, in keeping with the scale of the problem
- further progress was required

Details of the Japanese proposals to July 1982 are in the *Bulletin of the European Communities* 15 (6) 1982 point 2.2.49.

Further information

General report on the activities of the European Communities
    Luxembourg: Office for official publications of the European Communities, annual
Hanabusa, Masamichi
Trade problems between Japan and Western Europe
    London: Saxon House for the Royal Institute of International Affairs, 1979. 125p. ISBN 0–566–00275–2
The European Community and Japan
    Brussels: EC Spokesman's Group and Directorate-General for Information, June 1981. 14p. (Europe Information, External Relations series no 47/81)
Blauvelt, Euan and Jennifer Durlacher
Sources of Asian/Pacific economic information
    London: Gower 1982. 2 v.

New Zealand

Basic information

Historically Britain had strong trading links with New Zealand from earliest times.

When Britain negotiated to join the EEC, in spite of opposition it negotiated Protocol 18 of the Act of Accession 1973. This guaranteed imports into the UK of quantities of butter and cheese for five years (1978). The period for butter was extended to 1980 and quantities are being negotiated on an annual basis (OJ C327/100–1 15.12.80) and (EP Working document 1–336/80).

Links with New Zealand

There are no trade agreements with New Zealand, but firm contacts are maintained by bilateral and multilateral negotiations.

Community's interest

The Community is concerned over New Zealand agricultural exports:

- a voluntary restraint agreement of sheepmeat exports to the Community. This has been limited to 245,000 tonnes a year with effect from 1981 (*Bulletin of the European Communities* 13 (10) 1980. point 1.4.4)
- in 1981 butter exports to the EEC (for the UK) have been increased in price up to 75% of the Community's intervention price against a 20,000 tonne reduction in quantity to 94,000 tonnes (*Bulletin of the European Communities* 13 (9) 1980. point 2.1.45)
- a further reduction in the quantity of butter exported to the EEC (for the UK) has been agreed commencing in 1982 when the total will be 92,000 tonnes and 1983 when the total is likely to be 90,000 tonnes (a decision to be made before 1.10.82)
- a general decision on the import of New Zealand butter will be made for 1984 and subsequent years before 1.8.83 and based on a report and proposals for the Commission

Further information

General report on the activities of the European Communities
  Luxembourg: Office for official publications of the European Communities, annual
Europe today, state of European integration 1980–1
  Luxembourg: Office for official publications of the European Communities, 1981. 617p.
  ISBN 92–823–0037–4. Catalogue number AX–30–80–972–EN–C

Turkey

Basic information

The EEC-Turkey Association Agreement (OJ L217 29.12.64) was signed in Ankara on 12 September 1963 and entered into force on 1 December 1964. It is based on article 238 of the Treaty of Rome.

Development of association

The treaty lays down different stages for the development of the association as follows:

- a preparatory stage (1964–73) during which time the Community helped Turkey to strengthen its economy by means of financial aid and tariff quotas opened for tobacco, dried grapes, dried figs, and hazelnuts which represent 40% of Turkey's exports to the Community
- a transitional stage enabling a customs union to be established in 12–22 years according to the product
- a final stage providing the possibility for Turkey to accede to the Community once the economic policy of both partners has been co-ordinated. Since the agreement was in the form of a framework agreement, it was implemented by a series of additional protocols

Institutions have also been set up between the partners:

- a Customs Co-operation committee
- an Association committee which is at senior official level and prepares the work of the Council
- an Association council at ministerial level which meets at least twice a year and which reports to:
- a Joint Parliamentary Committee consisting of 18 members of the European Parliament and 18 members of the Turkish Grand National Assembly

Objectives of the EEC – Turkey agreement

- to promote the strengthening of trade and economic relations between the two partners
- to promote the development of the Turkish economy
- to improve the living conditions of the Turkish people
- to improve the level of employment in Turkey

Scope of the agreement

Financial Protocols have been signed from time to time, the first, being on 12 September 1963, was for 175 million US $ (now the equivalent of 210 million US $) covering aid and loans to Turkey.

A supplementary protocol increased the special loans to 242 million ua. A third protocol dated 12 May 1977 was for 310 million EUA lasting until October 1981. Exceptional aid was voted by the Council in May 1979 and was for 75 million EUA. A fourth protocol entered into force 1 November 1981 was for 600 million ECU over five years (*Bulletin of the European Communities* **13** (6) 1980. point 1.4.7 and **14** (6) 1981. point 2.2.49).

ECSC

An agreement with Turkey was signed on 23 November 1970 and came into force on 1 January 1973. It was of unlimited duration (OJ C113/1–80 24.12.73) (Version in English).

Some progress has been made towards implementing the proposals listed above. Military governments taking over from Parliament have caused some delay in these steps towards association.

Further information

General report on the activities of the European Communities
  Luxembourg: Office for official publications of the European Communities, annual
Association between the European Economic Community and Turkey
  Brussels: The Association Council, 1977. 151p.
Turkey and the European Community
  Brussels: EC Spokesman's Group and Directorate-General for Information, June 1978. 7p. (Europe Information External Relations series no. 9/78). Catalogue number CC–AB–78–010–EN–C
Europe today, state of European integration 1980–1
  Luxembourg: Office for official publications of the European Communities, 1981. 617p. ISBN 92–823–0037–4. Catalogue number AX–30–80–972–EN–C

United States of America (USA)

Basic information

There are no trade agreements between the European Communities and the USA except as regards fishing.

Each party does co-operate through international organizations and by membership of international agreements.

The European Parliament maintains regular contacts with the US Congress through twice yearly visits, eg the May 1981 visit discussed US interest rates, the US/Japan automobile agreement, dual pricing of natural gas, initiation in the US of anti-dumping legislation affecting fine and special steels, the North-South dialogue, energy and nuclear questions, co-operation in the field of science and technology, etc (*Bulletin of the European Communities* **14** (5) 1981. point 2.2.42–2.2.48).

Agreement

A fishing agreement concerning the US coastal area came into force on 9 June 1977 and is due to last until 1 July 1984 (OJ L141/1 9.6.77) (Regulation 1220/77/EEC).

Contacts

Delegations from the EC visit the USA frequently to discuss trading and manufacturing problems. On 9 and 10 February 1981 there was the problem of a recent rapid increase in the export by the USA of certain textile products. As a result action was taken later that month to correct this change (*Bulletin of the European Communities* **14** (2) 1981. point 2.2.28).

Study groups have been set up concerning certain industries. One of these is the EEC–US Study Group on petrochemicals (*Bulletin of the European Communities* **13** (12) 1980. point 2.2.40).

On 9 and 10 July 1981 Gaston Thorn visited the US President to prepare for the Ottawa Economic summit meeting held later that month (*Bulletin of the European Communities* **14** (7/8) 1981. points 1.1.1–1.1.6).

On 11 and 12 December 1981 the US Secretary of State, Secretary of Agriculture and the US Trade representative visited Brussels to discuss current problems with the EC President and members of the Commission. Discussions took place on resistance to protectionist pressures regarding steel, an exchange of views was recorded on the differing attitudes regarding agriculture. Finally, discussions were also held on the Multi-Fibre arrangement, Japan and GATT questions.

Further information

General report on the activities of the European Communities
   Luxembourg: Office for official publications of the European Communities, annual
Europe today, state of European integration 1980–1
   Luxembourg: Office for official publications of the European Communities, 1981. 617p.
   ISBN 92–823–0037–4. Catalogue number AX–30–80–972–EN–C

China (People's Republic of)

Basic information

The People's Republic of China has shown interest in the EC since the early 1970s. In 1973 correspondents from the New China Press Agency were accredited to the Commission Spokesman.

Sir Christopher Soames (now Lord Soames), when Vice-President of the Commission with special responsibility for external relations, was invited to China by the Chinese Institute for External Relations. With other senior officials, he was there from 4–14 May 1975 and during that time China decided to appoint an ambassador to the Community. The first Ambassador, Li Lien–Pi, presented his credentials on 15 September 1975.

Trade with China

A trade agreement between China and the EC was initialled in Brussels on 30 January 1977 and signed in Brussels on 3 April 1978. It took the place of certain bi-lateral trade agreements between individual Commission members and China which had been due to expire at the end of 1974. This new agreement came into force on 1 June 1978. (OJ L123/1–3 11.5.78) (Regulation 946/78/EEC). It is a five year agreement, with tacit renewal every year. It may be terminated by either party at six months' notice. The provisions of this agreement include:

- most-favoured-nation treatment in matters of customs duties and formalities and the granting of licences
- China will give favourable consideration to EC exports
- the EC will liberalize imports from China
- consultation over problems and visits by both sides
- market related prices and rates

At a meeting on 19 September 1978 the Council of the EC gave its approval to a special regulation on these common arrangements, which came into force on 1 January 1979. An agreement on trade in textiles of the GATT Multi-Fibre arrangement (MFA) type, but which takes account of the situation in China and gives common rules for the import of textile products (OJ L345/1–51 31.12.79). In force from 1 January 1980 to 31 December 1983.

In 1980 China became eligible for the, Generalized system of preferences (GSP) (qv) scheme.

The EEC–China joint committee meets approximately every year to review progress under the agreements between the two parties.

The President of the Commission, Mr Roy Jenkins, made an official visit to China in February 1979. A Community delegation headed by Mr Davignon visited China from 12 to 19.6.82. Concern over a reduction of the Community's share of the China market was expressed and a number of suggestions for strengthening co-operation were made and accepted. Areas of co-operation in scientific and technological subjects were explored and the Chinese showed an interest in exchanging information.

Further information

General report on the activities of the European Communities
   Luxembourg: Office for official publications of the European Communities, annual
The People's Republic of China and the European Community
   Brussels: EC Spokesman's Group and Director-General for Information, February 1979. 15p. (Europe Information, External Relations series no. 17/79) Catalogue number CC–NA–79–R17–EN–C [includes both the Regulation and the Trade agreement with China]
The People's Republic of China and the European Community
   Brussels: EC Spokesman's Group and Director-General for Information, 1981. 15p. (Europe Information, External Relations series no. 42/81). Catalogue number CC–NA–79–R17–EN–C
Europe today, state of European integration 1980–1
   Luxembourg: Office for official publications of the European Communities, 1981. 617p. ISBN 92–823–0037–4. Catalogue number AX–30–80–972–EN–C

Council for Mutual Economic Assistance (CMEA) Countries of Europe

Since the end of 1969 the Community rather than member states has been responsible for trade policy and since 1 January 1975 for agreements with the State trading countries of Eastern Europe (COMECON or the Council for mutual economic assistance CMEA). These include, the USSR, Bulgaria, Hungary, Poland, Czechoslovakia, Roumania and the GDR. Albania joined in 1949 but withdrew, de facto, in 1961.

In October 1972 at a conference of heads of EC member states, it was resolved to promote a policy of co-operation with East European countries. In November 1974 the Council set out a draft trade agreement with a Comecon country (Parliamentary support in EP Doc 425/74). This agreement due to replace existing bilateral treaties, was sent to all state trading countries linked to member states through agreements, due to expire. An additional proposal was made for textiles.

Roumania was the first country to give a positive reply and a textile agreement was initiated with this country on 16 December 1976. This was part of the Multi-Fibre arrangement (MFA).

The first MFA expired in 1977 and a new agreement was initiated with Roumania on 16 December 1977. Other agreements were signed with Hungary 30 November 1978, with Poland on 25 January 1979. They were applied with effect from 1 January 1978 and 1 January 1979 and lasted for 5 and 4 years, respectively. An agreement with Bulgaria was initiated in

1979 going into 'de facto' effect on 1 January 1979 and being valid until 31 December 1982. Czechoslovakia was also included in these negotiations. In June 1982 negotiations had already commenced on a renewal of these textile agreements.

In the fisheries sector the Community extended its fishing limits to 200 miles. On 12 November 1976 the Community informed the USSR, GDR and Poland of its action, and its readiness to negotiate a fishing agreement with them. Talks began in February 1977 between the two parties to conclude a framework agreement. Negotiations were suspended at the end of September 1977 and from 1 December 1977 no vessels from Eastern European countries have been allowed to fish in Community waters.

Steel sector

During its meeting of 19 and 20 December 1977 the Council proposed that all countries exporting steel to the EEC should conclude bilateral arrangements to ensure that the steps taken to assist the European steel industry were not undermined. On 12 April 1978 Czechoslovakia concluded a steel agreement with the EC. Similar agreements were concluded with Hungary on 1 May 1978, Roumania on 31 May 1978, Poland on 17 July 1978 and Bulgaria on 24 January 1979.

Industrial sector

On 6 February 1979 the council authorized negotiations with Roumania for an agreement on industrial products excluding iron and steel, and creating a joint committee. The two agreements were signed in Bucharest on 28 July 1980 (*Bulletin of the European Communities* **13** (7/8) 1980. points 1.4.1. to 1.4.9.).

Community CMEA relations

The first talks took place on 4 to 6 February 1975. In 1976 the President of CMEA proposed that an agreement be concluded covering relations between the two organizations. Subsequent talks were in Brussels and Moscow and by 1980 the drafting stage had been reached. A committee of experts tried to resolve difficulties at this stage and met in October 1980. In March 1981 letters from both parties showed concern at the failure to reach a conclusion.

Poland, emergency humanitarian aid

The aid is designed for the poorest section of the population, those who are affected by the scarcity of supplies. It consists of foodstuffs, and medicines. Supplies were sent in December 1981 (2 million ECU) January-February 1982 (8 million ECU) June 1982 (7.5 million ECU). In addition non-governmental aid during the first six months of 1982 totalled 9,000 tonnes of food and hygiene and medical products.

Further information

General report on the activities of the European Communities
    Luxembourg: Office for official publications of the European Communities, annual
Shlaim, Avi and G N Yannopoulos
The EEC and Eastern Europe
    Cambridge: CUP, 1978. 251p. ISBN 0-521-22072-6
The European Community and the countries of Eastern Europe
    Brussels: EC Spokesman's Group and Director-General for Information, December 1979.
    10p. (Europe Information, External Relations series no 26/79)
Europe today, state of European integration 1980-1
    Luxembourg: Office for official publications of the European Communities, 1981. 617p.
    ISBN 92-823-0037-4. Catalogue number AX-30-80-972-EN-C

Association of South East Asian Nations (ASEAN).

Basic information

Established by Indonesia, Singapore, Malaysia, Thailand and the Philippines on 8 August 1967 it covers a population of 236 million. It has 83% of world rubber exports and 70% of world tin exports.

Its purpose is economic development, social progress and the cultural evolution of the area.

In February 1976 at Bali, the five states concluded a Treaty of Amity and Co-operation and signed a Declaration of ASEAN Concord.

The 1976 trade returns showed that Japan takes 26% of all ASEAN exports, USA 20.3% and the EC 14.5%. ASEAN trade as a percentage of EC external trade has grown from 2% in 1972 to 2.3% in 1976 and 2.4% in 1977. In money terms it has grown from $2,342 million in 1970 to $10,331 in 1978. The UK percentage from $811 million in 1970 to $2,365 million in 1978.

Historic links between individual EC and ASEAN states include Commonwealth membership and the links between Holland and Indonesia.

Co-operation with the Community

Commonwealth preferencies and other individual trade agreements, were merged in the EC's Generalized System of Preferences (GSP) (qv).

It was found that it was not always possible for developing countries to utilize fully the GSP facilities open to them. Seminars have been organized in all ASEAN countries to work out ways and means to assist actively in training local staff to utilize more fully the resources available to their countries and to take full advantage of them. Particular care has been made to assist Singapore with its large entrepôt trade.

A joint study group (JSG) between the EC and ASEAN was set up after the September 1974 EC delegation to ASEAN led by Sir Christopher Soames, now Lord Soames. It held its first meeting in Brussels in June 1975, then Manila in December 1976, Brussels in October 1977 and Bangkok in April 1978. Trade was the main but not the only theme discussed. An EC/ASEAN trial meeting was held in Brussels 20–21 November 1978, at which Foreign Ministers were present and in addition the EC President Roy Jenkins and Vice-President Haferkamp. It was the Commission's intention in 1979 to open a delegation within the ASEAN region on 8 March 1980. An EEC–ASEAN co-operation agreement was signed at Kuala Lumpur on 7 March 1980. It entered into force on 1 October 1980 (OJ L144/2–8 10.6.80) and is due to last for five years. Its objectives are:

1 Most favoured nation treatment
2 Commercial co-operation
3 Economic co-operation
4 Development co-operation

To further this a Joint Co-operation Committee was set up.

The EC agreement complements the ASEAN framework agreement with USA and Japan, giving most favoured nation treatment to signatories.

Further information

General report on the activities of the European Communities
  Luxembourg: Office for official publications of the European Communities, annual
The European Community and ASEAN
  Brussels: Spokesman's Group and Director-General for Information, February 1979. 14p.
  (Europe Information External Relations series no. 16/79). Catalogue number CC–NA–79–R16–EN–C. [Rather later information in the 'Financial Times', for Friday, 7th March 1980. p.3]
ASEAN and the European Community
  Brussels: Spokesman's Group and Director-General for Information, July 1981. 11p.
  (Europe Information, External Relations series no. 51/81)
Europe today, state of European integration 1980–1
  Luxembourg: Office for official publications of the European Communities, 1981. 617p.
  ISBN 92-823-0037-4. Catalogue number AX–30–80–972–EN–C

Association of South East Asian nations (ASEAN) Inter-Regional Ministerial Meetings

Basic information

The first meeting of the ASEAN with the European Communities in this series was held in Brussels on 20–21 November 1978. It was at Foreign Minister level.

It started a series of meetings and covered the following aspects of relations between the two parties:

- external relations
- regional integration and co-operation
- development co-operation
- cultural co-operation
- the general framework of future co-operation

From this ministerial level meeting, was developed the pattern of future discussions. They guide the successful relationship between the EC and ASEAN (qv).

Further details of the ASEAN and EC ministerial meetings together with the names of those attending, can be found in the, European Community and ASEAN, noted below.

Further information

General report on the activities of the European Communities, Chapter III, Section 2, 'External relations'
   Luxembourg: Office for official publications of the European Communities, annual
The European Community and ASEAN
   Brussels: EC Spokesman's Group and Director-General for Information, April 1979. 14p.
   (Europe Information, External Relations series no 16/79) Catalogue number CC–NA–79–R16–EN–C. [text of the EEC–ASEAN co-operation agreement]
ASEAN and the European Community
   Brussels: EC Spokesman's Group and Director-General for Information, July 1981. 11p.
   (Europe Information, External relations series no. 51/81)

Indonesia

Basic information

Indonesia became an independent republic in 1949. It has an area of 203,000 sq. km. and a population of 135 million (1976 estimate). Its balance of trade has remained favourable but changed from + 107 million US $ in 1970 to +2872 million US $ in 1976. In the last year mentioned the EC took 7.2% of Indonesia's exports (559 EUR million) and sent to them 21% of their imports (939 EUR million). It is a member of ASEAN (qv).

Co-operation with the Community

Indonesian trade veered toward Japan and the USA, in the second half of the 1970s. However the Community has broadened the scope of its General System of Preferences (GSP) applicable to Indonesia as to other countries. The EC has co-operated in a major pilot soya bean plantation project in Sumatra (1 million ECU). It contributed to a migration project in Sulawesi under the 1977 aid project (2 million ECU) and a further 3 million ECU in the following year). A flood control and drainage project at Talungagund in Java in 1979 (6.1 million ECU). A crop development study in 1979 (3 million ECU). A husbandry development project with Italy in 1980 (4.4 million ECU). An irrigation project in 1980 (3.8 million ECU), etc. It has provided skimmed milk powder under the 1977 Community food aid programme, every year and in 1981 this aid was running at 1,350 tonnes of milk and 5,000 tonnes of cereals.

Trade agreements

As a member state of ASEAN (qv) at the end of 1977 Indonesia signed a five year agreement restraining textile exports under the International Multi-Fibre arrangement. This arrangement was confirmed with the Community and is in force from 1 January 1978 (OJ L350/27–58 31.12.79). (Regulation 3072/79/EEC)

An, Agreement on trade in certain hand-made products, which entered into force on 1.1.81 (OJ L337/50–139 13.12.80) (Regulation 3182/80/EEC). An, Agreement on trade in handwoven fabrics of silk and cotton, which entered into force on 1 January 1978 (OJ L337/1–49 13.12.80) (Regulation 3181 80/EEC).

A, Co-operation agreement between the European Community and the five states of ASEAN, (which includes Indonesia) was signed at Kuala Lumpur on 7 March 1980. It entered into force on 1 October 1980 (*Fourteenth general report on the activities of the European Commmunities in 1980,* point 690) (OJ L144/1–8 10.6.80) Regulation 1440/80/EEC).

On 10 July 1967 Indonesia opened diplomatic relations with the EC.

Further information

General report on the activities of the European Communities
   Luxembourg: Office for official publications of the European Communities, annual
The European Community and ASEAN
   Brussels: Spokesman's Group and Director-General for Information, 1979. 13p. (Europe Information, Development series). Catalogue Number CC–NA–791–DO3–EN–LC. [text of the EEC–ASEAN co-operation agreement]

Europe today, state of European integration 1980-1
   Luxembourg: Office for official publications of the European Communities, 1981. 617p.
   ISBN 92-823-0037-4. Catalogue number AX-30-80-972-EN-C
ASEAN and the European Community
   Brussels: Spokesman's Group and Director-General for information, July 1981. 11p.
   (Europe Information, External relations series no. 51/81)

Malaysia

Basic information

Malaya became independent and a member of the Commonwealth in 1957. In September 1963 the Federation of Malaysia was formed and consisted of Malaya, Singapore, Sabah and Sarawak. Two years later Singapore became an independent nation.

During the years 1970 to 1975, industrial production was increasing at 11% per year, though as late as 1976 manufacturing industry only employed 12% of the work force. During the period 1970-6 the average growth rate of the GDP was 7.8% per year. Malaysia is self sufficient in oil and there have been a number of recent new discoveries of oil and natural gas. Other important industries include timber and textiles as well as the production of tin in which Malaysia is the world leader. Other established industries include crude oil and rubber to which should be added a growing palm oil industry.

Co-operation with the Community

Malaysia is a member of the Association of South East Asian Nations (ASEAN). Trade with the EC shows a favourable balance for Malaysia. In EUA millions this was 138 in 1972, 291 in 1973, 318 in 1974, 258 in 1975 and 601 in 1976. About a quarter of all Malaysian exports go to the Community and a high percentage to the United Kingdom. Manufactured goods exported to the EC whilst small in volume, are growing and include clothing, sports shoes and textiles.

Trade agreement

At the end of 1977 Malaysia signed a five year agreement restraining textile exports under the International Multi-Fibre arrangement. Under ASEAN, Malaysian agreements with EEC include an agreement on trade in textile products (OJ L357/1-50 31.12.77) (Regulation 3019/77/EEC) currently (June 1982) being renegotiated plus an agreement, on trade in certain hand-made products which entered into force on 1.1.81 (OJ L337/50-139 13.12.80) (Regulation 3182/80/EEC) and a, Co-operation agreement which was signed at Kuala Lumpur on 7 March 1980 between the EC and ASEAN and entered into force on 1 October 1980 (*Fourteenth general report on the activities of the European Communities in 1980.*

point 690) (OJ L144/2–8 10.6.80). EC exports to Malaysia are mainly machinery, transport equipment, chemicals and fertilizers.

Malaysia opened diplomatic relations with the Community on 20 May 1968.

Further information

General report on the activities of the European Communities
   Luxembourg: Office for official publications of the European Communities, annual
The European Community and ASEAN
   Brussels: EC Spokesman's Group and Directorate-General for Information, February 1979 14p. (Europe Information, External Relations series no 16/79. Catalogue number CC–NA–79–R16–EN–C. [text of the EEC–ASEAN co-operation agreement]
ASEAN and the European Community
   Brussels: EC Spokesman's Group and Directorate-General for Information July 1981 11p. (Europe Information, External Relations series no 51/81)

Philippines

Basic information

The country became independent in 1946. It has an area of 300,000 sq. km. and a population of 43.7 million with a GNP of US $ 400 per head per year (1976).

The economy of the country is heavily based on agriculture, forestry and fisheries, with 50% of the population engaged on these industries and producing 26% of the GSP. Mining is the fastest growing sector of the economy with copper the most important mineral though there are other large mineral deposits. Industry is expanding albeit slowly.

Co-operation with the Community

The EC exports to the Philippines were 12% in 1976 and its imports for the same year 19%. In EUR millions these figures in 1971 were, EC exports 218 and imports 151. By 1976, however, these figures had changed to 338 and 410 respectively.

The Philippines opened diplomatic relations with the EC on 12 May 1964. On 18 December 1979 the Council approved a five year Co-operation agreement with ASEAN – which includes the Philippines (OJ C 18/5–8 24.1.80) [See also Europe Information, External Relations series 16/79 for the text of this agreement]. Under the Community's food aid programme the Philippines up to 1976 received 1.2 million US $ of skimmed milk powder and in 1977, 1.5 millions. Two trade missions visited Europe in 1977 under the EC trade promotion programme. In 1977 the two Communities concluded a five year Hand-made products agreement (OJ L337/50–139 13.12.80) (Regulation 3182/80/EEC) and a textile agreement within the framework of the International Multi-Fibre arrangement currently (June 1982) being renegotiated. In 1977 the Community accounted for 11% of total foreign investment in the country, well behind the USA and Japan.

EEC projects in the Philippines include the Mindanao irrigation study 1976 (116,000 ECU), the Bicol river irrigation development 1979 (4.5 million ECU), a crop protection programme for 1980 (3.5 million ECU), etc.

Further information

ASEAN and the European Community
  Brussels: EC Spokesman's Group and Directorate-General for Information, December 1979. 11p. (Europe Information, External Relations series no. 27/79) (revised edition, July 1981 no. 51/81)

Singapore

Basic information

A republic in the Commonwealth with an area of 586 sq. km. and a population of 2.2 million. Its GNP is US $ 2,574 per head (1974).

An entrepôt port, which accounted for one third of its trade in 1976, with a fast expanding economy and undergoing rapid industrialization particularly in export orientated goods. Its growth rate in 1976 was 8%. Petroleum refining grew in the 1960s and in terms of value is now the largest single industry. The electronics industry is having an outstanding growth in the 1970s.

Co-operation with the Community

Singapore is a member of the Association of South East Asian Nations (ASEAN). Trade with the EC in EUA millions showed Singapore exports to the EC in 1971 as 138 with imports from the EC as 391. In 1976 these figures were respectively 450 and 894. Half the EC imports go to the United Kingdom and 40% of EC exports are from the UK (Figures for 1976 from the EC Statistical Office).

Singapore became accredited to the Community on 19 May 1972. The EC's Generalized System of Preferences (GSP) applies to Singapore. As the country has a large entrepôt trade, in 1974 the EC exempted eight products which were exported through the country. Singapore sent trade missions to Europe in 1977 and 1978 through the Communities trade promotion programme. Within the framework of the International

Multi-Fibre arrangement, the EC and Singapore concluded a five year textile agreement (1978–82 inclusive) for the limitation of textile exports (OJ L350/99–138 31.12.79) (Regulation 3074/79/EEC). Currently this agreement is being renegotiated. In 1980 a Co-operation agreement between the European Community and ASEAN (which includes Singapore) was signed and brought into force on 1 October 1980 (*Fourteenth report on the activities of the European Communities in 1980*, point 690) (OJ L144/1–8 10.6.80) (Regulation 1440/80/EEC).

Further information

General report on the activities of the European Communities
   Luxembourg: Office for official publications of the European Communities, annual
The European Community and ASEAN
   Brussels: EC Spokesman's Group and Director-General for Information, February 1979.
   14p. (Europe Information, External Relations series no. 16/79). Catalogue number
   CC–NA–79–R16–EN–C. [text of the EEC–ASEAN co-operation agreement]
ASEAN and the European Community
   Brussels: EC Spokesman's Group and Director-General for Information, July 1981. 11p.
   (Europe Information, External Relations series no. 51/81)
Europe today, state of European integration 1980–1981
   Luxembourg: Office for official publications of the European Communities, 1981. 617p.
   ISBN 92–823–0037–4. Catalogue Number AX–30–80–972–EN–C

Thailand

Basic information

An independent Kingdom with an area of 514,000 sq. km. and a population of 42 millions. Its GNP in US $ is 370 per head per year (1976).

It has deposits of many minerals – coal, iron, copper, tin, gold, silver as well as rubies and sapphires. Tin is the main mineral mined and about 30,000 tonnes are exported annually. There are small oil resources and extensive areas of oil bearing shales. Agriculture accounts for 80% of the work force and 27% of the GNP.

Co-operation with the Community

EC trade with Thailand show imports into the Community as 149 million EUA in 1971 with exports running at 217 million. In 1976 these figures had become 510 million EUA and 198 million respectively, according to the EC Statistical Office. The imbalance of trade in 1976 was due to increased exports by Thailand of rice and tapioca.

Thailand opened its relations with the Community on 28 August 1962. The EC and Thailand concluded a textile agreement under the International

Multi-Fibre arrangement (OJ L337/1–49 13.12.80) (regulation 3181/ 80/EEC) Europe has been visited by two Thai trade missions. Thailand was included in the ASEAN co-operation agreement (OJ L144/1–8 10.6.80) (Regulation 1440/80/EEC). EEC projects in Thailand include the, Inland fisheries study 1976, a pig breeding centre project and an Inland fisheries project 1977, an, Integrated rural development project, a seed production centre study and a crop diversification study in 1978, a Winged bean crop development project, Rubber small holdings development, Pa Mong and Lam Chiiang SA irrigation and Crop development for the NE region for 1979, an agreement on the production, processing and marketing of Manioc in 1980 and a framework agreement on rural development 1981.

Further information

General report on the activities of the European Communities
   Luxembourg: Office for official publications of the European Communities, annual
ASEAN and the European Community
   Brussels: EC Spokesman's Group and Directorate-General for Information, December 1979. 11p. (Europe Information, External Relations series)
ASEAN and the European Community
   Brussels: EC Spokesman's Group and Directorate-General for information, July 1981. 11p. (Europe Information, External Relations series no. 51/81. [text of the EEC–ASEAN co-operation agreement])

African, Caribbean and Pacific States (ACP), and OCT Trade Agreements

Basic information

Agreements linking together over 60 ACP countries and the 10 EEC member states, were signed at Lomé (qv) and are currently in operation and expanding. They were not the first of these trade agreements and a number of members participate in other regional, etc groupings which link them to the EC. Also a number of other developing countries in these areas are linked to the Communities as part of the, Overseas countries and territories (OCT).

Historic development of trade agreements

1964 – The first Yaoundé convention, the Association of African States and Madagascar (AASM), was signed in 1962 and entered into force on 1.6.64 having a duration of five years (OJ 93/1429–1506 11.6.64). It covered Madagascar and 18 African states.

1971 – The second Yaoundé convention was signed in 1969 and entered into force on 1 January 1971, again lasting five years (OJ L282/1–53 28.12.70). States participating in the second convention were the same as for the first with the addition of Mauritius (1972). With both Yaoundé conventions a free trade area was agreed between the two contracting parties. A system of reciprocity in trade relations caused certain problems with developing countries. Through the EDF (qv) and the EIB (qv), financial and technical co-operation was arranged under the two conventions. Guidance to the development of the convention was provided by a, Council of the Association. A, Parliamentary Conference of the Association, linked the parliamentary institutions of the member states. An, Arbitration court of the Association was set up to resolve disputes concerning the interpretation and application of the Conventions.

1971 – The Arusha agreement with the three East African countries (Kenya, Uganda, Tanzania) was signed in 1969 and entered into force on 1 January 1971 (OJ L282/54–82 28.12.70). This was the second Arusha Convention, the first (1968) having not entered into force.

The trade arrangements were similar to the second Yaoundé convention. There was an Association council and a Parliamentary committee.

1966 – Lagos agreement with Nigeria was signed on 16 July 1966 but did not enter into force having failed to be ratified by all EEC members due to the outbreak of the Biafran war.

1976 – First convention of Lomé (qv) was signed in 1975 and entered into force on 1 April 1976 (OJ L25/1–177 30.1.76) having a duration of five years. States participating in this first convention included the EC member states, the 19 AASM members, the three East African states and those African, Caribbean and Pacific countries who had comparable economies and wished to join. Initially there were 46 member countries. Trade relations are no longer based on reciprocity of trade advantages, as with the Yaoundé agreements. STABEX (qv) was introduced. The EDF (qv) is the main agency for development programmes. Special provisions have been introduced for certain products – No. 3–sugar, No. 6–bananas, No. 7–rum, beef and veal. As with Yaoundé there is an ACP–EEC Council of Ministers. There is also an ACP–EEC Committee of Ambassadors, an ACP–EEC Consultative Assembly and an ACP–EEC Joint Assembly. Subsequently aid to ACP states continued via the EDF and those interested are advised to obtain the last item under, Further information, at the end of this section.

1981 – Second convention of Lomé (qv) was signed in 1979 and entered into force on 1 January 1981. At the time of entry into force there were 61 members and the second convention continued the work of the first with certain changes and developments. Special provisions were as in the first convention. A Recommended Council regulation (OJ C93/8 16.4.80) was published.

1958 – The Association of, Overseas Countries and Territories (OCT) consisted of the dependent territories of the Community member states.

Under the Treaty of Rome, provision is made for OCT countries in the preamble and articles 3(k) and 131. The duration of the first agreement was five years. At the end of this period certain countries had become independent and became eligible in 1964 for first Yaoundé convention. The objectives of the Community were in line with those of the United Nations for dependent territories. In addition, it was concerned to increase their trade and promote their economies and social development.

1964 – Decision of 25 February 1964 formed the second association of, Overseas countries and territories (OCT). It entered into force on 1 June 1964 and lasted five years. It was a development of the first agreement of 1958.

1971 – Decision of 29 September 1970 formed the third association of, Overseas countries and territories (OCT). It entered into force on 1 January 1971 and lasted five years. It was a development of the first agreement of 1958.

1976 – Decision of 29 June 1976 formed the fourth association of, Overseas countries and territories (OCT). It entered into force on 1 April 1976 and lasted five years. It was a development of the first agreement of 1958 and takes into consideration UK dependent territories.

Individual agreements have been made with a number of other developing countries.

Further information

General report on the activities of the European Communities
   Luxembourg: Office for official publications of the European Communities, annual
EEC-ACP trade relations
   Brussels: Spokesman's Group and Director-General for Information, December 1978. 30p. (Europe Information, Development series). Catalogue Number CC-AB-78-024-EN-C
Guide to EEC legislation, Chapter 26.3 'Food aid agreements', Chapter 44.2 'Multilateral agreements'
   Amsterdam: North Holland Publishing Company, 1979. 2 v. ISBN 0-444-85320-0
Europe today, state of European integration 1980-1
   Luxembourg: Office for official publications of the European Communities, 1981. 617p. ISBN 92-823-0037-4. Catalogue number AX-30-80-972-EN-C
How to participate in contracts financed by the European Development Fund
   Luxembourg: Office for official publications of the European Communities, 1981. 42p. (Collection Dossiers, Development series no. 3). ISBN 92-825-2301-2. Catalogue number CB-NX-81-003-EN-C
British Overseas Trade Board
Business guide to the European Development Fund
   London: BOTB, December 1981. various paginations
ACP states yearbook
   Brussels: Editions Delta, 1981. 600p. ISBN 2-8209-0014-5
Blauvelt, Euan and Jennifer Durlacher
Sources of Asian/Pacific economic information
   London: Gower, 1982. 2 v.

Lomé Conventions

Basic information

Between 1958 and 1962 the EC progressively unified its trade relations with a large part of the African Continent. This was the period of the first European Development Fund (EDF) which had resources of 580 million units of account. On 20 July 1963, 18 African countries signed the first Association Convention of Yaoundé, marking the beginning of the Associated African States and Madagascar (AASM). This Convention, which lasted from 1963-8, developed trade relations by a system of mutual preferences. The second Yaoundé Convention was signed in July 1969 by the same group of AASM countries plus Mauritius, and provided additionally, aid for trade promotion and emergency aid. After the enlargement of the Community in 1973 there was a meeting at Nouakchott in April of the same year to consider the enlargement of the Association. In May 1973 the trade ministers of the African countries held a meeting at Abidjan where for the first time they voiced their interest in a 'bloc to bloc' negotiation with the EC.

First convention

A draft Association Agreement had been compiled in Brussels as early as April 1973 and owed much to the Yaoundé formula but added a new system for the stabilization of export receipts for basic products. On 25 July 1973 delegations from 43 African, Caribbean and Pacific countries (ACP) came to Brussels. Negotiations started in October 1973. In February 1974 a further conference of Africa trade ministers was held in Addis-Ababa followed by a conference at Ministerial level (Kingston, Jamaica) in July 1974. Here the EC finally abandoned any reciprocity requirement on the trade side, they also agreed that industrialization should be given a place of priority in future co-operation. The ACP memorandum at the Kingston Conference served as a draft for the Lomé convention provisions. On 31 January 1975 the Yaoundé Convention became a thing of the past and its place was taken by the 'Convention of Lomé between the EEC and the ACP', it entered into force on 1 April 1976. The Lomé Conventions were each to last for five years. The first Lomé convention ceased on 1 March 1980. For detailed information about this agreement and the printed text see: *Lomé Dossier*, in the 'Courier', special issue on 31 March 1975; and the, *Lomé convention, Europe–ACP analytical guide to the terms of the Lomé convention* in European Commission document no. 129/76/X/F.

Second convention

On the 31 October 1979 the second Lomé convention was signed. It entered into force on 1 January 1981 and lasts until 28 February 1985. It links over 300 million people in more than 60 countries, in a privileged aid and trade relationship with the 270 million people of the EC. The human rights issue put forward by Britain in Lomé 1 was dropped in Lomé 2. It included a new system of support for mineral producers.

Details of the Conventions

- Lomé's main features are as follows:
  - trade relations are no longer based on reciprocity of trade advantages, but entail additional advantages for the ACP
  - creation of a system of stabilizing export earnings (STABEX) for certain ACP products (qv).
  - technical and financial co-operation: ACP participate increasingly in implementation of programmes or projects. The European Development Fund (EDF) is the main agency for these
  - industrial co-operation: to develop and diversify industry
  - special measures on behalf of least developed states within framework of STABEX and EDF
  - provisions relating to establishment, services, payments and capital movements: these safeguard equal treatment of companies and nationals of participating States
  - institutions direct and manage activities of Convention
- Finance

3,500 million ECU in the form of grants, loans, risk capital and STABEX, to be made available under Lomé II. 66% to be spent on industrial and rural development projects. The EDF allocated in July 1981 a further 95 million ECU from its fourth and fifth funds to ACP and Overseas Countries & Territories (OCTs) on top of the 3,000 million from the fourth fund originally allocated. Those wishing to participate in EDF aid to Lomé countries are advised to obtain the last item under, Further information, at the end of this section.

- Trade

Remaining .5% of Agriculture exports outside Lomé I to be given slightly better benefits:

- Caribbean and African sugar producers will continue to be able to export at guaranteed prices 1.4 million tonnes to the EC
- rum importers have slightly improved terms for a fixed amount
- bananas – no exporter to have less favourable import quota than in the past
- beef and veal imports to continue at previous rates
- duty free imports to the EEC from ACP countries for 99% of their exports

- Minerals

STABEX· not extended to Minerals (except iron ore) but a special scheme set up instead. This is the, System for mineral products (SYSMIN). It covers copper, cobalt, phosphates, bauxite and alumina, manganese and tin.

- Stabilization of export earnings (STABEX)

  Designed to compensate for any shortfall in the export earnings of ACP states (qv STABEX).

  Number of agricultural products covered is raised from 34 to 44 items.

  Under Lomé II the qualifying threshold covering reduced earning, has been improved. £350 m. allocated to STABEX for the next five years.

- Agricultural co-operation and technical aid

  Includes rural development projects, irrigation, crop development, stock farming, fish farming and research matters.

- Fisheries and sea transport development.

Countries participating in Lomé conventions are:

- the ten of the EEC
- in Africa: Benin, Botswana, Burundi, Cameroon, Cape Verde Islands, Central African Republic, Chad, Comoros, Congo, Ivory Coast, Djibouti, Equatorial Guinea, Ethiopia, Gabon, The Gambia, Ghana, Guinea, Guinea Bissau, Kenya, Lesotho, Liberia, Madagascar, Malawi, Mali, Mauritania, Mauritius, Niger, Nigeria, Rwanda, Sao Tome and Principe, Senegal, Seychelles, Sierra Leone, Somalia, Sudan, Swaziland, Tanzania, Togo, Uganda, Upper Volta, Zaire, Zambia, Zimbabwe
- in the Caribbean: Bahamas, Barbados, Dominica, Grenada, Guyana, Jamaica, Santa Lucia, Surinam, Trinidad and Tobago, St Vincent and the Grenadines, Belize (Proposal to Council 23.10.81)
- in the Pacific: Fiji, Kiribati, Papua New Guinea, the Solomon Islands, Tonga, Tuvalu, Vanuatu, Western Samoa

Parallel agreement with the ECSC: entered into force and expires at the same time as the Lomé Convention.

Further information

Exporting to the European Community, information for foreign exporters
    Luxembourg: Office for official publications of the European Communities, 1977. 71p. Catalogue number CB-23-77-526-EN-C
The Second Convention of Lomé
    London: Central Office of Information, December 1979. 3p. (Fact sheet no. 38/FS/79 Classification 7 (c))
Industrial co-operation and the Lomé Convention
    Brussels: EC Spokesman's Group and Directorate-General for Information, July 1978. 9p. (Europe Information, Development series 10/78)
Community aid to the Third World: the Lomé Convention
    Brussels: EC Directorate-General for Information, 1979. 7p. (European File 17/79. Catalogue number CC-AD-79-017-EN-C)

Europe today, state of European integration 1980-1
   Luxembourg: Office for official publications of the European Communities, 1981. 617p.
   ISBN 92-823-0037-4. Catalogue number AX-30-80-972-EN-C
How to participate in contacts financed by the European Development Fund
   Luxembourg: Office for official publications of the European Communities, 1981. 42p.
   (Collection Dossiers, Development series no. 3). ISBN 92-825-2301-2 Catalogue number
   CB-NX-81-003-EN-C
British Overseas Trade Board
Business guide to the European Development Fund
   London: BOTB, December 1981. various paginations

Mauritius and the African, Caribbean and Pacific (ACP) States

Basic information

In May 1972 Mauritius became the 19th member of the Association of African and Malagasy States, thus linking itself to the EEC under the provisions of the Yaoundé II Convention (qv), the only ex-British colony to join this Convention.

Mauritius signed the ACP/EEC Convention of Lomé (qv) in February 1975 and became one of the then 46 states to have signed. This Convention offers duty free access to the Community markets for nearly all ACP products. Reciprocity of trade which was a feature of the Yaoundé Convention was abolished under the Lomé Convention.

Co-operation with the Community

Of particular benefit to Mauritius was a special sugar protocol no. 3 under the first Lomé Convention which guaranteed access to Community markets up to 1 March 1980, at an accepted minimum price and for a certain guaranteed quantity. This same convention made provision for industrial development of ACP countries including the development of small and medium sized firms. Under the original Lomé Convention, Mauritius was scheduled to receive over 15.3 million units of account from the European Development Fund (EDF) (qv). The second Lomé convention, 1981, continued this programme.

The EC aid programme to Mauritius was discussed in May 1976 when it was agreed that of the EDF support 37% should go towards road infrastructure, 32% to agriculture, 21% social programmes, 4.5% education, 4.5% for industrial and trade promotion, etc.

The European Investment Bank (EIB) (qv), in its May 1976 mission, became concerned with major projects, the second extension to the thermal power station at Fort Victoria, the setting up of a bleached bagass pulp mill, the construction of a ship yard. Previously EIB had made a loan to the Mauritian Development Bank. A second loan of 2 million units of account was to improve electricity supplies.

Further information

General report on the activities of the European Communities
  Luxembourg: Office for official publications of the European Communities, annual
Mauritius and the Lomé Convention
  Brussels: Spokesman's Group and Director-General for Information, 1979. 13p. (Europe
  Information, Development series). Catalogue number CC–NA–79–003–EN–C
Europe today, state of European integration 1980-1
  Luxembourg: Office for official publications of the European Communities 1981. 617p.
  ISBN 92–823–0037–4. Catalogue number AX–30–80–972–EN–C

Sudan

Basic information

Sudan became independent in January 1956 and has a population of 18 million (mid 1975 estimate).

As the largest country in Africa, and one which is the most linguistically and geographically diverse, Sudan acts as an important bridgehead. It held the post of Presidency of the Organization of African Unity (OAU) until July 1979, when President Nemery had an important role to play in promoting peace. As one of the original members of the 1975 Lomé Convention, Sudan favours close economic ties with the EC. However, its annual average per capita income is only US $ 314 (1977). As part of a financial reform and economic stabilization programme, in July 1979 the Sudanese pound was devalued and the current six year development plan 1977–83 was slowed down. The aim of this latest plan was to raise the GDP to US $ 877 per capita. Under the 25 year master plan (first phase 1976–80) of the, Arab authority for agricultural investment and development (AAID) the aim is to turn the Sudan into an Arab granary. It is currently classified as one of the least developed countries.

Co-operation with the Community

The EC is Sudan's most important trading partner accounting for about half of its total imports and exports.

The EC aid programme is currently running at US $ 167 million of which 129 million is given under the Lomé Convention and the remainder in food aid. With STABEX the Sudan received 13.4 million ECU for its Groundnut support, under the EC 1980 transfers of funds.

EC aided projects include the Jonglei Canal to bypass the Sudd swamps, which besides increasing the flow of the Nile, will provide water to irrigate 4 million acres. A French company is digging the canal. The EC through its European Development Fund (EDF) is contributing 2.1 million EUAs to finance ecology studies in the canal area. At Juba the first national university to be established outside Khartoum will start after a comprehensive development plan and architectural studies have been completed. The EC, EDF resources, may contribute almost 10 million

EUA to the University project. To encourage agricultural production in the Babanousa area a railway is being built with an EC contribution of 9 million EUA the agreement for which was signed in Brussels in October 1978. Under the Lomé convention 3,390 millions EUA were allocated to the African, Caribbean and Pacific states (ACP) for the period from 1975 to 1 March 1980, and Sudan's share of this sum was 90.6 million EUA,

Further information

Sudan-EEC relations
  Brussels: EC Spokesman's Group and Directorate-General for Information, April 1979. 11p. (Europe Information, Development series no 2/79). Catalogue number CC–NA–79–DO2–EN–C
General report on the activities of the European Communities, Chapter III, Section 2, 'External relations, Developing countries'
  Luxembourg: Office for official publications of the European Communities, annual

Latin America

Basic information

Between 1968 and 1976 annual EC imports in millions of US $ of Latin American goods amounted to 2,450 at the beginning of the period and 9,164 at the end. EC exports in the same period rose from 2,711 to 8,240. It should be noted however that on a percentage basis there was a decline in the Latin American share of total EC imports during this period.

Regional organizations

Following the 'Buenos Aires declaration' (1971), which enabled those Latin American countries grouped together within the Special Commission for Latin America (CECLA) to call for the setting up of a system of co-operation between Europe and Latin America, the Community recognized the important place Latin America deserved in the sphere of its external relations. The two parties agreed that an EEC–Latin American dialogue should be held at regular intervals at Ambassador level. Its purpose is to provide an initial forum for examining problems of mutual interest. After having built up its contacts with the Latin American Free Trade Association (LAFTA), the EC is concerned to develop its relations with Latin America as a whole. This it is undertaking through the foundation of the Latin-American economic system (SELA) which was set up on 18 October 1975. SELA's aims are:

● to co-ordinate existing integration mechanisms (Andean Group, Central-American Common Market, Caribbean Community, etc)

- give new impetus to intra-regional co-operation
- organize producers of raw materials and basic agricultural products
- co-ordinate positions and strategies of member countries towards the outside world

States participating in this co-operative effort are: Argentina, Barbados, Bolivia, Brazil, Chile, Colombia, Costa Rica, Cuba, Dominican Republic, Ecuador, El Salvador, Grenada, Guatemala, Guyana, Haiti, Honduras, Jamaica, Mexico, Nicaragua, Panama, Paraguay, Peru, Trinidad and Tobago, Uruguay, Venezuela.

Negotiations are also in progress with the Andean Pact countries (Venezuela, Colombia, Peru, Ecuador and Bolivia). In the case of Bolivia these negotiations were broken off during 1980 after the latest revolution and this had an effect on all Pact countries. Negotiations are now being resumed (*Bulletin of the European Communities* **14** (10) 1981. point 2.2.57).

EC – Latin America co-operation

Existing lines of development were bilateral agreements between the EC and various Latin American states. These are included in EC trade agreements: with Argentina in 1971 (OJ L249 10.11.71), Brazil in 1973 (OJ L102/24–35 11.4.74) and Uruguay in 1973 (OJ L333/2–14 4.12.73), which were replaced by a framework agreement in 1980 to last for five years (*Bulletin of the European Communities* **13** (4) 1980 points 1.3.1–1.3.4) signed 18 September 1980. The original agreements were all based on most favoured nation treatment and were for three years with annual extensions. All three covered beef and veal and additionally the treaty with Brazil covered cocoa, butter and soluble coffee. In 1975 there was an agreement with Mexico (OJ L247/11–16 23.9.75) which was for five years with possible extensions. It is non-preferential and is founded on commercial and economic co-operation. In more specialized spheres there are agreements concerning the peaceful uses of nuclear energy with Argentina in 1963 (OJ L186/2966–8 21.12.63) and Brazil in 1965 (OJ L79/7–10 31.3.69); linked to the textile trade the EC has concluded agreements with Argentina, Brazil, Colombia, Guatemala, Mexico, Peru and Uruguay. These all became applicable 'de facto' on 1 January 1978 (OJ L357/1–50 31.12.77) and will last for five years. In May 1982 negotiations opened for the renewal of these bilateral textile agreements. In craft products export quotas have been opened since 1975 for Uruguay, since 1976 for Bolivia, Chile, Ecuador, Panama and Paraguay, since 1977 for Honduras and Peru and since 1978 for El Salvador (OJ L307/42–123 30.11.77) (Regulations 2636/77/EEC).

A second line of development is linked to the EC's Generalized System of Preferences (GSP) 1971 (qv). Under this agreement a large number of manufactured or semi-manufactured products from developing countries are allowed to be imported duty free. This includes the Latin American countries of the Yaoundé (qv) and subsequent Lomé conventions (qv). According to 1975 figures, EC imports of Latin American products included under the GSP were agricultural products 55%, industrial products 25% (less textiles, coal and steel products).

Export promotion aid is a third way in which the Latin American businessman is assisted in the EC market. In 1977 there were from Latin America 45 appearances in about 20 trade fairs and exhibitions in Europe, 20 EC trade promotion experts were made available to those in Latin American countries who wanted them, there were nine missions for Latin American exporters to Europe, three missions of European buyers were made to Latin America, etc. In addition the Community pursued measures aimed at giving aid for regional integration in Latin America slanted towards larger economic units with greater trading possibilities. Finally the EC has given financial and technical aid to the area.

Emergency food aid at a cost of 980,000 ECUs has been allocated to Nicaragua, and at a cost of 125,000 ECUs to Honduras, in June 1982. Exceptional aid for flood victims in Nicaragua costing 200,000 ECU and Honduras costing 100,000 ECU were also sent in the same month via relief organizations.

Since July 1974 interparliamentary conferences have been held between the EP and the Latin-American interparliamentary conference. Joint meetings were held in Bogota July 1974, Luxembourg November 1975, Mexico July 1977, Rome February 1979. For details see, Europe today.

Argentina, political affairs

The 1982 attempt by the Argentine to take over the Falkland Islands in the South Atlantic, which were at that time one of the Overseas countries and territories (OCT) and under the United Kingdom's responsibility, led to a united front by all member states. The Foreign ministers of the ten, the Commission and Parliament all urged Argentina to comply with the UN Security Council's resolution 502. The Community imposed an embargo for one month on imports from Argentina and on the export of arms and military equipment to that country under a Commission proposal of 9.4.82 which was accepted by the Council (*Bulletin of the European Communities* 15 (4) 1982. points 1.1.1–1.1.7 and 2.4.5). The embargo was extended indefinitely (OJ L146/1 25.5.82) however, Denmark accepted these measures until such time as they were succeeded by national regulations whilst Italy and Ireland revoked article 224 of the Treaty (*Bulletin of the European Communities* 15 (5) 1982. point 1.1.5). The suspension of imports orginating in Argentina was lifted on 22 June 1982 with the Argentine surrender (OJ L/177/1 22.6.82). A second Parliamentary debate on the Falklands took place on 12 May (*Bulletin of the European Communities* 15 (5) 1982. point 2.4.11).

Further information

General report on the activities of the European Communities
Luxembourg: Office for official publications of the European Communities, annual
Latin America and the European Community
Brussels: Spokesman's Group and Director-General for Information, September 1979. 8p.
(Europe Information, External Relations series no. 21/79). Catalogue number
CC-NA-79-R21-EN-C
Europe today, state of European integration 1980-1
Luxembourg: Office for official publications of the European Communities, 1981. 617p.
ISBN 92-823-0037-4. Catalogue number AX-30-80-972-EN-C

Maghreb States

Basic information

Algeria, Morocco and Tunisia form the Maghreb states.

Treaty agreements with these states fall under article 113 of the Treaty of Rome.

In 1969 Morocco and Tunisia signed association agreements with the EEC. These entered into force on 1 September of that year and were for a period of five years. They were renewed on 1 September 1975.

First steps towards a comprehensive agreement on trade as well as technical, economic and financial matters were taken in 1972 when talks were held between Algeria and the Communities (10-11 July 1972). Later that year the Commission recommended that formal negotiations be opened with all three states. The Co-operation agreements which resulted were signed in 1976 and are of unlimited duration:

- Algeria (OJ L263/1-127 27.9.78) (Regulation 2210/78/EEC)
- Morocco (OJ L264/1-127 27.9.78) (Regulation 2211/78/EEC)
- Tunisia (OJ L265/1-127 27.9.78) (Regulation 2212/78/EEC)

These were due for review in 1979 and again in 1983. They cover the following:

- economic co-operation
- financial co-operation
- technical co-operation
- trade
- labour matters
- encouragement of private investments
- co-operation in scientific fields
- co-operation in environmental protection
- co-operation in agriculture and fisheries
- co-operation in energy production as far as Algeria and Tunisia are concerned

Development of co-operation

In 1977 representatives of the Commission and the European Investment Bank (EIB) went to Algeria and Tunisia to select projects suitable for investment finance. Similar action in Morocco was taken in the following year.

Algeria, Morocco and Tunisia implemented the 1976 agreement on 1 November 1978 and Co-operation councils were established. In the case of Tunisia the first meeting of its council was held in late 1978. Commission delegations were established in each of the Maghreb states in 1979.

In the case of Morocco and Tunisia agreement was reached on the voluntary restraint of textile exports to the EC during the period 1978 to 1981. This restraint was under the International Multi-Fibre agreement.

EIB loans were made in 1969 to:

- Morocco 43.84 million EUA
- Tunisia 30.61 million EUA

These were enlarged in 1980 and covered the period to mid 1981. They were for:

- infrastructure projects
- help for small and medium sized firms
- technical assistance

The financial protocols were renewed on 27 July 1981. At the same time a new development finance proposal was being worked on. This was to cover a five year period (*Bulletin of the European Communities* **14** (7/8) 1981. point 2.2.47). In the case of Morocco a new financial protocol was signed on 10 June 1982 (*Bulletin of the European Communities* **15** (6) 1982. point 2.2.55).

In spite of the Co-operation agreement, there was no change in the volume of trade between the Maghreb countries and the EC and each of the three countries showed a trade deficit during 1980.

Under the Co-operation agreement the first meeting between European and Moroccan members of Parliament took place in Strasbourg on 10–12 March 1981. The Co-operation agreement, and the implication for Morocco of Spain's entry into the Communities, were discussed.

Further information

General report on the activities of the European Communities
  Luxembourg: Office for official publications of the European Communities, annual
Europe today: state of European integration 1980-1
  Luxembourg: Office for official publications of the European Communities, 1981. 617p.
  ISBN 92-823-0037-4. Catalogue number AX-30-80-972-EN-C

Mashreq States

Basic information

Egypt, Jordan, Syria and the Lebanon form the Mashreq states.

As early as 1965 an agreement on trade and technical co-operation between the EC and Lebanon, was signed. It lasted five years and was renewed in 1970 and again on 1 July 1975.

Individual preferential trade agreement by the EC with each of these countries started in the 1970s, for example, on 18 December 1972 a preferential trade agreement with Egypt was signed. On the 8–9 November 1973 exploratory talks with Jordan were started leading to a similar agreement.

Negotiations for a series of Co-operation agreements, for all the Mashreq states, similar to those signed with the Maghreb countries in 1976, were started in February 1976. A series of interim agreements were signed in 1977 and the final agreements entered into force on 1 November 1978. These were:

- Egypt (OJ L266/1–103 27.9.78) (Regulation 2213/78/EEC)
- Lebanon (OJ L267/1–88 27.9.78) (Regulation 2214/78/EEC)
- Jordan (OJ L268/1–93 27.9.78) (Regulation 2215/78/EEC)
- Syria (OJ L269/1–87 27.9.77) (Regulation 2216/78/EEC)

Development of co-operation

In 1978 the Commission and the European Investment Bank (EIB) visited the Mashreq states to identify projects suitable for investment finance.

During 1979 the EIB took a number of investment decisions on the projects identified during the previous year and allocated sums as follows for the period up to 1981:

- Egypt 76.33 million EUA
- Lebanon 1.34 million EUA
- Jordan 17.96 million EUA
- Syria 34.31 million EUA

These were for:

- infrastructure development
- agricultural development
- industrial development
- training, etc

These financial protocols were renewed in 1981 and a second series of financial protocols were proposed (*Bulletin of the European Communities* **14** (7/8) 1981. point 2.2.47). The second series was signed in June 1982 (*Bulletin of the European Communities* **15** (6) 1982. points 2.2.55–6).

Progress in the Mashreq states is not generally as fast as in the Maghreb group.

Emergency food aid at a cost of 5.5 million ECU has been allocated to the Lebanon and exceptional aid to victims of the war in that country, costing a further 700,000 ECU, were both made in June 1982, as part of a continuing humanitarian project.

Further information

General report on the activities of the European Communities
  Luxembourg: Office for official publications of the European Communities, annual
Europe today: state of European integration 1980-1
  Luxembourg: Office for official publications of the European Communities, 1981. 617p.
  ISBN 92-823-0037-4. Catalogue number AX-30-80-972-EN-C

Israel

Basic information

Under the Treaty of Rome, article 113, the EEC is encouraged to sign agreements with other countries which will support its own agriculture, industry, etc.

In 1970 a trade agreement with Israel was signed which was administered by an EEC/Israel joint committee.

A new agreement was signed on 11 May 1975 and entered into force on 1 July of that year (OJ L136/1-190 22.5.75) (Regulation 1244/75/EEC). It replaced and broadened the 1970 agreement and is for an unlimited period. It is for the progressive development of a free-trade area between the two parties and was the first step towards fulfilling a 1972 Communities decision aiming towards a free trade area covering the whole of the Mediterranean. In 1978 a financial protocol and an additional protocol to the 1975 agreement, was signed and entered into force on 1 November 1978 (OJ L270/1-19 27.9.78) (Regulation 2217/78/EEC). A second financial protocol was negotiated in 1982 but owing to the Lebanon war the signing of this new protocol was suspended in June 1982.

Development of co-operation

A Co-operation council, to develop the 1975 agreement was set up at the time it was ratified. In 1978 it progressed to its first Ministerial level meeting which was held in Brussels (*Bulletin of the European Communities* 11 (12) 1978 part 2 chapter 2).

A Commission delegation to Israel was established in Tel Aviv.

The first step towards a free trade area between the EC and Israel was taken in 1979 when a mutual 10% reduction on customs tariffs was made. Owing to financial problems in Israel certain products were excluded from this agreement.

European Investment Bank loans to Israel were in the order of 30 million EUA in 1979. These were for the development of small and medium sized industrial firms.

Further information

General report on the activities of the European Communities
   Luxembourg: Office for official publications of the European Communities, annual
Europe today, state of European integration 1980-1
   Luxembourg: Office for official publications of the European Communities, 1981. 617p.
   ISBN 92-823-0037-4. Catalogue number AX-30-80-972-EN-C

Third World

Basic information

The Third World consisted in 1977 of 2,800 million people living on 51% of the Earth's surface. On average they had an annual income of US $ 300 or less than the monthly average income in industrialized countries. This Third World consists of more than 110 developing countries whose exports consist of raw materials which are processed and largely consumed elsewhere. The Bandung Conference in 1955 established the concept of the Third World. The poorest countries with a gross national product (GNP) of less than US $ 265 per capita. Their problem is survival, they consist of 1,000 million people subject to the vagaries of the climate and to recurrent catastrophies. They usually have a population increasing faster than their food supply, they lack exploitable raw materials, they have environmental deterioration and their purchasing power is falling. The average income countries tend to be more favourably endowed with natural resources some of which bring in sizeable revenues for high populations. Financial and technical aid and above all industrial and technological co-operation are of importance to these countries. A few of the Third World countries have high incomes usually as a result of a spectacular rise in the price of their raw materials – most oil exporting countries fall into this category. These countries are still dependent on the industrialized countries for their outlets and have embarked on a rapid industrialization policy.

Community action in the Third World

In the area of financial aid specifically, Community policies complement the bilateral policies of the Member states as well as their multilateral contributions outside the Community as for example to the World Bank, the United Nations Development Programme (UNDP), etc. The EC's Third World policy combines firstly, special contractual agreements on a regional basis and secondly, action at world level. It has concluded a wide range of regional agreements such as the Lomé conventions (qv) which set up special relations between the EC and African, Carribbean and Pacific (ACP) countries. Other somewhat similar agreements are with the

Maghreb states (qv) and with Mashreq states (qv). These regional and country arrangements combine all types of financial, technical and commercial action to bring about economic change, with the developing countries deciding the purposes to which this development is to be made. The agreements so formulated are written into international treaties thus making a judicial obligation on both sides. At world level the action taken consists of:

- commercial agreements
- the EC's generalized tariff preferences
- financial aid
- technical aid to non-associated countries
- food aid (see last item under Further information)
- an emergency fund
- the work of non-governmental organizations

Under the 1982 amending budget a 184 million ECU programme of action against world hunger was welcomed by a meeting of Development Ministers from Member states on 15 June 1982. The programme combines emergency measures, support for food policies and a number of specific campaigns. A summary of this plan and the Parliamentary debate on it appears in *Bulletin of the European Communities* **15** (6) 1982. points 1.3.1–1.3.7.

Further information

General report on the activities of the European Communities
   Luxembourg: Office for official publications of the European Communities, annual
Europe – Third World
   Brussels: EC Spokeman's Group and Directorate-General for Information, July 1979. 27p.
   (Development series) Catalogue number CC–NA–79–705–EN–C
Europe today, state of European integration 1980–1
   Luxembourg: Office for official publications of the European Communities, 1981. 617p.
   ISBN 92–823–0037–4. Catalogue number AX–30–80–972–EN–C
The European Community and world hunger
   Luxembourg: Office for official publications of the European Communities, 1982. 7p.
   (European file 14/82) ISSN 0379–3133
The Community and the North–South dialogue
   Luxembourg: Office for official publications of the European Communities, 1981. 7p.
   (European file 14/81) ISSN 0379–3133

⑧ Additional Information

In the course of compiling this publication, the author found a small number of additional items thought likely to be of assistance to users of the book. These have been brought together as an additional chapter.

- Summer time (pages 361–2)
- Chronology of the European Community (pages 362–382)
- Abbreviations (pages 383–5)
- Public holidays within the Community (pages 386–7)

Summer Time

Basic information

The question of harmonizing the dates when summer time is in operation throughout Community countries has been of interest to Parliament for most of the 1970s.

Work undertaken

In 1979 (26 September) the matter was raised again under the heading of energy conservation. A written answer from the Council stated the position in member states and mentioned that a new initiative by the Commission was under way. (Debates of the European Parliament no. 245 September 1979 p 207).

The European Peoples Party Group, presented a motion for a resolution on the introduction of a uniform summer time. This was withdrawn on the subject being referred to the Committee on transport. (Debates of the European Parliament no. 248 13 November 1979 p 4).

FOR A DETAILED INDEX SEE THE YELLOW PAGES.

As a result of pressure, the Council approved a directive on 22 July 1980 under which, summer time in 1981 and 1982 began on the same day throughout the Community (OJ L205/17 7.8.80) (Directive 80/737/EEC). The agreed time and date was 0100 hours GMT on 29 March 1981 and 28 March 1982.

Whilst the Council laid down the start of summer time, it was the Commission which has proposed that the end of summer time should be the second Sunday in October (in, *Bulletin of the European Communities* **14** (3) 1981. point 2.1.148).

A proposal for a second Council directive covering 1983 onwards has been submitted, whereby summer time would begin on the last Sunday of March unless that day is Easter day in one or more member states. In which case summer time would commence on the previous Sunday (OJ C84/3 14.4.81).

A second Council directive on summertime arrangement made provision for 1983, 1984 and 1985 with summertime commencing Greenwich meantime (GMT) at 1 am on the last Sunday in March and ending at 1 am GMT on 25 September 1983, on 30 September 1984 and on 29 September 1985; except for Ireland and the UK when the dates will be 23 October, 28 October and 27 October respectively (OJ L173/16–17 19.6.82).

A Chronology of the European Communities

1946

In a speech at Zurich, Sir Winston Churchill declared 'We must build a kind of United States of Europe'. These words were taken up and became a slogan for those wishing to build a united Europe. (see 1–2 June and 13 October 1955)

1948

Two inter-governmental bodies were set up in Europe, the Organization for European Economic Co-operation (OEEC) whose original purpose was to share Marshall Plan aid, and the European Payments Union (EPU) (see 13 February 1957). The OEEC later became the Organization for Economic Co-operation and Development (OECD). (30 September 1961)

1949

5 May

The Council of Europe was set up in Strasbourg, but it has little power and now serves as a forum of European Parliamentary opinion.

1950

The Council of Europe's European convention on human rights, signed. (see 29 January 1981)

9 May	In the Salon de l'Horloge at the Quai d'Orsay, the French Foreign Minister Robert Schuman announced a proposal from his Government, drafted to a large extent by Jean Monnet, to pool the coal and steel resources of France and Germany in an organization open to all European countries.

The plan had two aims:

- to reconcile France and Germany
- to set up an economic community as the first step towards a European federation

And the means of achieving them can be summarized as follows:

- to begin by creating de facto solidarity between Europeans through concrete achievements, rather than by attempting to unite Europe in one move
- to lay the foundations of economic unification in Europe by pooling basic production – coal and steel
- to set up for this purpose common rules and institutions, notably a High Authority which would be independent of Governments but whose decisions would be binding on them.

The Governments of the Federal Republic of Germany, Italy, Belgium, the Netherlands and Luxembourg are quick to declare their acceptance in principle. The British Government, however, cannot accept a commitment to set up an authority with sovereign powers. Europe therefore begins as the Six.

24 October	French Prime Minister René Pleven puts forward a plan for a European Defence Community (EDC). (see 27 May 1952)

1951

18 April	The Six – Belgium, France, Luxembourg, Italy, Federal Republic of Germany and the Netherlands – sign the Treaty establishing the European Coal and Steel Community (ECSC) in Paris. They declare themselves solemnly 'resolved to substitute for age-old rivalries the merging of their essential interests; to create, by establishing an economic community, the basis for a broader and deeper community among peoples long divided by bloody conflicts; and to lay the foundations for institutions which will give direction to a destiny henceforward shared;' (see 27 July 1952) (see also 10 February– 1 May 1953)

The ECSC set up its first European institution – the High Authority – to which member governments agreed to transfer a part of their sovereignty. This Authority was controlled by an assembly consisting of representatives from the Six.

A court of Justice was created to deal with disputes between members of ECSC.

1952

27 May	The Governments of the Six sign the Treaty establishing the EDC (see 24 October 1950). This was later rejected by the French National Assembly. (see 30–31 August 1954)
27 July	The ECSC Treaty enters into force. During the year the institutions are set up in Luxembourg, with Jean Monnet, Paul-Henri Spaak and Massimo Pilotti presiding over the High Authority, the Common Assembly and the Court of Justice respectively.

11 August	The British Government expresses its intention to establish an association between the United Kingdom and the ECSC. (see 21 December 1954)
10 September	The Foreign Ministers of the Six ask the ECSC Common Assembly to co-opt a number of additional members into an ad hoc Assembly to draft a Treaty establishing a European Political Community.
13 September	The ad hoc Assembly is formed and appoints a Constitutional Committee to prepare the groundwork.
11 December	The Dutch Government puts forward a plan for integrating the economies of the Six, on the basis of a customs union and common market.

1953

1 January	ECSC High Authority imposes levies on coal and steel production – the first European tax.
10 February–1 May	The common market is established for ECSC products – coal and iron ore (10 February), scrap (15 March) and steel (1 May). (see 10 February 1958)
10 March	The ad hoc Assembly approves the draft Treaty establishing the European Political Community and submits it to the six Governments.

1954

30–31 August	The EDC Treaty is rejected by the French National Assembly. Discussions on the planned Political Community are cut short as a result. (see 27 May 1952)
11 November	Jean Monnet announces that he will not seek a further term as President of the High Authority.
21 December	The ECSC/UK Association Agreement is signed in London. (see 11 August 1952) (see 23 September 1955)

1955

1–2 June	The Foreign Ministers of the ECSC Member States, meeting at Messina, decide to press on with building a united Europe 'in order to maintain Europe's place in the world, to restore her influence and prestige, and to ensure a continuous rise in the living standards of her people'. The Ministers instruct an intergovernmental committee, chaired by Paul-Henri Spaak, to report on the possibilities of general economic union and joint development of the peaceful uses of atomic energy.
23 September	The ECSC/UK Association Agreement enters into force.
13 October	Jean Monnet sets up the action Committee for the United States of Europe. (see 20 November 1959)

1956

29 May	The Foreign Ministers of the Six, meeting in Venice, decide on the basis of the Spaak Committee's report to go ahead with negotiations for the conclusion of two Treaties which will set up a European Economic Community and a European Atomic Energy Community (see 1–2 June 1955) (see 25 March 1957). (see 1 January 1958)

26 June	Negotiations for the new Treaties open at Val Duchesse in Brussels.
3 October	The United Kingdom, which had refused to take part in the negotiations (see 26 June 1956) proposes the setting-up of a free-trade area. (see 20–21 July 1959)

1957

13 February	The Council of the Organization for European Economic Co-operation (OEEC) decides to begin negotiations for the creation of a European free-trade area in which the Six agree to participate. (see 29 May 1956)
19–20 February	The Heads of Government of the Six, meeting in Paris, reach agreement on a number of outstanding problems, notably the conditions for the association of overseas territories with the Common Market.
25 March	The Treaties (known as the Rome Treaties) establishing the European Economic Community (EEC) and the European Atomic Energy Community (Euratom) are signed in Rome. Both Treaties are ratified before the year's end by the Parliaments of all six member countries, with even larger majorities than when the ECSC Treaty was ratified. (see 29 May 1956) (see 1 January 1958)

1958

1 January	The EEC and Euratom Treaties enter into force. (see 29 May 1956 et seq)
7 January	The Members of the EEC and Euratom Commissions are appointed by the Governments of the Member States. Walter Hallstein becomes President of the EEC Commission and Louis Armand President of the Euratom Commission.
10 February	The ECSC reaches the end of its transitional period. (see 10 February 1953)
19 March	Robert Schuman is elected President of the European Parliament, all the first session.
3–11 July	The Agriculture Conference in Stresa lays the foundations for the common agricultural policy. (see 30 June 1960)
14 November	The French Government declares that it is impossible to create a European free-trade area (between the Six and the eleven other OEEC countries) without a common customs tariff and some harmonization of economic and social measures; the negotiations break down. (see 1 July 1968)

1959

1 January	The first steps – 10% cuts in tariffs – are taken in the progressive abolition of customs duties and quotas within the EEC. (see 1 July 1968)
4 February	Britain and Euratom sign a co-operation agreement.
8 June	Greece applies for association with the EEC. (see 1 November 1962) (see 1 January 1981)
20–21 July	Ministers of the Seven (Austria, Denmark, Norway, Portugal, Sweden, Switzerland, United Kingdom) agree, following the breakdown of negotiations, to establish a European free-trade area (see 3 October 1956) (see 3 May 1960)

31 July	Turkey applies for association with the EEC.
20 November	The Action Committee for the United States of Europe (Monnet Committee) proposes a merger of the Executives of the three European Communities (ECSC High Authority, EEC Commission, Euratom Commission) and the three Councils. (see 13 October 1955)

1960

13 February	The EEC Council approves the common customs tariff on which the Member States are gradually to align their own tariffs during the transitional period (see 1 July 1968)
3 May	The Convention establishing the European Free Trade Association EFTA enters into force. (see 20–21 July 1959)
12 May	The EEC Council decides to speed up the implementation of the Treaty.
17 May	The European Parliament approves a draft convention on direct elections (based on a report by Fernand Dehousse). (see 7–10 June 1979)
30 June	On the basis of the conclusions reached by the Stresa Conference and following discussions on the intiial guidelines put forward in November 1959, the Commission sends to the Council its proposals for implementing the common agricultural policy. (see 3–11 July 1958)
20 September	The European Social fund Regulation enters into force.
19–20 December	The EEC Council approves the basic principles governing the common agricultural policy.

1961

10–11 February	The Heads of State or Government of the Six decide at a summit meeting in Paris to work towards political union.
9 July	The EEC–Greece Association agreement is signed in Athens. (see 8 June 1959)
18 July	The Heads of State or Government at a summit meeting in Bonn issue declarations on cultural and political co-operation. They agree to closer political co-operation of the Six and undertake to hold regular meetings to concert their policies.
31 July	Ireland applies to join the EEC. (see 29 January 1963)
9 August	The United Kingdom applies to join the EEC. (see 29 January 1963)
10 August	Denmark applies to join the EEC. (see 29 January 1963)
1 September	The first regulation on the free movement of workers within the Community enters into force. (see 29 July 1968)
2 November	The French Government submits a draft Treaty establshing a political union of the Six (Fouchet Plan). (see 18 January 1962)
8–9 November	Accession negotiations begin with the United Kingdom.
30 November	Accession negotiations begin with Denmark.
6–7 December	At a ministerial meeting between the EEC Member States and Council, and the Associated African States and Madagascar (AASM) (formerly dependent territories associated with the EEC which had

gained their independence since the signing of the Treaty of Rome), the objectives and principles of an association convention are defined.

December | Sweden (12 December), Austria (12 December) and Switzerland (15 December) ask that negotiations be started with a view to agreements with the EEC that will be compatible with their neutrality. (see 29 November 1971)

1962

14 January | The Council finds that the objectives set out in the EEC Treaty for the first stage in the establishment of the common market have been achieved in the main. The second stage begins with effect from 1 January.

The Council adopts the basic regulations for a common market in agriculture (common organization of the markets in a number of products). European Agricultural Guidance and Guarantee Fund set up (CAP) (see 1 July 1964)

18 January | The French Government produces a new version of the Fouchet Plan. (see 2 November 1961)

1 February | France's five partners advance an alternative proposal for political union.

9 February | Spain seeks to open negotiations for association with the EEC.

17 April | At a meeting of Foreign Ministers, negotiations on political union are abandoned, chiefly because no agreement can be reached on the United Kingdom's participation.

30 April | Norway applies for membership of the Community. (see 29 January 1963)

15 May | The Six decide a second time to speed up the establishment of the Common Market.

18 May | Portugal applies for association with the EEC.

July | First CAP regulations take effect.

1 November | The EEC–Greece Association Agreement enters into force. (see 8 June 1959) (see 21 April 1967)

1963

14 January | The French President, General de Gaulle, declares at a press conference that the United Kingdom is not ready to join the EEC.

22 January | France and the Federal Republic of Germany sign a Treaty of Friendship and Co-operation in Paris.

29 January | The accession negotiations with the United Kingdom are broken off at the insistence of the French Government: negotiations with the other countries which have applied for membership or association are suspended too. (see 31 July 1961, 9 August 1961, 10 August 1961 and 30 April 1962) (see 10 May 1967, 11 May 1967 and 25 July 1967)

2 April | The EEC Council declares its readiness to conclude association agreements with other African countries comparable with the AASM in terms of economic structure and production. (see 20 July 1963 and 1 June 1964)

11 July	The EEC Council proposes regular contacts with the United Kingdom through Western European Union (WEU).
20 July	The Association Convention between the EEC and eighteen African States and Madagascar is signed in Yaoundé, Cameroon. To last five years. (see 1 June 1964)
12 September	The EEC–Turkey Association Agreement is signed in Ankara. (see 1 December 1964)
24 September	The Councils of the three Communities decide to begin preparations for merging the Executives. (see 8 April 1965 and 1 July 1967)
25 September	The countries of the East African Common Services Organization (Kenya, Tanganyika and Uganda) seek to open negotiations with a view to establishing formal economic relations with the EEC. (see 26 July 1968)
14 October	A trade agreement between the EEC and Iran is signed in Brussels. This is the first such agreement with a non-member country.

1964

15 April	On a proposal from the Commission, the EEC Council agrees to a medium-term economic policy programme being prepared for the Community.
4 May	The Kennedy Round of multilateral tariff negotiations under the General Agreement on Tariffs and Trade (GATT) opens in Geneva. (see 30 June 1967)
1 June	The Yaoundé Convention enters into force. (see 20 July 1963) (see 1 January 1971)
1 July	The regulations establishing the first Common agricultural market organizations and the European Agricultural Guidance and Guarantee Fund (EAGGF) enter into force. (see 14 January 1962)
1 October	In a memorandum entitled *Initiative 1964* the EEC Commission proposes a timetable for speeding up customs union.
1 December	The EEC–Turkey Association Agreement enters into force. (see 12 September 1963)
15 December	The EEC Council for the first time determines common prices for cereals.

1965

31 March	The EEC Commission puts before the Council its proposals for financing the common agricultural policy, proposals for replacing the Member States' contributions to the Community budget by the Community's own resorces and reinforcing the European Parliament's budgetary powers.
8 April	The Six sign The Treaty merging the Executives of the EEC, the ECSC and Euratom thereby establishing a single Council and a single Commission of the European Communities. (see 24 September 1963) (see 1 July 1967)
30 June	Maurice Couve de Murville, French Foreign Minister and President of the EEC Council, breaks off Council discussions on the Commission proposals for financing the common agricultural policy, for providing the Community with its own resources and agreeing Parliament's budgetary powers, noting that the Council

has failed to reach agreement on financing arrangements by the appointed time (the January 1962 decisions were taken on the understanding that the new Financial Regulation would take effect on 1 July 1965).

1 July

The French Government issues a communique stating that the Community is undergoing a 'crisis'.

6 July

The French Government informs the Member States that it is recalling its Permanent Representative and that the French Delegation will not be taking part in meetings of the Council or the Permanent Representatives Committee nor in proceedings of committees and working parties which were preparing for economic union or the resumption of earlier negotiations. This lasted six months. (see 28–29 January 1966)

26–27 July

The EEC Council meets for the first time without France, affirming that it is not prevented from meeting and deliberating by the absence of one delegation.

9 September

At a press conference General de Gaulle voices his concern at the working of the Community institutions, especially with regard to majority voting in the Council and relations between the Council and the Commission.

26 October

In a statement from the Council, France's five partners reaffirm their continuing respect for the Treaties and call on France to resume her place in the Community institutions. They propose that the Council hold a special meeting without the Commission, to attempt to resolve the Community's problems.

1966

1 January

The EEC enters the third and final stage of the common market transitional period: one consequence of this is the replacement of unanimity by majority vote for many Council decisions.

17–18 January

The Council holds a special meeting in Luxembourg without the Commission; France takes part.

28–29 January

Resuming its special meeting in Luxembourg, the Council issued statements on relations between the Council and the Commission and on majority voting which are commonly called the 'Luxembourg Compromise'. It was designed to avoid majority voting on any subject which a member state felt to be of vital national interest to it. France resumes her place in the Community institutions. (see 6 July 1965)

11 May

The EEC Council sets a firm date (1 July 1968) for the completion of customs union and the introduction ahead of schedule of the Common Customs Tariff for industrial products. It also adopts a timetable that will bring about free movement of agricultural products by the same date.

July

The EEC – Nigeria Association Agreement is signed

10 November

British Prime Minister Harold Wilson announces to the House of Commons that his Government intends to make a new approach with a view to the United Kingdom joining the Communities.

1967

9 February

By adopting Commission proposals for a common system of value

	added tax and the procedure for applying it (first and second VAT Directives), the EEC Council embarks on the harmonization of turnover taxes.
21 April	Democracy in Greece is overthrown by a military coup d'état; the Community then 'freezes' the Association Agreement, confirming its operation to day-to-day matters. (see 1 November 1962) (see 22 August 1974)
10 May	The Governments of the United Kingdom and Ireland make fresh applications to join the Communities. (see 29 January 1963) (see 23 July 1969)
11 May	The Government of Denmark makes a fresh application to join the Communities. (see 29 January 1963) (see 23 July 1969)
29–30 May	The Heads of State or Government of the Member States celebrate the tenth anniversary of the signature of the EEC and European Treaties in Rome. The Community's first five years economic programme, 1966–70, was adopted.
30 June	The Final Act of the Kennedy Round is signed in Geneva by the Commission (for the Community) and the other contracting parties. The participants undertook to reduce their tariffs on industrial goods by a maximum of 40% in stages over five years. (see 4 May 1964)
1 July	The Treaty merging the Executives of the European Communities enters into force. It created a single Council of Ministers and Commission for the EEC, ECSC and Euratom. (see 24 September 1963 and 8 April 1965
6 July	The fourteen-member Commission of the European Communities takes office, with Jean Rey as President.
25 July	Norway makes a second application to join the Communities. (see 29 January 1963) (see 23 July 1969)
26 July	The Swedish Government asks the Six to open negotiations to enable Sweden to take part in the Community in a form which would be compatible with her neutrality. (see December 1961) (see 29 November 1971)
29 September	The Commission delivers an Opinion expressing itself in favour of opening negotiations with a view to the United Kingdom, Ireland, Denmark and Norway joining the Communities. (see 10 & 11 May 1967) (see 19 December 1967)
27 November	General de Gaulle gives a press conference and declares that the United Kingdom is not in a position to join the Community.
19 December	The Council fails to reach agreement on the reopening of negotiations with the applicant countries.

1968

1 July	Customs union is completed eighteen months ahead of the Treaty schedule: customs duties between Member States are removed and the Common Customs Tariff replaces national customs duties in trade with the rest of the world. (see 1 January 1959 and 13 February 1960) (see 1 July 1977)
26 July	The Association Agreement between the EEC and the countries of the East African Community (Kenya, Uganda and Tanzania) is signed in Arusha, Tanzania. (see 25 September 1963) (see 25–26 July 1973)

| 29 July | The regulation securing complete freedom of movement for workers within the Community is adopted (more than a year ahead of the Treaty schedule). (see 1 September 1961) |
| 18 December | The Commission lays before the Council the 'Mansholt plan' for the reform of agriculture in the Community, which aims to modernize farm structures. (see 21–22 April 1970) |

1969

23 July	The Council resumes examination of the applications for membership from the United Kingdom, Ireland, Denmark and Norway. (see 10 May, 11 May and 25 July 1967) (see 30 June 1970) (see 22 January 1972)
15 October	The Commission sends the Council a proposal to provide the Community with the instruments it needs to implement a regional development policy.
1–2 December	Conference of the Heads of State or Government at The Hague, where they agree to lay down without delay a definitive financial arrangement for the common agricultural policy, to allocate to the Community its own resources and to strengthen the budgetary powers of Parliament. They also agree to open negotiations with the four applicant countries, to press forward with economic and monetary union and, lastly, to introduce a system of co-operation in foreign affairs (see 18 December 1968) (see 21–22 April 1970)
31 December	The twelve-year transitional period provided for in the EEC Treaty for the establishment of the common market ends.

1970

9 February	The Governors of the Central Bank sign an agreement establishing a system of short-term monetary support within the Community. This takes effect the same day.
21–22 April	Honouring the undertakings made at The Hague, the Council adopts definitive arrangements for financing the common agricultural policy (CAP) and makes a decision on the replacement of financial contributions from Member States by the Communities' own resources. The Ministers sign a Treaty amending certain budgetary provisions of the Treaties establishing the European Communities which gives the European Parliament wider budgetary powers. (see 18 December 1968) (see 1–2 December 1969)
30 June	Negotiations with the four countries applying for membership formally open in Luxembourg. (see 23 July 1969)
2 July	A new Commission, composed of nine members and presided over by Franco Maria Malfatti, takes office.
7–8 October	A working party chaired by Luxembourg Prime Minister, Pierre Werner, adopts the report on the attainment by stages of economic and monetary union. This it had been instructed to draw up by the Council following The Hague summit. (see 1–2 December 1969)
27 October	The Foreign Ministers, meeting in Luxembourg, adopt the Davignon report on 'the best way of achieving progress in the matter of the political unification of Europe'. (see 23 July 1973)
19 November	First 'political co-operation' meeting of Foreign Ministers is held in Munich. (see 23 July 1973)

1971

1 January	The second Yaoundé Convention and Arusha Agreements enter into force. (see 1 June 1964) (see 25–26 July 1973)
22 March	The Council and representatives of the member governments adopt a resolution on the attainment by stages of economic and monetary union, the first stage to start on 1 January 1971 (see 18 February 1974). The Council also decides to strengthen co-ordination of Member States' short-term economic policies and co-operation between the central banks, and to set up machinery for medium-term financial assistance.
12 May	Following the floating of several Member States' currencies, the Council introduces a system of monetary compensatory amounts for trade in agricultural products between Member States, with the aim of maintaining the unity of the common agricultural market.
21–22 June	The Council adopts the Commission's proposals to grant generalized tariff preferences to 91 developing countries.
15 August	The United States Government suspends the convertibility of the dollar into gold.
29 November	The Council invites the Commission to open negotiations with the EFTA countries not applying for membership of the Communities: Austria (see 12 December 1961) Finland, Iceland, Portugal, Sweden (see 12 December 1961) (see 26 July 1967) Switzerland (see 15 December 1961) The negotiations begin in December.

1972

22 January	The Treaties and related documents concerning the accession of Denmark, Ireland, Norway and the United Kingdom to the European Communities are signed in Brussels. (see 23 July 1969) (see 25 September 1972) (see 1 January 1973)
21 March	Introduction of the currency 'snake': the Council of the Communities and the Governments of the Member States decide to limit the spread between the Member States' currencies to a maximum of 2.25%. The applicant countries also join the 'snake'. (see 23 June 1972 (see 13 February 1973) (see 11–12 March 1973) (see 21 January 1974)
21 March	Franco Maria Malfatti resigns and is replaced by Sicco Mansholt as President of the Commission.
24 March	The Council adopts three Directives on the modernization of agricultural structures, following Commission proposals for the reform of agriculture.
19 April	The Convention setting up a European University Institute is signed in Florence.
23 June	The pound sterling and the Irish pound (pund) leave the 'snake'. (see 21 March 1972)
1 July	Portugal signed a trade agreement with the EEC.
25 September	In Norway's referendum on joining the Community, 53.5% vote against. The Norwegian Government asks to negotiate a free-trade agreement with the Community. (see 22 January 1972) (see 1 January 1973)

19–21 October	The nine Heads of State or Government of the enlarged Community hold a summit conference in Paris. They define new fields of action for the Community (concerning environmental, regional, social and industrial policies, etc) and ask the Community institutions to draw up the appropriate programmes. They reaffirm the determination of Member States irreversibly to achieve economic and monetary union (see 4–5 December 1978). They undertake to transform by 1980 'the whole complex of their relations into a European union'. (see June–July 1975)

1973

1 January	Denmark, Ireland and the United Kingdom formally join the European Communities. The thirteen Members of the new Commission are appointed. (see 22 January 1972)
	Free-trade agreements with Austria, Portugal, Sweden and Switzerland come into force. Agreements with the other three non-applicant EFTA countries take effect later (Iceland on 1 April, Norway on 1 July, Finland on 1 January 1974). (see 29 November 1971) and 25 September 1972)
11 January	The Commission of the enlarged Community, with François-Xavier Ortoli as President, holds its first meeting.
16 January	The European Parliament convenes for its first session since enlargement. The British Labour Party sends no representatives to Parliament, and the British trade unions do not take the seats allocated to them on the Economic and Social Committee. (see 7 July 1975)
13 February	The Italian lira leaves the 'snake'. (see 21 March 1972)
11–12 March	The Council holds a meeting on the monetary situation. The United Kingdom, Ireland and Italy having decided to let their currencies float independently, the 'snake' is retained by the other Member States (Belgium, Denmark, Germany, Luxembourg, Netherlands and France until 21 January 1974) and now floats against the dollar. (see 21 March 1972)
3–7 July	The Conference on Security and Co-operation in Europe (CSCE) opens in Helsinki.
23 July	The Foreign Ministers present their second report on political co-operation (Copenhagen report), calling for more active co-operation. The report is subsequently approved by the Heads of State or Government. (see 19 November 1970)
25–26 July	A ministerial conference is held between the Community and the AASM, the Commonwealth developing countries referred to in the Act of Accession and certain other African countries, as a prelude to negotiations for what will be the Lomé Convention with the African, Pacific and Caribbean (ACP) countries. (see 26 July 1968 and 1 January 1971) (see 28 February 1975)
12 September	The Tokyo Round of multilateral trade negotiations under GATT opens.
6–27 October	Yom Kippur War. The Arab oil-producing countries announce that oil exports to certain Western countries will be cut or stopped. The Organization of the Petroleum Exporting Countries (OPEC) decides to raise oil prices substantially.
6 November	The Nine issue a declaration setting out principles on which to

	base a peace settlement in the Middle East; this is to guide their policy in the years ahead.
14–15 December	The Heads of State or Government of the Member States confer in Copenhagen. On instructions from the Arab Summit in Algiers (26–28 November), the Foreign Ministers of four Arab countries deliver a message to the Conference. The decision is taken to put together the initial components of a common energy policy and set up a European Regional Development Fund by 1 January 1974. The Council then fails to act on these directives, which puts the Community under strain.

1974

21 January	The French franc leaves the 'snake'. (see 21 March 1972) (see 10 July 1975)
8 February	During Britain's election campaign, the Labour Party announces that it will ask for 'renegotiation' of the United Kingdom's membership of the Communities.
18 February	The Council fails to decide on transition to the second phase of economic and monetary union. (see 22 March 1971)
1 April	The newly formed British Government asks for 'renegotiation' of the United Kingdom's membership. (see 18 March 1975)
25 April	Portugal's dictatorship, in power since 1928, is overthrown. (see 28 March 1977)
24 July	The Greek Colonels' junta falls.
31 July	The Euro–Arab Dialogue open in Paris. The Community is represented by the Presidents of the Council and the Commission. It is agreed to set up a Euro–Arab General Committee and a number of working groups.
22 August	Greece asks the Community to 'unfreeze' the Association Agreement (confined to routine business since the Colonels' coup d'état). (see 21 April 1967) (see 17 September 1974)
14 September	At the invitation of French President, Giscard d'Estaing, the Heads of Government of the Nine and the President of the Commission meet for informal talks at the Elysée Palace. France drops her objections to direct election for Parliament and presents a package of proposals on the political organization of Europe.
17 September	The Council reactivates the Association Agreement with Greece. (see 22 August 1974) (see 12 June 1975)
11 October	The United Nations General Assembly grants the Community observer status.
9–10 December	At the Paris Summit Conference the Heads of State or Government take a number of important decisions concerning the Community's institutions:

- Parliament to be elected by direct universal suffrage from 1978 onwards; (see 14 January 1975)
- the Heads of Government to hold regular meetings 'in the Council of the Communities and in the context of political co-operation' (subsequently baptized 'European Council'); (see 10 – 11 March 1975)

- Leo Tindemans, the Belgian Prime Minister, to compile a report on European Union by the end of 1975. (see 29 December 1975)

The meeting also produces many policy decisions including one on the structure and endowment (for the next three years) of the European Regional Development Fund.

1975

14 January	Parliament adopts the new draft Convention (based on a report by Schelto Patin) on the election of its members by direct universal suffrage from 1978 onwards. (see 9–10 December 1974) (see 20 September 1976)
28 February	The Convention between the Community and forty-six African, Caribbean and Pacific States is signed in Lomé following the enlargement of the Community and the expiry of the Yaoundé Convention. (see 25–26 July 1973) (see 1 April 1976)
4 March	A joint declaration is signed by Parliament, the Council and the Commission instituting a conciliation procedure between Parliament and the Council, with the active assistance of the Commission, for Community acts of general application which have appreciable financial implications.
10–11 March	The European Council holds its first meeting in Dublin. On the basis of a Commission proposal it works out a solution to the problems raised by the United Kingdom in connection with her contribution to the Community budget, thus paving the way for the conclusion of the 'renegotiation' exercise.
18 March	Following the conclusion of the renegotiations the British Government announces its intention in the House of Commons to organize a referendum on UK membership of the Community (see 1 April 1974) (see 5 June 1975)
4–11 May	Sir Christopher Soames, Vice-President of the Commission with special responsibility for external relations, visits the People's Republic of China at the invitation of the Chinese Government. The Chinese Government states that it wants to establish official relations with the Community and announces plans for a trade agreement. (see 16 September 1975) (see 3 April 1978)
11 May	The Community signs a co-operation agreement with Israel.
5 June	The referendum results show a large majority in favour of the United Kingdom remaining a member of the Community. The total vote showed 67.2% in favour (of which 68.7% in England, 64.8% in Wales, 58.4% in Scotland and 52.1% in Northern Ireland) in a 64.5% turn-out (see 18 March 1975)
12 June	Greece applies to join the European Communities. (see 17 September 1974) (see 28 January and 9 February 1976) (1 January 1981)
June–July	Reports on European Union are adopted by the Commission on 25 June and by Parliament on 10 July, the two reaching similar conclusions. (see 19–21 October 1972)
7 July	Following the positive outcome to the referendum, eighteen British Labour Members take up their seats in the European Parliament. British trade unionists also take their places on the Economic and Social Committee. (see 16 January 1973) (see 5 June 1975)

10 July	The French franc rejoins the 'snake'. (see 21 January 1974) (see 14 March 1976)
22 July	The Treaty strengthening the budgetary powers of Parliament and setting up a Court of Auditors is signed in Brussels. (see 25 October 1977)
1 August	In Helsinki the Final Act of the Conference on security and co-operation in Europe is signed by the thirty-five States taking part. Italian Prime Minister Aldo Moro acting in his capacity as President of the Council, signs on behalf of the Community.
16 September	Official relations are established with China and a Chinese ambassador is accredited to the Community. (see 4–11 May 1975) (see 3 April 1978)
18 November	The first Tripartite Conference on the economic and social situation is held, attended by Community representatives (Commission and Council), the ministers responsible for economic policy and employment in the Member States and representatives from both sides of industry.
29 December	Belgian Prime Minister Leo Tindemans transmits his report on European Union to the other Heads of Government of the Community and to the Council (see 9–10 December 1974) (see 29–30 November 1976)

1976

28 January	The Commission endorses Greece's application for Community membership but expresses the view that there should perhaps be a waiting period before accession in view of the structural changes that will have to take place. (see 12 June 1975)
9 February	The Council comes out in favour of Greece's application to join the Community; it is agreed that negotiations will open on 27 July (see 12 June 1975) (see 1 January 1981)
16 February	The Council for Mutual Economic Assistance (CMEA) proposes an agreement between CMEA and its members, and the Community and its members. (see 21 September 1977)
14 March	The French franc leaves the 'snake' again. (see 10 July 1975)
1 April	The ACP–EEC Convention, signed at Lomé on 28 February 1975, enters into force. (see 28 February 1975) (see 24 July 1978)
25–27 April	The Community signs comprehensive agreements with the Maghreb countries (Tunisia on 25, Algeria on 26 and Morocco on 27 April).
13 July	Roy Jenkins is designated President of the Commission by the European Council thus giving effect in part to a suggestion made in the Tindemans Report (see 29 December 1975). In the months following, prior to taking up office on 1 January, he holds a series of consultations with the Governments of the Nine on the composition of the new Commission.
20 September	The instruments concerning election of Parliament by direct universal suffrage are signed in Brussels. (see 14 January 1975) (see 7–8 April 1978)
30 October	Foreign Ministers meeting in The Hague decide that Member States will extend fishing limits to 200 miles off their North Sea and North Atlantic coasts from 1 January 1977 and agree a number of common guidelines and procedures. These decisions, formally

adopted by the Council on 3 November, mark the beginnings of the common fisheries policy.

29–30 November   Meeting in The Hague, the European Council publishes a statement on the Tindemans Report and calls on the Foreign Ministers and the Commission to report to it once a year on the results obtained and the progress which can be achieved in the short term towards European Union. (see 29 December 1975)

1977

6 January   The Jenkins Commission holds its first meeting.

18 January   Co-operation agreements are signed with three Mashreq countries (Egypt, Jordan and Syria), to be followed by the agreement with Lebanon on 3 May.

28 March   Portugal applies for Community membership. (see 25 April 1974) (see 19 May 1978)

5 April   The European Parliament, the Council and the Commission sign a joint declaration on the respect of fundamental rights.

7–8 May   At the third Western Economic Summit in London (the 'Downing Street Summit') the Community participates, as such, for the first time in some of the discussions. (see 16–17 July 1978)

17 May   The Council adopts the sixth VAT Directive (establishing a uniform basis of assessment for value added tax) thus arranging for Community own resources to be operated in full.

15 June   In a communication to the European Council (shortly to meet in London) the Commission proposes a New Community borrowing instrument to finance structural investment serving the Community's priority aims.

1 July   Customs union is achieved in the enlarged Community. (see 1 January 1959)

28 July   Spain applies for Community membership. (see 29 November 1978)

21 September   A CMEA delegation led by Mihail Marinescu, Chairman of its Executive Committee, meets in Brussels Henri Simonet, President of the Council, and Wilhelm Haferkamp, Vice-President of the Commission – the body responsible for the negotiations on behalf of the Community – to discuss negotiations for an agreement. (see 16 February 1976)

25 October   The Court of Auditors of the European Communities, replacing the EEC and Euratom Audit Board and the ECSC Auditor, holds its inaugural meeting in Luxembourg. (see 22 July 1975)

27 October   Roy Jenkins makes a statement in Florence in the prospects for monetary union.

1978

3 April   The Community and China signed a trade agreement which came into force on 1 June. (see 4–11 May 1975)

7–8 April   The European Council, meeting in Copenhagen, agreed that the first direct elections to the European Parliament would be held between 7 and 10 June 1979. These dates were endorsed by Parliament and formally approved by the Council on 25 July (see 20 September 1976) (see 7–10 June 1979)

19 May	The Commission adopted a favourable Opinion on Portugal's application for Community membership. The Council came out in favour of the application on 6 June and decided to open negotiations. (see 28 March 1977) (see 17 October 1978)
6–7 July	The European Council, meeting in Bremen, agreed on a common strategy to achieve a higher rate of economic growth and approved the plan to set up a European Monetary System. (see 18 February 1974) (see 4–5 December 1978)
16–17 July	The Community as such participated in the Western Economic Summit in Bonn. (see 7–8 May 1977)
24 July	Negotiations opened between the Community and the ACP countries for a new Convention to replace the Lomé Convention which expires in 1980. (see 1 April 1976) (see 1 January 1981)
16 October	The Council agreed to create a New Community borrowing and lending instrument. The Commission was empowered to contract loans of up to 1000 million EUA and on-lend the proceeds to finance energy, industry and infrastructure projects contributing to priority Community objectives.
17 October	Negotiations for Portugal's accession to the Community were formally opened (see 19 May 1978)
20–21 November	The first ministerial meeting between the Community and ASEAN countries (Indonesia, Malaysia, the Philippines, Singapore and Thailand) took place in Brussels.
29 November	The Commission adopted a favourable opinion on Spain's application for Community membership. The Council came out in favour of the application on 19 December and negotiations were formally opened on 5 February 1979. (see 28 July 1977)
4–5 December	The European Council, meeting in Brussels, decided to set up a European Monetary System based on a European currency unit (the ECU) (see 6–7 July 1978). The EMS comprises an exchange and intervention mechanism, credit mechanisms and a mechanism for the transfer of resources to less prosperous Community countries. Eight member states – Ireland and Italy after a period of reflection – decided to become full members of the EMS. The United Kingdom opted to remain outside the EMS for the time being (despite a limited involvement in some of the credit mechanisms). Because of the link subsequently established by the French Government between the EMS and the phasing-out of Monetary Compensatory Amounts under the Common Agricultural Policy, introduction of the EMS was deferred from the initial target date of early January 1979 to 13 March 1979.
4–5 December	The European Council, meeting in Brussels, decided to set up a three-man committee to consider essential adjustments to institutional mechanisms and procedures in the context of enlargement. The 'three wise men' are Mr Barend Biesheuvel, former Prime Minister of the Netherlands, Mr Edmund Dell, former UK Minister, and Mr Robert Marjolin, former Vice-President of the EEC Commission.

1979

17 January	Tuvalu (formerly Ellice Islands) accedes to Lomé Convention (55th ACP State).

5 February	Spanish accession negotiations formally open in Brussels. (see 29 November 1978)
13 February	Mr Jenkins presents 1978 General Report on the Activities of the European Communities and the Commission's programme for 1979, to Parliament.
22 February	Commission approves second report on Community environment.
26 February	Dominica accedes to Lomé Convention (56th ACP State).
13 March	European Monetary System (EMS) enters into force. (see 4–5 December 1978)
16 March	Jean Monnet dies.
9 April	Council agrees on Regulation introducing ECU in Common Agricultural Policy.
23 May	Commission lays down guidelines for management of European Social Fund from 1980 to 1982.
28 May	Acts relating to Greece's accession to Communities signed in Athens. On completion of ratification procedures Greece will become 10th member state on 1 January 1981.
7–10 June	First elections to Parliament by direct universal suffrage. (see 17 May 1960)
15 June	Commission sends Council communication on, Community energy objectives for 1990 and convergence of member states' policies.
28 June	St Lucia accedes to Lomé Convention (57th ACP State).
11 September	Council adopts four year indirect action energy R and D programme (1979–83)
11 September	Council adopts four year programme (1979–83) for development of data processing.
30 October	Kiribati (formerly Gilbert Islands) accedes to Lomé Convention (58th ACP State).
31 October	Second ACP–EEC convention signed at Lomé.
12 November	Council adopts four year research programme on recycling of urban waste.
13 December	Parliament, for the first time, rejects draft budget for 1980. (see 9 July 1980)
18 December	Council adopts multiannual programme of research (1980–4) in climatology.

1980

13 February	Inauguration of EURONET–DIANE; the Community's direct access information network.
27 February	St Vincent and the Grenadines formally accede to Lomé convention (59th ACP state).
13 March	Council adopts new JRC multiannual research programme 1980–3.
21 March	Commission sends Council report on overall forecasts for coal supply and demand up to the year 2000.
30 May	Package agreement by Council on UK contribution to financing Community budget, farm prices 1980–1, market in sheepmeat, common fisheries policy.

9 July	President of Parliament declares general Community budget for 1980, finally adopted. (see 13 December 1979)
14 July	Signature of Euratom–Spain co-operation agreement on controlled fusion.
1 October	EEC–ASEAN Co-operation agreement enters into force.
4 November	Zimbabwe accedes to Lomé convention (60th ACP state).
24 November	Queen Elizabeth visits EC headquarters.
3 December	Exchange of letters with Portugal form agreement on pre-accession aid.
4 December	Council directive on Community driving licence.

1981

1 January	Greece becomes 10th member of the Community. Second Lomé Convention, signed 31 October 1979, comes into force.
6 January	Mr Gaston Thorn becomes President of the Commission.
13 January	Death of Mr Finn Olav Gundelach, Vice-President of the Commission.
20 January	Council adopts decision on exceptional Community aid for reconstruction of areas devastated by earthquake in Italy in November 1980.
29 January	Parliamentary Assembly of Council of Europe passes resolution expressing the wish that the European Communities will make a formal application to adhere to the European Convention on Human Rights in the very near future. (see 1950)
11 and 12 February	Mr Thorn presents 1980 General Report on the Activities of the European Communities and Commission's programme and priorities for 1981 to Parliament. After debate, Parliament passes resolution approving appointment of Commissioners and reiterates its request to participate in these appointments in future.
16 February	Council agrees on adjustment of Community loan mechanism to support balances of payments of member states.
20 February	Commission sends Council communication on steel restructuring policies.
25 February	Commission sends Council report on energy policy objectives for 1990 and on member states' investment programmes.
	Commission agrees in principle to grant emergency aid for victims of earthquake in Greece on 24 and 25 February.
18 March	Republic of Vanuatu (formerly New Hebrides) accedes to Lomé Convention (61st ACP State).
23 March	Commission sends Council communication on Community's policy in North–South Dialogue.
26–7 March	Council adopts resolution on steel recovery policy.
30 March	Council decides Community should sign International Cocoa Agreement.
30 March (to 2 April)	Council reaches overall agreement on 1981–2 farm prices and related measures and on package of other measures (mainly structural policy).

10 April	Parliament passes resolution on interinstitutional dialogue relating to budgetary matters.
18 April	Celebration of 30th anniversary of signing of ECSC Treaty.
29 April	Economic and Social Committee issues own-initiative opinion on revision of Regulation setting up European Regional Development Fund.
4 May	Board of Governors of European Investment Bank authorizes loans to Spain.
19 May	Council approves continuation of Super-Sara project.
	Council adopts second consumer protection and information policy programme.
	Council adopts Community food aid programmes for 1981.
20–1 May	IMF interim committee meeting and Group of Ten ministerial meeting held in Libreville.
25 May	Commission adopts preliminary draft budget for 1982 and preliminary draft amending budget No. 1 for 1981.
11 June	Council decides to extend to Spain Community's guarantee for EIB loans to non-member countries.
15 June	EIB Board of Governors decides to double Bank's capital.
23 June	Agreement for commercial and economic co-operation between Community and India signed.
24 June	Commission sends Heads of State or Government, its report on mandate of 30 May 1980 (UK financing Community budget).
1 July	Commission sends Italian Government recommendation on economic policy measures.
22–3 July	After conciliation meeting with Parliament, Council agrees draft budget for 1982.
23 July	Commission sends Council proposal for decision adopting a five-year (1982–6) programme in field of controlled thermonuclear fusion.
27 July	Council agrees to renew financial protocols with Maghreb and Mashreq countries and Israel, due to expire on 31 October.
	Council adopts third action plan for information and documentation.
29 July	Commission recommends all member states to sign during 1981 and ratify in 1982 draft Council of Europe Convention for protection of individuals with regard to automatic processing of personal data.
5 August	As part of 30 May 1980 mandate exercise, Commission sends Council its new regional policy guidelines and priorities.
21 September	Euratom–Australia agreement on transfers of nuclear materials signed.
23–5 September	Annual session of ACP–EEC Consultative Assembly.
30 September	As part of its work on 30 May 1980 mandate, Commission sends Council communications on:
	strengthening the internal market developing Community energy strategy scientific and technical research industrial innovation policy development of industry in Europe

	guidelines for European agriculture Mediterranean programmes – lines of action job creation: priorities for Community action.
4 October	Ministers and Central Bank Governors of member states agree to adjust central rates within EMS (revaluation of German mark and Dutch guilder; devaluation of French franc and Italian lira).
9 October	French Government memorandum on revitalizing Europe.
13–14 October	Community and ASEAN Foreign Ministers meet in London.
29 October	As part of 30 May 1980 mandate exercise, Commission sends Council proposal concerning reshaping of Regional Fund Regulation.
9 November	Commission sends Council and Parliament third five-year programme for environment.
23 November	Message from France, Italy, Netherlands and United Kingdom to Governments of United States, Egypt and Israel on their participation in international peace force in Sinai, and statement by the Community.
26 and 27 November	London, European Council.
14 December	Commission sends Council communication on new Community programme to promote equal opportunities for women.
17 December	Statement by Mrs Thatcher on European Council in London. For first time European Council President addresses Parliament.
21 December	President of Parliament declares general Community budget for 1982 finally adopted.
22 December	Commission sends Council report on poverty in Community.

Select List of Common Market Abbreviations

Notes. Standard lists of abbreviations will be found on the shelves of most libraries. Many of these will contain Common Market abbreviations and will supplement the following short list.

A number of the following abbreviations refer to the French form of the title. As France was a member of the EC many years before Britain the abbreviation of the French form of the title is now in standard use. An example is COREPER, below.

AAID	Arab Authority for agricultural investment and development
AASM	Association of African States and Mauritius
ACP	African, Carribbean and Pacific countries
ACPM	Advisory committee on programme management
ASEAN	Association of South East Asian nations
ASOR	Agreement on the international carriage of passengers by road by means of occasional coach and bus services
ATD	Aide à toute détresse
AWES	Association of West European shipbuilders
BOTB	British Overseas Trade Board
BTN	Brussels tariff nomenclature
CADDIA	Community system of computerized data collection
CAP	Common agricultural policy
CAS	Chemical abstracts service
CCC	Customs co-operation council
CCCN	Customs co-operation council nomenclature
CCT	Common customs tariff
CEDEFOP	European centre for the development of vocational training
CECLA	Special commission for Latin America
CERD	European committee for research and development
CIDST	Scientific and technical information and documentation committees (see also STIDC)
CIRD	Inter-departmental committee on research and development
CISI	Compagnie internationale de services en informatique
COM	Computer output in microform
COM	Commission (documents)
COMAC's	Committees on concerted action
COREPER	Permanent representatives committee
COST	European co-operation in the field of scientific and technical research
CREST	Scientific and technical research committee
CRM	Committee for medical research
CRONOS	Community statistical office computerized economic data bank
DIANE	Direct information access network for Europe
EAEC	European Atomic Energy Community
EAGGF	European agricultural guidance and guarantee fund
ECE	Economic Commission for Europe
ECOIN	European core inventory [Chemicals]
ECR	European Court reports
ECSC	European Coal and Steel Community
ECU	European currency unit
EDC	European documentation centre
EDF	European development fund
EEC	European Economic Community
EIB	European Investment Bank

EINECS	European inventory of existing commercial chemical substances
EMP	European Member of Parliament
EMS	European monetary system
EP	European Parliament
ERDF	European regional development fund
ESA	European space agency
ESC	Economic and social committee
ESF	European social fund
ESTI	European solar testing installation
ETUC	European trade union confederation
EUA	European unit of account
EUDISED	Automated multilingual thesaurus of Eurydice
EURATOM	European Atomic Energy Community
EURONET	European Information Network
EFTA	European Free Trade Association
EURONORM	European standards
EUROSTAT	European Communities statistics
EUROTRA	European advanced machine translation system
FADN	Farm accountancy data network
FAO	Food and Agriculture Organization
FAST	Forecasting and assessment in the field of science and technology
GATT	General agreement on tariffs and trade
GDR	German Democratic Republic
GSP	Generalized system of preferences
IATA	International air transport association
ICES	International council for the exploration of the sea
ICFTU	International confederation of free trade unions
ILO	International labour office
INSIS	Interinstitutional information system
JET	Joint European torus
JRC	Joint research centre
LAFTA	Latin America free trade association
MCA	Monetary compensatory amounts
MFA	Multi-Fibre arrangement
NCI	New Community instrument
NET	Next European torus
NIMEXE	Nomenclature of goods for the external trade statistics of the Community and statistics of trade between member states
NIPRO	Common nomenclature of industrial products
OCT	Overseas countries and territories
OECD	Organisation for European Economic Co-operation
OEEC	Organisation for Economic Co-operation and Development
OJ	Official journal of the European Communities
PREST	Working party on scientific and technical research policy
qv	Quod vide (a reference to related sources of information)

SCAR	Standing committee on agricultural research
SEC	Secretary-General (documents)
SEDOC	European system for the international clearing of vacancies
STABEX	Stabilization of export earnings
STC	Scientific and technical committee (of Euratom)
STIDC	Scientific and technical information and documentation committee (see also CIDST)
STRC	Scientific and technical research committee
SYSMIN	System for mineral products
ua	Units of account
UN	United Nations
UNCTAD	United Nations conference on trade and development
UNDP	United Nations development programme
UNICE	Union of industries of the European Community
VAT	Value added tax

Public Holidays in the Community (Portugal, Spain)

1980		Austria	Belgium	Denmark	Eire	Finland	France	W. Germany	Greece	Iceland
January	1 Tue	*	*	*	*	*	*	*	*	*
	2 Wed									
	12 Sat					*				
February	18 Mon							b*		
	19 Tue							b*		
	25 Mon								*	
March	17 Mon				*					
	19 Wed									
	25 Tue								*	
April	3 Thur			*						*
	4 Fri			*	*	*		*	*	*
	7 Mon		*	*	*	*	*	*	*	*
	17 Thur									*
	25 Fri									
	30 Wed									
May	1 Thur	*	*			*	*	*		*
	2 Fri			*						
	5 Mon									
	9 Fri	EEC commission								
	10 Sat					*				
	14 Wed									
	15 Thur	*	*	*			*	*		*
	17 Sat									
	24 Sat					*				
	26 Mon	*	*	*			*	*	*	*
	27 Tue							* Frankfurt		
June	2 Mon				*					
	5 Thur	*						b*		
	10 Tue									
	13 Fri									
	17 Tue							*		*
	20 Fri					*				
	21 Sat					*				
	23 Mon									
	24 Tue									
July	12 Sat									
	14 Mon						*			
	21 Mon			*						
	25 Fri									
August	4 Mon				*					*
	15 Fri	*	*				*	b*	*	
	25 Mon									
September	1 Mon									
October	27 Mon				*					
	28 Tue								*	
November	1 Sat	*	*				*	b*		
	11 Tue		*							
	19 Wed							*		
December	1 Mon									
	5 Fri									
	6 Sat					*				
	8 Mon	*								
	24 Wed					*				*
	25 Thur	*	*	*	*	*	*		*	*
	26 Fri	*	*	d*	*	*		*	*	*
	31 Wed									*

Compiled by the EEC Information Unit of the Department of Industry, 11th Floor Millbank Tower, Millbank, London SW1P 4QU

* Holidays   a. Half days.   b. in some or all of the Catholic Länder.   d. Government Departments only

Italy[1]	Luxembourg	Netherlands	Norway	Portugal	Spain	Sweden	Switzerland[2]	UK
*	*	*	*	*	*	*,	*	*
								*Scotland
	*							
				*				
					*			
			*		*	a*		
		d*	*	*	*	*	*	*
*	*		*			*	*	* Not Scotland
*				*				
		*						
*	*		*	*	*	*		
		*						*
						a*		
	*	*	*		*		*	
			*					
	*	*	*			*	*	*
				*	*			
				*				
				*Lisbon				
						*		
	*							
				*Oporto				
								* N. Ireland
					*			
								* Scotland
*	*			*	*			
								* Not Scotland
	*							
*	*			*		*		
				*				
		a*						
*				*	*			
				*				
*	*	*	*	*	*	*	*	*
*	*	*	*	*	*	*	*	*
						*		

Italy – local Saints days not included.   [2] Switzerland – local holidays not included